OF ARTHOUR AND
OF MERLIN

VOLUME II · INTRODUCTION
NOTES AND GLOSSARY

EARLY ENGLISH TEXT SOCIETY
No. 279
1979

OF ARTHOUR AND OF MERLIN.

EDITED BY

O. D. MACRAE-GIBSON

VOLUME II

INTRODUCTION, NOTES

GLOSSARY

Published *for*
THE EARLY ENGLISH TEXT SOCIETY
by the
OXFORD UNIVERSITY PRESS
1979

Oxford University Press, Walton Street, Oxford OX2 6DP

OXFORD LONDON GLASGOW
NEW YORK TORONTO MELBOURNE WELLINGTON
KUALA LUMPUR SINGAPORE JAKARTA HONG KONG TOKYO
DELHI BOMBAY CALCUTTA MADRAS KARACHI
NAIROBI DAR ES SALAAM CAPE TOWN

© *Early English Text Society 1979*

British Library Cataloguing in Publication Data

Of Arthour and of Merlin
   Vol. 2: Introduction, notes, glossary –
   (Early English Text Society. Original
   series; no. 279)
   Bibl.
   1. Macrae-Gibson, Osgar Duncan 2. Series
   821'.1   PR2065.A4
   English poetry
   ISBN 0–19–722281–1

*Printed in Great Britain
at the University Press, Oxford
by Eric Buckley
Printer to the University*

PREFACE

THIS volume completes the edition of which Volume I appeared
in 1973. The Introduction gives main attention to the literary
procedures by which the poem in its different versions developed
from its French source. It treats the equally important matter
of the language much more summarily, because this poem, and
other comparable texts, have already been the subjects of detailed
linguistic studies by others; but the Glossary seeks to provide as
full a key as pressure on space has allowed to all its linguistic
features. A number of individual linguistic points are also discussed
in the Commentary, whose main aim, however, is to explain
what the poet meant, especially where details of the sources (not
all fully published) can help to make this clear.

My work on this edition was begun more than twenty years
ago, at the very start of my scholarly career. Parts survive from
then; much is the product of successive partial revisions since.
Idle to dream of a leisurely opportunity to harmonize the whole
before sending it to press; I can only hope that readers may be
inclined to forgiveness of the errors and inconsistencies which will
certainly remain.

I ask forgiveness, too, from those who have helped me during
all this time and to whom I can offer only this general expression
of thanks, for they have been too many for me to name them all.
Some, however, it would be outrageous to thank only thus, and of
these first Professor G. V. Smithers, under whose supervision the
thesis-form of the work was begun, and whose influence will still
be evident throughout. Then Professor E. J. Dobson, under
whose most helpful supervision that form was successfully completed; and Mr. C. A. Robson, who gave me unstintingly of his
time and his profound knowledge of the varieties of Old French;
and Professor A. J. Bliss, whose criticisms and insights have been
of great profit to me (though I have ventured to cross swords with
him now and then); and Mr. C. A. McLaren, and Dr. D. B.
Johnstone, who have given me much expert help with the marginalia
of MSS. A and L, and without whom many of their obscurities
would have remained dark to me; and Professor Norman Davis,

who read a late draft of the typescript with great care, and saved me from more than one blunder, though I have not been able to accept all his suggestions.

I have already thanked in Volume I the Librarians and staff of the libraries holding manuscripts of my romance; now I must add grateful thanks to those of the Bibliothèque Nationale, particularly Monsieur J. Porcher and his staff in the Cabinet des Manuscrits, for much kindness, and tolerance of a foreigner's incompetence in the *démarches réglementaires*, while I was working on manuscripts of the 'Vulgate' *Merlin*. To the Early English Text Society, for me chiefly in the person of its Editorial Secretary, Dr. Pamela Gradon, I owe warm appreciation, both for giving the work an *imprimatur* and for guidance in its preparation for press; and to the Oxford University Press for all the care, patience, and helpfulness with which it has been put into print, particularly for valiant efforts to meet my technically inconvenient wishes as to precise lineation in the parallel text section of Volume I.

To my wife my obligations are of a different sort, not only for direct help, notably in some most laborious letter-by-letter proof-reading of the texts, to which much of the credit is due if these indeed prove, as I hope, relatively free of careless errors, but also for tolerating the thing spreading itself about the house, in one form and another, throughout the whole of our married life up to this time. And to Professor J. R. R. Tolkien different again, for the inspiration which I, like so many others, found in his warm-hearted and wide-spreading response to our early literature, creating a debt I sought to acknowledge in a Dedication which, to my grief, I was just too late to present to him in print.

Aberdeen, 1976

CONTENTS

CORRIGENDA TO VOLUME I

For the most part these represent desirable improvements in the interests of plausibility or consistency, rather than correction of actual errors.

p. 4; **L** 9 *for* Sum whyle *read* Sumwhyle

p. 14; **L** 154, 165, 166 *for* s⟨a⟩yȝe, ans⟩werde, man *read* s⟨e⟩yȝe, ons⟩werde, mon

p. 16; **L** 195 *for* [if] *read* [ȝef]

p. 24; **L** 285 *for* Eyþer *read* Eyþir

p. 30; Apparatus *delete note to* P 339

p. 42; **L** 501, 513, 515, 517, 522, 523, *for* askede, old, messengers, mani, þen, no⟩lde *read* asked, olde, messangeris, mony, þan, ne wo⟩lde

p. 44; **L** 529 *for* no thyng *read* nothyng; Apparatus, note to **L** 529 *delete* heo *would be an abnormal form in L and*

p. 48; **L** 602 *for* þondur lyȝt *read* þondur-lyȝt

p. 50; **L** 627 *for* afyled *read* a fyled

p. 56; Apparatus line 8 *for* 987 *read* 985

p. 57; **A** 728 *for* Whoso *read* Who so

p. 62; **L** 800 *for* feond *read* Feond

p. 64; **L** 845 *for* Ouer al *read* Oueral

p. 66; **L** 868 *for* feondes *read* Feondes

p. 76; **L** 1042 *for* no þyng *read* noþyng

p. 84; **L** 1165 *for* Belamy *read* Bel amy

p. 87; **A** 1107 *for* ping *read* þing

p. 100; **L** 1377 *for* for why *read* forwhy

p. 114; top line *supply line-number* 1610

p. 169; **A** 2190 *for* Lasse *read* lasse

p. 181; **A** 2639 *for* Whoso *read* Who so

p. 196; **A** 3250 *for* ⟨þe stirop tobent þe *read* þe stirop tobent ⟨þe

p. 230; **A** 4520 *for* sar[a]ins *read* Sar[a]ins

p. 290; **A** 6828 *for* euermore *read* euer more

p. 311; **A** 7646 *for* madame *read* ma dame

There are also two more cases which require a little argument; see below, Commentary, notes to lines **L** 162 and **L** 951.

INTRODUCTION

HEADNOTE

THE romance here edited exists in two quite distinct versions. For the earlier, longer, and better (A) the sole authority is the famous Auchinleck MS. The poem is there titled *Of Arthour and of Merlin*, which I have preferred to the hitherto usual editorial reduction *Arthour and Merlin*. Any reference to the romance below by the abbreviation AM is to this version, though with the reservation that A may not precisely represent what the poet of AM wrote. There also exists a late transcript of much of A, which has no real claim to be regarded as a 'manuscript of the romance'.

The later version is preserved in three manuscripts, a short fragment of transcript which is not of any of the three, and one early print which is likewise not from any of the surviving manuscripts; the earliest of these are a century later than A. Because of its close textual relationship to A I denote this version AM2, though in itself it would have no claim to the same title, since it is brought to an end before the birth of Arthur.

The romance was first edited by William Turnbull in 1838,[1] an expensively turned-out but hardly a scholarly edition, containing little editorial matter and many minor errors. Turnbull prints A, and the 'short fragment' (H) of AM2. The only satisfactory edition is that of Eugen Kölbing (1890); he prints A, the two leading manuscripts of AM2, and full variants from the others.[2] A few erroneous reports of manuscript readings survived his evidently thorough checking; I print a list as Appendix 2 (pp. 268–9 below), not from any wish to vaunt my text as superior but so that a reader using both can see whether a discrepancy is one I have taken account of or one which may reflect my error or carelessness. Kölbing's introduction is long and scholarly, and will always remain of main importance in the study of the poem, especially for its full treatment of all related versions of the story, in many languages; his notes and glossary are useful but very compressed;

[1] For details of this edition, as of all works cited summarily, see the Bibliography (pp. 258–65 below).
[2] As well as the first part of Louelich's *Merlin*.

his index of proper names is in intention complete, and almost so in fact, but marred by frequent confounding together of name-sakes and division of persons whose names have variant forms. I refer to this edition frequently below, usually as 'Kölbing' simply. Schipper took from Kölbing the extract, A 983–1170, which he inserted in the sixth edition (1901) of Zupitza's *Übungsbuch*,[1] under the title 'Aus "Arthur and Merlin". Das Wunderkind Merlin'. He emends freely, usually to improve metre. Besides these, the Percy (**P**) version of AM2 is edited by Furnivall, as 'Merline', in Volume I, pp. 401–96, of the Hales and Furnivall edition of the Percy ballads and romances,[2] with short extracts of the leading manuscripts of AM2.

The first modern printing of any parts of the romance in fact preceded all the above editions: in 1805[3] George Ellis included in his *Specimens of Early English Metrical Romances*, under the title 'Merlin', a number of extracts, derived variously from the Lin-coln's Inn MS. (**L**) of AM2 and from A, with linking summaries. There is no attempt to provide a scholarly text; the work would give the general reader, for whom it was intended, a very fair impression of the whole. Finally, in 1915 Jessie L. Weston printed in *The Chief Middle English Poets* unsatisfactory modern verse paraphrases of several extracts.

The main source of the romance is evidently a version of that part of the 'Vulgate' French prose Arthurian cycle known as the *Merlin Ordinaire*, the French Prose *Merlin*, *Lestoire de Merlin*, or simply *Merlin* (here denoted LeM), which was the source also of two much closer and less interesting Middle English versions, the English Prose *Merlin* (EPM), and a verse rendering by Henry Louelich the Skinner (Louelich). Since discussion of the affiliations of the texts of the romance turns in places on their relationship with this French source, I alter the usual order of sections in an Introduction such as this and deal with the source first.

---

[1] Schipper was responsible for revisions of this from the 5th to the 11th editions. Once inserted the extract was retained; I have used the 11th ed. (1915).

[2] The re-edition by Gollancz (1905–10) referred to in the 5th supplement to the Wells *Manual* is in fact merely a reprint, in a series under Gollancz's general editorship, of the text of this edition.

[3] The second edition (1811) makes inconsiderable alterations, at least in 'Merlin'. The third, revised by Halliwell (1848), makes a few textual corrections to the extracts, corrects some footnotes, and supplies a number more; it is in this form that the book is most commonly to be found.

SOURCE AND TREATMENT OF SOURCE

There is no critical edition of LeM, which survives in more than fifty manuscripts (besides six early printed texts); see accounts by Mead in the Introduction to his EPM, pp. clxi ff., and (more complete, though restricted to manuscripts containing the first part of LeM) by Micha in 'Les Manuscrits du *Merlin*'. I could not hope to make a systematic examination of these versions, therefore all references here to LeM must be in some degree provisional. I have, however, examined those manuscripts which seemed most likely to be relevant, accepting Mead's guidance on their relationship to EPM, since (as will appear) the source used by the AM poet must have been similar to that used by the EPM translator. It seems probable that the group of manuscripts denoted by Micha x' offers a text at most points closest in detail to that used by the AM poet, though it omits a number of passages which his source plainly had, in which matter Micha's group y³ gives the best text. The best manuscript of the x' group, according to Micha, is Bibliothèque Nationale fonds français (hereafter Bibl. Nat. f. fr.) 24394 (A'), but I have found this to contain numerous small omissions and confusions which would make its use as my main basis for quotation inconvenient. Very close to it, and better in this respect (though later, and inferior in some readings), is British Library (hereafter BL) Additional MS. 10292 (G'). This is the basis of Sommer's edition of LeM (part of his edition of the whole 'vulgate' cycle), and I therefore cite from Sommer (by page and line) unless otherwise stated, adjusting on occasion from A'. The best manuscript of the y³ group is unquestionably Bibl. Nat. f. fr. 105 (W); Sommer prints many variants from it in footnotes, to which, or to the manuscript itself, I refer in passages absent from G' and A', and when occasionally it is closer in detail to AM than these. Punctuation and capitalization in all quotations from LeM are my own.

LeM is composed of two distinct sections. The first section, which carries the story up to the coronation of Arthur[1] (equivalent to the first 3,006 lines of AM, although in AM the actual coronation takes place slightly later), is certainly in part, and probably wholly, a redaction of a poem by Robert de Boron, of which only

[1] i.e. *Artus*. I normally refer to persons and places by the accepted modern English form, if one exists.

a fragment of 502 lines survives. Two manuscripts of LeM[1] at this point claim authorship for Boron, probably merely reproducing a colophon which stood at the end of the poem. The second section[2] represents the most commonly found of several continuations of the story. It is rather clumsily joined to the first, for the first concludes *Ensi fu Artus esleus a roy, et tint la terre et le regne de Logres lonc tans en pais* (88, 17–18), while the second at once proceeds to describe the war against the rebellious barons and the many wars against the invading Saxons which follow. The derivation of AM is more clearly to be seen in this second section than in the first, for which reason I treat them in reverse order.

The Second Section of the Story

In this section at least it seems very probable that LeM was the sole source of AM. The form of the main story is closely similiar, although subsidiary episodes are sometimes absent in AM and the order in which events are described often differs somewhat. The comparatively few additions in AM are all such as an adapter could well have made without any particular source. There is in nearly all cases close correspondence, allowing for scribal botching, between the names of characters and places and the numbers in the different groups of knights. Two examples, of many, will suffice to illustrate this.

The kings who come to Arthur's court at his coronation, and rebel against him, are listed in LeM thus:

A cele cort . . . vint li rois Lot d'Orcanie, qui tint la terre de Loenois et vne partie de la terre d'Orcanie; cil vint a court atout v̂ cheualiers de pris. Et d'autre part vint li rois Vriens de la terre de Gorre, qui estoit iones cheualiers de pris, atout v̂. Apres vint li rois Nantes de Garlot, qui ot la seror Artu, atout vīj cheualiers. Apres vint li rois Carados Biebras, qui [estoit rois de la terre de̦ Strangorce et[3]] fu vns des cheualiers de la table roonde; cil amena vj̄ cheualiers. Apres vint li rois Agustans, moult bien a harnois, qui estoit rois d'Escoce; si estoit iones cheualiers et preus as armes; si amena v̂ cheualiers. [Apres vint li roys Ydiers, atout iiii̊ cheualiers.[4]] (88, 20–7)

---

[1] Bibl. Nat. f. fr. 747 (A), and BL Addit. MS 32125 (B).

[2] Micha refers to this section as the *Suite-Vulgate*, and elsewhere reserves to it the title of *la Vulgate de Merlin*. It is also sometimes known as the *Livre d'Artus*, but Sommer uses this title for the collection of stories of King Arthur which in Bibl. Nat. f. fr. 337 replaces the final part of LeM.

[3] Supplied from A[1], f. 141va, 15.   [4] Supplied from W, f. 162rb, 9–10.

In AM (3067 ff.) the names, territories, and numbers are closely similar, except for some confusion producing an absurdly large force with Urien, for a variation in the size of Yder's party, and for Yder's territorial designation *of þe marche*, although they are not given in quite the same order.

The heathens, and the Christians who strike them down, in LeM 151, 11 ff. and in AM 6160 ff. may be compared thus (certain of the forms are slightly closer to AM in A', f. 165ra, 9 ff, than in G'; where this is so I quote the A' form):

LeM			AM		
Bans	fells	Sornegrieu	Ban	fells	Sornegrex
Bohort	,,	Marganant	Bohort	,,	Marganan
Artus	,,	Sinelant	Arthour	,,	Sinalaut
Ulfins	,,	Balant (A')	Vlfin	,,	Sabalant
Bretel	,,	Cordant	Bretel	,,	Cordant
Keu	,,	Candenart	Kay	,,	Dan Deriard
Lucans	,,	Malec	Lucan	,,	Malard
Gyrflet (A')	,,	Mendap (A')	Grifles	,,	Menadap
Meragis	,,	Sardup	Meragys	,,	Sadap
Gornain Cadrus	,,	Dorilas	Gornenis	,,	Maupas
			Craddok	,,	Darrilas

The lists are evidently the same in substance.[1]

In many cases there is close verbal similarity between LeM and AM, apart from these names and numbers. Kölbing gives many instances in his Introduction, pp. cxxix–cxxxiv, though he was handicapped by having to rely on an early printed text of LeM which is quite often further from AM than readings now available. I print here only a few illustrative examples, chosen almost at random out of the large number which could be cited:

LeM	cf. AM
. . . que li rois Lot fu si estordis que il vole ius par desus la crupe del ceual a terre. (94, 19–20)	3271–4
Et par ce chastel dont uous oez parler orrent li Sesne tout le recouurier et tout le secours dou pays. (W; 131 note 4, 17–19)	4451–2
Et li rois Bans . . . salua le roy Leodegan . . . et li rois li dist que bien fust il venus se por son bien i venoit. (141, 25–7)	5504–6

---

[1] On *Sabalant* in AM see below, p. 71 n. 9; on *Maupas* and *Craddok* below, Commentary, notes to lines 5427–9 and 6187–8.

LeM	cf. AM

. . . car il estoit venus en lor ost en samblance de garchon
a piet, j tronchon de lanche en sa main. (186, 17–19)   7248–51

. . . quant il virent uenir l'auant-garde des Sesnes, atout
xv mil hommes . . . il ni porrent mie trop longuement
durer . . . ne iamais n'arestaissent tant qu'il venissent a
Bredigan se ne fust Gaheries qui leur vint poignant, atout
iiij hommes. (W; 195 note 1, 1–14)   8037–42

'Sacies', fait Merlins, 'qu'il n'a que iiij hommes en ceste
place qui les soustienent.' (242, 4–5)   9925–6

The source manuscript of AM was close to that of EPM;
they generally follow the same LeM tradition, and sometimes EPM
preserves matter underlying AM but not found in any form of LeM
which I have examined: thus the *king Adameins* of AM 4306 is
supported by a *kynge Anadonain* in EPM 173, 17–18, and the statement that the 'king of the hundred knights' *ladde* neuer lasse rout
þan *an hundred kniȝtes about* (3739–40) by the qualification preserved in EPM that he had always with him a hundred *whan he
hadde leeste peple* (185, 2). Therefore on occasion one can appeal
to EPM as well as to LeM in the criticism of AM—yet with caution,
for there are also cases in which AM and EPM follow different
traditions, a striking instance being AM's statement in lines 8903–
7 that *þis Nacien . . . seþþen hadde Launcelot in his ward*. This
accords with the x¹ tradition in LeM, *icil Nasciens ot puis Launcelot
. . . en sa baillie* (221, 38–9), whereas EPM's *This knyght hadde
after Galaad the sone of Launcelot . . .* (326, 28–9) follows the y³
tradition, *icist ot puis . . . Galaad le filz Lancelot* (W f. 233ᵛᶜ, 21–
3). Notable also is one case in which AM seems to preserve a more
original form than either EPM or any text of LeM which I have
examined: *Normaga of Sorailes* in line 4302, though corrupted,
must rest on a tradition including both *le roy de Noruaga* who
appears in LeM (W; 125 note 2, 2–3) and *the kynge of Sorloys* who
appears in EPM (173, 13).¹

The Author's Use of his Source in the Second Section

As the above shows, it is impossible to be certain at any point
exactly what form of the source the AM poet knew, and all discussion of changes which he appears to have made are therefore sub-

¹ See further below, Commentary, note to line 4302.

ject to reservation. Particularly is this so where he seems to have added material; his source was evidently fuller than any available version of it at one or two points, so it may well have been so at others. Nevertheless, since AM differs far more from LeM than any of the versions of it which I have seen do from each other, the majority of the differences are probably due to the AM poet, and an analysis of his literary practice based on this assumption will be sound generally, if not in every detail.

The most obvious difference is that the original has been much contracted in AM. This contraction is by no means uniform. For one thing, while the main events of the story are all taken over, various digressive episodes are entirely omitted.[1]

In LeM 99, 2–12 Ulfin and Bretel, seeking Ban and Bohort, come first to Ban's castle of Trebes, where they meet Ban's wife Helaine, but learn that Ban himself is with Bohort at Benoyc. On their way thither they meet the seven robber-knights. This visit to Trebes would occur in AM between lines 3446 and 3447; its absence is a gain to the coherence of the story, since nothing of importance arises from it.

In LeM 159, 19–31, Guinevere is compared for wisdom and beauty with Elaine, daughter of king Pelles of Listenois, and the author digresses to speak of Elaine and of her uncles, king Alain and king Pollinor, all of whom are involved in the story of the Grail. The equivalent point in AM would be, approximately, between lines 6577 and 6578, but in fact the whole passage, quite irrelevant to the immediate story, is omitted.

The account of the birth of Ywain *li auoutres*, got by Urien on his steward's wife, which occupies LeM 165, 25–42, is also omitted in AM, though the character appears later as Ywain the bastard. It occurs in LeM as a digression from the account of Urien's help to Aguiscan which is rendered in AM 6847 ff.; this Ywain was one of those whom Urien left to guard his city. It again is irrelevant to the main story, and it is too like the important story of Leodegan and Cleodalis' wife; its elimination is a gain.

On a rather different footing is the excision of a great deal of material in LeM 168–78 dealing with the wars of Nantres, Brangoires, Karados, Clarion, and Escan against the ravaging Saxons,

---

[1] Not all, of course. The story of Arthur's lying with Liʒanor (4179–92) and the long account of Naciens and his family (8883–926) are retained, for instance, though they might with advantage to the movement of the story have been cut out.

for which the AM poet substitutes a brief, new, link-passage (lines 6977-90). This cannot be regarded as digressive material, since the fact that the rebels soon had too much to do in their own lands to prosecute their feud with Arthur is a major element of the story, but the poet may well have felt that their wars were of less importance than Arthur's and those of the young bachelors, and ought not to be allowed to overweight the story. We may feel that he would have done better to have gone further in reducing them; what he has done is certainly an improvement.

In some cases, of course, he may have intended not to excise but to include at a more appropriate point in his work, after AM as we now have it breaks off. Thus in having Merlin go straight from Blaise to Arthur in lines 8577-8 he omits a long stretch of material which appears at this point in LeM. But Merlin's visit to Leonce of Paerne to warn him of impending attack (LeM 207, 23-208, 36) might well have been dealt with later, when the attack itself was to be described; the assembly of the rebels at Lincestre, where they agree to come together for one great battle against the Saxons (212, 13-213, 14), could fitly precede the description of the battle; Merlin's meeting with Vivian (208, 37-212, 8) could have been reserved so that the whole story of his involvement with her could be told as one. In this last case, however, the fact that the only reference to Vivian which is taken over into AM is quite garbled (see below, Commentary, note to line 4446) may suggest that the poet had little interest in the story and would not have treated it at all; it is in any case clear from the other instances that an important part of his literary technique was the elimination of digressive episodes to give a more straightforward story line.

A particularly interesting case of omission concerns Mordred. LeM first presents him as a full brother of Gawain, etc. (73, 22), but then as a bastard half-brother, sired by Arthur (96, 31-2), and the story of how Arthur got him on his half-sister, the wife of king Lot, when neither was aware of the relationship, is given at length in 128, 26-129, 28. AM omits all of this, and makes only a brief reference to Mordred as Gawain's infant brother when, later, the main story requires it (lines 8406 ff.), at a point where LeM again refers to his incestuous begetting (201, 33-4). In this case it is possible that the AM poet knew and followed a specific tradition of Mordred's legitimacy, in opposition to what became the established romance tradition (the two traditions became politically important in later disputes between England and Scotland[1]). But since the omission and simplification would be entirely in accord with his general style of treatment, it is at least as likely that his work helped to establish the tradition of legitimacy.

The same stylistic tendency can be seen in the relative degree of compression of different aspects of the story. It is the main scenes of action which receive fullest treatment; chiefly battles and other violence, though feasting also attracts the poet. In such scenes AM is often little shorter than its source, and there are long passages of fluent, skilful, but quite close translation. Sometimes the poet seems even to have expanded, though as noted above that can never be said with complete certainty. Passages, necessary to the plot, linking these scenes are in contrast heavily (and often expertly) compressed, as are passages of personal description. The effect is to produce a story close-packed with action, which the poet no doubt knew would appeal to that English taste for 'the adventurous, sensational part of the French romances' long since pointed out by Ker in *English Literature: Medieval* (p. 72). It is easy to take a patronizing view of this taste. Modern readers often find the battle-scenes boring. But this is largely because the proper pace is lost by imperfect fluency in reading Middle English. Here the first battle of Carohaise, particularly (lines 5585–6430), is most attractively presented; the scene shifts repeatedly between the groups involved, but we never lose the feeling of the steady onward drive of the whole battle.

To exemplify fully the poet's practices one would have to print LeM and AM as parallel texts; here a few examples must suffice. As an instance of quite close, though by no means word-for-word translation, we may compare the encounter of Arthur and Ionap,

---

[1] See an admirable survey by Flora Alexander in her 'Scottish Attitudes to . . . Arthur'. The Mordred of Wace and Laȝamon is clearly legitimate; they expand Geoffrey of Monmouth's simple statement that he was Arthur's *nepos*. It seems probable that in the first section of the story the AM poet incorporated a number of details from the form of it of which these are the main representatives (see below, pp. 26–32), so he could have done the same here. The tradition of Mordred's bastardy presumably comes from an assumption that a traitor was unlikely to be of pure blood, so *nepos* in GM was euphemistic. A manuscript of the *Chronicon de Regibus Angliae* ascribed to Peter Ickam (probably late thirteenth century), which is derived from GM, makes him Arthur's son by a concubine (see Fletcher's *Arthurian Material* . . ., pp. 174 and 188); the full tale is apparently first developed in LeM.

and the fighting which follows, in AM 8855–82 and in LeM 221, 9–23:

Et il uindrent tost et roidement, et li rois Ionap feri le roy Artu si durement en l'escu que sa lance, qui roide estoit, li passe outre vne brachie [res a res del coste senestre[1]], et li rois Artus feri lui si durement que parmi l'escu et parmi l'auberc li conduist le fer trenchant, parmi l'espaule. Mais li Sesnes fu de grant orguel et de si grant force que onques n'en fist samblant qu'il fust de riens greues; ains s'entrehurtent si durement des cors et des cheuaus qu'il s'entreportent a terre, les cheuals sour les cors, et iurent moult grant piece si estourdi qu'il ne sorent noient li vns del autre. Et lors poignent a la rescouse d'ambes ij pars; iluec ot grant froceis de lances et grant capleis sour hiaumes et sour escus. Iluec perdirent plus li iaiant que li Crestien, et non porquant il se traueillierent tant d'ambes ij pars que releue furent li ij roy. Si recommencha li estors fors et merueilleus. Illuec firent merueilles li cheualier de la table roonde et li xlij compaignon; encontre cels ne pot nule esciele durer, tant fust seree. Ains les amenerent al estandart; si furent si durement esfree la maisnie Solinas qu'il n'atendent fors al fuir.

In the usual terms of praise applied to a translation, the version in AM 'reads like an original', though the action is faithfully reproduced. The elimination of the period when the two kings lay stunned speeds up the movement, as does the jettisoning of the reference to the greater loss of the *iaians* than the Christians. The urgent but confused action before the kings are remounted is caught better in 8873–4 than in the French; the sudden and complete flight of the enemy is more successfully conveyed by the brief monosyllabic statement of 8882 than in the more steady-paced original. Many other instances of close but far from slavish translation can be found, notably in the battle-descriptions between 4795 and 5314 (LeM 135, 36–140, 24).

When contracting, the poet in some cases makes great reductions with no significant loss of sense. Thus, the approach of Galescin (AM Galathin) to his mother appears thus in LeM 127, 27–35:

Icil Galescins dont ie vous parole oi la nouele que li rois Nantres s'estoit combatus encontre le roy Artu, son oncle, et il auoit oi la grant proece que el roy Artu estoit; si en vint a sa mere et li dist: 'Bele mere, dont ne fustes vous fille al duc de Tintaioel et a la roine Ygerne, qui puis ot a seignor le roy Vterpandragon, qui engendra en lui, si comme i'ai oi conter, cel hoir qui est apeles li rois Artus, qui tant est preus et

---

[1] Supplied from A[1], f. 191rb, 6–7.

boins cheualiers, qui xi princes a descomfit a si petit de gent comme il auoit, si comme i'ai oi conter? Por Dieu dites moi la uerite s'il fu fiex Uterpandragon, qui fu a son tans li plus preudons del monde.'

The skilful précis in AM 4569–74 gives all the substance of the longer passage, and the elimination of the doubling which arises when Galescin is described as putting to his mother what he has just been described as learning is certainly a literary gain.

Not all is gain, of course. The breathless eagerness of the young man cannot be conveyed in the shortened speech, and he is to that extent less a character. Similar, but more serious, is the loss of subtlety in the exchanges between Galescin and Gawain before they agree to set out together to seek Arthur:

. . . et Gauaines li dist: 'Biaus cousins Galescin, vous me mandastes par j message que ie venisse a vous parler, iou et mi frere, et sacies se ce ne fust por ce que ie voloie prendre congie a vous ie m'en fuisse ales en vn lieu ou i'ai moult a faire, et ie ne desire nule riens autant comme ce que ie i fuisse.' 'Sire,' fait Galescins, 'ou deues vous aler?' 'Sacies', fait Gauaines, 'que ie m'envois ueoir la proece et la merueille et toute la larguece del monde, et dont iou ai oi dire plus de bien.' 'Dieu merci,' fait Galescin, 'qui est ce donques? Ore doinst Diex que ce soit por quoi ie vous auoie mande.' 'Certes,' fait Gauaines, 'ses nons ne doit pas estre celes, ains doit estre noumes deuant tous preudomes: il a anon li rois Artus, et si est nostre oncles et le vostre . . .' (133, 30–134, 5).

The reduction of this to the simple speech of AM 4657–64 certainly makes the action swifter and more direct, but the loss of these fencing exchanges is to a modern judgement a heavy price to pay. Yet such losses are not very many. Often AM seems simply well rid of repetitiousness in its source. The AM poet disposes in the four lines 8227–30 of Gawain's inquiry of Ywain concerning the letters which had brought him to Ywain's help; LeM takes ten much longer ones:

. . . si vint Gauaine a Yuonet le grant et li dist: 'Biau cousins, comment seustes vous qui nous estiens ici assamble, et par quel consel m'enuoiastes vous vos lettres l'autre soir?' 'Quels letres?' fait Yuonet, 'certes, ie ne vous enuoiai onques letre iour de ma vie, ne ie ne sauoie de vous nules noueles quant Diex nostre sires vous i enuoia en tel point comme vous me veistes, car tout y fuissiemes ochis ou prins et retenus se si tost ne fuissies venus.' 'Comment, biaus cousins,' fait Gauaine, 'le dites vous a certes que vous ne m'enuoiastes onques lettres?' 'Sire,' fait il, 'voirement le di iou, si ne vous mens de rien.' Quant Gauaine entent

que Yuones ne li enuoia onques letre ne message s'en a moult grant
merueille, et tout cil qui l'oirent s'esmerueillent dont la letre pot venir
. . . (198, 3–13).

The contraction has happy effect, eliminating the unnecessary
reference back to the events of the battle and the tiresome repetition of *ne . . . onques letre*. How far the poet was aware of such
points, of course, one cannot tell. Very probably to him this
passage was on all fours with the one previously quoted, just an
unduly long interruption to the story of action which he was
writing. He would have had the same motive in cutting such
passages of personal description as that of the transformed Merlin
who advises Gawain to return to Arundel after his successful
battle in association with Keus Destraus, Kehedin, and the squires
from the city. In LeM (200, 37–41) this is quite elaborate; in AM
8302 he is described simply as *an eld kniȝt*.

The poet's judgement in deciding, among many scenes and
incidents of action, which are deserving of full treatment and
which should be compressed is less easy to analyse, but seems to
rest on the same principles: in particular his compression of
certain incidents within long battles usually gives quicker and
more direct flow to the main action.[1] Thus the encounter of Rion
and Bohort, and the fighting which follows involving Aroans,
Herui, and Adragenis, is little shorter in AM 9007–30 than in
LeM 223, 29–224, 4, but Bohort's previous fight against Fansaron
is considerably reduced. In LeM this is presented in two long
'flash-backs' interrupting Rion's attack on Bohort, the beginning
of which is again described between them (222, 30–223, 13). The
poet probably found it too detailed compared with the fight
against Rion to which it serves as introduction, and the flash-back
technique did not suit his preference for direct narration; he gives
the fight briefly and straightforwardly in lines 8981–93. A similar
reason may account for his suppression of several other killings
after Ban has felled Sortibran (6379–82, cf. LeM 155, 3–8); he is

---

[1] This will hardly account for the heavy contraction of Arthur's first fight
against the fleeing Rion. In LeM 229, 32–232, 10 this is given at length, with
descriptions of the marvellous swords of the two kings and of their exchange of
accounts of their lineages, all of which is reduced to the few lines 9349–66 in
AM. Here, however, the AM poet probably included much of the material in
the later fight in which Arthur wins Rion's sword (compare his practice discussed
below, pp. 14–15), and it would be found on the missing f. 254A.

thus able to link more directly Ban's success with Ban's peril. Similarly, again, he compresses the bloody vengeance taken on Thaurus' body by Gawain's brothers (LeM 204, 13–16) into the two lines 8493–4 to allow him to keep the reader's attention on Gawain and his mother.

His compression of whole battles of subsidiary importance is particularly interesting. Here we sometimes find the entire sequence of events altered, yet with some incidents and turns of phrase clearly reflecting the source, as though he had looked at the relevant part of LeM, decided not to translate closely, and then without further reference to the French had constructed his own account. Such incidents and phrases from the original as were running in his head reappear, but not necessarily in the original context. Thus in the battle between Ulfin and Bretel and the seven robber-knights, in LeM 99, 37–100, 27, first the leader of the seven attacks, and Bretel thrusts him through the left shoulder, felling him. Then two more attack, of whom Bretel kills one by a thrust through the throat and Ulfin thrusts the other through the shoulder. Two more are dispatched, one thrust through the body by Bretel and the other breaking his neck when felled by Ulfin, and the two survivors flee. The version in AM 3452–88, perhaps half the length, has a different number and distribution of killings, but the unusual thrust through the throat is reproduced,[1] as is the neck-breaking, though the latter is combined with a wound through the *membre* which is not in the original. Similarly, in the battle against the eleven rebel kings (LeM 114, 40–121, 23; AM 3865–4052), LeM's description of the felling of Kay (*Keu*) by the king of the hundred knights is reproduced, but placed much earlier in the battle than in LeM, following Kay's striking down of Yder; in LeM Kay had just felled Lot.

This same practice of sometimes translating rather from memory than with the original open before him probably accounts also for some of the poet's apparently casual alterations of his source. Thus in LeM 143, 12–14 we are told that Cleodalis used to carry Leodegan's principal banner, but that when the Round Table knights came it was given to Herui, and Cleodalis bore a small one. The statement in AM 5638–9 that Cleodalis at that point bore the *maister gomfainoun* can hardly have arisen otherwise than from an

---

[1] AM 3455–6 is close to LeM 100, 13–14: . . . *et Bretel . . . enouie a celui le glaiue parmi la gorge et l'abat mort a terre del cheual tout estendu.*

imperfect memory of the French. Again, what else but imperfect memory can have changed Guiomar, Leodegan's nephew (LeM 218, 4 = AM 8695), who is with Leodegan in the pursuit of Rion in LeM 229, 13 into *Goionard, Riones nevou* in AM 9330–1 ?[1]

Other cases of apparently casual alteration may, however, be deliberate. Thus when the barons will not have *un homme de si bas lignage* for their king, and refuse Arthur's gifts, LeM says that *quant li rois Artus oi les manaces si issi hors la de maistre forterece* (88, 39–89, 1). In AM we are told in lines 3161–6 that Arthur and his friends drove out his enemies; the intention was doubtless to increase the impression of Arthur's power. A similar desire may have led the poet to have Ulfin and Bretel each fight two of the robber-knights at once, in the passage already referred to, instead of one each, to make Goiomar and Balinas kill four heathen each (9717–18) instead of only one each as in LeM 239, 16–17, to make Arthur go to seek further adventures at 9665 instead of missing his way in the darkness while making for Daneblayse as in LeM 238, 38–40, and to take every opportunity of defining the huge height of the *geauntes* where LeM for the most part merely calls them *grant et fort* or the like.[2]

More clearly deliberate is the way in which the order of narration in AM sometimes varies from that in LeM, bringing together matter which in LeM is dispersed. I have already mentioned (p. 12 and n.) one minor and one uncertain instance of this; the most striking series of instances concerns the 'young bachelors'. In every case LeM deals first with the resolve to seek knighthood of Arthur, and in some cases with the setting out,[3] and only after describing other events returns to say what happened on the resultant expedition;[4] in almost every case AM places the resolve immediately before the expedition.[5]

---

[1] See also below, Commentary, note to line 9670.

[2] Specified heights do sometimes occur in LeM, however, thus 230, 10–12 *il [Rion] . . . auoit bien, ce dist li contes, xiiij pies de lonc, des pies qui lors estoient.* Here AM (8975) removes the proviso, and adds three more feet!

[3] Galescin 127, Gawain and his brothers 130, Sagremor 132, Ywain 167–8, Kay *Destraus* and Kehedin 173–4.

[4] Galescin, Gawain and his brothers 134 ff., Sagremor 179 ff., Ywain 190 ff., Kay and Kehedin 198 ff.

[5] Galathin (= LeM Galescin), Gawain and his brothers 4569 ff., Ywain 7643 ff., Kay *Destran* and Kehedin (whose resolve is only briefly alluded to) 8238 ff. The references to Sagremor remain divided (4483–8, 6991 ff.); details of his resolve are cut out altogether.

In these rearrangements, as in his omissions, the poet is plainly seeking—and with skill and success—a coherent and straightforward narrative. It is his constant wish. In his version the rebels, after their first defeat by Arthur, swear vengeance (3363–4), and their oath connects this first with their second battle against the king. In LeM the equivalent oath comes during the first battle,[1] where there is no particular need for a link. While describing the embassy of Ulfin and Bretel to Ban and Bohort, LeM gives on pp. 98–9 a good deal of information about the previous wars of Claudas and about the seven knights of his who now attack the ambassadors. In AM such of this as is retained is reserved to follow the battle against the seven, and appears in lines 3491–3502; the expedition and encounter of Ulfin and Bretel can thus be recounted continuously, and the information about Claudas introduced by a reference to the knights whose actions have just been described. In LeM the curious nature of Gawain's strength is described at 129, 42–130, 3, where he first enters the story; to the poet of AM it seemed more appropriate to recount it where it first affects a fight, and it appears in lines 4781–94, at the equivalent point to which LeM merely says that *bien estoit midis passes* (135, 37). At 148, 1–23 LeM breaks into the account of Arthur's and Leodegan's fight against the Saxons to give the names of Arthur's party, *car moult font bien a nomer deuant tous preudommes.* Rather than have the action here interrupted by a long list, the AM poet incorporates it instead, in lines 5403 ff., at the point where the party arrives before Leodegan and there is no rapid action to be broken into, as an extension and modification of LeM's statement here that they *se tindrent tout main a main et en vindrent deuant le roy Leodegan l'un apres l'autre, et li rois Artus fu soi xli^{ime} auoec Merlin* (141, 18–20). In LeM the beginning of Yder's engagement against Soriondes' rearguard is described at 190, 27–31; then the account is broken off and the encounter of the brothers Ywain with the vanguard is dealt with; then the story turns to Merlin's message to Gawain and the array of Gawain's forces, and only then, at 192, 28, returns to Yder. In AM the whole of Yder's battle is described consecutively, in lines 7743–73. These are but a few of the many cases which could be cited. Vinaver has regarded a similar tendency in Malory as reflecting his date at the close of

[1] 95, 23–4; the equivalent placing in AM would be between 3345 and 3346.

the age of Romance (*Rise of Romance*, 127), but as Benson points out[1] it is in fact general in Middle English. Similar procedures can be demonstrated in the Stanzaic *Morte Arthur*, in *Ywain and Gawain*, and elsewhere.

The poet's capacity for neat adjustment of his original goes beyond mere rearrangement of order, to unobtrusive adjustment of substance where his excisions would otherwise leave loose ends. Thus his cutting of the story of Mordred's begetting, mentioned on p. 8, leaves him without the particular reason why Mordred's mother hates the war against Arthur which LeM supplies at 129, 34–6, namely that after the birth of his child the mother finds herself with a great love for Arthur in her heart. He makes her reason for urging Gawain to go to Arthur merely her general desire for reconciliation between Arthur and her husband Lot (4619–22), and, to balance this, at 4587–92 gives to Blasine a similar desire for which there is no warranty at all in LeM, where the whole initiative in this case comes from Galescin (127, 29 ff.). The most striking example of such neat readjustment arises from the elimination of a series of engagements of Nantres and others against the Saxons which was noticed on pp. 7–8. The story in AM is resumed with the landing of Sagremor. In LeM, having landed at Dover, he encounters a large group of Saxons from Oriel's force, which is ravaging in the area of *Norhaut*. This Oriel, *vns iones cheualiers qui moult estoit preus et hardis* (175, 1–2), is probably the same who at 164, 9 was among the conductors of booty whom the AM poet identified with *les x rois* of 165, 8 (see below, Commentary, note to line 6770). He certainly identifies the present leader with his king Oriens, and he supplies an effective link with the previous battle which he had described by making the survivors of that battle flee to Oriens (6955–8), where LeM 167, 1–3 merely had them fleeing to woods and forests, and by making it Oriens' desire for vengeance which leads him to embark on the ravaging expedition on which he meets Sagremor (6978–90); his anger at being worsted in this encounter is then made the reason for his embarking on the further burst of rapine which at 7271 ff. brings

[1] 'Sir Thomas Malory's *Le Morte Darthur*', 107–19. When the present work was in form for press there also appeared his *Malory's Morte Darthur*, in which he develops the theme further, illustrating English romance practice with an analysis of the AM poet's treatment of his source (pp. 52–7) which is generally similar to that here, though worked out quite independently (he has not used the original thesis form of the present edition).

Estas and Clarion into the field against him.[1] Oriens' continuing angry activity between his engagements against Sagremor and against Estas and Clarion is emphasized in the passage 7265–8, in which the poet has reversed the sense of LeM, which explains (186, 29–31) that the squires were left in peace because the Saxons had disappeared into Northumberland and into the territory of the Duke of Cambernic. Thus he neatly joins up his story, using the person of Oriens and his desire for vengeance as a link, so that one could not tell without reference to LeM that any matter had been omitted. The action makes geographical nonsense, of course, moving casually from Scotland to Sussex, but the action of LeM does not take place in any real Britain,[2] and amorphous topography is as licit in AM as in its source.

For the most part, then, the adaptation of LeM is made with considerable skill directed to a clear purpose. There is a price to pay, as we have seen, in the loss of some of the few subtleties of the original,[3] but since they are few the general gain in pace may seem worth it. More unfortunate are certain instances in which the action becomes obscure,[4] but they are neither many nor serious enough to affect one's general judgement of the poet's skill, unless

[1] In LeM (186, 36 ff.) Oriel merely joins a battle against Escan and Clarion which some of his men are already conducting.

[2] Oriel, for instance, reaches the area of *Norhaut* after setting out to plunder provisions in Northumberland, going thither by the river Severn and returning by the Humber.

[3] Two examples above, p. 11. We may also note the loss of Leodegan's courteous anxiety lest, not knowing his guests' degree, he may treat them with less honour than their status calls for, *car vous estes par auenture plus haut homme que ie ne soie* (142, 12–15). In the more direct statement of AM 5545–6 this light on Leodegan's character is lost; moreover the *for* which introduces the statement, rendering *car*, makes no sense. Again, in LeM 149, 6–13 Leodegan, forcing his love on Cleodalis' wife, threatens her with his sword if she makes a sound, and *asses se desfendi la dame par paroles, mais ele n'osa parler en haut; si li valut moult petit sa desfense*. This skilful little touch is lost in the brief account of AM 6492–4. Yet again, in LeM 218, 40–219, 26, when Guinevere helps Arthur to arm before the great battle against Rion, and herself buckles on his sword and spurs, Merlin observes that she has now invested him anew with the order of knighthood, except for one thing, the ceremonial kiss, and they then embrace *comme iouene gent qui moult s'entramoient*. This pleasing and delicately drawn scene is coarsened in AM 8677–80; the idea of conferring knighthood anew is lost and the kissing crudely multiplied (on this, however, see Commentary, note to line 8679). I cannot agree with Mead (EPM, p. lvii), who regards this 'pretty little by-play' as a valuable addition to AM.

[4] See below, Commentary, notes to lines 4625–7, 6343, and 6569.

in one particular case. In LeM III, 20–112, 11, while advising Arthur, Bohort, and Ban before their battle with the rebels near the forest of Bedingran (which appears in AM here as Rok(e)ingham), Merlin takes occasion to advise Arthur on the necessity of generosity, and to tell him that he will not lack the wherewithal because of a vast treasure buried in the earth just there. If this appeared in AM it would probably be between lines 3784 and 3785, but it does not appear, and with its loss is lost the main point of the tale of the two birds shot by the transformed Merlin, namely that Merlin wishes to force on Arthur's attention that he is not following the advice to cultivate generosity. The story of the birds is nevertheless retained in AM (4133–74), including a reference to buried treasure which would mean nothing to one who did not know the fuller story. Excision of this story would be in line with the AM poet's practice elsewhere, since it would be an interruption of a direct narrative of military dispositions; but the clumsy management seems well below his usual level of skill, and the failure here may rather be in the more difficult task of correcting an obscurity in his source. In Malory, too, Merlin's advice about generosity, with revelation of the treasure, is absent;[1] at one other point AM and Malory can be shown to go back to a common source different from any other known version,[2] and here also both probably derive from a version of LeM defective in omitting Merlin's advice.

In contrast with his numerous contractions, cases in which the poet seems to have expanded his source are infrequent, but scenes of battle, cruelty, lamentation, and feasting are sometimes extended, either by the insertion of further conventional description or by supplying deeds for knights not individually mentioned in LeM.[3] The general effect is of intensification, of the prowess of Christians, the bloodiness of battle, the bitterness of misery, and

---

[1] It would appear on p. 26 of the Vinaver *Works*; Malory however adjusts the remaining reference to the treasure so that it becomes a quite natural first reference (p. 38). See Benson's *Malory's Morte Darthur*, p. 60 and n. 33.

[2] See below, Commentary, note to line 3405.

[3] So 3333–8, 4819–34, 4941–50, 4999–5029, 5181–98, 5615–18 (and other such passages; LeM has much less of this sort of thing, though there is such a passage at 164, 11–18), 5693–5702, 5801–10, 5815–20, 6859–80, 6914–20, 7017–28, 7497–7505, 8132–98, 8641–6, 9157–83, 9319–28, 9675–90, and a good many others. All these are absent, or much shorter, in at any rate those versions of LeM I have been able to examine.

so on—often, it must be admitted, of crude exaggeration. Touches of circumstantial detail may also be added. Some are lively and appropriate,[1] others crude or at best unsubtle,[2] or even so exaggerated as to be silly,[3] and in two cases they are very doubtfully apposite to the context.[4] Some supply a useful link of motivation,[5] others merely make needlessly obvious what is clearly enough implied in the original.[6] The same direct, lively, but unsubtle mind which was responsible for the larger alterations examined above can be seen at work here (most of these additions would probably prove to be the poet's own had we his precise source), in occasional comments on the action, lively but sometimes obvious,[7] and in two outbursts against the wickedness of heathens.[8] Some of the poet's other interventions *in propria persona*, however, are of a different sort and of much greater interest, forming part of what Smithers describes as 'the apparatus of the epic style', but as these are discussed in detail on pp. 68–71 below, in considering whether AM and certain other works are of common authorship, all treatment of them is passed over here.

The First Section of the Story

Here the question of source is less simple. In the first place, though the general form of the story accords with LeM the resemblance in detail is less close; moreover at a number of points AM resembles rather the earlier form of the story which is found in Geoffrey of Monmouth's *Historia* (GM)[9] and is substantially taken over in Wace's *Roman de Brut*, and thence in Laȝamon's

---

[1] 3176, 4633–6, 4686, 6799–6800, 7090–6, 7305–8, 9070, 9275–6.

[2] 5166, 6371–2 (and others similar), 7241–2 (in LeM 186, 5 they merely *esgarde li vns l'autre, si commenchent a rire*), 7352–6, 7357–60, 8417–20, 8733–9.

[3] 5203–5, 5612–14, 7715–16.

[4] 8393–4 probably merely misapplies the usual hope of booty to an expedition which is in fact to rescue Belisent, though it could be argued that *wining* is used with deliberate ironic intent of Gawain's mother. 8768 is probably a conventional image of battle inserted without thought for the silence of which LeM speaks here and which appears also in AM in the next two lines, though again *also stilly so þai miȝten* could be taken for deliberate irony.

[5] 3413–17, 5401–2.

[6] 3989–90, 9384, 9873–4. In the last case, in LeM Leodegan merely *li tent s'espee comme forfais et li prie que son droit en preigne* (W; 240 note, lines 33–5).

[7] 3307–8, 5167–8, 5911–12, 6817.   [8] 8432–3, 9078.

[9] GM quoted from Griscom's edition; I cite, however, merely by book and chapter since this allows reference to most editions and translations (though there is no evidence that Geoffrey intended this division, as Griscom points out, pp. 26–30).

Brut as well as in a number of other works.[1] In the second place,
for much of this section one or more texts of AM2 exist beside
A, and where they diverge it is open to argument which most
nearly represents the original AM. However, in most cases of
fairly close similarity to LeM, A is the closer; I continue therefore
to cite AM in the A form, but whenever the AM2 texts differ sufficiently from A to affect the point at issue, I record the fact.

On the first point, the most striking instances of resemblance
rather to LeM than to the earlier form of the story[2] are:

(i) In the earlier form a vassal Pict murders the old king Constantine, Picts are invited to court by Vortigern and induced to
murder Constantine's son Constans, the monk turned king, and
only after this do Hengest and Horsa arrive in England, to be
hospitably received by Vortigern. In AM, as in LeM, there is no
mention of Picts, the old king is not murdered, and his son is
killed by disaffected barons after his defeat by Angys.

(ii) In the earlier form Arthur is readily accepted as Uter's son
and succeeds to the throne without opposition. AM, like LeM,
has the fostering of Arthur, the machinery of the sword in the
stone, and the reluctance of the barons to accept him.

(iii) The whole elaborate and circumstantial story of the conception, birth, and early childhood of Merlin, which AM shares
with LeM, is absent in the earlier form, where Merlin is merely
described as begotten by a mysterious comer, actually an incubus,
who took the form of a youth.

There are also a good many quite close verbal parallels between
LeM and AM, thus:

LeM	cf. AM[3]
A cest afaire furent doi preudome qui gardoient les autres ij enfans . . . lors prinsent consel li doi . . . Lors s'acordent li doi preudome qu'il s'en fuiront et menront les ij enfans en estraigne terre . . . (21, 36–22, 5)	281–2 and 286–7

---

[1] For a convenient summary of works derived directly or indirectly from GM,
see Parry and Caldwell's chapter 'Geoffrey of Monmouth' in the collaborative
Arthurian Literature in the Middle Ages, ed. Loomis.

[2] See further Kölbing, pp. cxii ff.

[3] In most of these cases the equivalent passages in AM2, if they exist, are
less close to the French; though in the equivalent to A 589–92 it is possible that
the reference in L 535 (similarly P 510, D 612) to the child's birth *fyue winter
perbyfore* may derive from a variant of LeM's *de vij ans*, which is not rendered
in A, and for a somewhat similar case see below, Commentary, note to L 252.

LeM	cf. AM
. . . mais . . . il voent j enfant de vij ans qui estoit nes sans pere d'omme terrien . . . (24, 26–7)	589–92
Ensi enmaine Merlins les messagiers . . . a l'ostel sa mere en vne religion de nounains . . . (26, 14–15)	1275–6
. . . si arresta Merlins et commencha a rire, et cil qui le menoient li demandent por quoi il rioit. (29, 25–6)	1319–22
Et Merlins trait Vter a une part et li dist: 'Pense d'estre preudome, car tu n'as garde de mort en ceste bataille.' Et quant Uter l'oi, si li esioi tous li cuers. (51, 12–14)	2119–24
Bretel prinst la coupe et s'en uint a la table ou Ygerne seoit; si se mist a ienols deuant lui et li dist: 'Dame, li rois vous enuoie ceste coupe . . .' (61, 6–7)	2275–80
'. . . et si te di que tes fiex sera chief de ton regne apres toi, par la uertu de Ihesu Crist, et il sera acomplisables de la table roonde . . .' (79, 22–4)	2747–50

One can also demonstrate, as in the second section, a probable special connection with EPM. AM's phrase at 256 *oȝain say* closely resembles EPM *ageyn hem seide* (25, 9–10), though not used at precisely the same point in the action; the specific sense of 'speak in opposition' which the phrase probably has here[1] is not in any of the LeM texts I have examined, thus . . . *si ne trouerent onques qui grantment en parlast* (21, 27). Again, AM's reference at 2034 to being *vnder his* [Merlin's] *ȝemeing* resembles rather the form of wish in EPM that Merlin should be the brothers' *lorde and gouernour* (48, 35) than the only form I have found in LeM, that Merlin should be *entor mon frere* (43, 33). EPM translates closely throughout, so these are probably further examples of verbal parallelism with the form of LeM which the poet knew.

However, as noted above, such similarities between AM and LeM are not as many or as close as in the second part, and long passages closely rendered are not to be found (although there are passages which appear to be précis of LeM, as instanced on p. 33

---

[1] It could, however, merely mean 'make reply', reflecting the quoted LeM reading (cf. *seyd* . . . *oȝan* 7217, though the usage is not exactly parallel). This, however, would lose the neat connection with line 253: few were opposed, none dared express opposition. The sense of opposition is explicit in the AM2 texts.

below). This difference in treatment between the two parts must be explained if one is to argue (what *a priori* is the most attractive, because most economical, hypothesis) that for the first part as for the second a manuscript of LeM was the principal source. It can hardly have been the sole source, unless in a form so different from those known to me as to amount to a distinct and unrecorded stage in the transmission of the story, because of the fact mentioned above that there are cases in which AM is closer to one or more of the versions of the earlier form of the story than it is to LeM, and which can hardly be due to the poet's independent alteration.

The most important of these concerns the names of the sons of the old king Constantine (or Costaunce). It is also, unfortunately, the one in which the evidence is the most complicated and confusing, so I postpone consideration of it.[1] More straightforward, and only a little less striking, is the matter of the falling of Vortigern's tower. In LeM it is thus described:

> Et quant il l'orent ouure iij toises ou iiij de sus terre en haut si rechai tout ius, et ensi rechai iij fois ou iiij. (23, 14–15)

The description in W is slightly different, but gives no more warranty for the statement in AM 541–56 that the work fell nightly. This could conceivably be the poet's own exaggerating modification, but is more plausibly to be related to the similar statements in all versions of the earlier form of the story,[2] though the further assertion in AM 554 that this nightly falling continued for six months is probably an independent exaggeration.[3] In the reason given for the falling of the tower, that it was caused by the nightly attempt of the two buried dragons to fight, AM (1459–62)[4]

---

[1] See below, pp. 27–32.

[2] GM VI, XVII; Wace 7333–8; Laȝamon 7725–8. Benson has drawn my attention (in a draft of his *Malory's Morte Darthur* which he was kind enough to send me, though pressure of space kept the passage out of the published work) to a similar statement in Heldris' *Roman de Silence* 5789, in a section based on LeM, and thinks it likely that this and AM go back to a variant form of LeM which had it also. That is possible, but if Heldris took the reference to the fall of the tower from LeM, he transplanted it to a new context, and the transplant could as well have been from another source altogether; he certainly knew and used more than one. On other possible connections between AM and *Silence* see below, p. 27 n. 1, and Commentary, note to line 1342.

[3] Wace speaks of *plusurs jurnees* (7337); GM has merely *set quicquid una die operabantur, absorbebat tellus in altera, ita ut nescirent quorsum opus suum euanesceret. Cumque id Uortegirno nuntiatum fuisset . . .*

[4] In AM2 the attempt becomes an actual fight.

specifically resembles Laȝamon (7956–7, possibly, of course, derived from a version of Wace not preserved); in LeM 31, 38–40 the dragons are merely disturbed by the weight erected above them. It is, again, possible that the poet, devising a more plausible reason than the transmission of pressure through the water, hit by chance on the same one that appears in Laȝamon, but not likely. AM (2413–15) also specifically resembles Laȝamon (9292–8) in the statement that the duke Tintagel (in Laȝamon the Earl of Cornwall), after leaving the king's feast, sends for supporters from far and wide, and assembles 15,000; it is unlikely that the numbers are the same by chance.

Independent modification is a more plausible explanation, to a greater or less degree, in the following cases, though taken together and in association with those given above they are strongly suggestive:

(i) LeM starts with the council of demons and the begetting of Merlin, and only after Merlin's redeeming of his mother are the old king (here Constans) and his sons introduced. AM, like all versions of the earlier form, introduces Merlin only after the messengers have set out to seek the fatherless child.[1]

(ii) In LeM it would seem that the Saxons who make war on king Moine are already in the land; at all events nothing is said about their having landed. In the earlier form of the story the Saxons under Hengest and Horsa are described as landing,[2] as Angys is in AM 109 ff. The circumstances of the landing, however, are quite different in AM, and only slight modification would be needed to give the AM form from that of LeM:

Et li Sesne guerroierent le roy Moine, et chaus qui estoient de la loy de Romme si vindrent plusor fois combatre as Crestiens . . . li Sesne . . . s'asamblerent et vindrent a grant ost sor les Crestiens (20, 25–7 and 33–4).

(iii) AM 485–8 states that not only did Vortigern marry Angys' daughter but many other similarly accursed unions were contracted. These other marriages, which do not appear in LeM, may reflect no more than the poet's liking for added circumstantial detail of an exaggerated sort, but may be (inaccurately)

---

[1] Kölbing would scout the possibility of independent modification here; the point is discussed on p. 27 below.
[2] GM VI, X; Wace 6704 ff.; Laȝamon 6879 ff.

inferred from a statement like that of Wace (Laʒamon 7255–7 is similar):

> Tost furent si paien munté,
> As Crestiens entremeslé,
> Avisunques conuisseit l'un
> Ki ert Crestien e ki nun (7063–6).

(iv) AM 1891 says that Vortigern was burned with *wiif and child*; LeM 36, 14 mentions Vortigern only. The modification in AM is slight, but it is notable that one manuscript of Wace adds:

> N'i remest dame ne pucele,
> Et sa feme arst qui molt fu bele.[1]

(v) In LeM 35, 16 Vortigern, warned by Merlin of the arrival of the heirs in three days *al por* [sic] *de Wincestre*, gathers his forces and goes thither to await the landing. In AM 1715–25 Merlin's warning mentions no specific time, and after an unspecified interval a message arrives that the heirs have come and are almost at Winchester;[2] the idea of news of the landing coming to Vortigern may reflect the account as given in Wace, 7599–600, *Vortiger, ki cel plai oi,* | *En Guales fu* ..., though in Wace as in GM Vortigern makes no attempt to give battle but at once prepares for defence.

(vi) In LeM 68, 38–9 Uter expresses sorrow at the death of the Duke of Tintagel: *li rois . . . lor dist que moult li pesa de la mescheance au duc*. In AM 2591–2 he is glad, a minor change which might well have been made independently, but joy as well as sorrow is referred to in GM, *Cumque omnem euentum didicisset, ob necem Gorlois doluit, set ob Ygernam a maritali copula solutam gauisus est* (VIII, XX); or Wace's *Semblant fist que mult l'en pesast,* | *Mais poi i out qui ço quidast* (8801–2) could easily be modified into a straight-forward statement that he was glad.

Besides the above, we may note a few cases in which the phrasing of AM perhaps echoes that of one of the versions of the earlier form, though applied either to a variant form of, or at a different point in, the story:[3]

[1] Bibl. Nat. f. fr. 1416 (denoted by Arnold *J*), following 7652.

[2] The poet has not been skilful here; by the time a disembarked army is almost at the town it is rather late to start writing letters summoning support, as in lines 1731 ff. Even if the messengers sent in AM2 (L 1844 ff.) represent the original AM, this is not much better. See further below, Commentary, note to line 1728.

[3] See also below, Commentary, note to lines 400–1, where, however, the echo turns on an emendation.

(i) Laȝamon (7199, MS. Otho.): . . . *þat þe king makede feste, on mid þe meste.* Compare AM 489, though in AM the reference is general and follows the account of the spread of heathendom in Britain, while in Laȝamon it is specific and precedes.

(ii) Wace 7446–51:

> Par tut l'eir unt lur [the *incubi demones'*] regiun,
> E en la terre unt lur repaire.
> Ne püent mie grant mal faire;
> Ne püent mie mult noisir
> Fors de gaber e d'escharnir.
> Bien prenent humaine figure . . .

AM 651–6 is nearer to this[1] than to the brief statement of LeM 17, 26–7, *et saces que tel maniere d'anemi ont a non esquibedes et repairent en l'air,* though in a different position from the equivalent passage in any other version, being the poet's assertion *in propria persona,* whereas in Wace (as in GM and Laȝamon; Wace is closest verbally to AM) it is an explanation given to Vortigern by a wise clerk, Magant, and in LeM it is Merlin's own statement to the judge who has been trying his mother.

(iii) Wace 7535–42:

> Dunc dist Merlin les prophecies
> Que vus avez, ço crei, oies,
> Des reis ki a venir esteient,
> Ki la terre tenir deveient.
> Ne vuil sun livre translater
> Quant jo nel sai interpreter;
> Nule rien dire ne vuldreie
> Que si ne fust cum jo dirreie.

This is to excuse Wace from rendering the long and highly obscure prophecies, uttered by Merlin when asked by Vortigern concerning the significance of the fight of the dragons, which constitute book seven of GM. LeM at the equivalent point (34, 19–35, 12) inserts a fairly short and quite different interpretation of the fight, making it portend Vortigern's death (which is separately prophesied in GM VIII, I in a form substantially taken over in Wace 7548 ff.). AM 1635–64 has the same interpretation as LeM, though followed by an additional reference to Vortigern's kindred and the heirs' supporters; then, as in LeM, Merlin goes to Blasy, and (as he does

---

[1] The AM2 texts are here slightly nearer still; L 609–16 is representative.

not in LeM[1]) prophesies further to him, and this further prophecy
is referred to and cut off in lines 1697–1706[2] in terms reminiscent
of Wace's.

(iv) GM: *Preualebat autem albus draco, rubeumque usque ad
extremitatem lacus fugabat. At ille, cum se expulsum doluisset, im-
petum fecit in album, ipsumque retro ire coegit* (VII, III). Laȝamon
7976b: *Ne isæh heom seoððe na mon iboren.* The version of the fight
in AM, longer than and different from that of any other version,
yet shows in lines 1525–36 the driving and driving back of GM
(though with the roles reversed), and in 1543–4 the mysterious dis-
appearance found in Laȝamon (though applied to the one survivor).

Now these various similarities between AM and versions of the
earlier form of the story can evidently be explained either by the
poet's having conflated (or, of course, having worked from a
source which conflated), or by his having worked from a source
representing a stage intermediate between the earlier form of the
story and that found in LeM. Conflation seems the more likely
explanation, in view of the displaced similarities. The author of an
intermediate version, particularly, if he moved the prophecy of
Vortigern's death to fill the gap left by Wace's refusal to translate
the dragon-fight prophecies, would surely feel that that had disposed of the refusal, and it would not occur to him to include it
elsewhere. But an author working chiefly from LeM might well
have some recollection of the refusal-passage in his mind from
an earlier reading of Wace, unconnected with the prophecy which
appeared in his chief source. Kölbing, however (p. cxxvi), argues
strongly that AM derives from an 'übergangsstufe'.[3] He does not
consider the dragon-prophecies; his main reason lies in the placing

---

[1] LeM refers later (48, 15) to *li contes des profecies Merlin* as a collection of
obscure sayings of Merlin begun by the barons of Pendragon and Uter; this
reference is not reproduced in AM.

[2] The specific refusal to tell more (1706) is not in L or P, but D 1231 has it.

[3] Bülbring's review of Kölbing opposes this argument at length. Several of
Bülbring's arguments are similar to those presented here; a further one, at first
sight powerful, is from the supposed inconsistency in AM by which the old
king, when dying, is made to ignore his promise to permit his eldest son to
forgo the succession and enter a monastery. This would strongly suggest a clumsy
combination of forms with and without the monk-story rather than derivation
from an intermediate version. But Bülbring was evidently treating *graunted*
(54) as indicative, denoting consent, even if reluctant, by the king to his heir's
wish, whereas it is better taken as subjunctive (see below, Commentary, note
to lines 53–4).

of the account of Merlin's birth. Boron, he says, placed it first because for him Merlin was the principal character of his work, while in the earlier form of the story he was merely one character among many in the long history of the British kings. Kölbing then inquires: 'Welches motiv sollte nun aber der verf. von E [AM] bewogen haben, dessen dichtung genau dieselbe tendenz und denselben haupthelden hatte, wie das werk des R. de Boron, diese durchaus zweckmässige anordnung zu redressiren?' Apart, however, from the general point made above that alterations of order to keep related matter together are common in AM, Merlin in fact receives considerably less attention, proportionately, in AM than in LeM, for the elimination or compression of digressive incidents and passages of personal description discussed and illustrated above removes a good many of his actions, mystifications, and transformations; he is not the clear 'haupthelden' of AM. Moreover, the reason why Boron opened with the story of Merlin's birth was very probably that this made an effective link with the 'Joseph' which 'Merlin' was intended to follow, a reason which did not, of course, weigh with the AM poet.[1]

What may seem a stronger argument for the 'übergangsstufe'-hypothesis is also indicated by Kölbing (p. cxxii), though not stressed or fully developed; it turns on the question of the names of the king's three sons, to which we must now return. In all versions of the earlier form of the story,[2] allowing for minor variants of form, they are Constans, Aurelius Ambrosius, and Uter, (later) surnamed Pendragon, of whom the eldest becomes a monk. In LeM, where they are first named in 20, 17–18, they are Maine or Moine, Pandragon, and Vter, who after his brother's death assumes the name Vterpandragon (52, 16–17). This change could well be explained by imperfect memory or faulty copying of Wace's version or one much like it.[3] In Wace 7571–4 Merlin prophesies to Vortigern that:

---

[1] Benson (unpublished draft) suggests that the AM poet's placing of the diabolic story may have been prompted by a reference to Merlin, in connection with Vortigern's tower, as specifically *fil al diable*, as in Heldris' *Silence* 5792; probably then in the version of LeM whence AM and *Silence* both derive (see above, p. 22 n. 2). If so, that reference could have prompted also AM 1207–8; but there is certainly no need to postulate it to account for the form of AM.

[2] So GM VI, V; Wace 6445–51; Laȝamon 6437–46.

[3] There is no certain evidence, unfortunately, that the first part of LeM rests in any degree on transmission through Wace, though it is perfectly plausible. Margaret Phelan is convinced that both parts of LeM make use of Wace

Aureles primes rei sera
E par puisun primes murra.
Uther, sis freres, Pendragon[1]
Tendra emprés la regiun.

No great confusion would be needed to turn this into *Uther e sis freres, Pendragon*, thus creating two princes out of one and leaving any succeeding reworker to make what he could of one more prince than the story had room for. Let us assume that this re-worker concluded that Aureles was the interloper; as a mere guess, if an intervening version had already substituted death in battle for death by poison, but had neglected to adjust this prophecy, the discrepancy might have led him to that conclusion. He would next meet the name in lines 7597–8: *Bretun se sunt ensemble trait, D'Aurele unt rei e seinur fait.* Now at this point the W version of

(Arnold and Phelan, *La Partie Arthurienne du Roman de Brut*, p. 36), but she gives no specific reasons. Paris and Ulrich (to whom she refers) observe in their edition of the Huth *Merlin*, pp. xii n. 1 and xvii, that 'c'est probablement par Wace que Robert a connu l'histoire des Bretons' because 'le nom de Gorlois, mari d'Igerne dans Gaufrei, est omis par Wace et ne se retrouve pas non plus dans Robert; le second des amis de Gorlois, celui dont Merlin prend la figure [AM alters this] se nomme *Britillus* dans Gaufrei; Wace en fait *Bretel* ou *Bertel*, et Robert lui donne le même nom.' Of these reasons the second is hardly significant, and the first is inaccurate, for Wace at 7807 speaks of *Gorlois, li cuens de Cornoaile*, and at 8465 *Gorlois, uns cuens cornoalleis* (MS. *J*, Bibl. Nat. f. fr. 1416 . . . *uns cuens de Cornewaille*), though the count is not named in the passages dealing with Uter's love for Ygerne and the events which followed.

Boron's source probably resembled Wace in omitting the dragon-prophecies, or Boron would hardly have expelled them in favour of his own different ones; it was related to Wace also in dealing with the Round Table, though had it been identical with Wace here there seems no reason why Boron should have made Uter the founder rather than Arthur. In support of a source for Boron closely related to Wace we may note that Robert Mannyng's chronicle, which clearly derives from Wace or from a closely related source, gives the same reason for the fall of the tower, that the weight of the work above the dragons disturbed them (8184 ff.), which is found in LeM; and that an unnamed hermit whom Merlin often visits in a wild place is referred to in Laȝamon (9378–81), quite probably taken over from the source version of Wace, from which hermit Boron may have constructed the character of Blaise.

In the second part of LeM, whose sources are for the most part very various (see Micha's full discussion in 'Les Sources de la *Vulgate* . . .'), there is one section, that towards the end dealing with Arthur's fight with the giant of Mont St. Michel and his campaign against the Romans, which rests closely on a version of Wace (see Freymond's 'Artus Kampf mit dem Katzenungetüm' and Micha's 'La Guerre contre les Romains . . .').

[1] The surname here is anticipated; elsewhere in Wace, both before and after this point, he is Uther simply, except on the actual occasion of his assuming the surname (8404), though in GM anticipation is general.

LeM introduces Aurelius: *Aurelius Ambrosius fist roy Pandragon, si leur fu moult loiaus* (f. 141ʳᵇ, 45–7), which looks very much as though the Wace line or some corruption of it had been understood to mean that the Britons invested their king by the agency of Aurelius. EPM 42, 19–20 has the same: *Aurelius Ambrose made Pendragon kynge, whiche was a iuste man and a trewe.*

Most of the other references to Aurelius in Wace are not by name, but simply as *li reis*, which would cause our reworker no trouble, but a few occurrences of the name (two before and three after the points just dealt with) would have to be ignored or explained away. There are in fact curious passages in LeM (W), and in Louelich, at some of these points, suggesting that they did indeed cause difficulty to one or more reworkers. At the first of them Louelich introduces the second son of the old king thus:

> The secund Awrely Ambros was cleped ryhte
> Owther Pendragon, whethyr ȝe wylen haue. (1684–5)

At the second, where the young princes' guardians *Unt pris Aurele e pris Uther* (6680) to take them overseas, Louelich speaks of *þe tothere tweyne bretheren . . . Bothen Awriele and ek Vter* (1800–1), in a passage otherwise, as is usual with him, close to LeM. LeM as I know it reads here . . . *les autres ii enfans, Pandragon et Vter* (21, 37), but Louelich's source manuscript probably had Aurelius, and his alternative naming earlier may well go back to it too; he gives no signs of being an imaginative innovator. He makes no further mention of Aurelius, but LeM (W) does, in a new piece of alternative naming, for after Pandragon's death we are told that Uterpandragon (who is in W so named from the beginning) *fu par droit non apelez Aurelius Ambrosius* (f. 147ᵛᵇ, 9–11). W (f. 141ʳᵇ, 32–4) also introduces Aurelius with Pandragon and Uterpandragon at the burning of the castle of Vortigern (here *Vertigier*), naming him first but not indicating his degree.

We cannot hope to recover all the details, but it is clear that the names of the two younger princes in LeM could derive, by way of corruptions and confusions, from Wace. So, too, could that of the eldest. In Wace, the Picts, wishing to be rid of their monk-king, are made to say '*Cest fol rei, cest moine ocium*' (6647), or in a variant reading[1] '*Cel fol moine ocium*'. An intermediate variant *Cel fol rei moine ocium* could well have existed, creating the appearance

---

[1] BL Addit. MS. 32125 (*F*).

of an actual king Moine. Other passages, too, could be carelessly misread, or have minor variants, giving the same sense. At 6496 the barons are reluctant *Que li moines reis devenist*; at 6523 Vortigern *Les dras de moine li toli* (to vest him in royal robes); at 6651 the Picts refer simply to *Cist fols moines*. One has to admit that when the true name and monkish order of the eldest son are elsewhere in Wace clearly stated (6445–8), and he is crowned explicitly under his proper name (6535), it is puzzling that this name should be lost from a reworker's memory; one would be tempted to postulate a version which, after describing how the prince became a monk but was later raised to the throne, said that he was nicknamed *li reis Moines* and thereafter regularly referred to him so, for such repeated references might displace the true name from later memory.[1]

That postulated version would in this matter be identical with AM,[2] and the hypothesis that it was the source of AM would naturally follow. One would most simply, then, assume that it retained the other features which AM shares with the earlier version of the story; also that it predated the confusions which removed Aurelius and created the separate Uter and Pendragon, since in this too AM (A) agrees with the 'earlier version'. Certain difficulties about such an assumption have already appeared, however, and AM's treatment of Aurilis Brosias and Uter Pendragon offers more, for it is not consistent. Aurilis, the second son at 45–6, clearly ought to be the heir after the death of his elder brother (in the earlier version he is indeed made king after the successful landing of the princes).[3] Merlin's statement in line 1180 that '*to kinges foure y worþ maister*' should imply a reign for Aurilis, for the four must be Vortigern, Aurilis, Uter, and Arthur; the equivalent in LeM is certainly explicit that *le quart*

[1] A further possibility of transmission is suggested by Louelich, where the eldest son is neither a monk nor named Moine; the account is that of LeM but the name is *Costantyn, Constans*, or *Costance*. If this goes back to a LeM variant, that variant would be intermediate between the earlier form of the story and LeM as we know it, having the name retained but the monk-story dropped. It could not be in a direct and simple line between them, but if beside it there existed such a version as I have postulated above, copying of the form of the one with the name 'corrected' from memory of the other would yield the LeM form. But this is, of course, highly speculative; Louelich himself, though no great innovator, may have adjusted this name.

[2] i.e. A. The AM2 readings represent a further complication here, on which see below, pp. 32 and 57–60.

[3] GM VIII, II; Wace 7597–8; Laȝamon 8060–62.

roi . . . aura anon Artus (28, 4–5). Yet from 1721 on the poet writes
as though Uter were the elder brother and natural heir, and it is
Uter who is crowned king at 2049–50. Aurilis, killed at 2138, is
thus deprived of his reign, and Merlin of one of his *kinges foure*.
It is hard to explain this if AM simply derives from a source which
maintained the consistent treatment of the earlier version. But it
is explicable if the poet was attempting to correct his source, a
manuscript of LeM, on the basis of his knowledge of his earlier
version. LeM first introduces the princes in explicit order of
seniority: . . . *li autres auoit non Pandragons et li tiers ot non Vters*
(20, 17–18); the poet, in lines 45–8, identified them with the princes
of the earlier version in the proper order of seniority as he remem-
bered it from the latter. In lines 57–8 (no equivalent in LeM) he
retained this order; the other order in 245–7 is probably simply
for convenience in rhyming, seniority here being of no importance.
When next he took over a reference to the names from LeM, at
the point where ships arrive belonging *a Pandragon et a Uter son
frere* (35, 37–8), he would seem in lines 1721–2 to be identifying
them with his princes the other way round, and certainly that
identification established itself, so that when in LeM 50, 40 ff.
Uter places himself between the Saxons and their ships and
Pendragon attacks from the other side, in AM 2093 ff. Aurilis
fights on the seaward side of the enemy and Uter on the landward.
But he obviously could not go so far in this identification as to kill
his Uter Pendragon, since everyone who knew anything of the
story would know that he survived to become Arthur's father, so
when in LeM 51, 12–14 Merlin promises Uter life, and he rejoices,
the equivalent lines in AM (2119–24) also have Uter (in the
ensuing battle AM is not close to LeM, and 'equivalent lines' do
not occur, so one cannot say that an identification once more
reversed is thus established). The change in identification between
45–8 and 1721–2 may reflect mere forgetfulness on the poet's
part (he had of course between the two turned aside from the
story of the princes to deal with the birth of Merlin), or he may
have been confused by variants in his actual source manuscript(s)
of LeM, for as we have seen there are certainly oddities to be
found among them.[1] Some future full critical edition of LeM may

[1] A simple error, like the *iter* for *uter* actually present in MS. G[1] at 35, 38
would in fact suffice. The corrupted word might well not be recognized as a
name at all, and faced with a named Pendragon and an apparently unnamed

throw light on the problem; provisionally I accept derivation
from LeM as a more plausible explanation of the inconsistent
treatment of the two princes in AM than derivation from a version
which itself derived from the consistency of the earlier version
and yielded the quite different consistency of LeM. Whether the
AM poet's king Moyne is also a (more successful) correction of his
source on the basis of the earlier version, or derives from the
postulated intermediate version, remains of course an open question; neither the 'conflation' nor the 'übergangsstufe' hypothesis
need be accepted or rejected *in toto*.

Unfortunately, the complications attending the names of the
two princes in AM are not at an end yet. The fact has still to be
taken account of that all the AM2 texts have the names in the
regular LeM form, and one obvious explanation for that would be
that the English original of our poem, the 'Ur–AM', had them in
that form, taken over directly and simply from LeM, and that they
were maintained in AM2 but 'corrected' in A[1]—with, of course,
just the same reversal of identification as if the original English
poet, working from LeM, created the forms found in A. Such a
reversal, however, with the loss of one king's reign, seems less
likely to have occurred in the course of copying or revising an
English poem than of translating and reworking a French source,
nor could one then appeal to possible confusions in a source manuscript of LeM as a cause. On a broad view, it would be easier to
assume that forms as in A were 'corrected' in AM2 on the basis of
acquaintance with LeM by the AM2 reworker.[2]

The Author's Use of his Source in the First Section

It remains to be explained, if the first part of AM, like the
second, derives from LeM, why the second is closer to the source.
A plausible explanation is not far to seek. In the second part AM is
on the whole closest to its source in scenes of battle and the like,
which are even expanded on occasion; other matter is more

brother one would naturally tend to identify the former with Uter Pendragon
rather than with Aurilis Brosias, thus establishing a practice.

[1] Bülbring takes this view, in his review of Kölbing, pp. 258–62. Kölbing
(p. clxxi) had accepted that 'correction' occurred rather in AM2, a necessary
conclusion if, as he believed, the names as in A derive directly from the French
source (see above, pp. 27–30).

[2] There are counter-arguments, however. See more detailed discussion below,
pp. 57–60, under 'Affiliation of Texts'.

cavalierly treated. In the second part the poet found in his source a story full enough of vigorous action to be made, with this sort of modification, to suit his purpose. But in the first part there is very little detail of combat in LeM; yet this is too important a section of the story to be as heavily contracted as merely linking passages can be. Much more thorough-going revision was therefore needed.[1] Where LeM neglected an obvious opportunity of introducing, or describing in detail, an exciting fight, the poet supplied the lack, whethert he combatants were men or dragons,[2] though he suppressed the battle which appears in LeM 78, 33–8, in which the Saxons are defeated by the Britons under the command of the dying Uter, borne in a litter; it presumably did not suit his vigorous taste.

For the rest, the general lines of adaptation are the same in the first as in the second part. We can demonstrate competent précis of the same sort. For example, LeM 67, 19–34 thus describes the expedition which led to Arthur's conception:

. . . lors monterent et cheualchierent tant qu'il uindrent a Tintaioel. Lors dist Merlins au roy 'Ore, demores ici j poi, et nos irons cha entre mi et Ulfin.' Lors s'en vont d'une part et se dessamblent entre lui et Ulfin; si s'en retournent au roy, et Merlins aporta vne herbe et li rois la prinst, si s'en froia. Et quant il s'en fu froies si ot tout apertement la samblance del duc. Et lors dist Merlins 'Or, vous souiegne se vous ueistes onques Iordain?' Et li rois dist 'Iou le connois moult bien,' et Merlins li monstre Vlfin en la samblance de Iordain. Et quant Ulfins uit le roy si dist 'Biaus sire—Dieux! Comment puet ce estre que nule samblance d'omme peust estre muee en autre?' Et li rois li demande 'Que t'est il auis de moi?' Et Ulfins dist 'Ie ne vous connois por nul homme se por le duc non,' et li rois li dist qu'il resamble apertement Iordain. Et quant il orent vn poi ensi parle, si vint Merlins, et lor fu auis que ce fust Bretel. Ensi parlerent en samble et atendirent iusqua la nuit, et quant il fu j poi anuitiet si s'en vindrent a la porte de Tintaioel . . .

AM 2507–20 gives all the necessary sense, though the feeling of real characters conveyed by the dialogue is, of course, lost. The

---

[1] A further reason for the greater variation in the first part may be that when the poet wished to vary in the second he had to rely on conventional phrases or his own limited imagination, since the variant continuations after Arthur's coronation, even if he knew any others, are too different to allow conflation, while in the first he had alternatives in his mind from his acquaintance with the GM–Wace–Laȝamon form. Mere weariness, leading to greater willingness to leave the source unaltered in the later stages, may also have been a reason.

[2] 301–54, 387–96, 432–74, 1511–44, 1797–1878, 2103–32.

general tendency, in the first as in the second part, is for AM to be made more direct than LeM, whether by the total suppression of digressive material,[1] or by simplification in the course of contraction,[2] or by rearrangement of order.[3] Merlin's part is somewhat reduced by elimination of some of his wonders and mystifications.[4] Occasionally motivation is lost in the course of contraction;[5] quite often subtlety and delicacy are lost.[6] Similar, too, are touches of lively circumstantial detail not in LeM[7]—but not infrequently crude or unsubtle[8] and in one case quite inappropriate to the context.[9]

[1] Thus all reference to the history of Joseph of Arimathea, which in LeM 19–20 Merlin tells Blaise is to be joined to Blaise's own book, is removed in AM.

[2] Thus in LeM 23, 17–24, 5 Vortigern first summons *tous les sages hommes que on pooit trouer*; they can tell him nothing of the fall of the tower, but recommend the summoning of those who may know *par force de clergie*. The clerks again cannot tell, but think it possible that some among them may know astrology and so be able to discover the reason, and they are bidden to select from among their number those who know that science. AM 566 ff. has a much more straightforward action.

[3] Thus in LeM 73–6 Merlin's advice on the disposal of the infant Arthur is placed between Uterpendragon's discovery of the pregnancy and the action he undertakes in accordance with Merlin's plan; in AM 2635 ff. Merlin's instructions are given first and the action then proceeds uninterruptedly.

[4] Most notably his miraculous bringing of Stonehenge from Ireland (LeM 52, 20–53, 14), and the elaborate story of his prediction of three different and apparently incompatible forms of death to a sceptic seeking to test his powers (45–7).

[5] Thus at 2449–50 there is no particular reason for the king to go *to plaien him on þe plain*; in LeM 64–5 this follows Ulfin's advice to the king to send for Merlin to help him in his wretchedness, and the ensuing appearance of an old man who makes an assignation with the king, to keep which they are riding when they meet *vn contrait* (AM *an beggere*).

[6] Thus, in the course of the lengthy negotiations preceding Uterpendragon's marriage with Ygerne, in LeM 72, 21–35 Ulfin is made to represent to the council that it is the king's duty, in order to restore peace to the kingdom, and in fairness to the duke, whose offence was not so grave as to deserve death, to marry Ygerne and to see her daughters also well married. The brief reference to the negotiations in AM 2593–2600 has no room for this; the poet probably thought it small loss. Again, when Ygerne asks the duke to leave the king's feast there is in LeM 61, 29–62, 1 a delicately drawn scene of love between them, which is much coarsened in AM 2341–50.

[7] Thus 530–4, 559–60, 565, 1687–8, 1768, 1935, 1937–8, 2366–72. Many of these are absent or weaker in AM2.

[8] Thus 1031–2, 1207–8, 1328–32, 2139–40 (as contrasted with 2123–4, which is from LeM; see above, p. 21), 2387–94.

[9] A *water swift and stepe* (1450) cannot be drained by building two walls across it and removing the water from between them. LeM 31, 35 ff. uses the words *aigue* or *iaue*, meaning evidently 'lake', although the words can also mean 'stream', which is the usual sense of ME *water*, the literal equivalent of *iaue*. AM2

There are also two much longer additions, namely the third demonstration of Merlin's powers on his journey to Vortigern, concerning the queen's chamberlain; and the account of Uter's conquest of king Harinan, Ygerne's first husband. In each case an account which seems to be related is to be found elsewhere, later in LeM in the first case and in Wace in the second.[1] Incorporation in a new position of material from elsewhere in LeM is, as we have seen, a feature of the second part also. Incorporation from a subsidiary source is not a very different procedure; had the 'earlier version' continued parallel with the second part of LeM we might have expected the same there. It may also be worth calling attention to a case where matter from the first and second sections of LeM is assembled together in the first part of AM; see below, Commentary, note to lines 2601–19.

I conclude that LeM probably stands throughout as the main source of AM, and that it was treated in a fundamentally similar way by the AM poet throughout.

MANUSCRIPTS AND EARLY PRINT

A *The Auchinleck MS.* (National Library of Scotland, Advocates' 19.2.1)

This is a parchment manuscript, containing now 332 leaves, measuring 19×25 cm. It was assembled in normal eight-leaf gatherings (except for one of ten leaves); there are now forty-six, complete or partial. Of the various leaves and gatherings wanting as the manuscript now stands, ten leaves have recently turned up in different places (not, however, including that missing from AM), and others yet may. Trimming has in places wholly or partly removed the running numbers (which stood at the head of each page and distinguished the various items), the marginal annotations, and the modern pencil folio numbers. At least 6 mm. has been cropped at the top, as can be seen from part of the strip which survives of the leaf following f. 72 and which was evidently folded in when the manuscript was trimmed.

has here a variant treatment, which may perhaps better preserve the original form of AM, but it still has the rushing stream, which makes absurd the methods adopted to drain it. See discussion below, p. 57.

[1] See below, Commentary, notes to lines 1342 and 2172.

The hands of six scribes appear, but the manuscript was designed as a unit, a more or less uniform format being imposed on them all. The usual page-layout is of two columns, each of forty-four lines, about 20 cm. high and up to 6 cm. wide; the initial letter of each line is set some two letters' width to the left of the beginning of the rest of the line.[1]

The accepted argument for the dating of the manuscript has been put by Bliss (in his *Sir Orfeo*, pp. ix–x) with a clarity and succinctness on which I cannot improve:

> The date of the manuscript can be established by internal evidence. Other manuscripts of the *Short Metrical Chronicle* bring the history of England up to the accession of Edward II, and conclude with a short prayer for *our ʒong king Edward*. In the Auchinleck MS. a passage is inserted between the accession of Edward II and the prayer, briefly relating the troublesome reign and death of the king and the accession of his son; *our ʒong king Edward* is now clearly Edward III. Since the manuscript contains two other articles concerned with the troubles of the reign of Edward II, it may be confidently dated about 1330, shortly after the accession of Edward III.

Mrs. Loomis has persuasively argued that it was produced in London, as a commercial venture ('The . . . MS. and a . . . London Bookshop . . .'). Nothing is certainly known of its history until 1740, when it came into the hands of Alexander Boswell of Auchinleck (father of Johnson's biographer), by whom it was given to the Advocates' Library (now the National Library of Scotland) in 1744.

AM bears the original running number xxxi. Five items have been lost at the beginning of the manuscript. There are also discrepancies between the original and the accepted modern numeration of the surviving items, but the effects of these on the numbering of AM cancel out, as it happens, and AM is now reckoned as the twenty-sixth item. It begins at the top of f. 201rb, on the third leaf of the twenty-eighth surviving gathering;[2] the previous

---

[1] For a full description and discussion of the MS., including the recovered leaves, see Pearsall and Cunningham's Introduction to the facsimile *Auchinleck MS*. See also Kölbing's 'Vier Romanz Handschriften', 178–91, considerably amplified and corrected in Bliss's 'Notes on the Auchinleck Manuscript', and with further minor corrections in Cunningham's 'Notes . . .'; and Guddat-Figge's *Catalogue of Manuscripts*, pp. 121–6. (with full references to other mentions of the MS). Smithers gives an account of the recovered leaves in 'Two Newly-discovered Fragments . . .' and 'Another Fragment . . .'.

[2] No. 29 in Bliss's analysis; he convincingly demonstrates the loss of one gathering after the fourteenth surviving one.

column contains the end of *Beues of Hamtoun*. The title *Of Arthour and of Merlin*, in red, stands at the head of the column, and was followed by a miniature, which is now cut out (like so much of the illumination of the MS.) so that only the top right-hand corner of the frame remains. Immediately below this the text begins with an illuminated I. The loss of the miniature has also almost completely removed lines 34–44 from the verso of the leaf. One whole leaf has been completely lost, following f. 254, at the beginning of the last gathering of AM (the thirty-fifth surviving gathering, Bliss's no. 36). There is therefore a lacuna in the text following line 9446; since the lost leaf was presumably in the regular layout there are 176 missing lines, of which we can restore only so much as the catchword at the end of f. 254, *fleand his sw*, tells us, and the name *Sir Antour* with which the last missing line probably ended.[1] The poem comes to an end on f. 256ᵛ; the last eight lines are at the top of the second column. The title of the following piece stands at the head of this column, above the last eight lines of AM.[2] Immediately after the end of AM comes the miniature belonging to this next piece, and then the piece itself starts *It bifel whilom ich vnderstond*.[3]

AM is written by the scribe denoted α in Kölbing's article and 1 in Bliss's. Besides the full facsimile specimens of his hand appear in frontispiece i to my Volume I, in the frontispieces to Brunner's edition of *The Seven Sages of Rome* (f. 89ʳ, lines 824–916 of that text) and Leach's of *Amis and Amiloun* (f. 55ᵛ, lines 1241–1328 of that text), and in Bliss's 'Notes on the . . . MS.', plate 1 (part of f. 16ᵛ, lines 1a–13a and 23a–35a of *Seynt Mergrete*). It is a simple textura book-hand, clear and professional, and is rarely

[1] Inferred from LeM, and from comparison of lines 9623–7 with 9743–4 and 9751–5.

[2] There is a similar arrangement at the beginning of *Hou our leuedi saute was ferst founde* on f. 259.

[3] Title, miniature, and the first part of the text of this piece have been heavily erased; the next leaf, which contained the rest of it, has been cut out so as to leave only the initial letters of the lines. Kölbing ('Vier Romanz Handschriften') read and conjecturally completed the title as *þe wenche þat ⟨lou⟩ed ⟨a k⟩ing*, but between *ed* and ⟨*a k*⟩*ing* is space for about twelve letters, of which I read the first two as probably *to* and the last two as perhaps *bi*; the stroke of the *i* is at any rate clear. With rather wide spacing, the whole might have been *þe wenche þat loued to ligge bi a king*. The miniature can be seen to represent a bed or couch, but the figure, or probably figures, on it are completely removed. Kölbing's suggestion in this article that somebody removed the piece as obscene is very plausible, though too little of the text can be read to provide evidence.

difficult to read, though in a few places the ink has run and smudged the letters. The scribe made a considerable number of errors, but usually corrected them, either by rewriting over erasure, or by altering an incorrect letter, or the first stroke of such a letter, into the correct one; both these methods lead here and there to uncertainties of reading. There are also letters and words deleted by striking through or subpuncting. In addition to running corrections by the scribe there is also a later stratum of corrections, on which see Volume I, p. xii.

The letters *m*, *n*, *u*, and *i* are of course formed of separated minims; *i* is frequently distinguished by a stroke, but this is sometimes displaced to the right in a series of minims, and apart from this these letters can be told apart only by context. Of the other letters *c* and *t* cannot always be distinguished. In the ninth line of my frontispiece facsimile is a *c* with the top stroke extending slightly to the left of the upright (*ich*), and a *t* with only slightly greater leftward extension (*aboute*). Elsewhere there are some undoubted cases of *c* with greater leftward extension than some undoubted cases of *t*, for instance in line 7074 *swiche vertu*. As a result, it is impossible to be sure whether the *rect* which appears in Turnbull's text and mine in line 7241, or the *rett* of Kölbing's, is correct; or whether the duke whom Turnbull and I name throughout *E(u)stas* is not on at least some occasions meant to be *Escas*, as Kölbing has it, which would be closer to LeM's *Escans*; or whether the sword which we all three agree in naming *Estalibore* in line 2817 was not in fact meant as *Escalibore*.[1] Difficulty also arises, though less often, with *v*. The scribe's usual form can be seen in the ninth line from the bottom of my facsimile (*vp*), but it can also appear with the left-hand stroke more vertical, when it tends to become indistinguishable from his *b* (illustrated in *bigonne* five lines above). This tendency can be seen in the *Amis* facsimile, tenth line from the bottom (*bitvixen*); identity is complete in *bitvene* in AM 2595. As a result, though I have a duke *Vargon* in line 6768, Turnbull's and Kölbing's *Bargon* is also a possible reading. More rarely still uncertainty is possible between *l* and the long form of *s*; and, especially in the initial letter of a line, between *a*, the short form of *s*, and *g*. Scribal abbreviations are sparingly used and present little difficulty. Letters of special capital form

---

[1] The vexed question of *þurth* or *þurch* can, however, probably be settled; see below, Commentary, note to line 249.

are rare, though *L* and *A* occur sometimes as initial letters of lines,[1] *C* in numerals, *R* in *Rion* and other proper names, and *O* in *Orien(s)*.

Major divisions of the text are marked by a large illuminated capital, which the scribe directed by placing a guide-letter to the left of the column and setting in two lines of text, and the rubricator realized in blue ornamented with red. Minor divisions, and sometimes significant lines even where no division can be said to occur, are indicated by the mark (illustrated in my facsimile) represented in the printed text ¶, which the scribe directed by a stroke to the left of the column and the rubricator realized[2] in red or blue at his taste.

Various hands have written on margins at different points in the manuscript and on the largely blank f. 107. Most of these marginalia are little more than 'doodles', having nothing to do with the adjacent text, and could be of value for the study of the manuscript only if one could identify any of the hands or signatures and thus throw light on its history between its composition and 1740; this I have so far failed to do. However, with the beginning of AM a new marginal hand, of some small interest, appears. In this hand there are a number of glosses, the first three in English and the rest in Latin, varying from single words to such short summaries of the action as the one which appears (together with various of the other types of marginalia) in my facsimile. The same hand has also drawn attention to several points in the text by underlining or by marginal marks of different sorts, and in four places[3] seems to me to have made textual corrections, though three of these are merely single strokes of deletion, which cannot of course be certainly attributed to a particular hand. This hand is of about 1600, and it at least tells us that during the long blank in the history of the manuscript some scholar read with attention the first 2,000 lines of AM (the last gloss is beside lines 2001–2). He was evidently interested in the supposed early history of Britain, for he made similar notes to the first part of the *Short Metrical Chronicle*, beginning on f. 304 (and nowhere else in the manuscript). Parts of some of his glosses have suffered badly from rubbing of

[1] In this position there is also a tendency to use the more ornate alternative forms of *i*, *m*, and *s*.

[2] Occasionally he mistook his instructions; see lines 3509, 5346, 6768, and 7796. At 7397 the instructions themselves were confused.

[3] See lines 102, 820 (and below, note in Commentary), 981, and 1865.

the manuscript edges, and some have lost too much by its trimming
to be confidently reconstructed, but as full a transcription as possible of those relating to AM appears in Appendix 1 (pp. 266–7
below).

S *Scott's Transcript* (Bodleian Library, MS. Douce 124)

This was made from A, under Walter Scott's supervision and
partly in his own hand, to supply George Ellis with a continuation
of the romance, which he already knew up to Vortigern's death
from the Lincoln's Inn MS. (L) of AM2, for use in preparing his
Specimens of . . . Romances. It has no more value for the study of
the romance than that of supplying another opinion on doubtful
readings—a minimal value since the transcription was not, by
modern standards, very careful. I have identified and discussed
it in my 'Walter Scott . . . and MS. Douce 124';[1] it does not
warrant detailed treatment here.

L *The Lincoln's Inn MS.* (Lincoln's Inn Library, Hale MS. 150)

This[2] is a parchment manuscript, containing now 125 leaves,
measuring 13×31 cm.; it was assembled in twelve-leaf gatherings.
Several leaves have been lost from AM2 and the preceding item;
there have also evidently been extensive losses before and after the
surviving matter. There are now nine complete gatherings, preceded by two and followed by one[3] which are incomplete. Some
leaves were displaced in what was evidently an early binding, to
judge by the wear on the leaf which thus became f. 1; the modern
folio numbering follows the resulting incorrect order. The leaves
were reordered (but not renumbered) when the manuscript was
rebacked in 1972; my Volume I already stood in print, and uses
the disordered folio numbers as all earlier scholars had done, and
as I continue to do here.

It is dated *c.* 1450, and confidently located in Much Wenlock,
Shropshire, in Moore, Meech, and Whitehall's 'Middle English

---

[1] Of which Guddat-Figge gives a somewhat inaccurate summary, p. 126
n. 18.

[2] Described by Kölbing in 'Vier Romanz Handschriften', 194–5, and by
Guddat-Figge, pp. 228–31. On the gatherings see Mills's ed. of *Lybeaus
Desconus*, p. 4.

[3] Described by Mills merely as four leaves of which no two are conjunct,
but the text is continuous: they are the first four leaves of a gathering.

Dialect Characteristics . . .', 54, on the evidence for which see
Barnicle's edition of *The Seege or Batayle of Troye*, pp. x–xiv.

The contents are: (i) the last part of *Lybeaus Desconus*; (ii)
AM2; (iii) *Kyng Alisaunder*; (iv) *Seege or Batayle* . . .; (v) the
first part of *Piers Plowman* (A-version). AM2 begins, with a plain
blue capital H,[1] at the top of f. 13^r, which was originally the ninth
leaf of the second surviving gathering, and continues through the
tenth and eleventh leaves (ff. 2 and 3). A lacuna follows, implying
the loss of the last leaf of the gathering, and the text is then completed unbroken on ff. 14–17.

The whole manuscript is in one hand, except for the *explicits* to
(i) and (iii), which differ from the main hand and from each other;
in single column, with between forty-eight and sixty lines to the
page. A specimen appears in frontispiece ii to Volume I of the
present edition; others in the frontispiece to the Barnicle edition
of *Seege or Batayle* . . . (part of f. 90^v, lines 1–14 of that text), and
in plate II, facing p. 104, vol. I, of Smithers's edition of *Kyng Alisaunder* (part of f. 45^v, lines 1827–61 of that text). The hand is a
typical Anglicana hand of the period, not as careful as that of the
Auchinleck text, but clear and offering in itself small difficulties
of reading, except that *e* and *o* are sometimes difficult or impossible
to distinguish. In the second line of my frontispiece facsimile the
o in *strong* tends towards an *e*-like form; in lines 1288–9 the
second letters of *rown* and of *messangeres* are quite indistinguishable except by context; and my footnotes record a number of
cases in which Kölbing and I take opposite views of uncertain
readings. Much more serious is the fact that the manuscript has
evidently had hard usage; certain parts are badly rubbed, and in
three places portions of leaves have come clear away and are lost.
There are fewer corrections than in **A**, and those less clearly
(though still probably) to be divided into strata; see Volume I,
p. xii. There are also fewer abbreviations.

There are marginal comments to AM2, and to KA, comparable
with those in **A**, but all in English; there are perhaps two hands.
The writing is a spidery secretary hand, often difficult to read, as
can be seen from the specimen in my facsimile; again, as full a
transcription as possible of the AM glosses appears in Appendix 1.

[1] There is no other rubrication in the manuscript, though in several other
places the scribe has indicated an illuminated capital; there may of course have
been illumination at the lost head of *Lybeaus Desconus*.

There is also what may be a proper name, only partly legible, at
the foot of f. 16ᵛ.

D   *MS. Douce 236* (Bodleian Library)

Another parchment manuscript,[1] it contains now thirty-six
leaves, measuring 12 × 16 cm.; of the eight-leaf gatherings two
survive complete and four partially. It contains only AM2, though
there may of course originally have been other matter preceding
or following this. The original layout as regards AM2 can be
reconstructed confidently from the gatherings and catchwords and
from comparison of the text with other versions of the romance,
as follows (Kölbing's description, in his edition pp. xvii–xviii, needs
minor correction):

Gathering			Folios					
1	x	1	2	3	4	5	6	7
2	8	9	10	11	12	13	14	15
3	16	17	18	19	20	21	22	23
3a	x	x	x	x	x	x	x	x
4	24	x	25	26	27	28	x	29
4a	x	x	x	x	x	x	x	x
5	x	x	30	31	32	33	x	34
6	x	x	x	35	36	x	x	x

The text began on the lost first leaf of gathering 1; at the end any
likely conclusion would more than fill the last three leaves of
gathering 6, so there was no doubt a gathering 6a. Beyond that
one can only conjecture.

MED dates it in the last quarter of the fifteenth century, though
Kölbing assigned it to the beginning of that century and Moore,
Meech, and Whitehall to *c.* 1400.[2] They locate it in Tolpuddle,
Dorset. It was certainly there at one time, for on f. 14 (but in a
hand considerably later than that of the manuscript) appears:
'This is Robert Jones his booke recorde of Steven Jones[3] and of
Robert Webbe and of Mistoris Caterne Jones and of many mo
good people in the parishe of Tolpudle'. There also appears on

---

[1] Described by Guddat-Figge, pp. 264–5.

[2] *MED Plan and Bibliography*, p. 26; Kölbing, p. xviii; Moore, *et al.*, p. 55.
Guddat-Figge would seem to prefer the later date (but does not discuss it).

[3] Guddat-Figge 'Jaro', but 'Jones' is to be preferred.

f. 22, however, a note in a sixteenth- to seventeenth-century hand which Dr. Hunt and Miss Barratt of the Bodleian Library have kindly made out for me as reading: 'Your frindes[1] John Martin of the place of Admaston geve these with speade', which might suggest a connection with Admaston in Staffordshire.

It is all in one hand (probably including all corrections), in single column, with between 14 and 22 lines to the page. The hand again is a typical Anglicana of its period, clear, and in the way of difficulties of reading offering only the familiar problem of various forms of stroke or flourish on the ends of words which may represent -*e*; in my quotations I have been more ready so to interpret them than Kölbing was. There is very little decoration.

P *The Percy Folio MS.* (British Library, Additional MS. 27879)

This seventeenth-century paper manuscript is described by Furnivall in the Hales and Furnivall edition, vol. I, pp. xii-xiv;[2] being well known, and of comparatively minor importance for the study of AM, it does not call for detailed treatment here. AM2 is the forty-first item, and runs from f. 72[v] to f. 89[r]. There are occasional difficulties of reading comparable with those in **D**, the question being whether a downward hook is to be interpreted as a mere flourish or as the sign, properly for -*es*, which would indicate a plural and which one would expand in this case -*s*.

H *Stow's Transcript* (British Library, Harleian MS. 6223)

This[3] is a paper manuscript in the hand of John Stow the chronicler, and accordingly of the sixteenth century. The cover (numbered f. 1) titles the two items *The Life of Merlin in vers* and *A Histori of Englan taken out of y[e] Booke of Eaton Collegg* (followed by the initials of Stow's son, R S, and the date 1615).[4] The first

---

[1] A plural can hardly be intended, however; the -*es* is represented by a mark of contraction, and this would not be the only occasion on which one would wish to discount such a mark. The difficulty is frequent in **P**; for a case in an annotation to **L** see below, p. 267 n. Guddat-Figge reports the following 'John' as 'Joseph', but again this would not seem to be sound.

[2] Further by Guddat-Figge, pp. 151-9.

[3] Described by Guddat-Figge, pp. 208-9.

[4] Brunner's statement ('Romances and their Audience', 225) that 'fragments [of AM] were inserted . . . into . . . MS. Harley 6223 . . .', which he offers as one piece of evidence demonstrating that some Middle English romances 'must have been believed to contain real history' because they 'were copied into MSS.

item, however, contains merely the opening sixty-two lines of a version of AM2, breaking off part way down f. 2^v. It starts as though marked for an illuminated H; it seems unlikely that Stow intended to have it illuminated, so probably he was carefully copying an original on which the intended illumination was never performed. The whole scrap indeed has the air of a careful transcript.

W *Wynkyn de Worde's* Marlyn (Unique complete copy, Pierpont Morgan Library)

First printed *c.* 1500,[1] one of this printer's many unassuming popular issues, it is catalogued from its title-page *Here begynneth a lytel treatyse of ye byrth & pphecye of Marlyn*, and the fact that it is a text of AM2 had not been generally recognized; certainly not by me until Mr. P. N. G. Pesch, of the Utrecht University Library, most kindly drew my attention to the facts. Printing of the present volume was by then well in hand, and I have been able to make only limited use of W.[2] I have however sought to check all points at which it might affect my argument; where I do not mention its reading it may be taken that it does not. Mr. Pesch intends to deal with it in a forthcoming article. It opens with twelve tail-rhyme lines unrelated to any version of AM, but thence gives a full text of AM2 from line 5 of **L** to the end of **P**, followed by a concluding couplet similar to **L** 3–4. I print specimens as Appendix 3, on pp. 270–6 below.

AFFILIATION OF TEXTS

The general lines of affiliation are clear. First, the AM2 texts are not grouped together merely in having the shorter form of the story (we cannot in fact say confidently where **D** or the progenitor of **H** may have ended); they all clearly belong to a tradition distinct from that of **A**, and must surely derive from a common original, an 'Ur–AM2'. There are many cases in which they agree against

containing historical matter', suggests that the two items are more intimately connected than they are.

[1] Only fragments of this edition survive. Complete copy 1510, with many minor variants (all my quotations are from this, since first ed. does not survive at any relevant point); reproduced University Microfilms reel 1178. Further ed. 1529, again with variants; only fragments survive. I examine these eds. in a short note to be published in *The Library*.

[2] That I have been able to make any use of it is thanks to the Pierpont Morgan Library, and especially to Dr. Paul Needham, Curator of Printed Books, who responded instantly to my request for assistance; I am most grateful.

A. The most striking is the one already noticed on p. 32:[1] all five texts of AM2 are in accord, against **A**, in the names of the old king's sons. All agree, too, in passing straight from the naming of these sons to the old king's sickness, without any equivalent of **A** 49–62. Apart from this, in the short section of text for which they all exist agreement of all four manuscripts against **A** can be demonstrated only in small matters, and of all five texts not at all.[2] However, in the section lost in **D** on the missing first leaf the first ten lines of **L**, **P**, and **H** are closely similar and quite distinct from anything in **A**, and the fifth to ninth of these lines have close equivalents also in **W**; while after **H** breaks off one can pick almost at random and find passages in which **L**, **D**, **P**, and **W** agree together against **A**.

Second, as a glance will show, there is nevertheless so much verbal agreement between the **A** and AM2 texts that independent descent from the French source is out of the question. Either, then, Ur–AM2 derives from **A**, or **A** and the AM2 texts derive from a common English source. In the latter case, since there will be little dispute that **A** is the superior text, this common source is more likely to have resembled **A** than AM2; that is to say **A** and Ur–AM2 both derive from an Ur–AM rather than **A** from Ur–AM2 (even supposing the latter to have continued so far beyond any of the surviving AM2 texts). A further reason to believe this lies in the closer verbal resemblance of **A** than the AM2 texts to LeM in a number of passages, as noted above.[3] The question whether Ur–AM2 derives from **A** or goes back to an Ur–AM is discussed on pp. 51–60 below.

Third, within the AM2 group both **D** and **W** are distinctive. Each contains many lines resembling **A** which are different, or absent, in the other AM2 texts; the majority of these they have in common but each has quite a number of independent ones also. I have recorded most of **D**'s in the textual apparatus in Volume I

---

[1] See further below, pp. 57–60.

[2] The rhyme *anon*:*euerychon* of **L** 59–60 appears, in that order, also in **D** 48–9, **P** 57–8, and (:*echeone*) **H** 54–5, but in the reverse order in **A** 99–100. The couplet **L** 67–8 has close equivalents in **D** 56–7 and **P** 65–6, and its first line in **H** 62, immediately before **H** breaks off in mid-couplet; but there is no equivalent in **A**. **W** lacks the passage in which these occur.

[3] p. 20 and n. 3. There are also a number of cases in which material peculiar to **A** appears to derive from LeM, but unfortunately in all the more convincing ones **D** is wanting; if we had it we might find the material preserved there, which would suggest that it was in fact in Ur–AM2.

(I was then unaware of **W**). Each contains also many variants and additional lines not related to **A**, a substantial number shared but by no means all. Those peculiar to **D** often suggest mere local expansion, and many are metrically inferior. Peculiar to **W** are couplets or longer groups suggesting reminiscence of earlier passages, or in one case anticipation of a passage shortly to come;[1] there are also readings which seem clearly to represent deliberate emendation.[2] Much of this can be illustrated in the passage equivalent to **A** 71–2. **P** and **H** agree with **L** in having the lines in reverse order from **A**, and in having a variant phrasing in their second one (**H** has some further verbal variations); **D** and **W** both have the order of **A**, **D** having almost identical wording in the first line but a considerably modified second line. **W** has minor divergencies from **A** in both lines, making it further from **A** than **D** is in the first line, but closer in the second. Then **D** has an independent couplet *And þat no treson be зow among | For his loue þat suffrede deþ on þe croys wiþ wrong*, before continuing, in common with the other AM2 texts, with a line substantially identical with **A** 73.

Fourth, **P** is very close to **L** as far as **L** goes, to such an extent that material lost from **L**[3] can confidently be restored from **P**. **P** agrees with **L** in one almost certainly erroneous reading, *Lett make accompackement* (249 = **L** 261), where **D**'s *Let make a comoun parlement* (**W** 256 identical except for spelling) preserves the correct form (cf. **A** 292); and is close to **L** in two others for

---

[1] Of lines 1639–42, for which no other text has equivalents at that point, the first two are almost identical with 1677–8, (see Appendix 3, p. 274 below). The second two are almost identical with 40–1.

[2] Thus 188–9 *Vortyger sayd without stryfe | But ye byreue his lyfe* (= **L** 199–200) can hardly be anything but an ill-judged attempt to mend what was naïvely seen as a discontinuity between the lines. A very interesting case is the passage 25–8 (see Appendix 3, pp. 270–1 below), which may well reflect a wish to establish which prince was the senior by a reworker who knew it must be Pendragon but realized that the form of his exemplar suggested the reverse (see below, p. 59 and n. 1). Here however a possible textual connection with **A** 45–8 could suggest that the passage comes from Ur–AM2, though it is hard to see how the other AM2 texts would derive from it (**D** is close to **L**).

[3] See above, pp. 40–1. I have followed Kölbing in continuing my line numbering of **L** through its missing leaf, following the restored text, even though since **P** sometimes omits couplets (once a single line) found in **L**, and contains one couplet which is not (following **L** 310), and since **L** has not a uniform number of lines to the page, it may well be that this restored line-numbering does not exactly represent the original text. Nothing similar can of course be done for **D**.

which **D**'s equivalent is unfortunately lost:[1] *Till I haue asked wiffes 12* (881) would seem an attempt to mend what appears in **L** 926, and *On 12 wiues shee did her anon* (888) agrees closely with **L** 933. It agrees also with **L** in almost all cases in which, though **L**'s reading is not prima facie erroneous, **D**'s and/or **W**'s readings are closer to that of **A** and therefore probably more original. The great majority of its differences from **L** are explicable as casual alterations in the course of transmission.

Fifth, although **P** preserves the formula with which **L** concludes,[2] it then picks up the story again, plainly now deriving from a different source,[3] and a source of a quite different type, for though in this section there is still clear textual connection with **A** there is also enormously more additional matter than any of the AM2 texts have earlier presented, matter moreover of much superior imaginative quality. This new source probably derived from our Ur–AM2. **L** 1806–15 promises an account of the death of Angys as well as of Vortigern; the passage appears almost identically in **P** 1706–15, and with only minor variations in **D** 1244–53 and **W** 2035–44, so doubtless goes back to Ur–AM2. The conclusion of **L**, after the death of Vortigern only, represents therefore abridgement of Ur–AM2, which itself continued further, so the obvious postulate is that this continuation underlay the source of the latter part of **P**, though this source amplified it extensively. This same source must also be that of the latter part of **W**, which accords more closely with **P**, both in proportion of lines substantially identical and in detailed correspondence within these lines, than in the earlier part. **W** however has no equivalent of **L**'s concluding formula, but passes from a line equivalent to **L** 1975 (**P** 1861) to one equivalent to **P** 1868, by way only of the

---

[1] W's *Tyll the haue Iuged* . . . (1031) may represent the original (in which case my emendation of **L** is to be rejected), or merely a better mending; its . . . *they dyde her* . . . (1038) will be a different but equally erroneous reflection of an original . . . *he dide hir* . . .

[2] P 1864–7, equivalent to **L** 1978–81:

> Now pray wee all the heauens kinge
> And his mother that sweet thinge
> He blesse vs all with his hand
> And send vs peace in England.

[3] Holland has independently (he was evidently unaware of the original thesis-form of the present edition) pointed out the distinct derivation of the end of **P**, in 'Formulaic Diction and the Descent of a Middle English Romance', 92–3.

independent couplet 2247–8 (reminiscent of the earlier 1830–1, equivalent and close to L 1634–5). This portion of W appears in Appendix 3, p. 275 below. Whether the joint source of L and the first part of W had the abridgement, and the writer of an antecedent of W also turned to the same version of the continuation as underlies P, but leaving out any now inappropriate conclusion; or whether the source to which P turns was simply the source of W, which had at an earlier stage been continued with change of source (or by a new hand treating his source differently), one cannot of course tell. But that there is a change behind W at this point is certain. Apart from the change in imaginative quality, there is objectively demonstrable a change of vocabulary and idiom, most obviously in the appearance of *ver(a)y* as an intensive, and of the phrase *Marlyn the chylde* (these new features appear in P also, though not always in equivalent lines).

Sixth, H, like P, is close to L, the great majority of its divergencies being explicable as casual alterations in transmission. Typical of the relationship between L, P, and H (though chosen as showing more variation than most) is the couplet L 23–4. P has the lines in reverse order and with a casual variant:

> That they durst him not abyde
> And droue them out of feild that tyde.

H has the order of L, with a different casual variant:

> And drove them out of the londe that tyde
> Ther was none durst hym abyde.

In seeking to establish the manuscript affiliations more exactly, Kölbing draws attention in his edition to a number of correspondences not dealt with in the above general statements: 'P steht L im wortlaute sehr nahe; aber doch kann es nicht eine . . . abschrift davon sein . . . denn an mehreren stellen stimmen die varianten von P zu D. H geht meist mit L, stimmt aber doch in einigen lesarten zu P gegen L. Alle drei hss. weisen demnach auf eine gemeinsame vorlage (*a*) zurück, welche ebenso wie D direkt oder indirekt auf der ersten niederschrift dieser fassung [AM2] basirt' (p. xviii). We can add some cases in which P agrees, against L, not with D but with A, D being independent or wanting, in support of the completion of Kölbing's proposed stemma which the relationship of D with A would in any case speak for (leaving it open at present whether 'AM' is identical with A or represents an Ur–AM from which A also derives):[1]

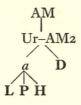

It is, however, dangerous to assume that the mere existence of parallel readings points to a joint source, and in fact as a full explanation of all the variants which Kölbing records his proposed stemma breaks down at once.[2] He records ten cases of agreement of H with P against L. In four of these D, A, or both support P and H, and in three more D and A are either wanting or have readings distinct from any other manuscript, but in the remaining three A and D agree with L against P and H.[3] This could imply simply a joint source *b* for P and H, deriving from *a*. However, in one of the three cases of agreement of P with D against L to which Kölbing draws attention in the section of text for which H exists, H agrees with L against P and D,[4] which would have to be a coincidental agreement (of the other two, in one the line is omitted in H and in the other H has a distinct variant). Further, Kölbing draws attention to three cases of agreement of H with D against L, though he does not bring them into his argument on affiliation. In one of these the agreement is against L and P (A having a distinct variant), in one against L, P, and A together, in one with A but

---

[1] Further refinements would in fact be called for. The distinct derivation of the latter part of P is not shown; the new source might derive from *a* or might be a parallel derivative of Ur–AM2. It is also highly probable that at least one stage intervenes between Ur–AM2 and D (see below, pp. 64–5). But these points are irrelevant to the present discussion.

[2] Holland has again independently observed this; he points out particularly that H, P, and D agree on the name Constantine for the old king, against L's Costaunce ('Formulaic Diction', pp. 90–1). However, since casual variation in the forms of the name is evidently possible (see A's naming of the elder son at 49, 75, and 103, and Louelich's at 1709 and 1844 beside 1683, etc.), and since the old king is named but twice in L (14, 159) and P, and once in H and D, I would attach less importance to the point.

[3] The most substantial of these involves the name for which L has once *Angys*, regularly *Aungys*. A has regularly *Angys*, *Angis*; D once *Aungis*, regularly *Amygys*, *Amygis*. Against this H has *Anguish*; P once *Anguish*, regularly *Anguis*.

[4] L 44 *þat*, H *al that*; D *what*, P *in what*.

against **L** and **P** together; and clearly a good deal more coincidental agreement now has to be assumed.

The line in which the latter two of these three occur, **L** 62/**A** 102,
well demonstrates the impossibility of arriving at a reliable stemma
on the basis of such minor points of agreement and disagreement as
Kölbing is arguing from. **D** 51 reads *To make Moyne here kyng*, **P** 60
They made Moyne lord and kinge, and **H** 57 *To make Moyne theyr lord
and kynge*. The four AM2 manuscripts agree together in the major
matter of the name *Moyne* against **A**'s *Costaunce*; **H** and **D** agree
against **A**, **L**, and **P** in opening with an infinitive; **H**, **D**, and **A**
against **L** and **P** in having a possessive; and **H**, **P**, and **L** against
A and **D** in having *lord and*. The only grouping that could be
extracted from this is of **L** with **P**, and this is the grouping against
which Kölbing offers most cases.

My own opinion is that **P** and **H** probably had a distinct common source, which derived from a close ancestor of **L**, but it
would be a waste of paper to set out the accumulation of subjective
judgements about readings more and less likely to have arisen by
descent rather than independent alteration on which this rests,
since in any case many similarities not arising from common
descent must remain. It is plain that the various versions were not
produced by scribes copying with close and constant attention
fixed on their exemplars; often their attention was at best casual
and intermittent, and of the variants thus introduced it is not
surprising that some were independently similar, either by true
coincidence or because the copyist concerned had come across
different versions, from which turns of phrase had remained in
mind.

There are moreover the possibilities of deliberate eclecticism
and intelligent emendation. The shift from one source to another
in **P** after the point where **L** concludes is plainly deliberate; in his
edition of *Lybeaus Desconus* Mills concludes that 'the textual history of P has been . . . radically confused by eclecticism and rational-
ization' (p. 27). One clear case of deliberate emendation is worth
record. For the couplet 1844–5 the scribe of **L** originally wrote
Opir messangeres he sent anon | To þe hepene kyng Aungys. **P** 1742–
3 reads *Other messengers he sent anon | To kinge Anguis soone*.
This suggests that the scribe of **L** was here following closely a
source substantially identical with the source of **P**. The scribe of
P or an antecedent restored the rhyme by adding *soone*, but since

this would have produced a hypermetre he eliminated *þe heþene* (yielding in fact a rather poor line). The scribe of **L** noticed that what he had written did not rhyme, so he struck out *anon* and substituted *ywis*, a superior reconstruction and in fact 'correct' in the sense of restoring what an earlier version had, as in **A** 1733–4. Had he made the correction before putting *anon* on parchment, his *ywis* would have seemed to descend directly from **A**, or from Ur–AM.[1] There may have been many similar cases in which he and other scribes did just this; details will never be recoverable.

It is no more possible to place the antecedent of (the first part of) **W** precisely in a stemma than it is to place those of **L**, **P**, and **H**. The mere fact that **W** more closely resembles the group which these three constitute than it resembles **D** does not mean that there existed a joint source of **L**, **P**, **H**, and **W**, parallel with the source of **D**; it may simply reflect greater individual variation in the descent to **D** than to any other text. Similarities between **W** and **L/P** against the agreement of **D** and **A**, between **W** and **D** against **L/P** and **A**, and between **W** and **A** against **L/P** and **D**, can all be readily found, and some in other groupings also, including one even between **W** and **P** against all the other manuscripts.[2] All that can be said is that the **W** tradition represents a descent from **A**, or Ur–AM, separate or separating from those of the **L/P/H** and **D** traditions.

The final, probably the most important, question in the affiliation of the texts concerns the existence and status of my 'Ur–AM,' for if Ur–AM2 can be shown to descend from it rather than from **A**, the AM2 texts can be used as authority for the occasional correction of **A**. Kölbing (p. clxxi) is confident that it does so derive, and he uses AM2 in this way. So do Zupitza (in his review of Kölbing, p. 91) and, especially, Holthausen ('A- und ME Texten', 198–207). Now plainly an English version antecedent to **A** existed, for authorial and scribal dialectal strata can be

---

[1] As the *ywys* of **W** 2081 may well do (**W** is close to the corrected **L**).

[2] They are most, and similarly, frequent with **L/P** against **D** and **A** and with **D** against **L/P** and **A**. Typical is **W** 1359 *And home he came by nyght*, **D** 1029 *And come by ny3t*, against **L** 1213 *Hit was by ny3t*, **A** 1125 *Bi ni3t it was*. The most substantial positive correlation (there are various cases of shared omission of couplets or short passages) is with **A** 417–18: **W** 398–9 has *Agayne his fomen that wolde hym slee | And he sholde haue halfe his fee*, where **D** 412 agrees closely with **P** 367 (the rhyme-line **D** 413 is independent). The agreement with **P** is in the trifling matter of initial *V*, not *F*, in the name given to Vortigern.

distinguished (see below, p. 62); also two awkward passages and
at least one curious form can best be explained by reference to an
antecedent version.[1] But its mere existence is of little significance;
evidence for the descent of Ur–AM2 must come from the AM2
texts.

Now from them one could construct, as an approximation to
Ur–AM2, an eclectic text based on L/P but preferring the agreement of any two of A, D, and W to L/P's sole authority, and, in
the portions for which we have a text of D, lines not supported
by either A, D, or W eliminated.[2] Such a text would be closer to A
than any of the actual AM2 texts, but would still differ very
considerably. Most of the differences, however, can be accounted
for on the assumption that a scribe, though deriving his text from
A, felt himself so familiar with the material that he did not make
constant reference to his exemplar but frequently ran on from an
imperfect memory. Thus we find couplets substantially reproduced
but with the lines in reverse order, as in A 1371–2/L 1461–2,
lines displaced further, as in A 578/L 503, and sometimes larger
passages displaced, as in A 718–34/L 689–704; occasionally
material from A appears twice, as with A 1330/L 1374 and 1392.
AM2 sometimes preserves verbal similarity to A though the sense
is altered, as in A 1213/L 1285; not infrequently the similarity
is restricted to identity of rhyme with the rest of the line quite
different, as in A 135–6/L 111–12, while in a few cases it is the
rhymes that differ with the rest of the line similar, as in A 1331–
2/L 1395–6. It is doubtful if actual oral transmission played any
significant part in any of the transmissions that produced our
AM2 texts; there are very few of the types of corruption so
plentifully demonstrated by Smithers in the Lincoln's Inn text
of *Kyng Alisaunder*.[3]

[1] See below, Commentary, notes to lines 378, 1196, and 9646; also to 9345,
where, however, the case is much weaker.

[2] In a few cases we can achieve a more sophisticated restoration by postulating
an antecedent from which the AM2 texts have diverged. Thus the antecedent
of L 316 *play*, W 329 *moche play*, and D 339 *noblay* was probably *noble play*
(as in fact in A 358). The antecedent of P 382 (= reconstructed L 400) *dighten*
and D 436 *raydyn* was very possibly *graiþeden* (in fact A 432 *grayþed*).

[3] His edition, vol. II, p. 12. A case which might go back to Ur–AM2 is L 774
made hire mong against A 792 *ȝede among* (D wanting, P 737 *was euer among* more
likely to be an improvement of an original like L than a preservation of the form
from which L derives). Of cases which cannot well go back to Ur–AM2 I
note D 28 *sayd* against A 79, L 49 *hadde*, P 47, H 46 *had*; D 31 *also* against A
82 *fals and*, W 49 *false and* (L, P, H have not the passage); and L 1539 *arered is*

Not all the differences between AM2 and A can be explained like this. Such a passage as L 1800–14 would justify Kölbing's view that 'der verfasser [of Ur–AM2] . . . hat . . . den ehrgeiz besessen, nicht nur für einen copisten gelten zu wollen, sondern vielmehr den rang eines umdichters, eines bearbeiters für sich zu beanspruchen' (p. clxxi), though he is more disposed than I to see variations as deliberate. Other variants, however, he sees as 'bessere lesarten' going back to what I call Ur–AM. Now among the many cases in which the AM2 texts differ from A it would be surprising if AM2 did not sometimes seem superior; even where this is clearly so, as in the *swyre* of L 715 for the clumsily repeated *hond* of A 745, the superior reading is not necessarily the more ancient,[1] and in several cases cited by Kölbing the superiority is much less certain. In my opinion, for instance, it would do the poem ill service to destroy the effective emphasis of the doubling in A 1135 by substituting *lyʒe ich* from L 1223 for the second *seystow*.[2] Similarly, of the additional passages in the AM2 texts[3] some are effective, some doubtfully so, some frankly bad, and many have the air of mere inflation of neutral quality, but for the most part there is no strong reason to suppose any of these types otherwise than additions. As an example of an effective addition

against A 1449 *a ʒerde*, D 1066 *a ʒerdes*, W 1733 *two yerdes* (P omits; probably a scribe was understandably baffled as to what a form like L's might mean). Holland is convinced that '[the later] manuscripts preserve the results of oral transmission of the original romance, or a part of it' ('Formulaic Diction', 94), but it does not seem to me that he critically distinguishes between oral transmission and reproduction wholly or partly from memory of a text originally read. He very fairly points out that many of the minor variations in the AM2 manuscripts may arise by incorporation of formulaic phrases from a common stock, not particularly from any version of AM itself, but to describe such incorporation as 'oral improvisation' represents an unwarranted jump in argument. He goes on to agree—indeed assert as though the contrary were the accepted view—that unoriginal phraseology need no more in Middle than in Old English point to oral composition.

[1] See below, Commentary, note to line 1196, for an instance in which what may seem a superior reading in AM2 is best explained as an attempted mending of a reading as in A. In the present case the curious *stronge myght* of W 807 could well represent an attempt at some stage of transmission to understand an original repeated *hond* as here in metaphorical sense.

[2] One might better justify *lyʒe ich* as the original reading here by comparing LeM 16, 42–3 '. . . *Ore dites se ce est uoirs ensi com ie le vous di . . .*', though neither version of AM is here so close to LeM as to make this a strong argument. For another case of an uncertainly superior reading in AM2, see below, Commentary, note to line 839.

[3] For an account of the more significant of these, see Kölbing, pp. clviii–clix.

we may take the couplet **L** 1093–4, which Kölbing holds to be original on stylistic grounds. But a wish to bring out the contrast, implied in **A**, between the silence of the expected defendant and the defence offered by the infant, could well be ascribed to the 'author' of Ur–AM2. The mother's silence does not, in any case, come from LeM, where she has a good deal to say at this point.[1] It seems quite likely that her speech was simply cut by the AM poet in accordance with his principles of contraction, thus producing accidentally the implication of silence which was seized on by the Ur–AM2 reviser. A more doubtfully effective addition, though in a passage where some expansion of **A** might well seem called for, is the description in AM2 of the observations of the astrologers, to whom the *sky* showed not merely the birth of a fatherless child but specifically that his blood would sustain Vortigern's castle (**L** 538–42). In **A** we are given no reason why, having seen the birth of the child, the astrologers decided to order his death. The reason given in LeM 24, 36 ff., however (that their observations showed that the child would cause their deaths, and so they decided at any rate to eliminate this threat) probably underlies **A** 611–12. Since the reason given in AM2 would not imply that the child was a danger to the astrologers, Kölbing's belief (p. clviii) that this reason derives from Ur–AM is unappealing; rather is it constructed, somewhat clumsily, from what the astrologers say to the king in **A** 597–600 and 607–9. As an example of a really bad addition in AM2 we may take the laboured obscene joke of **L** 1431–8; for a typical passage suggesting mere inflation **L** 1352–1402 against **A** 1316–38 (noting in passing the inappropriate *ioye and blis* of a priest's singing at a funeral in **L** 1387).

There are, however, a number of additional passages in the AM2 texts which contain matter also to be found in LeM. The similarity in several of these cases, including some mentioned by Kölbing, is comparatively slight, or, even when more considerable, could easily be coincidental.[2] But I note three, particularly, in

[1] 14, 36 ff. The reference in **L** to her holding the child *in hire arm*, on the other hand, is noticeably like LeM 14, 34–5 . . . *si le prist entre ses bras et vint ensi deuant les iuges*, and EPM 17, 17–18 implies an antecedent version of LeM giving a yet closer resemblance: . . . *and toke hym in her armes, and stode still*. Yet these are natural details which could be added independently.

[2] Thus **L** 627–8 is not really very close to LeM 4, 28–9 *Moult sont fol li diable quant il quident que nostre sires ne sace ceste oeure*, though Kölbing (p. clix) claims a connection. **L** 1109–10 has some similarity to LeM 15, 8–9, in which Merlin *dist que che ne sera mie si tost qu'ele sera arse*, and a similarity a good deal

which the similarity is substantial and coincidence seems unlikely. The first is Blasy's recommendation to the remaining sister not only to defend her bedchamber with the sign of the cross (as in A) but also to have a light burning there (L 794). Compare LeM 8, 19–20 *Et garde que la ou tu gerras ait clarte.* P duly has the line (757), with only trifling variation, D is unfortunately wanting here, but W has *But that she blyssed her a ryght* (884), which may be related to A 816. This suggests that the reference to light may be a reinsertion at some stage of transmission by a reworker who had come across it in LeM or a related text, though it could be that it descends from Ur–AM through Ur–AM2 but was for some reason eliminated in A, perhaps because the line it rhymed with (L 793) seemed otiose, and casually changed in the transmission to W. The second of these passages is peculiar to D. In it the fiend, before enlisting the old woman's aid, makes a direct attempt to pervert the eldest sister's virtue, but is repulsed because she is faithful to Blasy's confession of her: between lines equivalent to L 698 and 699, D has

> Was abouȝten ful long wyle
> þat eldeste mayden to beghyle
> And for nauȝt þat he myȝt do þan
> He ne myȝt bygylen þys goud wouman
> For ȝhe was schreue of dede and þouȝt
> þe feend myȝt do to hure ryȝt nouȝt (822–7).

Compare LeM 6, 15–27:

... a l'aisnee plot il moult bien ce que li preudons auoit dit ... et elle i mist moult grant cure; ... li diables ... l'en pesa moult et ot paor qu'il

closer to the form in EPM 17, 32–3, where the speech opens '*It is no right that she be deed for she hath it not deserued . . .*'; but the whole passage L 1107–10 could well have been inserted independently to supply what seemed to be a lack of argument in Merlin's speech in A 1041–4, and LeM is certainly not followed either in the placing of the lines or in the general theme of this speech of Merlin's. The note above (p. 54) records a rather similar instance. All these are supported as original AM2 readings by the general concurrence of D and W. Peculiar to D is a passage (738–49), appearing between variant equivalents of L 626 and 627, in which a fiend, amplifying the plan to beget an antichrist, sets out the facts of the Incarnation and Redemption. This has similarities to, and may reflect, LeM 3, 27–9, in which in the course of a very much longer diabolic debate on the plan a fiend explains how Christ *pour homme saluer est venus en terre et vaut naistre de feme et effetier les tourmens del monde*, but any expansion here would be likely to be on these lines. See further below, Commentary, note to L 252.

ne les perdist. Si se porpensa comment il les poroit engingnier. Illueques
pres auoit vne feme. . . .

A connection is very probable, but if the **D** passage goes back to
Ur–AM, unless we abandon the concept of Ur–AM2 altogether
it must have been dropped independently in **A** and in the antecedent, or antecedents, of **L/P** and **W**. That is not impossible.
Two, or even three, reworkers could independently have judged
such a reference to the eldest sister's virtue inappropriate when
she was about to fall with but little resistance, and that not on
moral grounds, when tempted by the old woman. But the LeM
passage is perfectly appropriate as it appears there. It appears
after the execution of the first of the sisters; the eldest is proof
against the old woman and later becomes Merlin's mother, but
the youngest, to whom the holy man's counsel had been much
less welcome,[1] is persuaded to become a prostitute. It seems to me
more likely that the AM poet, rearranging and simplifying the
temptations with the sisters attacked in order of seniority, very
sensibly discarded the specific reference to the eldest's virtue, and
that it was clumsily put back in **D** or an antecedent. The third
passage is the most likely to go back to Ur–AM2, since it is found
in both **D** and **W**. Between lines equivalent to L 1206 and 1207,
D has

> And yf þu wost forsake hit þanne
> I schalle tellen þe al þat y canne (1021–2).

W 1351–2 is very similar. This can hardly be independent of
LeM 16, 43–17, 1 *se vous ne le connoisies ie vous dirai encore autres
ensegnes* and/or 17, 3–4 *se vous ne connoisies ceste chose ie vous dirai
encore autre que vous saues bien que voirs est*. The latter of these
may also be the basis for **L** 1203–6, with 1208–10 resting on the
immediately following *et la dame se taist et li enfes dist* . . .; these
lines have the support of both **D** (1017–20) and **W** (1347–50),
but the similarity with LeM is less close. If any or all of this is
to be derived from LeM through Ur–AM2 to the preserved
texts, the natural assumption will be that it reached Ur–AM2
from Ur–AM, with the **A** version resulting from abridgement, but
once the possibility of later insertion of matter resembling LeM
has been entertained, one will be unwilling to dogmatize about the
antiquity of any small amounts of such matter.

[1] 6, 14–15 . . . *et la maisnee volsist bien qu'il fust ars en cendres.*

There is also a further and notable case of variation between A and the AM2 texts which at first sight seems much easier of explanation if AM2 preserves the reading underlying A. In LeM, when Merlin is asked how the water may be removed which, as he predicted, has been discovered, he replies '*On le fera toute coure en boins fosses*' (32, 17–18), and this is done. The puzzling *picke walles* of the equivalent passage in A (1474) could be explained if Ur–AM had the *deope welles* of AM2 (L 1566), with a possible, though here inappropriate, rendering of *fosses*; scribal corruption to *walles*, followed by 'correction' of the adjective to make sense, would then yield the form of A. If so, the introduction of the numeral 'two', presumably in Ur–AM since it appears in A and the AM2 texts, is merely casual. But an alternative explanation will account for the numeral, namely that the original English poet, baffled as to how an underground water might be caused to flow into *fosses*,[1] altered the story to the form found in A, in which walls are built across the channel, forming a sort of coffer-dam, and the water bailed out from between them.[2] For this operation *two* walls are clearly needed, and we may now suppose a corruption (or deliberate 'correction') of *walles* into *welles* in the transmission to AM2, with the numeral retained. The men who toiled *bi to and to* in A 1475–6 to remove the water, presumably carrying some sort of vessel between them, probably reflect the *hommes a col por porter loins* whom Merlin in LeM 32, 2–3 suggests as needed to carry away the earth which is above the water; this reference would be eliminated as meaningless in the AM2 form.

Finally, the most striking of all the ways in which AM2 resembles LeM against A is the one already referred to on p. 32: AM2 retains, or reverts to, the names Moyne, Vter, and Pendragon for the sons of king Constance. I argued briefly above for reversion,

---

[1] This method makes sense if the water is at the top of a mountain, as it is in the earlier versions of the story, and as it remains in the y³ tradition of LeM (though the point is not stressed): *l'ueure . . . trambloit si tres durement qu'il leur estoit auis que toute la montaigne deuoit fondre* (W f. 135ʳᶜ, 32–6). Cf. EPM 27, 23 . . . *the mountayne that the werke was sette on gan to tremble* . . . When the site of the projected work has been removed to Salisbury Plain, as in all forms of AM, it becomes silly. The method suggested in A at least makes some effort to resolve the difficulty; in AM2, after the *welles* have been made, we are merely told that *Al þe water þey brouȝt out þo* (L 1567), with no indication of how.

[2] Though in making his water *swift and stepe* earlier he in fact left an absurdity as great as the former (see above, p. 34 n. 9). The *welles* of AM2 would of course be no more efficacious in draining a *water . . . strong and steop* (L 1540).

but one might well be puzzled, if the AM2 form in fact derives from the A form, why so attractive a story as that of how
Moyne came by his name should have been abandoned by the
later redactor. Some further support[1] for the alternative supposition that the names in AM2 derive from Ur–AM, whence they
were altered in A, comes from a comparison of the lines in AM2
and in A following the death of the prince named Pendragon in
AM2 and Aurilis Brosias in A. A 2161–2 have at first sight the
form of a funeral tribute to Aurilis, but they in fact apply to
Uter (and Aurilis is rather abruptly dismissed); they could not be
applied to Aurilis, who was not at any time king and so could not
have *ful wele held his lond to riȝt*. But, as noted on pp. 30–1, it is
only the confusions arising from the alteration of names in A which
there deprive Aurilis of his reign. I suggested on p. 32 that this
alteration was an attempt to correct LeM rather than Ur–AM,
but the argument was one of probability only. If Pendragon (the
equivalent of A's Aurilis) duly had his reign in Ur–AM, the lines
whence A 2161–2 derive may well have been applied as a funeral
tribute to him, a state of affairs to some extent surviving in AM2,
where a line equivalent to A 2161 (P 2374, W 2777) is applied to
Pendragon. On this supposition, having changed the names and
abandoned Aurilis' reign, the redactor of A when he came upon
these lines in his source was obliged to twist them to make them
refer to the survivor.[2]

On the other hand since twisting must somewhere have occurred,
it can just as well be supposed in an adaptation of the A form to the
AM2 form, with the application of the lines changed to lead better

---

[1] See also below, Commentary, note to lines 2055–8.

[2] There is an attractive variant of this argument if we take W here to preserve
the general form of Ur–AM2, and hence of Ur–AM. Then in Ur–AM the
antecedent of A 2161 applied to the dead Pendragon, and that of A 2162
introduced the reign of Uter, which was to form the matter of the next section.
Between these lines came the antecedent of W 2779–80 (see Appendix 3, p. 276
below), which had however to be discarded in A (together with whatever was
the antecedent of W 2778, P 2375, and whatever rhymed on the antecedent of
W 2781). In P or an antecedent what had become a mere cursory reference to
Uter's reign seemed inappropriate, and the couplet was again discarded, the
whole concluding passage being adjusted to refer to Pendragon and all good men
instead of to the two kings. However, it would be quite in keeping with the
character of W if the distinctive couplet were a late addition, the phrasing
a partial reminiscence of 2638–9 *And sythe thrughe comyn radde | Pendragon
the crowne name* (= A 2048–9, appearing where P has 2240). Then P more
nearly preserves the antecedent form, and my argument which follows in the
main text above can stand.

into the conclusion which was immediately to follow. Further, it is notable that although in LeM the brothers are always named in order of seniority, with Pendragon preceding Uter, in the AM2 texts the other order is much commoner, many of the instances being most easily explained as adaptations of lines referring, as in **A**, to Uter Pendragon; thus in **L** 1948–50 *þer fauȝt Vter and Pendragouns . . . | And Vter . . . nouȝt forȝat . . .*, where the awkward second *and* looks very like a survivor from an earlier form as in **A** 1855–7 *. . . þer fauȝt . . . Vter Pendragon . . . | And his broþer nouȝt forȝat . . .* Particularly interesting is the first instance,[1] where a copyist's jump from the *oþer broþer* of **A** 45 to the *broþer* of 47 could easily have produced what was converted into the basis of **L** 29–30 and of the other AM2 versions[2] by a reworker who knew the LeM form of the names. If the derivation was from **A** itself, and if **A** had already lost its miniature,[3] this reworker would also have had to restore an apparently missing reference to the eldest son, for *Costaunce* in **A** 44 is not easily or confidently to be read, and even if read would naturally be taken as the name of the old king by one who thought he knew the name of the heir. His practice thus established, the reworker would suppress or adjust other cases as he came to them. Where the two brothers are

[1] The others are at **L** 221, 1855, 1867; **P** 1869, 2275. Even where the brothers appear in the order of LeM, the AM2 readings can readily be seen as a different adaptation of a reference as in **A** to Uter Pendragon: **L** 1964, **P** 1885; also (though from their different style one would attribute these rather to the particular source whence **P** derives its last section than to Ur–AM2) **P** 1896–7, at which point LeM refers to king Pendragon only (36, 33–4), and 1984–5, for which LeM has no close equivalent, referring in the whole account of the messengers' report (37, 22–40, equivalent to **A** 1961–2, **P** 1974–83) to the king and his counsellors without names, until in lines equivalent to **A** 1967 ff., **P** 1986 ff. . . . *lors dist li rois qu'il lairoit Uter son frere al siege . . .* (37, 40–1). Bülbring's review, however (pp. 260–1), makes a quite different inference from the commoner order of names in AM2. He supposes this order to have arisen in Ur–AM, simply because it made rhyming easier, and then, by falsely suggesting that Uter was the senior, to have confused whoever was responsible for the form preserved in **A** and so led to his omission of the reign of the prince he names Aurilis Brosias (see above, pp. 30–1). But in fact though rhymes for *Vter* may be scarcer than for *Pendrago(u)n* they are not really very difficult to contrive; any of those used for *Fortiger* would do. Bülbring's explanation seems to me less likely than mine.

[2] **P** is virtually identical with **L**. **H** has *The other tweyne of grete renoun | Hyghte Vter and Pendragon*; **D** *þe oþer children were of grete renoun | þat on hyȝte Vter þat oþer Pendragon*. One could speculatively reconstruct an Ur–AM2 text from these readings, but there would be no value in doing so. **W** is quite distinct; see above, p. 46 n. 2.

[3] See, however, below, Commentary, note to line 44.

separately treated in A, he would naturally identify A's Uter Pendragon, who is crowned king, with his Pendragon, whom he knew to be the heir, so that A's Aurilis Brosias would become his Uter. This would continue until it became clear that A's Aurilis was to die, when he would be forced by his knowledge of the story to reverse his identifications, producing the change of equivalences seen in A 2117–24/P 2318–21—and restoring the passage to the form it had in LeM 51, 11–13: . . . *et Vter apresta son oire et ses gens por aler entre le riuiere et l'ost, et Merlins trait Vter a une part et li dist 'pense d'estre preudome car tu n'as garde de mort en ceste bataille.'* If we were dealing with this passage only, of course, the assumption that the P form derives directly from LeM, through Ur–AM and Ur–AM2, and that the A form is an alteration of this, would be the natural one. The following passage, describing the battle, provides no useful evidence. Neither text of AM is close to LeM, nor are the correspondences between A and P everywhere clear. I have printed P 2332 as equivalent to A 2131, but P 2328 also seems related.

Thus it is impossible to say certainly whether the AM2 texts derive from an Ur–AM, antecedent to A, rather than from A itself. There is, however, some suggestive evidence in this direction; even if many of the similarities between the AM2 texts and LeM are insertions in the course of the transmission of AM2, some may none the less go back to Ur–AM. Accordingly it is reasonable to look to the AM2 texts to see if they offer guidance in a case where A is plainly corrupt (as is done in the present edition, for instance, at A 781–2; see below, Commentary, note ad loc.), but the AM2 texts cannot properly be taken as authority for emending A.

LANGUAGE

The Language of the Original

The language of the version underlying A, which is as near an 'original' as we can reach, has been analysed by Kölbing, pp. xxi–xxiii; the phonology, and the more important features of the accidence, are fully treated in Liedholm's *Phonological Study . . . of AM* (hereafter referred to simply as 'Liedholm'). The dialect is, moreover, very close to that of *Kyng Alisaunder* (KA), of which

Smithers has given an authoritative account in his edition, vol. II, pp. 40–55. Only a very compressed treatment is therefore called for here. The most noteworthy features are:

(i) As in KA, SE *e*-quality in words which had *ȳ* in OE (WS) is very common, though rhymes implying *i*-quality also occur.

(ii) As in KA, but in a much higher proportion of cases, the derivative of the *i*-mutation of Gmc *ă* before nasal appears in rhymes implying *a*-quality, beside others implying *e*-quality.[1]

(iii) The same appears to be true of the derivatives of IEᵤ *ē* (WS *ǣ¹*) and of the *i*-mutation of Gmc *ai* (OE *ǣ²*), though so many of the forms involved are capable of alternative phonetic explanation (see Liedholm, pp. 58–70) that there is no point in quoting figures unsupported by full discussion.

(iv) As in KA, singular and plural present indicative can inter-rhyme, implying -(*e*)*þ* as the poet's form; in contrast to KA singular -*es* does not occur in rhyme, but certain forms in **A** may suggest that the original had -*es*,[2] in which case two actual occurrences of -*es* within the line are probably preserved rather than introduced by the scribe.

(v) As in KA, rhymes establish alternative present participial forms in -*ind*(*e*) and -*ing*(*e*).[3]

(vi) The original probably used *he* as both 3rd sg. fem. and nom. pl. personal pronoun. These pronouns never occur in rhyme; the evidence is inferential from apparent false 'corrections' by the scribe of **A**,[4] so one cannot say whether *he* was common or occasional in the original. As objective plur. *hes*[5] is attested by rhymes as a rarer alternative to *hem*. These pronominal features are similar to what can be inferred for KA.

(vii) As in KA, though the evidence in AM is less striking, the vocabulary contains a number of words and phrases of distinctively SE provenance, of which *schriue* (*of*) 'care (sometimes "know"?) (about)', usually negated, may be specifically Kentish;[6]

---

[1] In AM 38 certain rhymes on *a*, 28 on *e* (accepting as certain rhymes on proper names whose original form is sufficiently established by other unambiguous rhymes, etc.); in KA 11 and 41 respectively (Smithers's ed., vol. II, p. 47).

[2] See below, Commentary, note to line 1647.

[3] Not absolutely, since -*nd* and -*ng* (= [ŋg]) can inter-rhyme, but such rhymes are few and rhymes tending to establish the participial forms are many.

[4] See below, Commentary, notes to lines 401, 988, 2506, 2656, 7005, 8012, 8343, and 8553–4. [5] See below, Commentary, note to line 732.

[6] AM 2533, 8780; KA 3892; William of Shoreham *De Septem Sacramentis* 1081, 1995, and (not negated) 1232, *De Decem Preceptis* 102; *The Seven Sages*

and many words and phrases taken over or adapted from French, a number of the words being rare in English.

AM, then, like KA, must have been composed in the London area,[1] by a poet well versed in French as well as English; the higher proportion of distinctive dialectal features as compared with what became standard English usage indicated in (ii) and (iii) above[2] suggests a rather earlier date than for KA. A *terminus ad quem* for both texts is given by the dating of the Auchinleck manuscript at about 1330 (see above, p. 36). Smithers suggests a possible upper limit of 1250 for KA on non-linguistic evidence (KA vol. II, p. 44); the presence in both texts of forms attesting retraction of OE *æ* before *ld*, etc. (beside more frequent ones attesting breaking) would make one put the probable dates later than this,[3] and so perhaps for AM would the reference in A 25–6 to noblemen who knew no French. One can hardly hope to get closer than a vague 'the end of the thirteenth century' as a probable date of composition.

The Language of the Manuscripts

The language of A, like that of the original, has been analysed by Liedholm. It represents, moreover, what has become recognized as a clear linguistic entity, an early stage of what became Standard English, the Type II of Samuels's well-known article 'Some Applications of Middle English Dialectology'. Analysis here is therefore unnecessary. Substantially, it is characterized by a tendency to eliminate all the more distinctive features of the original in favour of the developing standard. The only significant exception is the present participle, for which the scribe strongly prefers forms in -*and*. This 'northern form' has caused much trouble to commentators, but it should no longer be necessary to point out that it is not an exclusively northern form; it was regu-

---

of *Rome* (by a probable emendation) 1840. Also worth note in AM are *ablowe, al what, at þe first word, speruer, stiuour,* and (though by emendation) *crudand* 'hastening' (see below, Commentary, note to line 5984).

[1] Without trying to define the limits of this 'area' more closely than evidence warrants. Place-name evidence does not establish any phonetic differences between the dialects of London and Essex, and the lack of texts of assured Essex provenance makes lexical evidence of little value. The possible area of composition also extends somewhat west and north-west of London. Sklar argues for Sussex ('Dialect of AM'), but not soundly.

[2] On these features see Ek's *OE æ before Nasals and æ in S-E ME.*

[3] See particularly Mrs. Bohman's *Studies in the ME Dialects of Devon and London,* p. 90, on these forms in the London area.

larly used in the early fourteenth century in the London area, though how this came about remains open to argument.[1]

The language of **L** shows western colouring similar to that demonstrated by Smithers for the **L** text of KA (vol. II, p. 55), as does that of the other poems in the manuscript, but there are characteristic differences between the different poems which suggest rather carry-over from a collection of Western exemplars than importation by the scribe of **L** himself.

In AM2, as in the other poems, there are frequent *eo* spellings in cases where this might be expected in a Western text—in words from OE *ĕo*; or in which phonetic rounding is likely, as in *weore* 'defend' 126, 215 (:*dere*); or which suggest false accommodation of an unfamiliar SE form, as in *deone* 1039 (:*quene*). AM2 also shows such spellings frequently in the definite article *þeo*, beside *þe*[2] (a feature shared with *Lybeaus Desconus* and, though less strikingly, *Seege or Batayle of Troye*, against *Piers Plowman* and KA, in which *þeo* is rare), and in the negative adverb *neo* beside much rarer *ne*, *no* (*neo* is rare in the other poems, in which *no* is the usual form). The eccentric *oþreo* (29) is also notable. Such forms suggest a scribe used to copying *eo* in words where his own dialect had *e*, and sometimes mistaking a final *e* with a marked curl back on the right for *eo*. The existence of *seo* and *no* beside *þe* and *ne* would suggest to him that what he read as *þeo* and *neo*

[1] See Duncan's 'Notes on the Language of the Hunterian MS. of the *Mirror*', and my 'Auchinleck MS.: Participles in -*and(e)*'. Other supposedly northern forms, *walde* beside *wolde warld*, beside *world*, and *noiþer* (regular, *noþer* once), are no more exclusively northern than is the -*and* participle. Duncan, pp. 205–6, mentions *warld*, *noiþer* and *noþer*, as well as -*ande*, as 'Type II' forms, evidently quoting more fully from Samuels's findings than Samuels himself did; Samuels records *warld*, and also *wald*, as 'Type II' (p. 88, and p. 91 n. 13).

[2] The distribution pattern is curious. In the first 800 lines *þeo* is steadily the commoner form (by about 4:1); thereafter *þe* (about 2½:1). This suggests a change of hand here in a version at some stage of transmission, which may also account for the fact that in the earlier part of the text *nouȝt* adv. is predominantly used with another negative preceding, in the later part without; the much smaller number of instances make this a much less clear-cut change, however. A comparable distribution pattern for *þeo/þe* is also to be noted in KA, but here *þeo* dominates only in the first 200 lines (2:1) and then becomes sporadic. This could suggest that the scribe encountered a new shape of final *e* in his KA exemplar, which he first tended to interpret as *eo* but soon began to realize was not; *neo* is also concentrated in the first 200-odd lines (but exactly the same explanation will not do here since the ruling form thereafter is *no*, not *ne*). I have not been able to give enough time to the non-AM texts of **L** to offer definitive conclusions about all this.

were legitimate forms, hence their frequency beside the single casual *opreo*. The form *felleon* (608) could be a parallel case, but as non-final *e* would be less likely to have the confusing curl back it may more plausibly be seen as simply a slip in copying *feollen*. Influence from this word could have something to do with *feolle* 'cruel' (136), though *feole* 'many' is a more likely source of influence; or we may look to the preceding word *weore* as explanation, as to the preceding *peo* and following *preo* for *sustreon* (702, 709), to the following *heo* for *skapeode* (761).

The spelling *u* for the vowel derived from OE (WS) ȳ, and for the unstressed vowel which in 'standard' ME is represented *e*, is less common in AM2 than in KA, being in both cases largely restricted to the sequence *ur*; for *eo* it occurs occasionally, as in KA. As regards the vowel derived from ȳ, *Seege or Batayle* and *Piers Plowman* resemble KA, while in *Lybeaus* the *u*-spelling is rarer than in AM2; as regards the unstressed vowel *Seege or Batayle* resmbles AM2, while in the other two poems I have found no *u* spellings at all.

The KA text appears to be unique in this manuscript in having frequent use of *i, y* to mark vowel length; the spelling *o* in words having OE *a(o)* before single nasal is on the contrary general in the **L** texts (AM2 *mony* 8 etc., *mon* 12 etc.).

A north-westerly provenance for the form of AM underlying **L** could be inferred from the presence of *bydene* 576 (:*beon*; an original *bydeone would be a likely form, though nowhere recorded) and *til* 700.

The language of the **D** text of AM2 shows a less clear pattern. The three most striking features are:

(i) Some Western colouring comparable to that in **L**; not however expressed by *eo* spellings (which are regular in *eorth(e)* 720 etc. but otherwise appear only in *seo* 'see' 1084 and in the false 2nd person pronoun form *peo* which rhymes with it), but by a good many in *u* in words having OE (WS) ȳ (e.g. *dude* 43 etc., *hure* 534:*desyre*), *ie* (ȝut 68 etc., *hurd(e)* pt. 251 etc., and the obj. and possess. fem. and possess. pl. *hure* 477, 672, 770, etc.), and *ēo* (*buþ* 495 etc.).

(ii) A considerable number of *e*-forms also in such words (e.g. *ech(e)* 103, etc., *lest(e)neþ* 14 etc., *kende* 350 etc.); some doublets result with words under (i), as in *ferst* 557 beside *furst* 544, and *mery* 1254 beside *mury* 530, and there is the interesting rhyme *werch* 736:*church* 737. No *i*- or *y*-forms occur for such words. The southern past tense *fyl*, *fillen* 113, 693, etc. is also noteworthy.

(iii) A further range of *e*-forms in words having OE *ĭ* (e.g. *dreuen* pl. pt. 1247, *quek* 'alive' 985) or shortened OE *ī* (*gresly* 1122), beside others with the expected *i*, *y*. The exact phonetic and geographical limits of this apparent lowering remain somewhat uncertain, but in Dobson's *English Pronunciation 1500–1700* it is recorded as occurring in vulgar London speech (vol. II, § 80); a SE/London speech including both this and general *e* for OE *ȳ* is perfectly plausible. Since the western colouring of L, as we have seen, derives from an antecedent, and since D and L certainly derive from a common ancestor, a SE/London scribe working from a western exemplar seems more likely than the other way round. Unfortunately the rhymes peculiar to D help little, for they include some unlikely to have been perfect in any dialect, such as *als*:*castels* 128–9, and the remarkable *leme* 'limb':*keme* 'come' (inf.) 122–3, with which the scribe evidently did his best. As noted above (p. 46) a number of the lines peculiar to D are metrically lax; these rhymes are probably from the same hand, and so will be the replacement of the rhyme *beon*:*bydene* by *stylle*:*snelle* in a variant passage. There is nothing significant to say about the replacement of the *til* noticed above by *to*.

Nor is there about the dialects of or underlying H and P. Nonstandard forms are normalized, or replaced by substitute readings, or occasionally the whole couplet in which they occur dropped; peculiarities introduced are of minimal interest.

AUTHORSHIP

There is no external evidence for the authorship of AM, and the speculative construction of a shadow author from internal evidence is of little value. If common authorship with other works can be demonstrated, however, this is of value, for one can then argue from one work to another. Kölbing (pp. lx ff.) thinks it probable, and Smithers (KA vol. II, pp. 40–1) is convinced, that the author of AM also wrote KA[1] and *Richard Cœur de Lion* (hereafter RCL),

---

[1] Brunner, in 'Die Reimsprache der . . . *Sieben weisen Meister*' (p. 205), and Liedholm (p. xxi) also regard common authorship of AM and KA as quite

and Smithers also that he wrote *The Seven Sages of Rome*[1] (SS). In the cases of both RCL and SS it is necessary to define what is to be ascribed to the 'author', since the manuscript traditions are complicated;[2] caution prescribes restriction in RCL to passages common to both main groups of manuscripts, in SS to the poem as it appears in the Auchinleck MS.

That there is much similarity between these four poems is beyond question. As noticed above (pp. 60–2) the dialects of AM and KA are very similar; what differences there are are consistent with one author using a smaller proportion of forms which were going out of use in his later than in his earlier work. The original dialect of SS appears very similar to that of KA,[3] to the extent that the shorter length affords sufficient evidence; that of RCL[4] is again similar, but perhaps still later in view of the higher proportion (though still a minority) of *i*-rhymes for words having OE $\bar{y}$ and the rarity of *a*-rhymes for words having OE $\bar{æ}$.[5] The vocabularies of the four are also very similar: of particular interest are several words, phrases, and usages common to KA and AM but otherwise rare or unknown, thus:

	AM	KA
after þat hii ware ⎫ 'according to		2499
after þai were ⎬ their status'	6520	
being 'condition, personal circumstances'	5525, etc.	223
deþes 'mortal (*of wound*)'	2098, etc.	2369, 4602
fulrade 'narrate fully'	4258, etc.	4640
honteye, -eys 'shouting of insults'	6879	3827
ratel 'flutter? (*of banner*)'	7848	928, etc.
skecken 'make a raid'	7409	*implied by* 3558

possible. Heuser, in *Altlondon* (pp. 61 ff.) assumed two authors belonging to a group of contemporaries, but as Smithers points out Heuser had not all the evidence of similarity now available, since he had to rely on Weber's very imperfect edition of KA.

[1] Or at least (as with RCL) those parts which appear in the Auchinleck MS.
[2] See Brunner's eds. of RCL, pp. 11 ff., and of SS, pp. xvii ff., and Norman Davis's 'Another Fragment of RCL'.
[3] See Brunner 'Die Reimsprache . . .'. In addition to points made there we may note what was probably an original rhyme of *man* pl. on *woman* sg. at 1730–1 (A 1606–7), beside one certain rhyme in *e*-quality in *men:slen* 504–5 (A 385–6).
[4] See Brunner's ed., pp. 38 ff.
[5] Brunner records none, but note *shethe* n.:*scathe* n. 2149–50 (the author's form of *shethe* presumably had *a*, from OE *scæþ* beside *scēaþ*), and what is probably an original rhyme *drade* n.:*made* pret. 6103–4.

	AM	KA
talle v. 'cut (*with weapon*)'	5072, 6948	1883
wel wele 'in very good order'	5079	1747 (also SS 2456)

None of this, however, need point to more than a group of authors writing in the same area at the same time, using naturally therefore the same sort of language. Nor is it evidence for common authorship that the author of KA has clearly modified his source at one point under the influence of an episode which occurs in AM,[1] for even if he took it thence, which he need not have done, this merely shows that he knew AM (as he would be likely to know an earlier work written in his area), not that he wrote it. The same applies to a passage in SS which is plainly adapted from AM. In his French source the author of SS found an episode apparently confected in part on the basis of the story of the finding of Merlin as it appears in LeM. The empress is trying to persuade her husband, Diocletian, against the advice of his seven wise masters, to execute his son by his former wife. She tells a story of how the emperor Herodes' seven counsellors, unable to explain why the emperor becomes blind whenever he leaves his city, are told that a fatherless child can explain this. They find Merlin when his companions *li reprochierent qu'il estoit nez sans pere*;[2] in due course Merlin explains that excavation under the emperor's bed will reveal a cauldron containing seven boiling springs. The execution of the seven counsellors, who are deceitful, will quench these and cure the emperor. In rendering this episode the author of SS in several places uses phraseology reminiscent of AM, and the finding of Merlin appears thus:

> On a dai þai com þer Merlin pleid
> And on of his felawes him traid
> And he was wroþ and maked a res
> And cleped him sschrewe faderles
> And saide he was of þe fendes kinde
> His felawes euer misdoinde;

[1] In KA's source Alexander fixes a spear in the summit of Mount Taurus and threatens to kill anyone who removes it; the alteration in KA to a spear found fixed there which only he who should rule the earth could pull out (2621–32; see Smithers's ed., vol. II, p. 27) is plainly derived from the story of Arthur's sword.

[2] Compare LeM, in which one of his companions *commencha ... Merlin ... a reprochier qu'il estoit nes sans pere* (25, 37–8).

'Daþeit haue þou' quaþ child Merlin
'Al to loude þou spak þi Latin,
Seue maistres i se her come
þat han me souȝt al fram Rome . . .' (2379–88).

This cannot possibly be independent of AM (A) 1195–1220. Even
if SS did not appear to be later on dialectal grounds one would say
that the SS passage is rather a contraction of the AM one than the
latter an expansion of the former. It is particularly notable that
Merlin's anger against the playfellow who reveals his identity to
the messengers is reasonable in AM, where the messengers are
under instructions to kill him at once, but makes little sense in SS,
where the counsellors merely wish to bring him honourably to
the emperor. Whether this is more likely to reflect re-use of the
material by the same author or incompetent plagiarism by another
is arguable; the latter is at least perfectly possible, so that as
evidence for common authorship this episode takes us little
further.

What has chiefly convinced critics of common authorship is
extensive similarity in style of composition and in phraseology.
The evidence on the first point is not particularly strong in the
cases of RCL, because the source has not survived so that one
cannot be sure what is the author's own, or of SS, because this is a
quite different type of story from the others; but as between AM
and KA it is striking. The same sorts of modifications to the
sources appear in both poems: compare my analyses on pp. 6–19
and 32–5 above with those of Smithers in his KA, vol. II, pp. 26 ff.
Not all can be ascribed to general English taste; in both, particularly, the poet(s) made extensive use of what Smithers calls
'the apparatus of the epic style', a series of stylistic devices which
are not to any great extent taken over from the specific sources of
the poems but which evidently reflect a knowledge of French epic
tradition. The types recorded by Smithers from KA can almost
all be found also in AM. Similes comparing the actions of men
with those of animals occur eight times;[1] they are also compared
with natural forces six times[2] and with the flight of an arrow once,[3]
and men holding fast to each other in battle are once compared
with two burrs.[4] We may also note the comparison of flying

---

[1] 2008, 4047, 7000, 7972, etc., besides bare comparison with a *wode lyoun*
thrice and a *speruer* once.

[2] 4844, 5874, 5934, etc.   [3] 5920; cf. KA 5530.   [4] 8280.

weapons with motes in a sunbeam[1] and with a swarm of gnats.[2]
Blows given in battle are compared with those of a butcher,[3] a
carpenter,[4] and a smith.[5] Ironic metaphors are represented by
the ideas of 'reconciliation'[6] and 'tribute'[7] by weapon-stroke, as
well as by the commoner 'teaching a lesson'.[8] Foreshadowing
occurs several times[9] (Smithers notes only one case in KA, in
4813-14, but other, if perhaps less striking, examples do occur
there).[10] The deadliness of battle is expressed in terms of bereave-
ment of kindred in three passages.[11] There are several examples of
on the one hand litotes,[12] on the other hyperbolic description of
the size of armies or the extent of slaughter: the latter mostly
obvious ones, as in the repeated comparison of shed blood with
a river,[13] but the images of corpses strewed so thickly that for miles
around one could not avoid treading on them,[14] and of severed
parts of bodies thickly entangled like sticks in a crow's nest,[15] are
notable. Abuse, albeit of a rather unimaginative sort, is directed
at enemies in battle several times,[16] and the same thing is implied
by *honteye* at 6879. To only a small extent could all these devices
have been suggested to the poet by LeM, although comparisons
of an attack with a storm[17] and of weapon-strokes with carpenters'[18]
are to be found there, as is reference to bereaved women.[19]

Two of the other elements of the epic style call for more detailed
examination. The AM poet several times makes subjective
comments on the action[20] (as also in KA[21]); once[22] he goes further
and uses the action as an occasion for a piece of generalized moral-
izing:

> Amonges men it were ille
> 3if eueriche vnwrest hadde his wille (6963-4).

---

[1] 9159-60.　　　　　　[2] 9161-2.　　　　　　[3] 4802, 8202.
[4] 6044, 8838.　　　[5] 7520.　　　[6] 335-6 (very similar to KA 2923-4).
[7] 5219-20 (very similar to KA 3345-6), 7800.
[8] 9675, etc.　　　　　　　　[9] 91-4, 300, 2065-6, etc.
[10] 1745-6, 2658, etc.　　　　　　[11] 409-10, 457-8, 6915-20.
[12] 2784 (very similar to KA 3828), 2985, 6333, 6940.
[13] 5295-6, etc.　　　　[14] 2147-50 (very similar to KA 4439-42).
[15] 9171-4.　　　　　　[16] 6371, 8476-7, 8998, 9350, 9371.
[17] *si uienent bruiant comme tempeste* (147, 32-3).
[18] *. . . comme se che fuisent carpentier qui carpentassent el bos* (147, 35-6); this
underlies the simile in AM 6044.
[19] *il . . . ploroit . . . maint franche dame por lor freres et por lor fils et por lor
signors* (149, 33-4).
[20] 693-4, 737, 782-4, etc.　　　　[21] 413-14, 1124, 1771-2, etc.
[22] Besides the proverbial expression introduced by *men seyt* at 1895.

Such sententious asides are much commoner in KA,[1] and they
are also imported massively into the 'headpieces' which form one
of the most striking similarities, but also differences, between
AM and KA.

There are ten examples of the 'headpiece' in AM, all based on
a reference to a month or season. That at 4675–80 rests to a
considerable extent on a passage at the corresponding point of
LeM:

> Che fu a l'entree de Mai, au tans nouel que cil oisel chantent cler
> et seri, et toute riens de ioie enflambe, et que cil bos et cil uergier sont
> flori, et cil pre rauerdisent d'erbe nouele et menue et est entremellee
> de diuerses flors qui ont douce odour, et ces douces aigues reuienent
> en lor canel, et les amors noueles font resbaudir ces valles et ces puceles
> qui ont les cuers iolis et gais por la douchor del tans qui renouele. Lors
> auint que Gauaines . . . (134, 28–34).

LeM goes on to say that as it was hot the party started early, a link
between the season and the story abandoned in AM together with
the syntactic linking provided by *Che fu a . . .* and *Lors. . . .* The
piece in AM stands, like the others, as a separated lyrical insertion,
in function somewhat like a chapter-heading verse. All but one
of the other nine examples in AM are constructed with but little
originality on the same lines as this one, the seasons referred to
being once March,[2] once April,[3] thrice May,[4] twice June,[5] and
once merely *somers tide*.[6] The adjective *miri(e)* is used of every
one of these, and every one includes a reference to birds singing,
flowers blooming, or both. The references in the LeM passage
quoted above to the flowing of rivers and the love of young men
and women are paralleled in AM in one of the June pieces:

> þe riuer cler wiþouten sour,
> Boþe kniȝtes and vauasour
> þis damisels loue par amour (8660–2).

The descriptions show some variety, especially in the references
to human activity, but the mechanical nature of much of the construction is evident from the meteorologically unlikely description

---

[1] 1125–8, 1341–2, 3880–5, 4550, 4597–4600, 4717–18, 6982–7, and quite
possibly also 1045–6, besides proverbs introduced by *men seiþ* and the like at
161–2, 751–2, 1279–80, 4723–4.

[2] 5349–52.   [3] 259–64.

[4] 1709–14, 6596–6600, 7397–9.

[5] 3059–64, 8657–62.

[6] 7619–22.

of March as *hot miri and long*[1] and characterized by the usual singing birds and blooming flowers. The insertion of this particular headpiece was perhaps suggested by the statement in LeM that Arthur's party arrived at Carohaise *la velle de la Pasque Florie*[2] (141, 8). That at 7397 ff. rests to a much greater extent on LeM, where the British are established by *vne moult bele lande*, where *li oisel chantoient parmi le gaudine vertes feullu et feisoient moult douce saison comme el mois de May qui la estoit entrez . . .,*[3] a picture further elaborated in the following lines.

The unusual and striking headpiece at 4199 ff. also takes a hint from LeM, which tells us that *il fesoit moult grant froit et il auoit bien gele* (W; 124 note 3), but the development, contrasting the steadfastness of true love with the winter failure of natural beauty in bird, countryside, and man, appears to be the poet's own. It is the only considerable development in this genre in AM. In KA, however, the genre proliferates; there are twenty-seven instances. Some replace the spring scenery by effective vignettes of autumn.[4] Some add to the description of the scenery and events of the season sententious observations[5] or quick sketches of human behaviour.[6] Some omit the seasonal reference altogether and offer a morning-picture instead[7] (with or without similar added touches), and some are compounded entirely of human observation, *sententiae*, or both.[8] This further development is quite consistent with common authorship, provided KA is later than AM, and this is suggested as we have seen by linguistic evidence also. KA is in fact in many ways a better piece of work than AM. In almost all comparable passages it is stylistically superior, and it displays a more perfect understanding of French, with scarcely any of those misunderstandings of source which AM occasionally suggests.[9] On the hypothesis of common authorship, AM would stand to it as a highly promising prentice piece.

[1] The intention seems to be to say that the days are long, a statement explicitly made in other headpieces (1710, 3063, 4678, 6597).

[2] Though *la Pasque Florie* signifies simply Palm Sunday.

[3] W f. 217[ra], 40–8; portions illegible because of a smudge of spilt ink supplied from the closely similar Bibl. Nat. f. fr. 9213 (Y), f. 183[va–b]. The x[1] tradition has a much briefer equivalent of this passage (188, 8–10).

[4] 795 ff., 3289 ff., 5745 ff. (a fine example); 457 ff. is rather poor.

[5] 457 ff., 1843 ff., etc.   [6] 3289 ff.

[7] 911 ff., 1239 ff., etc.   [8] 235 ff., 1573 ff., etc.

[9] In at least three cases a spurious proper name seems to have been created by the addition to the original of what is in fact a distinct element: *Dorkaine*

RCL, as we have seen (above, p. 66), also appears to be later than AM, probably also later than KA. The development of the 'apparatus of the epic style' is, however, oddly different from that in KA, if all three poems are by the same author. Most of the devices occur, the ironic metaphor in considerable elaboration,[1] but in the parts which one can fairly judge to be original neither sententious interpositions by the poet nor the headpieces which in KA so often contain them appear at all.[2] Of course, an author need not keep on the same tack in every work, but these were effective devices, and in writing another poem in the same genre it is puzzling that our postulated author abandoned them.

Their lack in SS, on the other hand, may be thought sufficiently accounted for by its not being in the same genre. It is already sectioned by consisting of linked short stories, so sectioning by headpieces would be uncalled for; the stories are narrated by characters of the framing story, so interpositions by the poet himself would make a complicating third level; none of the stories are concerned with epic battle, so most of the other epic devices would be inappropriate. On this score nothing can be argued for or against common authorship.

Similarity of phrasing, also, is closest between AM and KA; least close, as would be expected (and yet still very noticeable) between SS and the others. Kölbing prints a large, though by no means exhaustive, collection of similarities in his AM, pp. lxii ff., lxxxii ff., and civ; others are pointed out by Brunner and Smithers

---

(3746) from (le roy Loth) d'Orcanie (110, 10), Sabalant (6181) from (Ulfins feri) si Balanc (qu'il . . .) (151, 22–3), Troimadac (9345) from li rois Maidrap (232, 14); also (but corrected) Sestas (3769) from li dus Escant (110, 5). In three more the same mere descriptive epithet li lais hardis (148, 19–20, etc.) has been converted into the proper names Blehartis (5483), Lectargis (9626), Beichardis (9753). See further below, Commentary, notes to lines 3290, 3733, 4165–6, 4298, 4602, 5406, 5459, 5979, 8713, and 9345, where other cases which may reflect imperfect understanding of French are discussed. KA is so free of cases suggesting this that Smithers describes the author as bilingual, but he admits the possibility of lapse of understanding at one point (KA vol. II, p. 27, and see below, Commentary, note to lines 8942–4); we could think of an author whose birth-tongue was English but who later developed an increasingly perfect mastery of French.

[1] Blows in battle constitute plenteuous payment (6153), a drynk of woo (6440), wesseyl (6816), and a drink off Kyng Richardis cuppe (7024); also in passages probably, but not assuredly, original a dole (3142), a warysoun (3144), and a means of giving a blessing (548). God is also besought to give a traitor grace of worldis schame (2719).

[2] One of each occurs in passages probably not original (5397–8, 3759–69). For reasons for rejecting these passages, see Brunner's ed., pp. 20–1.

in the course of the Commentaries to their editions of RCL and KA. The following are typical specimens:

> AM   Men hem serued of gret plente
>   Mete and drink of gret deynte (3117–18)
>
> KA   Hij weren yserued wiþ grete plente
>   Wiþ fresshe and salt of vche deynte (4169–70)
>
> RCL And were serued with grete plente
>   Of mete and drynke and eche deynte (1787–8).
>
> AM   . . . and gan to tere
>   Wiþ boþe honden hir ȝalu here (857–8)
>
> SS   Wiȝ boþe honden here ȝaulew here
>   Out of þe tresses sche hit tere (463–4, A 344–5).

No such particular similarities, of course, are individually important; comparable ones can be found without difficulty in poems for which common authorship is not in question, as Holland's 'Formulaic Diction' amply illustrates (pp. 99–109). What is important is simply their large number, at least as between AM, KA, and RCL, coupled with similarity of vocabulary even outside such phrasal parallels. To multiply instances here sufficiently to make the evidence convincing would occupy many more pages than could be justified; a parallel reading of the poems will quickly supply the lack. And yet however much similarity of all sorts can be found, in an age in which the notion of plagiarism as an offence did not exist it will still be impossible to distinguish in this way between common authorship and authorship by a 'school' whose members knew each others' work.

To attempt this distinction we would need to isolate personal minutiae of style of a sort unlikely to be imitated because unlikely to be identified by any ordinary reader, but it would be just such minute distinctions which would be most easily destroyed by casual scribal alteration. There is, however, one group of usages which one might expect to show a personal 'signature' and yet to be relatively immune to scribal corruption, namely the rhyming tags. A full investigation of these as a possible test of common authorship requires extensive display of evidence and detailed statistical analysis, and must be reserved for a special study which I hope to publish elsewhere. Briefly, however, the hypothesis is that since in general nothing in the matter being rendered constrains the use or non-use of particular tags, an author is likely to show a characteristic pattern of preference among them, and though another author may of course take over tag usages from works he has read, he is unlikely to take over a complete pattern of distribution. Ideally the hypothesis should be substantiated by appeal to several different works known to be by the author in question. Lacking these for our (or any contemporary) author we can do the next best thing by comparing different sections of the one work, provided it is long enough. It proves that of the most frequently used tags in AM, all except (*so*) *i*(*ch*) *finde* are distributed in a way consistent with my hypothesis. The reason for the exception is that the poet used this tag for virtually one purpose only, to accommodate an obligation to state the size of a military force: of its thirty occurrences twenty-eight are rhymes on *pousinde*.[1]

Comparison with the other poems of the 'group' shows a markedly lower overall frequency of tags in them. That would be consistent with their being later and superior works by the same author, but if so one might expect a general reduction in the use of all tags, which is not the case. There are far fewer examples of *apliʒt*, etc.,[2] *ich wot*, etc., *forsope to say*, etc., and (KA and RCL only) *sikerly* (*-liche*, *-lik*), whereas the two tags most frequent in AM, *ywis*, etc. and *saun faile*, etc., are just as freely used in the others. The distribution patterns in KA, RCL, and SS are in fact much liker to each other than any of them is to AM, though RCL shows a frequency of *saun faile*, etc.[3] markedly higher than in any of the other three poems, which is puzzling on the hypothesis of common authorship. SS similarly shows a higher frequency of *sikerly*, etc., but not sufficiently so to be clearly evidential considering the poem's comparatively short length.

[1] Not so of such extensions of the tag as *So ich in pe brout yfinde*; of the five such only one rhymes on *pousinde*. The reason seems to be that usually the numeral including *pousinde* occupies all or nearly all of one line, and the statement of which the numeral forms part occupies so much of the couplet line that only a short tag is needed to fill this. Nor is it so at all in the other poems of the 'group'; in KA and RCL the simple tag has a much more varied use, in SS it occurs only once, rhyming on *blinde*. This represents a real difference of tag-rhyming technique between AM and the others, of a different sort from that noted below.

[2] The 'etc.' in all cases is to include variants with the same rhyming syllable.

[3] Also of *i*(*ch*) *vnderstonde*, but here the distributions are too odd to allow confident argument. All the few instances in AM are in the second half of the poem; two-thirds of those in RCL in the first quarter. In neither case do the contexts provide any obvious reason for this.

Now of course a poet in improving his technique by the discard of routine devices might do so differentially, but the evidence of these tag usages must at least cast some doubt on the generally accepted view that AM and KA are by the same author. Added to other points made above it casts considerable doubt on the view that RCL is also by this author. It is harder to say anything confidently about SS because of its shorter length and different nature (apart from its particularly obscure manuscript tradition), but my own opinion is that SS could quite well be by the same author as KA, that this author might at an earlier stage in his career have written AM (though if so his poetic technique changed considerably as his career developed), but that RCL is in all probability of distinct authorship.

COMMENTARY

The Commentary is directed chiefly to the elucidation of the principal version, and all line-references are accordingly to **A** unless otherwise specified.

15–16 'and [can] clearly see, if they wish to, that there is no need for them ever to be lost', i.e. 'can see the means of grace . . . whereby God shall have no need to damn them'; taking *ysen* as infinitive, parallel to *witen and se*.

17–18 'In this matter they have everywhere advantages, (namely a knowledge of) French and Latin.' Holthausen's *Auauntages . . .*. [*of*] *Freynsch* ('A- und ME Texten', 199) is not necessary; the construction of the whole introductory passage 1–30 is clumsy, and suggests addition by a less competent poet than the main one.

21–6 Notable at this early date are the reference to noblemen who speak no French, as further evidence that the displacement of English by French was less than used to be supposed (see Wilson's 'English and French in England'); and the patriotic declaration that everyone born in England *ought* to understand English, evidently including those of French descent who would not yet be called Englishmen.

44 *Costaunc⟨e*: supported as a more probable reading than *Costentine* by the annotation recorded in Appendix 1 (p. 266 below), if the manuscript was still unmutilated at the time (but if so, of course, my speculation on p. 59 above that the mutilation might bear on the form of AM2 would fall).

53–4 '. . . begged his father . . . that (he) would grant . . .'; for omitted subject pronoun cf. lines 86, 295, 432, etc.

57 *maki*: probably infinitive; an illogical but quite understandable change of construction.

58 *no noþer*: in such cases, exceptionally (others in lines 75, 1502, 1897, 3984, 4573, 6893, 7663, 7667), I treat manuscript word-division as important enough to preserve. The feature is absent from **L**.

60 *toȝain his owen wille*: 'against [the king's] will'; cf. *Sir Perceval* 319–20:

> Bot to þe kynge I rede þou fare
> To wete his awene will.

86–90 Lines 86–7 may be read as one clause (cf. 723–4 *bihete gir ȝiftes . . . to wende . . .*); 88–9 then go together, with 90 a separate clause asyndetically linked. Alternatively 87–8 may be taken together, with 'postponed *and*' construction; 89–90 then form one clause, and the gifts in 86 are simply part of the king's general recognition of his steward's services. Whoever was responsible for the form preserved in AM2 (L 51–2, portion there omitted D 35–7) clearly understood his original in the latter way.

89 *go†uerny*: *goruerny*, and the similar *wincherster* 141, are defended by Kölbing (note ad loc.) and, hesitantly, by Liedholm (p. 161). Various examples of inorganic *r* in Middle English are given by Behrens (*Zur Lautlehre der französischen Lehnwörter*, p. 196) and von Feilitzen (*Personal Names of Domesday Book*, p. 84), but none in forms similar to the AM examples. Von Feilitzen moreover points out that in most of his examples 'the inorganic *r* seems to repeat an organic *r* in the preceding or following syllable', so that 'the possibility of dittography should . . . be considered'; I assume and correct such an error.

L 55 *So þat*: 'when', or perhaps 'as soon as'—cf. **D** 58, where *so þat* answers to **L** 69 *so sone as*. For senses of *so* simple approaching 'when' see below, note to line 2153.

L 92 *wiþ mouþ and cher*: perhaps we are to understand that he conveyed the urgency of his request by expression of face as well as words, but probably *cher* is no more than a near-doubling of an already conventional *wiþ mouþ*.

155 *Mani . . . so*: in effect 'many who'. Possibly '(as) many as', but probably we are to understand that some of the *fel kinges* accepted Angys' overlordship tolerantly enough.

180 *site*: metre and rhyme would both be improved by reading [*hem*] *s[e]te*.

L 162 *And of h⟩ys*: following **P**, and Kölbing prints *hys* as though clear, but the form would be unique in **L**, and the sense is poor. A better reconstruction would be *Of Den⟩ys* (there would not be room for *And of Den-*).

190 *don his hond*: *hond* here is equivalent in sense to *miȝt*, and the phrase to *dede his miȝt* 5971; similarly in *God . . . saue and kepe þi miȝti hond* 1377 beside *Crist saue þi miȝt and þi mayn* 7034, *of noble hand* 5464 beside *of miȝt cler* 6572. This extension of meaning is promoted by the fact that ME *main* represents both OE *mægen* and OF *main*, so that *hond*, its synonym in the latter function, would tend to be treated as a synonym also in the former. The same extension is suggested below, note to line 3091, for *mounde*, and a similar process in the note to *croice* 7305. For the present phrase cf. *dos hond to þ ilke* in *Ancrene Riwle* (Titus), Mack's ed., p. 158 line 23.

206 *conioun*: there are difficulties of form in the accepted derivation from the northern *can-* form of OF *chanjon*. Bliss ('Imparisyllabic Nouns', 4–5) believes that *cangun*, which is normally taken as a variant of our word, is in fact distinct, and that neither can be derived from *c(h)anjon*. The point is not important enough for full argument here; my view is that the distribution of the various forms in ME indicates that they were seen as forms of the same word, and that semantically they relate so well to *chanjon* that the accepted derivation remains the most satisfactory. Particularly notable is the quality ascribed to a *cangun* in *Ancrene Wisse* (Tolkien's ed., p. 58, f. 29ª, 15–16) of thriving *se lengre se wurse*, which is strikingly like that ascribed to a *chanjon* in the first recorded instance of that word, in one of the *Sermones Vulgares* of Jacques de Vitri: *puer quem Gallici vocant* chamjon *vel* chanjon, *qui multas nutrices lactando exhaurit, et tamen non proficit nec ad crementum pervenit* (quoted in P. Meyer, '*Chanjon*, enfant changé en nourrice', *Romania*, xxxii (1903), 452–3).

L 206 *rowned*: 'spoke' is possible here (the word does not necessarily imply secrecy in ME), but hardly in L 209; the form will represent scribal botching of a weak pa. t. form of 'run'.

249 *-þurth*: different scholars have with equal confidence asserted that the reading, here and *passim*, must be *þurth* or *þurch*. For reasons given above, p. 38, certainty is impossible, but on balance *þurth* seems the more likely, and it is confirmed by *þurth* in the Hunterian MS. of the *Mirror*, whose language, like that of our scribe, belongs to Samuels's Type II (see Duncan's 'Notes on the Language . . .', 206; he has kindly confirmed to me that the reading is certain). The word *furth* 5020, 8174 is then to be treated similarly.

256 *oȝain say*: 'speak in opposition' rather than 'make any reply'; see the discussion above, p. 21 and n.

264 *proudeþ*: I take the meaning to be the same as that implied in *maidens tiffen hem in pride* 7622; but *OED*'s 'be lively or wanton' and Kölbing's tentative 'einherstolziren' (Glossary) are also possible.

268 *wicked*: *OED* takes the word as formed from *wick* adj., as *wretched* from *wretch*. But in both cases the formation may be from the noun, with suffix signifying 'like a' (as in the early fourteenth-century *crabbid* and *doggid*, and already in OE *hōcede* 'shaped like a hook') beside the usual OE sense 'possessed of (thing or attribute)'. The noun *wicca(n)* is attested in OE, but no related adjective until EME.

284 *rewe*: perhaps transitive 'grieve', subject *blod*, and similarly in lines 3514 and 9050; in 6304 'grieve at', subject *men*, in view of the plural verb-form *gun*. The instance in 2283 could be taken either way, as could that in KA 2788 *þe slauȝtte miȝth vche man rewe*. Smithers renders this 'grieve at' (KA, Glossary), but his queried alternative explanation as impersonal seems preferable, and fits all the AM instances. In 6304 the plural verb is to be explained by attraction of the effective, though not syntactic, subject, an explanation in any case essential in *Costaunce ded gun hem rewe* 1772.

L 252 *heore*: would appear to mean 'the two barons' ', but is *heore blod* the heirs, whom the barons claim as kin; or can the line signify that they feared for their own lives; or could *reupthe of heore blod* imply 'deep, inward pity', with the antecedent of *þey* 253 eleven lines back (*breþere* 242)? Or has *heore* also this antecedent? However read, the expression is awkward, and **P**'s *the right* may preserve the more original form, *the right blood* signifying the legitimate heirs. L would then represent a botched attempt to correct what was not understood. In **P** itself the sense is made clear by the insertion (probably not original on metrical grounds) of *children* in the next line; the manuscript reading *they children* does not establish that *children* is a late insertion, with the original pronoun carelessly retained instead of adjusted to an article, for erroneous *they* for the article appears elsewhere (see below, note to **P** 330), but since this error is rare gives some support to the suggestion. The reading of **W** 245 . . . *reuth on the chyldrens blode* is straightforward, but if it represents the original the corruptions are puzzling; it seems more likely to be a correction. The **D** reviser completely rephrased the passage, making in passing an otiose alteration of the number:

> þe twelf barons þat were ful gent
> Gonnen to vnderstonde son
> Of Vter and of Pendragon
> þat þey schulden be ded (257–60).

If the reference here is to the children, then the **A** and **AM2** versions perhaps derive independently from the first and second parts respectively of a passage in LeM: '*li doi . . . disent 'Des que Uertiger a fait nostre signor ochire, si tost com il sera rois il fera ocire ces ij enfans . . .*' (21, 40–2). But the **AM2** version could equally derive from **A**, understood to refer to the prospective death of the heirs (*þe kinges blod*) instead of to the recent death of the king.

L 261 *compacement*: *MED*'s quotation *compacement | Of eorles and of barouns . . . | For to a slayn þeo childre*, jumping from 262 to 264, makes better sense than the actual text allows. The *compacement* has to be identified with the *parlement* of 263, implying 'conspiratorial assembly'. This is, barely, possible, but in fact the word almost certainly reflects a botch, **D**'s *comoun parlement*, supported by **W**, being correct (as noted above, p. 46).

295–6 *nouȝt:bicouȝt*: the original rhyme was probably *nauȝt:bicauȝt*; see Liedholm's discussion, p. 117.

324 *stiel*: this regularly carried-through spelling is best explained, with Liedholm (pp. 17, 101) as representing the AN spelling *ie* for *ẹ̄* noted in Jordan's *Handbuch*, § 51 Anm. 1 (though the *Aȝenbite* forms cited by Jordan as exhibiting this have all been otherwise explained in Wallenberg's *Vocabulary of . . . Ayenbite*). The spelling may have been systematized in this word from a wish to keep the derivatives of OE *stȳle* (in the sense 'bit of a weapon') and *stela* ('haft') separate, or may be a mere personal idiosyncrasy of the scribe; compare his predilection for the form *diol*.

356 *bost*: the citation by various authorities, including *MED*, of AN *bost* as the source goes back to Skeat, who in 1906 recorded in *The Athenæum* his discovery of the word in Walter de Bibbesworth's late thirteenth-century *Traité sur la langue française*. However, Owen in her edition of this work points out that Walter 'a fait passer . . . dans son vocabulaire un assez grand nombre de mots anglais', and she regards *bost* as probably one of them (pp. 28–9, and Glossaire); so the AN etymology is clearly unsafe. The word is probably related to dialectal Norwegian *bausta* 'rush forward violently' (cf. the ON by-name *bausti*, presumably 'one who rushes . . .') but in what way is obscure; the phonology forbids derivation directly from the Norse, for this should produce $\bar{o}$.

375 *lower*: Vortigern makes a deliberate play on the word. For its use, as here, of Christ's 'full and sufficient satisfaction' cf. the pseudo-Skeltonian *Image of Ipocrysy* 151–2:

> Thoughe Christ be the doer
> They force not of his looer.

378 Probably to be understood as 'you shall not serve me (any longer)', correlated with the asseveration of 377, rather awkwardly, by repetition of *so*. Alternatively, as certainly in AM2, 'you shall not treat me like that', looking right back to 369. Very possibly, in fact, 377–8 were preceded in an antecedent version by lines equivalent to L 333–4 which were eliminated in transmission as unnecessarily duplicating 379, the resultant disconnection being not noticed.

380 *todrawe*: If the word-order is significant we have here threatened dismemberment (or dragging about) of the body after hanging (cf. 2012, KA 2248), in contrast with, e.g., 469, and with what is actually done in 383–4; but the poet is probably just using a conventional phrase in whichever order suited his rhyme, with little thought for detail. In LeM there is no hanging, before or after 'drawing': Vortigern *les fist loier a keues de xij keuaus, et tant detraire et trainer que poi en remest en samble* (22, 19–20). L 1160 and L 1481 contrast similarly.

L 340 *traysed*: 'attached by a "trace"', a use of the verb earlier by two centuries than *OED* records (s.v. Trace *v.*²). For attachment by a trace cf. SS 1315–18:

> He let him drawe out of þe pit
> And his fet set faste iknit
> Wiȝ trais an two stronge hors
> And hete to Rome drawen his cors.

The verb is a natural formation from such usages.

P 330 *the*: this form for the 3rd plural personal pronoun would seem to represent an idiosyncrasy in an underlying version, sometimes retained though more often regularized by the Percy scribe, in view of the apparent false 'regularizing' of a definite article at P 1881. If so the version concerned included the whole content of the manuscript, for the form occurs *passim*; there are also other cases of false regularizing (e.g. *Eger and Grime* 1100, *Nutt Browne Mayd* 34, and see note to L 252 above). In any case it appears too often to make appropriate the treatment of each instance as an error calling for editorial correction.

394 *þe bal vp in þe hod*: Smithers suggests that such phrases may signify properly 'the testicle in the scrotum', though 'in most of the later contexts an original sense "scrotum" was misunderstood' and the phrase taken to mean 'head' (KA, note to line 6471); and in his Glossary he is positive for this sense (s.v. Balle, Hode). For wounds to the genitals as an item in a general description of carnage cf. KA 2409 *þere was kytt many a cod*, and for a 'ball in the hood' phrase very probably in this function (in view of the immediately following reference to *hede*) the Harley MS. of *Seege or Batayle* 1378 *k–m* (in Barnicle's ed.):

> . . . many on les þe hert-blode
> And many on þe ballis in þe hode,
> Many on brayned into þe hede . . .

The occurrence in KA, however, constitutes the sole reference to Alexander's losses in a campaign, which would seem more natural if it signified 'head':

> Ac many of his kniȝttes gode
> Loren þe balles in þe hode.

In the Auchinleck *King of Tars*, certainly not a 'later context', this interpretation is surely established when the threat in which the phrase occurs is fulfilled:

> He þat nold nouȝt forsake his lay
> He schuld forlesse þat ich day
> þe bal vp in þe hode
> .   .   .   .   .   .
> And cristen men wiþouten wene
> Striken of her heuedes al bidene. (1215–17, 27–8)

The use here of *vp*, and of the singular *bal*, would in any case speak for this interpretation, as they do in the AM instance. Comparison of the head with a ball is of course well established, as in RCL 4533–4:

> In þe nekke he hytte hym wiþal
> þat þe hed trendelyd off as a bal.

400–1 Can be interpreted unemended, if we assume that the *barouns* of 397 were among those who at 162 *speken wordes felle*, and that they now accuse themselves of having provoked by these treacherous words Vortigern's (vicarious) murder of Moyne. But this would be very strained; nobody would accuse himself of *tresoun* while seeking support. My emendation assumes that the scribe simply mistook a singular *he* for a plural and 'normalized' it (see above, Introduction, p. 61 and n. 4). Line 401 then means 'by means of the treacherous words which he (Vortigern) had spoken,' alluding to his words at 219–20 and 224–5, by which covert phrases he *procourd fro fer þe ded of Moyne*, as Merlin later puts it (1637–8).

Kölbing's note suggests rather to read *kinde* or *kinred* for *king* (*kin* might be best), which is attractive, and has the support of AM2 (**P** 344, **W** 371 *kynred*; **D** 387 *frendes*), but 401 is still awkward to interpret. The straightforward 'because of the treacherous words which they (the *kin*) had spoken' (alluding to 367–72) will not do, for the barons would no more thus have accused their kinsmen than themselves; the interpretation must direct the accusation against Vortigern. Kölbing suggests either 'wegen des verrathes, den sie erwähnt hatten,' or 'verrätherischer weise, desshalb weil sie gesprochen hatten'. Of these the second seems preferable, and its first part has some support from AM2 (P 343, D 386 and W 370 similar), but it seems a less straightforward solution than mine.

There is no useful equivalent in any version of LeM I have seen. Louelich, however, at a point equivalent to 239, has:

> But algates thus was the kyng ded
> Be thike xij fals mennes reed (1795–6).

Since he has just described the twelve as actually doing the killing this is otiose. It may result simply from a casual slipping of the numeral into what should have been a more general reference to the many conspiring barons, but could well represent mechanical rendering, or misrendering, of something in his source, which could then also be the source of our passage as in the manuscript. This, however, would require that the AM poet deliberately moved the passage into a context where it made no sense. I think it more likely that if he had a source it was a reminiscence of Wace, or a related text. When the princes arrived to take vengeance on Vortigern, Wace points out that he deserves his fate, because he

> Ocis out lur frere Constant . . .
> Senz main mettre, par traïsun (7621–3).

429 *were*: More likely 'make war' than 'defend', although this almost doubles the sense of the previous line, because LeM here speaks of an attack on the barons: . . . *et par maintes fois se combati Uertiger a aus* (22, 35). Compare note to line 3641, below.

453 *A boþe half*: there is, of course, no difference between the status of the element *a* here, in 1106 *a-game*, etc., and in 3880 *afot*, etc. Printing style represents *ad hoc* editorial decision in each case (cf. note to line 915, below).

455 *dast*: *MED* (s.v. Dashen) takes up the suggestion of *OED* (Dash *v.*¹) of an ON origin for this word, and adds a reference to German dialectal *tatschen* to the Swedish *daska* and Danish *daske* cited by *OED*. But as *OED* points out, the words may well represent independent, parallel, echoic formations. The verb appearing in 5614 *dusched*, etc. is probably related to this in the way Smithers calls 'ideophonic' ('Some English Ideophones'); *MED*'s derivation (s.v. Dushen) from OE *dwǣscan* with vocalization of *w* and shift of stress in the resultant diphthong is not very attractive. There is a similar relationship between the verbs *lasse* (9103) and that appearing in 6875 *ylust*, which are accepted as echoic. It may be suggested that the existence of the pair *cras(h)en/crus(h)en*, which can be regularly etymologized (OF *crasir*, *cru(i)stre*), encouraged the formation of others.

P 405 *For loue of*: merely an extreme example of the semantic development to 'for the sake of', 'because of', without necessary implication of affection, already to be seen beginning in A 27, 8823, and established in

L 1030, 1176, etc.; though Kölbing's note calls the present use of *loue* 'sinnlos', and suggests substituting *drede* from the equivalent line (467) in D. W 450 also has *drede*, but this still does not prove *loue* to be an error.

499 *afterclap*: probably formed on MLG *achterclap* in the same sense, and/or MDu *afterclap* beside *achter-* 'slander behind back'.

544 *vp so † doun*: the manuscript reading seems to result from a confusion between this phrase and *vp and doun*; metre as well as sense is improved by the emendation.

565 *bat*: Kölbing takes this as from the verb *biten*, here in the sense 'nagen', and refers to 'dieses aüssere kennzeichen des zornes' (note ad loc., and Glossary). But it is physically impossible to gnaw one's own elbow (apart from the fact that the pa. t. 3 sg. of *bite* is elsewhere in AM *bot*). It represents rather the rare contracted weak pa. t., with early shortening of the vowel, of the verb from OE *bēatan*, as in Capgrave's *Solace of Pilgrimes* (Mills's ed.) 14, 2 *bat oute þe dwelleres* . . . Vortigern struck his hand or fist on his elbow, in a gesture which Norman Davis tells me is still in use in Eastern Europe, not unlike our striking of the palm of one hand with the other clenched fist.

567 *wretþe*: -*tþ*- spelling of the word is a notable idiosyncrasy of this scribe; not, however, unique to him as Bliss believed ('Notes on the Auchinleck MS.', 654 and n. 6). for Duncan has since found a parallel ('Notes on the . . . Hunterian MS. of the *Mirror*', 206).

585 *astromiens*: for the form compare KA 136, and see Smithers's edition, note ad loc.

623 *clerk*: may be a genuine plural form, reflecting OF pl. *clerc* in *cas sujet* (though the usage here is objective). It could also be a scribal 'correction' of *clers*, which would be an adoption of the OF pl. in *cas régime*; or could of course represent mere casual omission of -*es*.

bihinde: '(to remain) behind', cf. line 6591; alternatively *lete we bihinde* may signify 'let us turn our attention from', as does *lete we ben* in line 5131.

636 *his miȝt*: can be taken as adverbial, 'and the Devil laid low in respect of his power'. But probably the general sense of the verb in the previous line is understood as carried forward, without regard for the niceties of grammar, into a construction in which *haþ* would be the proper auxiliary. Alternatively, of course, *Deuel his* could be taken as the equivalent of a genitive, but this usage is not elsewhere found in the KA group.

641 *pride*: I cannot parallel this application to a single leader, but it is not far from *OED*'s sense 5 for the noun; neither the *pr[u]de* suggested in Kölbing's note, nor the *[for] her pride [with] Lucifer* in Holthausen's 'A- und ME Texten', is required.

642–6 A widespread notion. See Bennett's note to *Piers Plowman* B I 122 ff., Mansikka in *Encyclopedia of Religion and Ethics* (ed. Hastings),

IV, 622, etc.; for its currency in the EME period compare *Cursor Mundi* 491–5. It clearly arises from the need to fit a general belief in nature spirits into the Christian cosmos, well discussed in Lewis *Discarded Image*, VI. The passage does not rest on LeM.

L 602 *þondur-lyȝt*: an awkward use to signify 'thunderstorm' at large; perhaps a nonce-usage for the sake of rhyme, but it probably recurs in L 1610, where *þe fuyr* from *þondur-lyȝt* would seem to signify 'lightning'.

651 *houen*: *MED* regards the verb as formed from the past stem of OE *hebban*, ME *hēven*, with original sense of poise in the air then extended in the much commoner terrestrial applications. Liedholm (pp. 39–40) suggests that it derives from an OE **hufian*, itself formed on a postulated **hufu*, related to *hof* as *lufu* to *lof*. Her discussion arises from the rhyme on *heraboue* 1573, which she suggests might have pure *ŭ*-value, but this has little force in recommending the derivation, since *houe* 7146 clearly rhymes in the quality *o* (though this does not of course forbid her derivation, since the word could exemplify the change *ŭ* > *ǭ* in open syllables). I had rather look to the recorded MDu *hoven* 'dwell'; to the extent that an aerial sense is genuinely present in the word in any of its applications this would represent influence from the past tense of *hēven*.

L 624 Probably '(such) that the world shall become afflicted' (*wo* to be seen as adj. rather than adv.; cf. L 860, contrasting with A 4002, etc.), with illogical shift of construction in the next line. If *þat* is subject, *wo* must have the unique sense 'grievous (to)'. The *wor[k]e* suggested in Kölbing's note is at first sight attractive, but requires an abnormal use of *ful* as intensive to a noun.

682, 3, 4 *hem*: the family; Kölbing's *he[r]* is unnecessary. Line 712 implies some degree at least of diabolic effect on the daughters; in LeM (4, 24 ff.) the husband is the first to be made angry (the wife is already in the Devil's power).

684 *yplỉȝt*: Kölbing takes this as pronoun plus verb, a reduction of *y ȝou plỉȝt*, but in view of the common *aplỉȝt* (which he has, with less plausibility, to take as a reduction of *y ȝou aplỉȝt*, a phrase which does not, in fact, occur in the KA group) it seems better to treat it as an adverbial use of the participle.

692 *diol*: the form, an idiosyncrasy of this scribe, is discussed by Liedholm, pp. 146–7, and Slettengren 'On . . . *diol*'. No fully satisfactory explanation has been put forward, but orthographic influence from such OF plural forms as *diaus*, *dieus*, yielding singular forms in *di-* (not, however, recorded in OF), seems more plausible than the transposition of vowels in the form *dōil* suggested by Slettengren.

694 *foule answere*: referring presumably to the *chideing* of line 683.

718 *fro aboue*: from the air, where his habitation was; compare lines 641 ff. and 651.

L 692 *or*: as though to say that she escaped prosecution if married *or* if undetected.

L 694 *heo scholden*: Apparently a casual and temporary shift into the plural, it may reflect a partial survival of the plurality of A 730–2; W 782, 4 has . . . *men sholde them take* . . . *they sholde* . . . K however sees *scholden* as a mere error.

729–32 Burial alive of the woman as a punishment for fornication is referred to by the late twelfth-century monk Jocelyn of Furness in his Life of St. Kentigern (Forbes's ed., p. 184) as a law among the ancient Saxons which continued almost down to his own day. LeM does not refer to a particular land, or assert that this was the general punishment for a fornicator who would not become a prostitute, merely that *en icel tans estoit costume . . . c'on en feroit iustice* (5, 32–4). The AM poet may then have modified his source on the basis of the same tradition that Jocelyn reports.

732, 52 *also quic*: all other instances of *quic* in AM are in the sense 'alive', and if so here we have the very unusual use of *also* as a mere intensive, equivalent to the *al* which AM2 certainly has (L 694, 726). I take the phrase, however, rather as equivalent to *also skete*, etc. (see below, Glossary, s.v. Also) 'at once', leaving burial *alive* merely implied; *quyk* occurs in KA in the senses 'quickly' and 'at once'. It is true that when in LeM the punishment is specified, in the judgement on the first erring sister, burial alive is explicitly specified, and there is no mention of immediacy of execution, indeed the judge's sentence *que il la enfuiront en terre toute uiue* par nuit (5, 40–6, 1) implies a delay; this, however, is not represented as the usual practice but adopted *por la honte des amis* (6, 1) because of the culprit's well-born family, so immediate execution could fairly be inferred as normal.

732 *hes*: a much discussed form; see Brunner *Die Englische Sprache*, 1st ed. II, p. 102 and 2nd ed. II, p. 108, and *MED* s.v. His *pron.* (4). A satisfactory explanation must account for both the quite frequent forms without *h-* and for the absolute restriction to the objective case. The latter is not sufficiently explained by identification with the same form as obj. sg. fem. (not in fact in identical distribution); would the restriction to obj. really be carried into the pl.? Crossing of enclitic with regular forms must be invoked; Bennett and Smithers (p. 293) are then surely right to prefer as source the MDu enclitic *-s(e)* to the postulate of an unrecorded native enclitic parallel with that in OFris.

739 *wailing*: the probable ON etymon is represented only by the noun *veilan*, which in Fritzner's *Ordbog* is glossed 'Jamran' and related to the postulated verb **veila* as *veinan* to *veina* and *vælan* to *væla* in similar senses. Craigie, however, in the supplement to the Cleasby–Vigfusson dictionary, glosses *veilan* 'weakness', relating it to *veill* 'diseased', and if this is accepted it makes **veila* a very unsatisfactory etymon for the English verb. However, as *veilan* occurs in the phrase *veinan ok veilan*, apparently similar to *veinum ok gaulum, væl ok veinan*, etc., Fritzner's view seems better. It is not disturbed in Hødnebø's *Rettelser* to the *Ordbog*.

750 *þe ioie*: this use of the definite article can be seen as a gallicism, or possibly an awkward reflection of LeM *ensi aues vous* la *ioie perdue de uostre biau cors* (7, 3), though AM here is not very close to LeM. The simple emendation *he* for *þe* 749 would give a better reading, *þe* 750 becoming the pronoun. The comparative rarity of the construction which this assumes in 749 (but cf. 340) would account for a clumsy attempt at scribal 'correction', or the error could be simple misreading.

770 *agile*: certainly an infinitive, as explained in Smithers's 'Notes on ME Texts', 209–10, though Kölbing treats it as preposition plus noun.

L 730 If *þar* has the normal sense 'needs to' the line must signify 'and while you do there is no need for any man to marry you' (because, as is explained after the parenthetic 731, there is no need for it to become known). The lines run more fluently, however, if *þeo whiles* is conjunctive; I suggest that *þar* may mean 'cares to', a plausible semantic extension though I cannot parallel it. The reading of P (695) implies a scribe who took the line in some such way: *Although noe man doe you wedd* (D is unfortunately wanting); W 822 *Tyll some man come the to wedde* looks simply like a late substitution.

782 *Tofolwe[d] hir bodi*: the manuscript reading is defensible; *to* would be a (rare) pa. t. form of *take*, and *folwe* a unique instance of the bare infinitive after this verb as an inceptive (itself a rare usage, even with *to* + infinitive, except in *Ormulum*). Kölbing's *to[k] folwe* accepts the latter; Zupitza in his review of Kölbing, p. 91, and in 'Zu Sir Torrent', 4–5, also the former, explaining the form as based on inf. *ta* and pp. *tan*. Zupitza cites, in addition to the present case, two examples from *Torrent* and two from variant manuscripts of minor poems of Lydgate. There may also be further examples in AM 5555 and 7581, but in each case I prefer other explanations (see below, notes ad loc.), and in the present case also the combination of a form improbable in a London text and a unique construction seems to me too unlikely to accept. I print the slightest emendation that will serve, at the cost of creating an unrecorded (though plausible) compound. Another reasonable emendation would be *[tok] to folwe*, accepting *take* inceptive. In any case *hir bodi* is a kind of synecdoche for 'her' rather than a mere conventional phrase, her body being what interested the *haras*; a usage not far removed from that in line 747.

I suspect, however, that there has been more serious corruption. The original may well have had the ideas both of low fellows 'following' her and of the 'fouling' (or perhaps 'discolouring', with the verb *falwe*) of her body, as in AM2 (L 762–4). One might conjecture that the original was something like:

> For ribaudes a gret haras
> Com folwe hir in þat cas;
> For ribaudye and gret trespas
> Tofouled [*or* Tofalwed] hir bodi. Allas . . .

A copyist then botched the two similar couplets into one, producing A 781-2. LeM has no equivalent of the passage.

L 766 *bygyle*: anticipating L 806 ff., if the couplet is not mere otiose repetition of L 745-6—W 856-7 passes straight from an equivalent of L 764 to an equivalent of L 767.

820 If I am right in identifying the late marginal hand as having struck through *þat he*, the deletion is of no authority; the least emendation which will then give a satisfactory reading is the elimination of *he*.

833 *Out*: an earlier instance of this usage by nearly a century than the first recorded by *OED* (s.v. Cry *v.*, 21), but there is certainly no need for the [*l*]*ou*[*d*] suggested in Kölbing's note.

833-4 *come*:*sone*: such rhymes, between consonants of different points, but the same mode, of articulation, are common in the KA group; cf. AM 2301-2, 2707-8, 4113-14, 9737-8, etc., and see Smithers's 'Notes on ME Texts', 211. There is a lengthy discussion of these, among other rhyme variants, in Gadow's Introduction to his edition of *Owl and Nightingale*, §§ 17, 18.

839 *hir*: Kölbing (note ad loc.) would then insert *dore* (so in fact W 929), or *fenster* (cf. 815), or *hous* (so L 841). But the crossing was after all to defend herself; also LeM (though AM is not very close to it at this point) speaks only of her being instructed to cross *herself* on going to bed and on rising, which on this occasion she forgot (pp. 8-9). On either ground the manuscript reading can stand, though emendation would certainly improve the metre.

L 849 *a streone of a child*: the phrasing no doubt reflects the long-held notion of the sperm containing all the elements of, and itself developing into, the child.

L 876 *after þan*: 'after that has happened', or if taken as outside the speech 'next', 'in reply'. Either way it is little more than a line-filler and rhyme-maker (cf. similarly empty use of *byfore* in L 955).

871-5 The sense may be taken as 'if I find you pregnant I shall help you; meanwhile (until I see whether you are) go home . . .'; or as 'if I find you pregnant I shall help you until I see the child (whose nature will give me more information and I can then decide my future actions); for now, go home . . .'. LeM is not close enough to give guidance as to which the AM poet intended.

885 'It profited her nothing to hide it'; *it* appears to represent both the impersonal subject of *gett* (cf. 4025) and the object of *hide*; for other cases of words apparently doing 'double duty' like this see below, notes to lines 3056, 4932, 5635, and 9078. The form *gett* is probably past tense, existing beside more frequent *gat* etc., but may be historic present. It would seem that in A this verb, derived from ON *geta*, is distinct from that exemplified in *ȝat* (line 8895), from OE -*g(i)etan*, though the occurrences are far too few for certainty.

L 902 *mou[þ]*: *mou* appears to be unrecorded outside Scots, and despite certain northerly forms underlying L (see above, Introduction, p. 64) is probably a mere casual error here.

915 *icham*: I have treated this as a fused form, parallel with the undoubted *ichil*, etc., except in line 73, where metre suggests otherwise. The choice is, of course, imposed purely by modern conventions of presentation, as in various other cases (see notes to lines 453, 3377, and 7469–70); to a scribe of the period the distinction between *icham* and *ich am* would represent no clear difference.

937 *Opon tvelue wiues*: this detail, together with the women's formal oath to their statement (942) is added in AM; in LeM the judges merely *apelerent femes a lor consel*, and their reply to the question put is introduced simply by *Et eles dient . . .* (14, 42–15, 3). The AM poet was no doubt influenced by the English legal system. In the reign of Henry II the procedure of the 'inquest of sworn recognition' became a usual one. Its function was to answer a particular question referred to it, usually one of title to land, though sometimes on some other more specialized matter. It was composed of twelve lawful men of the neighbourhood, variously knights or merely freemen, chosen as likely to know the facts of the matter, which facts they were to declare, unanimously, on oath. A variant of this procedure is here conceived. The question to be referred is that specified in lines 935–6; the persons most likely to know the facts would naturally be women. For the procedure of the inquest the *Tractatus de Legibus . . . regni Angliae* ascribed to Ranulf de Glanvill is the prime source; there is a convenient summary treatment in Jolliffe's *Constitutional History of Medieval England*, pp. 207–10, and see also Devlin's *Trial by Jury* (Hamlyn Lectures, series 8, London, 1956), p. 8.

945–6 'We can all realize that it is not possible for her to prove the truth of her story' (because in the nature of things there could be no witness to the event claimed to have occurred).

L 951 *[ʒ]i[f]*: but the regular form in L is *ʒef*. A better emendation would be to *þei*; a one-minim error would give *þen*, and 'correction' of this the manuscript *siþen*. W 1058 has *Thoughe*.

L 960 *here telle*: I cannot parallel the absolute use of the phrase, though it is acceptable. The emendation *here delue* confidently proposed in Kölbing's note, however, giving accurate rhyme and a sense close to A (960), proves to be supported by W 1067, which strengthens its claim for acceptance.

988 *fende*: a rather late example of this plural form, if indeed it is plural, but very possibly singular was intended, *þai* 899, 90 being a 'normalization' of *he*, falsely taken as plural (as in 401, etc.), by a scribe who gave little heed to the form *fende*. Compare, however, *helle-fende* pl. in line 8366, but this may represent mere adjustment for rhyme.

993 The infant was placed in a basket, which was tied to the rope, a fact made clear in LeM (13, 4–5), but not here.

L 1078 *wreke*: the proper sense is almost certainly 'cover' (*reke* < MDu *reken*, as in **A**, and **W** 1209), but the form has been adjusted as though it were the verb from OE *wrecan*, an understandable error if the sense 'thrust' survived for this verb, otiose if not.

1054 Reflecting Merlin's later explanation to Blaise in LeM that the fiends '*me misent en tel uaissel qui ne deuoit mie lor estre, car la boine uie de ma mere lor nuist moult*' (18, 35–6).

1071 *gabbest*: regularly derived from the comparatively rare ON *gabba* or the related OF *gaber*, but Smithers's connection of it with the root illustrated in OE *gaffetung* is probably preferable (his KA, Glossary, and 'Ideophones', 104–6); he plentifully illustrates the consonant substitutions involved. All the pre-ME forms appear to have the sense 'mock', but a semantic extension to 'lie' is easy to understand.

1150 *sende þou after*: 'send to follow (her)', or 'send for (in order to send . . .)'?

1159 *scippe*: the relationship of the vowel with that in the accepted parallels ON *skopa* 'run', MSw *skoppa* 'spring', is again explained by Smithers ('Ideophones', 82 and 101–2). The front vowel would imply a lighter, quicker movement.

1167 'and in view of the fact that he (Merlin) pledged himself on her behalf . . .' (and since Merlin had proved his powers of knowledge in other ways his assurance was reliable). LeM reads . . . *et li iuges dist, oiant tous, que li enfes a bien sa mere rescouse d'ardoir par raison* (17, 40–1). The suggestion in Kölbing's note that 'man würde etwa *jugged* erwarten [for *legged*]: "und dann fällte er um ihretwillen den urtheilsspruch"' is thus not supported.

1174 *wiþouten harm and schame*: 'without bringing harm or shame on him'. Merlin, as a mysterious being of diabolic ancestry, obviously might have power to do harm, unless conjured to the contrary; compare his mother's conjuration in lines 1006–7. The same idea is more explicit in LeM: . . . *et Blases respont 'Ie t'ai oi dire et ie croi bien que tu es concheus del Diable, si redout moult que tu ne m'engignes'* (18, 26–7). The collocation of *harm* and *schame* recurs in lines 5520 and 9878–9.

1180 *kinges foure*: Fortiger, Aurilis, Uter, and Arthur. On the confusions which deprive Aurilis of his reign see above, Introduction, pp. 27–32.

1184 *averray*: MED includes this instance under Averren (<OF *averer* 'corroborate', etc.), and glosses 'inform, instruct', but the form is difficult on this derivation. Liedholm, pp. 107–8, suggests three possible derivations: (1) confusion of *aver* (<OF *averer*) with *avay* (<OF *aveie*, pr. sg. of *avier* 'inform'); (2) from pr. sg. of OF *averier* 'prove'; (3) formation from *verray* (<OF *verai*) 'true, truly'. I prefer the third.

1196 *þo ich þre*: curious, since four groups, each of three, were sent out (602–3). The passage can be emended by comparison with AM2 (**L**

1263–70), as suggested in Holthausen's 'A- und ME Texten', 204–5, though with some violence to the text:

[Of] þo ich † sechers snelle . . .
Comen † þre [of hem] bi cas.

But it seems more likely that the form as we have it rests on LeM, though confusedly. In LeM the messengers are sent out in six pairs (25, 25–6), and two of these pairs have met by chance when they come upon Merlin, so that when they hear him abused as 'fatherless' by a playmate, crying because Merlin has hit him, *si alerent tout iiij cele part ou li enfes ploroit* (25, 38–9). In EPM, and probably then in the version of LeM which underlay AM, the reference to the number of the messengers comes slightly earlier, at a point equivalent to the present one in AM; *Thus thei reden in oon company, alle iiij, till on a day that thei passeden thourgh a feelde be-side a town where-in were grete plente of children, that ther-in were pleyinge* (30, 3–5). The present *þo ich* would be appropriate in reference back to an account of the coming together of this company. No such account has appeared, but it may be that 'Ur–AM' had it, with our text reflecting mechanical copying of the reference back despite previous contraction which had removed the account. The number then represents a simple error of *iii* for *iiii* at some stage in transmission, or a clumsy 'correction' in an effort to agree with line 603. It seems useless to try to correct the text since it is elsewhere quite uncertain how many messengers *did* find Merlin. In line 1230 Merlin addresses them as *boþe*, as though one of the original pairs were in question (it is hardly likely, though conceivable, that the word could come to be applied thus to more than two men, by extension from its occasional use as a conjunctive adjective linking more than two nouns); in 1292 when they set out with him they are *al fiue*, presumably the two pairs plus Merlin.

AM2 here seems to be a mere attempt to mend AM, and is not a good basis for emendation of the latter.

1228 *erne*: *OED* (s.v. Run) takes this form of the verb as properly derived from the OE causative *ærnan*, and so Liedholm, p. 14; but Mercian *eornan* (attested by *Vespasian Psalter* 57, 6 *eornende*, etc.) provides a suitable source. The verb derived from *ærnan* seems in AM still to be distinct (see below, Glossary, s.v. Arnand).

1230 *Wel comeþ*: the phrase derives from OE *wilcumian*, misapprehended as compounded of *wel + cuman* 'come with good fortune, etc.'

boþe: see above, note to line 1196.

1237 *worþ it*: probably to be seen as impersonal verb and object; in the next line *it worþ* must be understood, though as personal verb and subject.

1238 'never after (will it be) the better founded': his death will in fact destroy the possibility of securing it. Alternatively *neuer* may just be a negative modifier of *more* (regular would be *neuer þe more*, *þe* here either omitted to avoid the awkward doubling or haplographed out in copying), and the line a litotically negated comparative equivalent of *miche þe bet* (cf. line 10), simply strengthening the direct negative of 1237.

1252 *al þat schal be don*: nowhere else does Merlin claim this total knowledge of the future, but a five-year-old may be allowed a little boasting to the royal messengers! It does not rest on LeM.

1270 *dede*: for the sense 'story' see *MED* s.v. Dẹde 5 (a). The first example there given is AM 1182, but in that case the straightforward 'write down their deeds' gives good sense. The present case, however, seems clear, though more than a century earlier than *MED*'s next example.

1284 *his maister Blays*: LeM explains that *si le clama maistre por ce qu'il auoit este maistre sa meire* (28, 16–17).

1292 *fiue*: see above, note to line 1196.

1297 *a toun was chepeing*: '. . . where there was . . .', rendering LeM *vne uille ou il auoit marchiet* (28, 33).

1300 *loued schon to selle*: probably 'were appraising shoes which were for sale', see *MED* s.v. Lǒven v. (2), 3, though a usage without reference to the value at which appraised is abnormal, and one could alternatively understand 'were eagerly selling shoes', with slight weakening of the commoner verb's regular sense 'take pleasure in'. The emendation *haued* suggested by Holthausen ('A- und ME Texten', 203) is in any case unnecessary, though it is plausible; the scribe's eye could easily have caught *louȝ* 1299. LeM has no equivalent.

1329 *ginneþ wepe*: the emendation *wepeþ* suggested in Smithers's 'Notes on ME Texts', 210, is not essential, but would much improve the metre. The manuscript form would represent a clumsy 'correction' of what is in fact a quite admissible type of rhyme; cf. lines 1645–6, 3829–30, 4937–8, etc., and see, besides Smithers's article, his KA (note to lines 149–50), and Gadow, cited above in my note to lines 833–4.

1342 The story of Merlin's third laugh, and the testing of his knowledge by the examination of the chamberlain, does not occur in LeM at all. In a later portion of LeM, however (pp. 281–92), a story in many respects similar is found. Merlin is being brought to interpret a dream of the Emperor's in which twelve young lions lie by a crowned sow. On the way he laughs several times, but gives either no answers or entirely mystifying ones when asked why. He finally explains before the emperor that the sow represents his adulterous empress, and the twelve young lions twelve men whom she has disguised as maidens of her chamber so that she can have her pleasure of them at will. His other laughter has arisen from his knowledge that the emperor's steward, known as Grisandoles, is in fact a woman, Arenoble, and that beggars outside an abbey gate are in fact standing upon a buried treasure worth more than the whole abbey and all its possessions. The supposed maidens are stripped before the emperor

and his barons, and they and the empress are burned; the steward is
indeed found to be a maiden, and the emperor marries her.

Our 'third laugh' story is not the same as this, but if the AM poet were
seeking some more convincing proof of Merlin's wisdom to give Vortigern
than the mere word of the messengers (who would have a personal interest
in concocting a tale to explain their disobedience of the king's orders),
this later incident, in somewhat similar circumstances, might well have
come to his mind and led him to construct the present story. Benson
(unpublished draft of his *Malory's Morte Darthur*; see above, Introduction, p. 22 n. 2) suggests that he may have been influenced by Heldris de
Cornüalle's *Roman de Silence*, a work partly based on LeM, in which
also laughs from these two episodes of LeM are brought together, though
in a story equivalent to the later, not the earlier, episode. It is notable
that in *Silence* Merlin's revelation that the eponymous hero is in fact a
woman is followed by a reprise of the story of the queen's false accusation
from the earlier episode, in the form of an explanation obtained by the
king from Silence (6586 ff.). LeM has no such reprise, and our poet, who
makes this story the centre of Merlin's account of his laugh, might then
more easily have got the suggestion for his treatment from *Silence* than
merely from LeM. But his treatment is certainly not close to that in
Silence, and no influence need be assumed.

1391 *þat it may stond*: the implication seems to be that as a result of
Merlin's explanations the castle will afterwards be able to stand; it is also
possible that *destourbes . . . þat it may stond* is equivalent to *destourbes . . .
to stond* 'hinders from standing', but such a construction would be, as far
as I am aware, unparalleled. There is something to be said for the suggestion made in Kölbing's note and in Holthausen's 'A- und ME Texten',
206, that a negative has fallen out before *stond*. W 1673 (see Appendix 3,
p. 274 below) would then exactly represent the original (L 1478 similar).

L 1481 *mynt*: I treat as belonging to *mene* (L 1799, etc.), with raising of *ĕ*
or coalescence of the products of OE *mǣnan* and *myntan*, from either of
which *ment* A 7089, etc., could of course derive, as Zupitza points out
in his review of Kölbing, p. 90.

1450 *stepe*: *OED* (s.v. Steep *a.*, 3e) understands the sense here as 'having
a headlong course, flowing precipitately'. But the river referred to in line
7900 as having a *strem stepe* flows through a *mede* (7897) on which it is
possible to encamp (8054 ff.), so can hardly have a precipitous flow. The
word occurs once in OE of a river: *se stream ætstod swa steop swa munt*
(Ælfric's *Catholic Homilies*, ed. Thorpe, II, 212, lines 21–2). There is the
sense is evidently 'high'; and 'running high' seems the most likely sense
here and in line 7900.

1473–6 For a discussion of the confused engineering here described,
see above, Introduction p. 57, also p. 34 n. 9.

1479 *wa[re]*: the manuscript reading could easily result from a scribe's
misreading of *war⁹* as *wat⁹*.

1480 *schode*: the word elsewhere seems to be used only of the parting of the hair.

1486 *ybent*: 'imprisoned' (OE *bendan* 'set in bonds'). *OED*, however, interprets as 'braced, nerved or wound up for action' (s.v. Bent *ppl. a.*, 2), and *MED* as 'coiled' (Běnden, 2 (a)).

L 1578 *bryȝes*: possibly a mere error for the acceptable **bryȝnes* (cf. recorded *brihnes*, etc.), but a further reduction of the consonant group seems quite possible.

1492 *moþe*: for the form, cf. Dan Michel's *Ayenbite* (EETS ed. 256, 4), also *Cursor Mundi* (Cotton MS.) 1904 *moth*, 4358 *mothes*, but Kölbing may well be right in seeing the present case as a mere scribal error.

1494 *gastlich*: OE *gæstlic* 'fearsome', if present in *Wanderer* 73, as Smithers strongly argues ('*Seafarer* and *Wanderer*', first part, 141–2), provides a direct etymon.

1502 *heued*: the tail, being barbed (*hoked*, 1499), would have an end somewhat like an arrow- or spear-head, for which the word *heued* is regularly used.

1515 *kest*: such forms are best explained as formed by analogy from doublets like *lest* beside *last* in forms from OE *lǣstan*, and *fest* from ON *festa* beside *fast* from OE *fǣstan*.

1531 *arered miȝt*: 'exerted his strength'; see Smithers's argument for this sense in 'Notes on ME Texts', 210–11.

1576–7 'Of such a being . . . that by means of his blood . . .'.

L 1678 *heo*: probably simply miscopied from *he*, as with *þeo*, etc. (see above, Introduction, p. 63).

1605–6 The awkwardness of the change from direct to reported speech called for by *bitokneþ . . . þereafter* reflects the unsuitability of modern punctuation to ME text, rather than any awkwardness in the original which might prompt emendation. Kölbing's note suggests *bitokned*; better if one wishes to emend would be *herafter*, since LeM here has direct speech. The temptation to avoid the difficulty by rendering *þerafter* 'in accordance with it' is opposed by LeM *qui a uenir sont*.

Interpretation of *tokening* as 'remarkable event' gives good sense; I cannot parallel it, but OE *tācn* appears in this sense, an extension from '(significant) miracle' through 'work of power', 'heroic deed', in *Elene* 319, 645 (see Gradon's note). However, LeM has the elliptical phrase *ce sont tout senefiances qui a uenir sont* (33, 31) '. . . signs (of events) which . . .', and *tokening þerafter schuld falle* is very possibly merely a mechanical rendering of *senefiances qui a uenir sont*.

1630 *loke*: a synonym of *waite* 'watch' (<OF *waiter*), it comes to be taken as a synonym also of *waite* 'deal out' (<ON *veita*); see Smithers's KA, note to line 2154. The sense of the latter word was not improbably felt as

'watch for an opportunity to inflict', as though it were the same word as, not merely a homonym of, the former; this sense would be appropriate, for instance, in AM 352.

1637 *Whiche þou*: placing of personal pronoun in apposition to the relative presumably to make clear that the antecedent is *þe*, not *þi miȝt*. Kölbing's [*Bi*] *whiche* avoids the awkward construction, and the error would easily arise from a copyist's supposition that the sense should be '. . . your power which you have procured . . .', but it was hardly by means of 'all his might' that Vortigern procured, from a distance, Moyne's death.

1641 *Token*: as the subject clause describes a running fight, it was perhaps felt as a complex of events, hence the plural verb. But very likely one *þ* was carelessly omitted in transcribing an original *tokneþ þou*, and *tokne* then 'corrected'. Kaluza, in his review of Kölbing, col. 268, regards the word as a noun, used in the absolute sense 'this is a token that', and compares line 4315 *þe best conseil þat y can*, and Chaucer's *Troilus* 1002 *Ensample why*, but the present case, with a preceding as well as a succeeding noun clause in apposition to *token*, would be stranger than either of these supposed parallels.

1643 *cite toun*: we should perhaps read *cite-toun* (which certainly occurs in KA 5634, 6058, and 7537), as Kölbing's note suggests.

1645 *signifie[þ]*: so Smithers, 'Notes on ME Texts', 211. On the resultant rhyme see above, note to line 1329.

1647 *heldeþ*: the third person form may be explained by the fact that it stands in a relative clause. Compare, however, cases in lines 2637, 2680, and 6787. Separate explanations of each can be offered, but all four cases are best taken together as suggesting either such an extension of third person forms as Holmqvist notes in *English Present Inflections*, p. 86, or more probably that the scribe was in the habit of regularizing 3rd person -*es* of his exemplar, and falsely did the same in these cases. Compare his *fouleþ* in line 3064 (his *forþ* in 2089, 9280 is probably not comparable), and see above, Introduction, p. 61.

1663 *mene*: = *men*, not *meine*, for the latter always rhymes on stressed -*e*.

1669 *þi wiues fader Angys*: probably to be seen as part of a split genitive group with *þi* 1668, all qualifying *kin* (see below, note to line 7628).

1721 Here and in what follows the poet writes as though Uter were the elder brother and natural heir. On this confusion see above, Introduction, pp. 27–32.

1728 *hende*: the inorganic *h*- here may reflect a scribe's feeling that the present phrase is related to *neiȝe-hond*. The present line, taken as parallel to 1725, would suggest that the poet was following LeM in making Winchester a sea-port (see above, Introduction, p. 24), but lines 1761–4 clearly imply a land approach to the town. Line 1765 is probably a clumsy attempt to combine the sea-description in LeM with what the poet knew to be geographical fact.

1736 *miʒtes*: probably merely a copyist's 'correction' of *miʒt* for the sake of the rhyme, but for the plural used even of a single person see *OED*, s.v. Might *sb.*, 3c.

1791–2 'By means of (God's) grace and of powerful friends (namely the barons who had resumed allegiance), they (Uter and his associates) obtained there what was useful to them (namely the town of Winchester, freely surrendered).' For the construction, cf. 6866 *What þurth miʒt and Godes craft.* The emendation *Wharþurth* (Kölbing, though he prints as two words) gives the easier reading 'by which means they (the citizens of Winchester) obtained there thanks and powerful friends, which was useful to them', but it is not essential. Kölbing, in his note, also suggests *fredome* for *frende*, following AM2, but it is as likely that this is a modification introduced in the later version.

1816 *For he hem wende*: Vortigern's killing of his turncoat supporters is apparently said to be *because* he had supposed them to be his men, which is curious, though one can well imagine his anger the greater and his killing the more ruthless under these circumstances than if they had been avowed enemies. It may well be that line 1815 was originally . . . *he ran hem on*, not parenthetic, 'he ran on them with great fury because . . .'. If a scribe mistook this *he* for the plural and 'normalized' it to *þai*, 'correction' of *him* into *hem* might easily have followed. Kölbing's note suggests deletion of *For*, a straightforward way of avoiding the difficulty.

1846 *ariʒt*: emendation to *anon riʒt* would much improve the metre.

1857–8 L has the normal construction of an object clause after *forʒete*. 'Ur–AM' may well have had this with *þat* understood; in the derivation of L it was supplied, while in that of A a copyist did not recognize the construction and deleted what he took to be an erroneous negative. The A form could also be understood as having *forʒat* used absolutely, but this would be I think unparalleled. P and W both lack the couplet.

1859–60 '. . . clove, (striking) at the helmet, till . . .'. An awkward construction, moreover elsewhere *to* after a verb of striking governs the person struck, not the part of the body or armour; but preferable to the only other way of construing the text unemended, namely to assume a reversal of the elements in the compound *tocleue*, which would be most exceptional when the sense of *to* is so far removed from its usual prepositional or adverbial one. Very possibly, however, there has been a simple error by omission of one letter from the common phrase *cleue ato*. Alternatively, perhaps *to cleue*, meant as the compound, was misapprehended by a copyist, inattentive to the sense, as simplex with oddly placed *to*, whose position he 'regularized'.

1861–2 Either *ywued* or *yreued* must be emended to *þe heued*; it seems palaeographically rather more likely that *h* was misread as *w* than as *r*;

note that when the scribe accidentally repeated lines 4033–4 he substituted *weld* for *held*.

1863 *men*: the original probably had *man* singular, rhyming on *dan* with *a* for the *i*-mutation of Gmc *ǎ* before nasal (see above, Introduction, p. 61).

1895 *ʒere and oþer to*: a variant on the *ʒer and oþer* which appears in line 755, but it may well be that the original was *a ʒere oþer to* (cf. line 6483), corrupted under the influence of *ʒere and oþer* in the scribe's mind.

1896 *an hond go*: I cannot exactly parallel this phrase, but compare various usages recorded in *MED* s.v. Hŏnd(e 6 (c).

1917–18 'how it, (the phenomenon of) the dragons under the earth, was to signify the king's death'. While the doubling of a noun by a pronoun in apposition is quite common, the present case is exceptionally awkward and probably corrupt, but no suitable emendation suggests itself; the comment in Kölbing's note 'man würde etwa erwarten *þe kinges deþ bitokne schold*' hardly supplies (or is meant to) an emendation one could admit to text.

1935 *roue*: *OED* enters this as the only instance of Rove *v.*[4], but suggests no meaning; Kölbing's gloss 'zucken' is probably a mere contextual guess; Liedholm mentions, but does not treat, the difficulty on p. 186. I conjecturally identify the verb with *OED*'s Rough *v.*[2], regarding the spelling as an unusual case of *u* for expected *w* (on the usual circumstances for this see Liedholm, p. 159) if it is not simply a copyist's botch for the sake of the rhyme. The line then signifies 'he coughed against his shoulder', a (presumably vulgar) clearing of the throat before speaking. One might alternatively relate the word to ON *hrufla* 'scratch', assuming it a reduction of a postulated **rouel* as though this were a frequentative (cf. *roten* 3867, apparently formed on MDu *rotelen*), but this would give a less plausible sense.

1937–8 *haue:bismare*: Liedholm treats the abnormal rhyme simply as 'one of the quite numerous instances of assonance occurring in our text' (p. 3); it differs, however, from the accepted type of imprecise rhyme discussed above (note to lines 833–4). It is not an impossible extension of the type (cf. below, note to lines 3447–8, for a different extension), but since the metre also is abnormal corruption seems likely. Kölbing, p. xxxvi, suggests dealing with the rhyme by inserting *þare* after *haue*; or the original might have had the elliptical . . . *him schuld nouʒt þare*, with *þare* then misread as *haue* (cf. below, note to line 5977) and *him* 'corrected' accordingly; or the *[s]ha[r]e* for *haue* of Ellis's *Specimens of . . . Romances* is attractive, though it would be a use of *share* two centuries earlier than the first recorded by *OED*. To correct the metre we would then need to insert a word in line 1938; there would be many possibilities, e.g. *[staffe-] strokes*, or . . . *and [bisting and] bismare*, both apt for haplographic error.

1940 *nice*: 'idle, negligent'; in LeM Merlin says *'vous ne faites mie bien a besoigne uostre signor'* (36, 43). The same sense is appropriate in line

7218, and will fit also the occurrences in 2784 and 2985, though there we could as well understand that Brice and Antor are 'no fools'.

1941 *scorn*: the vowel is best explained as a lengthening-group development, the word (<ONF *escarnir*) having fallen in with native words in *ă*; so Wallenberg, *Vocabulary of . . . Ayenbite*, p. 213 n. 2.

P 1965 *befall*: use as a synonym of *become* is unparalleled. It is not an impossible extension of recorded uses, but one may suspect that *Where* is dittographed for original *what*, 'what had happened to . . .'.

P 2091 *wininge*: retained as giving a defensible sense, 'where would be most profitable for him, Pendragon (to seek Merlin)'. But probably, as Percy's own note on the manuscript suggests, an error for *woninge*, 'where he, Merlin, chiefly lived'; the *dwellynge* of W 2482 will represent substitution of a more familiar synonym, as quite often in this text.

1991–2 'in that same appearance of a yeoman which he had seen previously'.

1997 Uter's easy acceptance of the apparent *swain* as Merlin lacks verisimilitude, and results from compression of the story. In LeM Merlin comes before the king in the form of *vns moult biaus hons et bien uestus, que bien sambla preudons* (39, 9–10), evidently the same as that in which he had previously come, representing himself as a messenger from Merlin, to report the death of Angys—*vns preudoms . . . moult bien uestus et cauchies* (38, 23–4), but then changes his appearance to that known to the barons so as to demonstrate his identity.

2013 *his folk*: apparently Uter's. The use of *schilt* (<OE *scildan* 'protect') is odd, however; Uter's people are hardly in need of protection, since they have Angys firmly besieged. It is possible, therefore, that the verb is in fact from OE *scylian* 'separate', in the (admittedly unparalleled) sense 'separated from him', implying here 'deprived of their leader'; *his folk* are then, straightforwardly, Angys' people.

2022 *stet*: on this word, recorded only in AM and KA, see Smithers's KA, note to line 2258.

2032–4 'and he (Aurilis) thanked him (Merlin) . . . and offered him all his possessions if he (Aurilis) could be under his (Merlin's) care.'

2055–8 These lines come awkwardly here, whether *al þat oþer bodi* means 'the whole of Uter's body' (which makes the connection with the following lines passably smooth; *he* 2060 is Uter, who is, despite Merlin's partiality for his brother, a noble knight), or, conceivably, 'everyone else (put together)'. The latter could reflect Merlin's assurance to *both* brothers in LeM, at a somewhat earlier point in the story: '*en tous les lieus ou ie serai, serai ie plus remenbrans de vous et de vos oeures que del autrui*' (43, 36–7)—at the present point (48, 28) LeM's Merlin makes no comparison of any sort, but declares that he greatly loves both brothers.

The equivalent lines in AM2 (P 2288–91, W 2687–90 similar) occur much more appropriately. The royal names being restored to (or preserved in) the LeM form (see above, Introduction, pp. 27–32 and 57–60), the lines predict by implication that it will be Uter who will survive the battle, which in the AM2 placing is imminent. It is tempting to see this superior reading as going back to 'Ur–AM', which must then have had the names as in LeM (to be preserved in AM2), and not, as argued above, already changed to the A forms (to be restored in AM2). With the change to the A forms, what now asserted Merlin's partiality for the doomed brother was felt as intolerable immediately before the battle in which he was to die, so the reviser, not liking to delete it altogether or reverse its application, removed it to what was at any rate a less objectionable place, where an equivalent of LeM's statement that Merlin loved both brothers probably survived to attract the passage. However, I do not see the alternative supposition that A, clumsy as it is, represents the original AM, and the altered placing in AM2 a happy stroke by a reviser once the restoration of names had made the lines refer to the surviving brother, as in itself so much less likely as to outweigh my earlier arguments.

2084 *y say*: or, as suggested in Zupitza's review of Kölbing, p. 91, *ysay* 'was never seen'. But *y say* is a very common tag.

P 2289 *well*: comparative usages with the positive form were an early Germanic feature, and seem to have remained occasional in English; see Lehmann's 'Comparative Constructions . . .', 327–9, and two of *OED*'s instances s.v. Than, 3a. The present case is comparable; there is no need to see it as an error for a comparative form.

P 2326 *stryde*: retained as making good sense, but an error for *stryue* (so Kölbing's note) is very probable.

2129 *wald*: *OED* (s.v. Will v.[1], 26) takes such usages as weakened from the volitional sense. I suggest this may rather be from the sense of habitual action, implying that the landing had continued over a period, but it certainly approaches the status of a mere expletive auxiliary. Compare note to line 5825, below.

2153 'As night was falling', but the tendency for *so* to extend its applicability to a point event is probably shown here, the sense approaching 'when night fell'. Cf. KA 5766, where Smithers accepts this extension, though observing (note ad loc.) that 'there is admittedly no other example in the [KA] group or in ME of *so* in the sense "when"'; also L 55 *so þat* probably in this sense.

2161 *he*: Uter, not Aurilis. On possible reasons for this clumsiness see above, Introduction, p. 58.

2172 *Harinan*: evidently identical with the king Aramont referred to at the beginning of the *Livre de Lancelot* which follows LeM in the vulgate cycle. It might therefore be better to read his name, with Kölbing, *Harman*, but a trisyllable fits the metre, here and in line 2177, much better.

He is described in the *Lancelot* (part I; 3, 16-4, 7) as *sires de Bertaigne la Menour*, and overlord of *Gaule et Benoich et toute la terre iusque a la marche d'Auuergne et de Gascoigne*, as he should have been of Boorges also, but that Claudas would not acknowledge him. In return for help against Claudas he became Uter Pendragon's man, and together they defeated Claudas and ravaged his land. He was surnamed Hoel.

It would seem that he is identical, or has been identified, with the Hoel, king of Armorican Brittany, who appears in Wace 10107 ff. as instructed to conquer on Arthur's behalf various territories in Gaul: *Angou, Gascuine, Alverne*, and *Peitou*; this he does, as also *Berri* and *Toruigne*. Arthur himself resolves to conquer *Burguinne* and *Loherregne* (but only a slight misreading is needed to add these to Hoel's conquests) and is shortly recorded as possessing territories including *Angou, Normendie*, and *Buluine*. Thus of the territories listed in AM 2173-6 as won by Uter from Harinan only *Chaumpeine* does not appear in the passage from Wace. Wace in fact never refers to Champagne at all; in geographical fact, however, it is bounded to the east by Lorraine and to the south by Burgundy, and among its dependencies in the twelfth and thirteenth centuries was Touraine, and these three related names do appear in Wace.

This Hoel must in turn have been in some version of the story identified with his namesake the duke of Tintagel, the husband of Ygerne supplanted by Uter (named in LeM 127, 24, in a passage which could easily be read as making Ygerne his daughter, not his wife, but the status of *li dus de Tintaiel*, normally unnamed, is elsewhere clear), so that Aramont-Hoel also became known as a husband of Ygerne. In what form the AM poet knew of this, and whether he or his source identified Aramont (Harinan) with Ygerne's *premier seignor* referred to, but unnamed, in LeM 96, 27, we cannot tell, any more than we can tell whether he or his source varied the voluntary acceptance of Uter's overlordship into Uter's simple winning *þurth his miȝt* (2171), but both would be in line with modifications in parts of AM taken directly from LeM.

On further complications concerning Ygerne's husbands, and on the source of Hoel's title *of Cornewaile* in line 2181, see below, notes to lines 2239, 2445, and 2601-19.

2185-7 Uter's subjection of Ban and Bohort is not referred to in LeM, but is a reasonable inference from LeM's account (pp. 106-7) of how Merlin tells them, when they arrive at court, that Arthur is Uter's son and they ought to hold their lands of him, which they readily accept and swear allegiance.

2198 *Of kniȝtes*: the partitive reflects LeM *et il* [Merlin] *li dist '. . . iou i asserrai des plus preudomes de vostre regne . . .'* (55, 11-13). The suggestion in Kölbing's note that '*of* würde besser fehlen' is thus inappropriate.

2203 *wise*: 'expert in war' (cf. 3244 *wise in fiȝt*, 3758 *wise and hardi . . . in bataile*), or simply 'wise' (cf. 1823-4 *. . . wise wordes couþe speke | Stedes prike . . .*). There is similar uncertainty in line 8696.

2209–10 This close association of the knights is described in LeM as brought about by Merlin's arts. They notice with surprise that despite their various origins *'nous entramons tant ou plus comme fiex doit amer son pere, ne iamais ce nos est auis ne nous departirons se mors ne nous depart'* (55, 35–7). On their fighting as a separate body compare LeM's account of their preparations for Leodegan's first battle against Rion, when *icil furent en vne eschiele tout par els, car il ne voloient mie estre auoec les cheualiers del pais* (143, 8–9); AM's equivalent (5749, not at quite the corresponding point) is less striking.

2239 This curt statement is far from fulfilling the promise of lines 2183–4. There the poet must have seen Hoel as that husband of Ygerne who would die in the war brought on him by Uter, of which he knew he was to tell the story at length; his title *of Cornewaile* has been carried over at some stage in transmission from the equivalent character in Wace, *li cuens de Cornoaille* (8572, etc.). Now, however, we have apparently a new conflation of Wace's figure and LeM's *dus de Tintaiel*, ignoring their proper names (respectively Gorlois and Hoel), which in fact very rarely appear, producing Tintagel of Cornwall. The AM poet, it would seem, recalled here that he had formerly identified a duke Hoel as a husband of Ygerne, but forgot the circumstances in which he had referred to him, so he now ascribes to this Hoel the position as Ygerne's *premier seignor* which he there gave to Harinan, and he later (with some variations) assigns to Hoel the paternity of Ygerne's daughters by this *premier seignor*. See also above, note to line 2172, and below, to lines 2445 and 2605.

2262 *hiȝt Bretel*: to be understood as a relative clause without expressed relative pronoun. The frequency of the usage with *hiȝt*, however (four out of a total of eight relative clauses), suggests that this form at any rate was tending to a quasi-adjectival status. For the form *het(e)* the figures are two out of six.

2296 In LeM the king offers this gift by way of the duke, who replies *comme cil qui nul mal ni pensoit: 'Sire, grans mercis; ele le prendra moult uolentiers'* (61, 1–2). Ygerne's first refusal of the cup does not therefore appear in LeM; the AM poet has combined, rather clumsily, the gift of the cup and an earlier proffer of jewels, when *Ygerne s'en desfendoit et n'en vaut nul prendre* (60, 11–12).

2300 *algat*: the sense 'none the less' which the word acquires in later ME is here implicit rather than explicit.

2301 *wepe*: the rhyme is admissible (see above, note to lines 833–4), and Kölbing's emendation *grete*, though plausible, should not be admitted to text.

2316 *senche*: initial *s* where *sch*, representing [ʃ], would be expected (OE *scencan*), is rare in the KA group, but cf. KA 3903 *sanchiþ* (<OE *scand-*), and probably AM 5874, 7932 *singel*.

2327 *Oþerwise*: 'in any other way', i.e. 'with any other response'.

2333 *þo at arst*: rather expressing that *as soon as* he was alone the king was overwhelmed by love (in contrast to the *a-paise* above), than that it was *not until* he was alone that this happened (which would not contrast well); *at arst* takes on the sense regularly expressed by *at first*, an understandable transference. In lines 6720 and 9155 the phrase probably has its more usual shade of meaning.

2350 *aforce*: *MED* regards the sense as 'violate', a sense certainly developed in later ME, but here it is probably simply 'compel', as in KA 788 [Alexander] *a-forceþ it* [Bulcifal] *wiþ strengþe*. Completion of the sense as '. . . to commit adultery' is then to be understood from the context.

2435 [*a*] *roche of ston*: for the phrase *roche of ston* 'rock' see *King Horn* 79 *Vnder a roche of stone*; the emendation *roche and ston* suggested in Kölbing's note is not called for. The phrase, however, is used in *Horn* of a natural formation, and I cannot trace *roche* used of building-stone. The word in French can mean 'castle', however (as in LeM 126, 18–19 *j . . . chastel . . . que on apele la roche as Sesnes*), and I take this to be the sense here; perhaps also in line 5459, though there AM misrenders LeM (see my note, below). The original was perhaps *o roche of ston*, which would make 'correction' to *of* by a scribe who did not understand the usage particularly easy to understand.

2441 *ylay*: Kölbing's 'nachträge und besserungen' (p. 502) suggest emendation to *bylay*. *MED* (s.v. Līen 7 (a)) sees here the same verb and the same sense as (e.g.) *lay* 1909, but in a unique reflexive usage, which seems to me particularly unsatisfactory in view of the apparently parallel *him* 2443. I treat it as a distinct verb. OE *gelicgan* may well have had the transitive sense 'occupy', though it is not recorded (cf. *gesittan*), and a crossing of sense with *belicgan* 'surround' would be quite understandable.

2445 *cuntasse*: perhaps in a general sense 'noblewoman', but in Wace she is technically a countess, as the wife of *li cuens de Cornoaille*, one of the figures from whom her husband in AM seems to have been compounded (see above, note to line 2239).

2478 *glosing*: Kölbing glosses 'schmeichelei', and his note explains the line as meaning 'ich weiss genau, was du mit deiner freundlichkeit gegen mich erreichen willst'. But Merlin is rather saying that he knows Uter's stated reasons for hostility against Tintagel to be specious.

2481–2 *ar tomorwe | Y schal þe lese*: probably '(if) before tomorrow I release you'; for a conditional without either *ȝif* or inversion cf. line 7599 (see my note, below). It is of course possible to treat the question as ending at *me* and the rest as a statement; this is how Kölbing prints the passage. If so, this definite statement is followed by the same matter in interrogative form (2489), and then again as a statement (2492), which is very clumsy. The equivalent passage in LeM has a conditional, though a different one: *se vous m'osies douner ce que ie vous demanderoie, iou porcaceroie que vous auries s'amor* (66, 25–6).

2488 *Al þe biȝete*: probably 'everything that you obtain', reflecting though in altered form Merlin's unparticularized demand in LeM for '*ce que ie vous demanderai le matin que vous aueres la nuit gut auoec lui*' (66, 31–2). After the success of the operation Merlin specifies that the requirement is *j oir male* who has been begotten (68, 18). The AM form with its clearer implication allows this specification to be discarded; Uter's agreement in line 2490 is a sufficient basis for Merlin's statement in 2631–3 that the child has been promised to him. Alternatively, *biȝete* may be taken as specifically meaning 'child'; the phrase then literally means 'the whole child', and we should understand '(give me) the child unreservedly'. The expression on this basis is awkward, however.

2506 *þai*: probably an erroneous 'normalization' of *he*, as in line 401, etc., since only the king is actually going to be the lover.

2514 *gnidded*: Smithers ('Ideophones', 98–9) sees this form as reflecting a genuine doubling of the consonant in the pa. t. pl. and pp. stem of OE *gnīdan* (so also, with a different vowel, in OE *gnuddian*), having an emphatic force. This is attractive; we should perhaps translate 'rubbed briskly'.

2526 *he*: Merlin, the application continues acceptably from line 2519, though it seems awkward to a modern reader.

2558 *þat present*: the phrase *les presentes* and its English rendering *þeis presentes*, 'the present letters', etc., are recorded from the fourteenth century. An extension of the sense from 'letter bringing news' to 'news' generally, even if (as apparently here) oral, and a singular formation from the usual plural, are both easy to understand, though I cannot find another instance, and though Kölbing's note declares *present* here to be meaningless: 'würde man vielmehr *tidende* erwarten'.

2601–19 Assembled out of a good deal of dispersed and sometimes confused material in LeM (pp. 73, 96, 127, 128, 165), which is pruned and shaped effectively to present a fourfold wedding of the main characters (in LeM 73, 19–20 Lot is clearly said to have married at the same time as Uter, but it is not clear when the other marriages took place), uncomplicated by any detail about Ygerne's other daughters, who in LeM include Morgan *la fee*, a noted astrologer (73, 23–8). All mention of Gawain's brother, or half-brother, Mordred is also eliminated (see above, Introduction, pp. 8–9). Appropriately for this fourfold wedding comes a clear statement that the three daughters involved were by Hoel, Ygerne's earlier husband, so that we can readily accept them all as now of marriageable age; in LeM Blasine is daughter of Hoel of Tintagel (127, 23–4 and 29–30), and taken with that 96, 27–9 must probably be read to imply that the other two are also, but Hoel is the second husband, the one displaced by Uter (see above, note to line 2172). Elimination of unnecessary detail then allows the AM poet to escape what would be a consequential difficulty. LeM (96, 29) mentions the marriage of Karadan (or in a variant Carados) to another of Ygerne's daughters; she can be inferred to be by the earlier husband, but if this marriage appeared in AM she would be taken to be by Tintagel, making it difficult to see her son Aguiscant (or Agustans), king of Scotland, as old enough to appear among the rebels at Arthur's coronation feast, as he does both in LeM (pp. 88 ff.) and AM (3101 ff., as Angvisant).

A minor alteration in AM supplies a name for Lot's wife, and suppresses that of Urien's. Very possibly the poet knew of Urien's in a form like the *Hermesan* which Sommer, in the *Index* to his *Vulgate Version*, records from MS. Bibl. Nat. f. fr. 337 of LeM (see AM 7627 *Hermesent*), but finding here in his source some form of the *Brimesent* which appears in G¹ (165, 21) took this as another person, assumed it must therefore be misapplied, and so transferred it to Lot. Whether the form *Belisent* is his own casual alteration, or reflects a variant in his particular source, one cannot tell.

2605 *Galaas*: does not reappear under this name, or any obviously related variant, but is probably to be identified with Galathin, who is described as Nanters' son in line 4553, etc. In 4551 Nanters' *sones* are mentioned, if the manuscript is read unemended, and we could then suppose Galaas to be Galathin's brother, but in favour of emendation to a singular is not only that it is only about Galathin that we in fact hear *noble þing* (or anything), but also that LeM has a singular reference at the equivalent point, to *Galescin le fil le roy Nantre de Garlot* (133, 15–16).

2616 The original reading was very possibly *hende and noble kniȝt, certeyns*.

2637 *feleþ*: perhaps a slip under the influence of forms immediately above, but see above, note to line 1647.

2645 *man schal*: the original was probably *schul* (*man* plural), but a scribe took *man* as singular and 'corrected' the verb.

2651–4 A crux. Kölbing retains the reading and line-order of the manuscript, but assumes a lacuna before line 2651, where some lines (presumably a couplet) referring to Antour's wife are taken to have dropped out. Line 2653 (MS. order, my 2651) remains most abruptly inserted, and it is strange that the reference to the wife's milk should precede that to her being with child. My restoration is frankly conjectural, but avoids the need to assume a lacuna. Once the inversion of the couplets had occurred it is understandable that a scribe, confronted with a baffling passage including the unusual *biȝeten a quen* 'obtained a noble lady (as wife)', should have tried to mend it and produced what stands in the manuscript. The equivalent passage in LeM refers successively to (i) the nobility of Antor, (ii) the fact that he has a wife, (iii) her being brought to bed of a son, and (iv) her nobility: *'Il a en cest pais j des plus preudommes de vostre regne, et li miex entechies de toutes boines teches; s'a vne femme qui est acouchie d'un fil, si est moult preudefeme et loial'* (74, 28–31). This provides some slight support for the order of narration in my reconstruction, though AM is not textually very close to LeM here.

2656 *he*: the scribe first wrote *sche*, probably normalizing *he* of his exemplar, which he correctly took as feminine (see above, Introduction, p. 61 and n. 4. Subsequent 'correction' by subpuncting was probably under the apprehension that the masculine was intended, with *Antour* as antecedent.

2660 *an for an*: I cannot parallel the phrase, but compare the (much later) use of *knyght for knyght* in Metham's *Amoryus and Cleopes*:

> Bot off alle thise viij dayis, knyght for knyght, non so manly
> Hym qwyt as Amoryus, for noght onys he was reysyd
> Owte off hys sadyl . . . (905–7).

2671 *and y the*: 'if I (am to) prosper', i.e. 'if what I aver be not true, may I not prosper', a variant on regular *so mot y þen*, etc. (as in line 1048). Alternatively 'if I succeed (in doing so)', i.e. in proving that she took Uter for Tintagel, presumably by evidence from her people in the castle. This is the probable sense of *proue* 1239, and for the present phrase compare then 6996. But she makes no attempt to 'prove' in this sense.

2680 *findeþ*: possibly -þ by dittography in copying an original *finde þerat* (subjunctive), but see above, note to line 1647.

2683 *bleþeliche*: on the stem-vowel see below, note to line 2978.

2690 *þat*: commonly used in direct speech to introduce a request (as in line 2345); here unusually in indirect, but the sense 'and requested that he should keep it secret' is clear.

2715 *wiif*: uninflected genitive by analogy with other nouns of relationship, probably because such phrases as OE *sweostor sunu* or their ME derivatives were felt as compounds, just as, for example, *biche-sone* 8477 was, so one should perhaps print *wiif-child*.

2742 *fer*: 'for a long time', but I cannot parallel such a usage except in contexts which enforce a temporal sense (*fer biforen*, etc.). Error for *er*, by anticipation of *fer* 2743, is therefore quite likely, as suggested in Smithers's 'Notes on ME Texts', 212.

2773 *spouse*: cf. *The Owl and the Nightingale* 1334; Kölbing's *spous[had]e* is not called for.

2796–7 'May He vouchsafe to choose (a king) among us, and grant that we may have a sign thereof . . .'.

2816–70 LeM (at a later point in the story) has . . . *et les lettres qui estoient escrites en l'espee disoient qu'ele auoit non Escalibor, et c'est j non Ebrieu qui dist en Franchois 'trenche fer et achier'* (94, 28–30).

2820 *and al þing*: cf. 8911 *lete kniȝtschippe and al þing*.

2850 *tate*: the vowel can be explained by loss of the second element of the diphthong in OF *taite* (so Liedholm, p. 72; see Wallenberg's *Vocabulary of . . . Ayenbite*, p. 154 n. 1), but for regular *tette* (<Gmc *titta*) *taite* is itself perplexing, and may be a mere orthographic variant. An OF **tate* might be expected in the Lorraine district (see Pope's . . . *Latin to . . .*

French, § 1322, xvii); appearance of this dialectal feature in England would be remarkable, but not impossible. The form recurs in lines 2944 (within the line) and 8466 (in rhyme).

2871 *at side and at ende*: probably merely the usual device of indicating totality by a linked pair of opposites. But possibly lines 2871–2 refer to the individual fights which (one may well suppose) took place on the outskirts of the main mêlée, and in which an unproved knight might well wish to 'warm up' before plunging into the mêlée (*com amidward* 2873).

2973 *clop and cradel: MED* curiously renders *cradel* here 'bed'. One could understand 'first (in Arthur's infancy) he had provided him with swaddling-clothes and a cradle; later . . .', but it seems more likely that everything here belongs to the accoutrements of knighthood. I take the *cradel* to be an arrangement of straps on the horse's back to which the *clop* was secured; on the *clop* in turn the *sadel* rested. Medieval illustrations of the arrangement are conveniently reproduced in C. G. Trew *The Accoutrements of the Riding Horse* (London, 1951), plate xlix, and J. Hewitt *Ancient Armour and Weapons in Europe* (Oxford and London, 1855–60), vol. II, p. 320. I cannot parallel my suggested applications of the terms *clop* and *cradel*, but the former would be a natural reduction of *saddle-cloth* (though even the compound is not recorded so early), and the latter a quite understandable transference (like that producing the modern equestrian use of *cradle* for a structure on a horse, though a different one with a different function).

2975–6 *brini . . . hauberioun . . . aketoun*: the *brini* and the *hauberk* (of which garment the *hauberioun* is possibly a smaller version, but the words are probably used interchangeably) are both forms of mail-coat. The *hauberk* is regularly described in AM as *felefold*, but it was probably never more than double; LeM speaks of *les ij plois del hauberc* (139, 22–3), and describes it as *fors a double maille* (138, 35–6). Possibly the *brini* (and/or the *hauberioun*) was thought of as only of single mail, but the poet probably had no feeling of a critical distinction, and is here just piling up technical terms for general effect (as elsewhere with astrological terms; see below, note to line 3568).

The *aketoun* is quite distinct. It is worn under the mail-coat, and is not armoured, though probably padded or quilted. The word in OF also signifies a type of material, and doubtless this was the original sense, the garment being made from it. The material would be expected to offer some resistance to a weapon (the Tobler-Lommatzsch *Wörterbuch* quotes a reference by Aymeri de Narbonne to a stroke which *tresperça le hauberc . . ., mes li porpoinz fu . . . d'auqueton, qui de la mort garanti le gloton*), but not approaching that of armour (Godefroy's *Dictionnaire* quotes from Thomas of Kent *les haubers li falsa cum cil fut d'aketons*).

2978 *stef*: the form implies shortening of *ī* (OE *stīf*), followed by lowering. This is well known in polysyllabic compounds (and thus *blepeliche* 2683); see Wallenberg, *Vocabulary of . . . Ayenbite*, p. 35 n. 5. Here it is probably extended from such compounds; the alternative view that it could occur in early ME before single final consonants (see for instance Luick, § 388, A 1, 2) has been forcefully challenged by Burchfield, who points out that 'evidence that this tendency existed before the fourteenth century is drawn almost entirely from the *Ormulum*. It is a remarkable fact that nearly every one of the forms cited are either misreadings of the manuscript or obviously scribal errors' ('Language of Ormulum', 60–1.).

2983 *þat ich day*: rather '(that) on that very day' than 'that every day'.

3045 *wite*: I cannot parallel this intransitive use, but it is a quite possible extension from the regular reflexive one. The suggestion in Kölbing's note that the word is a casual error, perhaps for *arme*, by a scribe in whose mind such a tag-phrase as *þat wittu wel* was running is not needed; if emendation is to be considered we should simply regularize the construction by reading *ȝou* for *þan* (Norman Davis's suggestion).

3056 The construction seems to be a blend of *þai hem poruaid* (cf. 3714) and *hem alle among* (cf. 1473 *vnder hem alle*), with *hem* in effect doing 'double duty' (cf. above, note to line 885; for other possible examples close to the present one see below, notes to lines 3197, 3275, and 3451). Alternatively we may have simply *hem alle among*, with *poruaid*, as in line 1348, non-reflexive (though then the placing of *hem* is curious); or simply *þai hem poruaid*, with *alle among* a phrase (unparalleled as far as I know) signifying perhaps 'meanwhile'.

3072 *leue to fiȝtes*: the exact construction appears to be unparalleled. Regular would be *leue to fiȝt* or *leue of fiȝtes*, and this may be a blend, though probably the original had the former, with the infinitive converted into an apparent noun plural by scribal 'improvement' of the rhyme.

3081 Rather a pure partitive construction, 'a quantity of . . .' than implying *seuen hundred of* . . ., which Kölbing's note suggests. The original, however, was probably *On noble destrers* . . . (cf. lines 3761, 4498, 5394, etc.), with *of* dittographed from the previous line.

3091 *mounde*: the word in AM is regularly applied to knights, in the present phrase or *of gret (more, mest) mounde* (3704, 5490, etc.; seventeen instances). The usage is paralleled by similar ones with *power* (3098, 3398, etc.), and, less frequently, with *miȝt* (1736, 6572) and *main* (5478, 5754), and these words clearly have the sense 'might in battle'. It seems likely, therefore, that OE *mund* 'hand' has undergone a development of meaning similar to that of OE *hond* (see above, note to line 190), acquiring the sense proper to *main* <OE *mægen* as well as, and then, in this case, displacing, that of *main* <OF *main*.

The uses *not* of knights are in lines 3307 *dint of gret mound* (cf. 9378 *dint þat fro main cam*), 3354 *bi Godes mounde* (cf. 1832 *for Cristes hond*), 4478 *child of gret mounde*, 5906 *stede of mounde*, and 6495 *maide of gret mounde*. The sense 'might' is appropriate to all but the last (allowing for anticipation of future prowess in 4478), and that could be unthinking extension once the word had become conventional for a noble man.

KA, however, has a much more various usage of the word. There are cases like those in AM, thus 2424 *baroun of grete mounde*, but several others require the sense 'rich or high quality', thus 179 *orfreys of mounde*, 2203 *geste of mounde*, and 2651 *strate of riche mounde*. Smithers therefore (KA, Glossary, s.v. Mynde *n.*[1]) derives the word from an ON root **mund-* (cf. ON *mynda* 'weigh', ONorw. *mundr* 'bride-price'). A basic sense 'value' could underlie the usages in AM (compare 5824 *kedden þai were men of mounde* with 3480 *kidde þat he was auȝt* '. . . was worth something'), but the preponderance in AM of cases suggesting the sense 'might' persuades me that OE *mund* has made at any rate an important contribution to the semantic range of a word in which this and ON **mund-* have probably coalesced.

3120–1 *botors . . . crane*: both popular table-birds in earlier times; the bittern was still commended as late as the mid nineteenth century. See André Simon, *A Concise Encyclopædia of Gastronomy* (London, 1952), pp. 513, 548.

3176 An ingenious prevarication. Ygerne was, of course, Uter's queen when Arthur was born, though not when he was begotten, as the reader was reminded in line 2773. The poet unfortunately also reports (3147–8) the full explanation which Merlin gives in LeM (90, 6–41), thus spoiling the point of his innovation here.

3197 *drede*: elsewhere in AM reflexive, and probably in effect so here, with *hem* doing 'double duty' (see above, note to line 3056).

3203 *pauilou[n]s*: the reading *pauilons* is legitimate, but it would be a unique -*is* plural in this text (though -*is* gen. sg. occurs in lines 1456 and 2708); the supposed *i* has no stroke, which is rare beside minims; and omission of one minim in a sequence is a very slight error (cf. 6030). I take these points together as justifying emendation.

3227 *wenten oȝen*: 'turned back', i.e. 'ceased to flee'.

3237 *alle þai hadde wonne*: reflecting a phrase which in LeM is placed before the second battle, *quidoient auoir eu tot gaaigniet* (110, 19).

3249–50 'He thrust down his feet in the stirrups, forcing the stirrup taut (the horse quivered)'. Thrusting thus would naturally apply pressure with the legs to the horse's flanks—'put the legs on' in modern equestrian parlance. This would call the horse to attention, before the signal to go forward was given with the spurs (3251). Similarly in lines 6352–3.

3262 *nevou*: The AM poet regularly uses the word to render LeM *neueu*, *nies* (e.g. in line 5232, LeM 139, 21), presumably intending its most common sense, 'nephew' (possibly 'bastard son' in 6849; see my note, below); but also to render *cousin*, the relationship being clearly a cousin one (e.g. 4658, LeM 133, 31), a usage which I cannot trace outside AM. The only relationship between Nanters and Lot which emerges from AM is that of brothers-in-law (see lines 2601–8 and 4557–60); LeM, however, speaks of Lot's distress at Nanters' unhorsing *car il*

estoient andui cousin germain et si auoient ij serors a femes (94, 13–14), so
'cousin' is the probable sense here.

3275 *aforced*: I punctuate on the basis that this can be taken as intransitive, an extension (unparalleled but plausible) from its regular reflexive
usage, in the same sense 'strive'; but not improbably *him* here does
'double duty', as reflexive pronoun with *aforced* and object of *dere* (cf.
above, note to line 3056).

3290 *four launces*: the attackers were six, however. The numeral here
may be dittographed from line 3289, or it may arise from LeM *li vj roi . . .
prendent lances fors* (94, 37–40): in a thoughtless moment a translator
could have taken the last word for a numeral, or could simply have taken
over the word into his English version, to have it misunderstood and
'normalized' by a later copyist.

3302 *hauber*: if the form is genuine it is a back-formation from the
regular OF plural *haubers*.

3334 *rede*: *OED* treats as belonging to Rede *v.*² (<OE (*ge*)*rǣdan* 'arrange'),
and so also pa. t. *redde*(*n*) 7896, 8277, but the semantic change is then
remarkable. The senses suggest rather Rid *v.*; ON *ryðja* occurs as transitive 'clear (road etc.)', reflexive 'clear way for oneself', and intransitive
in the phrase *ryðja til* 'prepare for'. The pa. t. forms in *e* and *i* (5306)
offer no difficulty, nor would an inf. with *ĕ*; in the present case we may
have this (with a quantitatively inexact rhyme and, probably, scribally
adjusted spelling), or a formation by analogy with such verbs as *spede*,
pa. t. *spedde*, or perhaps coalescence with the verb from (*ge*)*rǣdan*.
Possibly we should see *red* 8596 'rescued' (OE *hreddan*) as also part of one
coalesced verb.

3363 *flegge*: Kölbing (Nachträge und besserungen, p. 503) relates the
word to OE *flēgan*, ME *fleien* etc., 'frighten', but the double consonant
makes this unsatisfactory; it relates rather to OE **flycge* 'fledged' (late
OE, once, *unfligge*). The exact sense is uncertain. *MED* renders the
present phrase 'winged words', which makes little sense; Liedholm (p. 46)
suggests 'high-flown'. My own suggestion 'eager' has the advantage of
suiting also the occurrence in a letter of Margaret Paston (1461): 'he and
alle his olde felaweship . . . arn right flygge and mery' (*Paston Letters . . .*,
ed. Davis, no. 158, line 10). In the present case the rebellious kings'
words were more eager than they themselves were.

3377 *fourtenizt*: possibly a mere error for the usual *fourtennizt*, but
simplification of the *nn* would be a natural development, especially if the
form were becoming felt as one word (though **L** 601 *seoue nyzt* shows
simplification in what can hardly have been felt, and is certainly not
written, as one). Probably the scribe of **A** did feel *fourtennizt* to be a close
unit; at any rate he wrote it as one four times in AM (2625, 3582,
4260, 4263), as two only in 4071 (whereas *seuen nizt* is written as two in
2053 and 5556, as one only in 2232). The poet, however, never uses it
with an article (unless the ambiguous *þe fourtenniztes end* 4263 be an

example), so probably did not feel it to be a genuine single noun. As in other cases (see above, note to line 915), an editor must make a somewhat arbitrary choice, and I have printed *fourten niȝt* as two words, though retaining the scribe's form here.

3391 *seyn Iones misse*: the feast of the beheading of St. John Baptist, 29th August. The present statement replaces that of LeM, 96, 7, that Arthur held court *le iour Nostre Dame en Septembre* (Nativity of the Blessed Virgin, 8 September); the reason for the change may simply be that none of the regular ways of defining the latter (*our leuedi day in heruest*, etc.) fitted the verse.

3396 *seriaunted*: the sense required here, 'provide self with servants', is not as far as I can trace elsewhere recorded, in French or English (OF *sergenter* is 'act as servant'), but is plausible. Kölbing emends to *His seriaun-tes*, and in his note renders lines 3396–7: 'Seine (d.h. Arthour's) diener zog um seinetwillen Merlin zu jedem geschäfte heran'. This requires an odd usage of *purth him*, and moreover transfers the actual ordering of the officers to Merlin, whereas in LeM it is clearly Arthur who does this, though under Merlin's instructions: *Li rois Artus . . . fist . . . asses cheualier nouiaus . . . et il ot garni toutes les forteresces de tiex gens comme Merlins li coumanda et enseigna* (96, 8, and footnote 2 (W)).

3405 *XI kinges and doukes on*: similarly in line 3637; in 3829 merely *xi kinges*. Ten kings and one duke are named in 3725–74. In LeM only ten names altogether appear, six first (see above, Introduction, p. 4), establishing a group then referred to as *li vj roy* (94, 37, etc.), and four more in 110, 5–13, including *li dus Escant de Cambenic*, after which the group becomes *les x rois* (113, 20, etc.), the fact that one of them was not of royal rank being presumably overlooked. Evidently in later transmission the ten kings thus created, and the one duke, have been taken to be separate, making eleven in all, thus *x roys couronnez et vn duc* in LeM (W) (111, footnote, 28, at a point equivalent to AM 3637), though this manuscript still has only the ten names, *xi princes* later in LeM (G¹) (127, 32), and *xj kynges* in EPM (152, 22, etc.).

In a further stage of transmission the cognomen which LeM attaches to Carodas seems to have been separated off to create an eleventh name, evidently in a form capable of yielding *Brangore* (whether as a new name or by identification with a character already known). This division is found in AM (3729 and 3749–50), and in Malory (the Vinaver *Works*, pp. 25–6), but not at the equivalent point in any form of LeM known to me. It probably occurred, however, in the form of LeM underlying both AM and Malory; its consequences certainly occur later in LeM, where Strangore is successively described as the principal city of Brangore and of Carodas (131, 23–4 and 132, 21–2), and later yet there is a specific reference to the *ij rois d'Estrangore* (199, 39). The AM poet does not accept this, but his adjustments are inconsistent. In line 3089 he had accepted Carodas as of Strangore; in 3729, etc. Brangore is of Strangore and Carodas merely 'of the round table'; in the passage equivalent to LeM pp.

131–2 Brangore is again of Strangore, though now in the form *Estrangore* (4461–2) and *Galence* is introduced as Carodas' city (4491), adopting a name which occurs in LeM, as *Galenice*, in an indifferent context (173, 3). At the present point the statement that the duke was additional to *eleven* kings is a further confusion unique to AM; Malory has merely the eleven kings (who include *the deuke of Canbenet*).

For other cases in which what was originally one person appears divided in AM see below, note to lines 5427–9.

3447–8 *aboue:come*: an abnormal rhyme, but paralleled in the couplet *Childhood of Jesus* 343–4 and in *Floris and Blauncheflour* (Cambridge MS.) McKnight's ed. 727–8; possibly also in AM 6369–70, 8385–6, and 9679–80 (see below, notes to first two of these). If it is to be accepted here, rather than Kölbing's *abone*, which gives a more normal rhyme but introduces a dialectally unexpected form, the same should be done in *Roland and Vernagu* (281), a text showing clearly SE rhymes, in which also the editorial *abone* would be unlikely.

3451 *Wiþ loude cri*: probably to be taken as qualifying *priken* rather than *bad*; LeM has *et s'en ua criant* (99, 25).

ȝeld: *OED* records as the first instance of this verb intransitive, but it may well be simply the regular reflexive with *hem* doing 'double duty', as reflexive pronoun with *ȝeld* and object of *bad* (cf. above, note to line 3056).

3490 *was*: the indicative is curious; the original was very probably *war*.

3528 *wiþ gret ferrade*: I take this to refer to the hospitable reception which the king gave to the envoys (described at some length, as by the two kings, who are already together, in LeM, pp. 100–1). But possibly it should be taken rather with the next line: 'sent quickly for Bohort (to come) with (a) large company'.

3534 *London of gret valoure*: 'the worthy city of London', but *of gret valoure* is probably a botching up of something missing or illegible in the exemplar; the original perhaps had *bi norþ and souþe* 'everywhere' (cf. line 3186)—this is close to one of the suggestions in Kölbing's note.

3546 *welcome*: as in line 8548, context demands pp., not adj. Not improbably the original in each case was *welcomed*, and the rhymes have been 'corrected'.

3568 *welken*: to be derived from OE *wœlcen* or *welcen* beside *wolcen*. Cf. *dœhter, dehter* beside *dohtor*, and see Bülbring, 'Erhaltung des . . . œ-Lautes', 102–7.

turned of herre: 'shifted from its hinges', i.e. the whole pattern of the celestial sphere was disordered; for the phrase cf. Gower's *Wherof this world stant out of herre* (*Confessio Amantis* bk. V, 346). Such an astrological upheaval would occur at some moment of cosmic calamity; compare the statement in the Towneley *Noah*, 345, that *the planettis seuen left has thare stall* at the time of the Flood. Probably no particular occasion is here in the poet's mind; he is merely making a display of astrological jargon (there is no equivalent in LeM).

3598 *Holias*: LeM *Belyas li amoreus del chastel as puceles* (103, 32); identical then with the *Belias* of lines 3956 and 5435—LeM's equivalent of the latter is *Belyas li amoureus* (148, 7–8).

3607 *sengours*: the manuscript reading is retained as conceivably genuine, though it more probably arises from scribal interchange of letters in the regular *segnours*; or perhaps we should read *sengnours* (a good OF form), assuming that a copyist intended to regularize the spelling but carelessly removed the wrong *n*.

3641 *were*: certainly 'make war', not 'defend'; LeM has '*Nous ne mouerons deuant che que nous aurons fait vne bataille encontre les barons de ceste terre*' (108, 5–7). Cf. above, note to line 429.

3652 Since all men were forbidden to move about, any man found doing so could confidently be captured as an enemy scout.

3657 *Rokingha†m*: the insertion of a superscript form which in this hand should signify *ra* (though in others it is also used simply for *a*) apparently reflects casual taking-over of one feature of LeM's *Bedingran* (108, 15), though the intention was to write the substituted name. On the curious double treatment of this name in AM see below, note to line 7342; where the present substitution is not made the *ra* appears, as in LeM, in line 7812 (see my note, below), and there is a confusion like the present one in line 8040. In 7391 *Rokingham* is written with *ha* superscript, as though the scribe had first in mind a superscript which would have given *Rokingram*, but then corrected himself. Unless we suppose him himself acquainted with LeM, he was presumably confronted with confused notation going back to the AM poet.

3659 *telt*: Liedholm's treatment of this as a noun (p. 86) is certainly wrong; she has missed the common 'postponed *and*' construction.

3660 *flesches*: the plural form impairs both sense and metre, and probably reflects simply dittography of *es*.

3676, 9 *Leonce, Farien*: in LeM they are not stewards; their conversion into these officers would seem to rest on a misreading of LeM's account of the preparations by Ban and Bohort for their expedition: *Si commanderent lor terres a garder a Leonce de Paerne, qui estoit lor cousins germains . . . si fu Phariens en sa* [Ban's and Bohort's] *compaignie, et li senescaus de Benoic et cil de Gaunes* (101, 23–6).

3677 *kinges Banes*: as far as I know an unparalleled usage; the normal ones are illustrated by 5492 *king Bohortes godsone* and 8014 *þe kinges sones Vrien*. I retain the manuscript form here as defensible, but probably *kinges* reflects mere dittography.

3689 *him*: Leonce. But it is very likely a corruption of *hem*, as suggested in Kölbing's note.

3712 *þe marche*: LeM has *vne marche qui estoit entre le roialme de Gorre et le roialme d'Escoche* (109, 41–2).

3721–2 *On Arthour . . . þai wold happen*: appears to render LeM 110, 1–2 *qu'il . . . s'en iroient sour le roy Artu*; but if so with an unparalleled semantic shift from 'come upon (by chance)' to 'fall upon (by intent)'. Particularly in view of *al aboute*, it is more likely that the poet intended rather the verb from OF *happer* 'seize'; the particular sense here may reflect the sense 'clamp' of the OF noun *hape* (compare the common metaphor of a vice in modern military descriptions). The *on* remains a clumsy reflection of *sour*.

3725–6 *To . . . Com*: equivalent to the compound which appears (as *tocomen*) in line 2840; the rendering of 3725 in Kölbing's note, 'Zu diesem verrathe, um ihm auszuführen', does not attract.

3733 *Norþ Wales*: reflecting misunderstanding of LeM's *Norgales* (110, 6), which is the king's *city* in 131, 21 (= AM 4430) and elsewhere.

3738 *bi riȝtes*: if genuine, this antedates by five centuries *OED*'s first recorded occurrence of *by rights*, but again the form is probably a copyist's; the poet would have used *bi riȝt*, possibly rhyming on an uninflected plural *kniȝt* (cf. 2365 etc.).

3746 *Dorkaine*: reflects misunderstanding of LeM's (*de Leonois et*) *d'Orcanie* (110, 10), but already in LeM the name has ceased to relate to Orkney: it is *la cite d'Orcanie* in 128, 16 (= AM 4385) and elsewhere.

3755 *þat*: the antecedent is rather *Nanters* than *Arthour*, though one cannot be sure.

3771–2 *Arundel . . . Cambernic*: this identity will rest on a corrupt or misunderstood statement in the source. At a point equivalent to line 4521, LeM has Cambenic, not Arundel, but W adds a reference to *le chastel Arondel qui estoit en la marche de Cambenic* (133, footnote 1). On confusion arising from the identification see below, note to lines 6660–2.

3798 *in her teþ*: not far from the usage recorded by *OED* from Robert of Gloucester; emendation is certainly not called for.

3801 *hard*: qualifies *sweuen* rather than *feren*; LeM speaks of *j soigne moult fort et moult espoentable* (113, 28–9).

3805 *Þiderward*: in the direction which line 3804 implies that Lot stated; the sense is quite clear, although Kölbing (note) finds the word 'nicht zu erklären' unless the direction had been specified, as in LeM (113, 38–9), and concludes that lines must have been lost.

3847 *folc*: elsewhere in AM spelt *folk*; very possibly here a miscopying of *floc*, the usual word in AM for a specific division of an army (though such a division can then be referred to by the more general word *folk*, as in line 7979).

3852 As observed in Kölbing's note, a couplet referring to the sixth company must have fallen out following this line. Lines 3939–40 suggest that its leader should be Antour, though his name does not appear in the equivalent passage in LeM (112, 22–30) as the others all do. However, the arrangement in AM is much modified from LeM, in which Arthur's forces are in three divisions only; LeM goes on at once to describe the four divisions of Ban's and Bohort's forces (similarly much modified in AM 3951–68), hence evidently the total of seven. Once this had been misapprehended as referring to Arthur's men only, new leaders had to be produced.

3859 *þe oþer*: Ban and Bohort and their men, held in reserve on Arthur's side just as Lot, Nanters, Urien, and Carodas are on the rebels'. In LeM they are not simply in reserve; Merlin instructs Arthur that *li rois Bans et son frere s'en iront par deuers la forest, si les assaudront par deriere la forest, et vous par deuant* (114, 33–5).

no miʒt ben ykidde: most easily understood with *miʒt* an auxiliary of permission, as it appears to be in line 2201; the plan of battle prohibited them from revealing themselves to the rebels yet. This is not the poet's normal sense for *may, miʒt*, however (even in 2201 one cannot be quite sure), and it is at least as likely that it expresses the inability of the rebels to observe them, with semantic drift of *ykidde* from actively 'revealed' to merely 'visible', 'seen'.

3867 *roten*: *OED* records as the only instance of Rote *v.*[3]. It is certainly related to the verb *ratel*, and may be a mere error for *rotlen* (see below, note to line 7848). If a genuine form, it is presumably formed on *rotlen* as though this contained a frequentative suffix.

3896–8 'They rode to the knights, (namely to) . . . Griflet and . . . Kay, (whom) they remounted . . .' If the manuscript is retained unemended, it is hardly possible to take the article as idiomatically omitted before *kniʒtes*, since several groups of knights are involved (contrast line 1227, where only one group of messengers is present); we are then forced to render 3895–6 'and they rode, two knights, with other knights as well', which is very awkward. From my suggested *he þe*, loss by rubbing or fading of the descender of *þ* could easily give the appearance of *he he*, which a scribe might take as dittography and 'correct'.

3910 *her alder powers*: cf. KA 1687 *hire aldre radd*. All other occurrences of *alder* in AM, however, are adverbial with superlatives and the line as it stands is metrically poor; the poet very probably wrote *alder mest*.

3912 *was*: agreeing with the nearest element of the compound subject; all four kings were *bihinde*, i.e. in reserve, as clearly stated in lines 3861–3.

3915 *frem*: as Smithers suggests in 'Notes on ME Texts', 212, this is probably a ghost-form, a mere scribe's botch after the original rhyme *fram:man* had become imperfect by the normalizing of the latter (cf. *men:fram* prep., 5271–2). But one cannot exclude the possibility of a back-formation from a verbal form (OE *fremman*, ON *fremja*), or from the comparative and superlative.

3929 *chalanged*: *MED* understands as 'spurred on by taunts', a sense not elsewhere recorded for the verb but presumably taken as extended from the usual 'rebuke'. This seems out of character for Arthur (though Merlin certainly spurs *him* on by taunts in line 6343), and it is not clear how such an action could be *bi riȝt*. One might, perhaps, interpret the line 'and rebuked those of his men that deserved it', but I prefer to assume here the sense 'exhort', or the like, which is recorded, though exceptionally, for OF *chalangier*; see Tilander's *Lexique du Roman de Renart*, p. 30.

3941 *seuen*: the omitted name is clearly Kay's, though it is not clear where it might have been fitted in.

3945 *sur carking*: compare 4454 *soure carked*. If, as Liedholm believes (p. 187), the present form represents an adoption of ONF *surcarquier* (= OF *surchargier*), of which 5941 *ouercarked* represents a half-translated adoption, then the form in 4454 is probably a scribal 'improvement' of an original *surcarked*. The recorded sense of the OF verb is simply 'overload', but it is rare, and the simplex *chargier* has the sense (among others) 'press hard, harass' (for the adoption of which into English see *OED* s.v. Charge *v.*, 10), so it is quite possible that the compound could signify 'press very hard, harass severely', which would suit the three AM occurrences. A verb *surcark* is not, however, recorded in English unless it be here; the only assured instance of such a form is as a noun in *Cursor Mundi* 9843 (Göttingen MS.; other MSS. *ouercark(e)*, *ovircark*), meaning 'excess'. The verb *surcharge* appears rather later, but *OED* records nothing nearer my suggested sense than 'make an overwhelming attack on' (late sixteenth century). I therefore follow Kölbing and *MED* in assuming, here and in 4454, that the first element is the separate word *s(o)ur(e)* 'bitter(ly)'; *ouercarked* could be a new ME formation rather than an adoption of *surcarquier*, though the form in *Cursor Mundi* must presumably be from the French.

3969–70 *þai* and *hem* are the rebels, engaged in the attack begun in lines 3911 ff. *þe oþer* are Ban's and Bohort's men; the slaughter described in lines 3971–2 is evidently that which grieves the rebel kings in 3979–81. Kölbing, retaining the manuscript unemended, is forced in his note to interpret *þai* as Arthur's men, *hem* as the rebels, 'ein auffalender beleg für die häufige unklarheit in der beziehung der personalpronomina in diesen romanzen'. Quite apart from the extreme awkwardness of this, the poet could not possibly have described Arthur's men as 'wailing', however hard pressed.

A possible alternative emendation would be *wai[t]ing*, in a postulated sense 'infliction of injury' extended from the regular 'infliction' (cf. 3936 *deden wo*); the unusual usage would account for the word's 'correction' by a copyist.

3986 An agile rider today will sometimes show off by doing this, but one doubts if it was ever really done in armour.

4006 *palet*: the etymology accepted by *OED*, from OF *palet*, a diminutive of *pal* 'stake', seems semantically very unsatisfactory, and the influence of ME *pel(le)* = *pal(le)* (<OE *pell, pæll*) which Liedholm (p. 133) invokes to explain the form *pelet* (AM 9353) is equally unattractive, for the senses are too far apart. A formally satisfactory etymon for *palet/pelet* would be OF *paillette*. Among the senses recorded for this in Littré's *Dictionnaire* is the shoemaker's usage 'morceau de cuir taillé au tranchet, servant a fortifier'. No such sense is recorded in the medieval period, but a tradesman's term might well escape record, and perhaps the word was also used for some leather piece in the lining of a helmet.

4030 Probably 'which they had previously put in position', though one could perhaps render 'which those in the lead (of the flight) had put in position'. The latter would accord better with LeM, which describes how they fled until *il vindrent a vne aigue bruiant ou li fuiant auoient fait j pont de raime et de buisce* (121, 21–2). AM is not precisely following LeM here, however (the equivalent of the rally described in lines 4031 ff. is in LeM a smaller affair, briefly interrupting the flight to the bridge), and the manuscript can be rendered unemended as 'in front of which they had been drawn up', but apart from losing all correspondence with LeM this would be an unusual use of the verb. For the rhyme as emended compare lines 4045–6; in the present case *legge* would have been 'corrected' for the sake of the rhyme on the scribal form *brigge*.

4035 *Sir*: a legitimate plural; in OF *sieur* can be plural, though *seigneurs* is usual.

4051 *mani slawe*: apparently implying that ten thousand is not many; the poet probably in fact wrote *mani mo slawe* or *mo yslawe*.

4074 *þat cas*: 'the state of affairs'; cf. 861 *þe cas*. The use of *þat* is unusual, however; the original was perhaps *in þat cas* (as in lines 2003 and 5142).

4085 *Sex hundred [þousand]*: adopting the emendation suggested in Kölbing's note. The manuscript figure is absurdly low; the British kings dispose altogether more than 100,000 men (lines 4357–4531), yet can only defend their own regions.

4119 *he*: plural, anticipating 4120 *Ban and Bohort*.

4146 *wold*: from the context one might guess this to be an error for *nold*, but LeM establishes that the positive is correct: . . . *si demande li rois s'il veut uendre ces oisiaus . . . et li vilains li dist que oil volentiers* (122, 28–9).

4148 *Hou*: 'for what price', an abnormal usage, found elsewhere only in the corresponding passage in EPM *How wilt thow yeve hem?* (168, 6). The line renders LeM *Et que les faites vous?* (122, 29) 'What do you reckon them at?'.

4155 *þi gold*: see above, Introduction, p. 18.

4165–6 These lines appear to mean that the king has had the birds but Merlin has had no money for them, but this makes little sense as a reason for Merlin's not caring that the king does not believe him. Kölbing, in his note, would render '"Denn, könig", sagte er, "du hast (viel) von mir, aber ich nichts von dir zu erwarten"', but the hardly justified addition of 'zu erwarten' does not really help. In LeM Merlin's reply is a play on words: '*Se vous uoles*,' *fait li vilains*, '*si m'en crees, et si non si ne m'en crees pas, car ie n'ai riens acreu a vous; si soions quite et quite*' (123, 5–7). He is punning on the senses 'believe' and 'obtain' (a likely extension, though I cannot find another instance, of the sense 'borrow on pledged word') of *acroire*. The AM poet rendered *car* by *for* (4165), but replaced the untranslatable pun by a passage making *for* inappropriate. The translator of EPM simply renders *car ie n'ai riens acreu a vous* by *for I ne leve yow nought*, and otherwise renders closely (168, 30–2), a more pedestrian way of failing to make sense of the passage.

4199 *alange*: the exceptional retention, within the line, of an *a*-form for the vowel derived from *i*-mutation of Gmc *ă* before nasal is probably because the scribe associated the word with *lang*, and similarly in the verbal form in line 4202.

4207 *hete*: the sense 'passion' which derivation from OE *hǣtu*, *hǣte* 'heat' would yield may seem more appropriate here than 'feeling of hostility' (<OE *hete*). But in the other two occurrences of the word (230, 5147) 'hostility' is very suitable, and I prefer to assume derivation from *hete* in all three cases.

4209 *Norhant*: Urien's city in line 4528 also (*Norham*, as in 4211), but elsewhere (line 2614, etc.) he is said to be king of *Schorham*. His apparent two cities arise from a confounding together of LeM's *Sorhaut* (perhaps as *Sorhant*), Urien's city, and the quite distinct *No(r)haut* (*No(r)hant*?); the latter appears correctly in AM 7380, where *A noble kniȝt, lord of Nohaut* renders LeM's *le segneur de Nohaut* (188, 4–5).

4268–70 As one might now say: 'God bless my soul, what's the use of . . .'.

4273 *oȝen*: doubtless for original *oȝan*.

4276 *schandliche werk*: 'black arts'; to Arthur's enemies Merlin's magic would naturally so appear. In 4275 *gode* is 'skilled', not 'morally good'.

4298 'until (the coming of) the knight highest of lineage'. An unparalleled, though understandable, extension of the use of *fort* prep., which is elsewhere used only with nouns defining a time (once a point in a prayer) at which one arrives. The sense, however, and hence the emendation, are established by LeM: '. . . *ne del roy Alain, qui gist malades, n'atendons nous nul secors, deuant ce que li mieudres cheualiers del monde uiegne a lui et li demant dont cele maladie li vint et quel chose li g[r]aus est que l'en sert*' (125, 12–15). The scribe's *for* is either dittographed from immediately above or represents an ill-judged 'correction' of a usage not understood.

   Kölbing's note suggests that a couplet has been lost after 4298, which gave the sense of the statement in LeM; if so *fort* has its normal sense. But it seems more likely that the Chosen Knight's inquiry has become corrupted into the assertion of AM 4299–4300, for which there is no warranty in LeM. Possibly the original form of these lines had *Fort þe best kniȝt* . . . *Haue yseyd wherefore* . . ., with the inquiry varied into a statement, and a copyist then took *yseyd* for pronoun and verb, and 'regularized' the word order; if so again *fort* has its normal sense.

4302 *Normaga of Sorailes*: LeM (W) reads '. . . *et de Pedru le roy de Noruaga ne poons nous auoir nul secours, car Galehous* . . .' (125, footnote 2, 1–3). EPM has '*And of the kynge of Sorloys no may we haue no socour, ffor Galehaut* . . .' (173, 13–14). The form of LeM underlying AM probably had both *Noruaga* and *Sorloys*; it read, perhaps, . . . *et de* . . . *le roy de Noruaga et de Sorlois* . . ., which was translated as though it were . . . *le roy Noruaga de Sorlois* . . . What chain of corruption connects *Pedru* with *of þe Marais* we can hardly hope to discover, but that there was corruption here in at least some versions of LeM is evident from the extraordinary reading *par de la de par* for *Pedru* in MS. Bibl. Nat. f. fr. 9123 (Y), a manuscript ordinarily so close to W as to suggest that it is a direct copy. Kölbing's *Nor Maga* would represent the only occurrence of *nor* in AM, and would imply further puzzling corruption.

4304 *Galaous*: LeM (Y) *Galehous li filz al iaiande*, identical then with the Galahos of line 8923, and distinct from the Galeus of line 4309 (LeM (Y) *Galchos li bruns*).

4321 *kepe*: *MED* curiously enters under Kẹpen 21 (a) 'remain in', etc. but LeM *garderons les voies et les trespas* (125, 30–1) confirms the commoner sense 'guard'.

4363 *[h]is*: compare lines 4375, 4403, and 4491; here the scribe's eye no doubt slipped to the next line.

4364 *wante*: Liedholm (p. 20) seems to favour the view put forward in Zupitza's review of Kölbing, p. 89, that this belongs to the verb from OE *windan* (whose pa. t. 3 sg. is *wond* in line 9388). For this verb of motion of a body of men cf. 5734 and 7956, but these uses are of sudden and forcible movement, in each case an attack; moreover the *t* would be unexpected. It seems better to treat *wante* as from *wende* (<OE *wendan*), which is used of all types of going; the *a*-form is unsurprising in rhyme.

4372 *hem*: Ider . . . | *Wiþ his folk* (4367–8); emendation to *him* is unnecessary.

4395 *VIII þousand*: the 3000 of 4386 plus the 5000 of 4388. The equivalent total in LeM is given before the references placed in AM in lines 4389–94; it specifically excludes *ceaus de la uille* (128, 20), and naturally excludes also the volunteers attracted by *li granz renons que il auoit de estre larges*, whose arrival is described next (*puis li enuint* . . .) (W; 128, footnote 2, 5–7). The rearrangement of order in AM has created obscurity. The figures in forms of LeM I have seen do not quite agree with AM, but those in EPM (p. 179) do, and so doubtless they did in the form of LeM underlying both English versions.

4444 *so[ster]*: the emendation is established as correct by LeM (W), *fors que Morgain, la suer le roy Artus, et Viuiane, que Merlins ama tant* (131, footnote 4, 14–15).

4446 *Niniame*: properly the famous sorceress; but the AM poet was not, it would seem, familiar with her story, and appears to have been misled into treating her as a place, with Morgan left as the beguiler of Merlin. His misunderstanding perhaps derives from a form of LeM which in the passage quoted in the note above read . . . *et fors que Viuiane* . . ., with *fors que* then corrupted into *fors de* 'outside'.

Whether the name should be *Vivian*, etc., or *Ninian*, etc. remains uncertain; see W. A. Nitze 'An Arthurian Crux: Viviane or Niniane', *Romance Philology*, vii (1953), 326–30, and E.P. Hamp 'Viviane or Niniane—A Comment from the Keltic Side', ibid. viii (1954), 91.

4451–2 'The Saracens had support from that castle, and much recourse (to it)'. *OED* regards *recour* here as a variant on Recover *sb.*, in some sense like 'help', and at least one of *OED*'s other citations has a sense proper to *recover* (from Usk's *Testament of Love*, perhaps rather 'remedy' than as glossed); but that from Louelich, certainly, and that from Barbour's *Bruce*, possibly, can be derived from OF *recors* in the regular sense 'ce à quoi l'on recort', and so can the present use in the equally regular sense 'action de recourir à qq'un, à qq'chose'.

4454 *soure carked*: see above, note to line 3945.

4468 *was*: the five thousand men are presumably felt as constituting a single body, hence the number of the verb; cf. line 9647.

4470 *panimes*: if genuine, the form antedates by a century and a half *OED*'s first record of the word with *pai*- reduced; compare perhaps *tate* 2850, etc. (but see my note above). Here we may simply have scribal omission of one in a series of minims.

4472 *douster*: for a summary of the distribution of (ȝ)*st* and other variant spellings for *ht* after a stressed vowel in early ME (as well as of *ht* appearing by inversion for various other consonants) see Mahling's *Tonvokal* + *ht*.

4484 *Com to kniȝt*: taking *kniȝt* as noun, compare the regular idiom 'come to man' for 'be born'. The rich provision of line 4486, however (see next note), would rather be for Sagremor's journey than for his future dubbing, and the promise of line 4483 would more satisfactorily refer to his appearance in lines 6991 ff. than in a much later part of the story (not in AM). Perhaps then *kniȝt* is verb, in the sense (plausible, though I cannot parallel it) 'become a knight', giving 'come in order to receive knighthood'.

4485 *Wherepurth*: if this has its normal sense 'as a result of which', we must take lines 4483–4 as parenthetic, and understand that it was because of Sagremor's high rank that the emperor arrayed him so richly. It was not, however, for that reason that he was sent to England; probably then *wherepurth* must, exceptionally, signify 'for which purpose'.

4487 [*fr*]*o*: the manuscript can be construed unemended, 'to Constantinople on his way to England'. But the emperor would probably be in Constantinople, and in LeM Sagremor is certainly in that city when Arthur's fame reaches him. The scribe's eye probably slipped to the line below (compare a similar erroneous *to* in line 5353).

4491 *Galence*: on the introduction of this name see above, note to line 3405.

4524–5 As the text stands, must be understood 'together with 7000 who had been guarding . . .'. But almost certainly some matter has dropped out, and the careful guarding of *pap and way* is intended to be by the whole force under the duke's directions. LeM (133, 3–4) records that he gathered men from near and far until he had 8,000 (it is not clear whether this includes the survivors of the battle or not), *sans cels qui en la cite estoient*, who numbered 4,000 (EPM, 188, 2–4, makes the figures 4,000 and 3,000 respectively). Line 4524 perhaps read originally *Wiþ seuen þousand of purchas, saunfaile*, and was followed by a couplet referring to the men found in the city. The suggestion in Kölbing's note (influenced by EPM's figure for the men of the city) to read *þer dwelled* for *wiþ* in 4522, and to link *wiþ* 4524 with *went* 4521, is a strange one; those who *ascaped fram þe batayle* would certainly come with the duke, not be found in the city.

4551 *sone*†: see above, note to line 2605.

4555 ff. The syntax is confused. It would seem that the poet began as though to say 'Of Ygerne Blasine and Belisent were born', or the like, inserted what would have been a parenthetic *þat ich . . . make* (4556–7), but then resumed after this with a different construction. Kölbing's emendation creates a unique case of a major section beginning in mid-couplet (it is rare even for the mark ¶ to split a couplet); besides, an invitation to 'listen concerning Ygerne' would be a poor introduction to an account of her daughters and grandson, in which she herself is never to be mentioned at all.

4594 *oȝain* [*him hold*]: my Apparatus credits the emendation to Kölbing's notes, but in fact it first appears as a correction in Walter Scott's hand to the portion of S transcribed by his amanuensis (see above, Introduction, p. 40).

4599 *sent*: the original was probably *ofsent*; or perhaps its rare variant *osent* (cf. line 2686), which might have confused a copyist.

4602 *þe newe faire*: LeM *la noeue ferte de Borceliande* (128, 7) 'the new fortification . . .' (not 'ford' as Sommer's marginal noter enders it on p. 133). Our *faire* may be a mistranslation, or the word may have been misread as *feste*, in either case with the 'new fair' of London probably in the translator's mind; or perhaps the source manuscript of LeM was corrupt, though if so the source of EPM, where the phrase is rendered *newe werke* (178, 33), evidently had not the corruption.

4625–7 No reason is given why the younger brothers should lay all the blame on Gawain. AM is in fact here a combination of the passage at the equivalent point in LeM, where the mother says '*Si faites moult a blasmer, vous et uostre frere*' (130, 18–19), with Agravain's later charge '*Vous en faites plus a blasmer que tout li autre, car vous estes li aisnes de nous tous*' (130, 40–1).

4676–7 *play:play*: on the self-rhyme, compare 2675–6 and 3843–4. The suggestion in Kölbing's note to emend to *lay* in 4676 is thus not necessary, though certainly attractive.

4681 To make the king participate in the equipping of Gawain is obviously a mistake; in LeM it is only his mother who is involved. Possibly Lot's presence here is an unthinking addition by the poet, or possibly the line is a corruption, perhaps of *King Lotes leuedi* . . . (cf. line 4694).

4686 *in sout of o clope*: 'in matching garb, made of the same stuff'. This is almost tautological, and perhaps *sout* should be taken to mean 'garb' simply, as in KA 182, but probably the present phrase is constructed under the influence of the more straightforward *in sout of* 'in the same style of dress as' and *of o sout* 'dressed alike'.

4716 *her*: the invaders'; the lack of antecedent has been overlooked.

4718 *sonne schining*: I treat this (and similarly in line 9164) as noun and present participle (cf. 6877 *þe sonne schineand briȝt*), but it could also be seen as compound noun (cf. 8799 *þe dayspringing*), or uninflected genitive and verbal noun.

4739 *schirsten*: compare *douster* 4472, and see reference in my note ad loc.

4757, 4761–2 'They said whose sons they were . . ., sons of castle-owners and of minor tenants—(who) afterwards did well in king Arthur's service.' That line 4761 must be linked with 4757, not (as Kölbing's punctuation would have it) with 4763, is clear from EPM . . . *the childeren that ther were come, with thise v cosins, and with other that were ryche mennes sones, as Castelleins and vauasours of the londe, that after were of grete prowesse in the house of kynge Arthur* . . . (192, 28–32). None of the manuscripts of LeM which I have seen has an equivalent passage, but Kölbing (p. cxxx) quotes from the printed version of 1528 *qui estoient filz des chastellains et des gentils hommes de la contree de Logres*, confirming that the EPM passage duly rests on LeM.

4769 *our sleiȝt*: 'the killing of our (i.e. British) people'.

4783–92 This account of Gawain's changes of strength is simpler than in LeM (129, 42–130, 3), where there is doubling at Terce as well as that at Prime. It is also complete and intelligible, whereas LeM in the form

I have seen omits two necessary changes. We cannot of course be sure whether the AM poet corrected a faulty source or followed a correct one, but very possibly the former, since both EPM (182, 1–8) and Louelich (12433–40) have the omissions (as well as other confusions of their own).

4820 *him*: Gawain.

4841 *arme*: *MED* records a single instance of this singular, from Robert of Gloucester; but there as here an error for the plural seems quite likely.

4849–51 '. . . who escaped, and of whom ten, fleeing with great haste, came . . .' But Kölbing's deletion of *And* (4850) has much to be said for it. The scribe's exemplar had perhaps *fleʒ*; he mistook this for verb and conjunction and normalized the order, then realized his mistake and completed the present participial form but neglected to delete the conjunction.

4857 *euerich man*: either a very poor rhyme, or the original had *men*. The very few apparent cases of *every* with a plural noun in ME all invite special explanation; here perhaps the poet, whose natural form of the plural was *man* but who recognized *men* as a permissible alternative, useful for rhyming, carelessly failed to notice that as he was using a syntactic singular the alternative was not properly available.

4886 *Of † fet*: I have followed Kölbing in treating the manuscript reading *of þo fet* as erroneous, but it is possible that the expression reflects a qualification in the source like that which LeM elsewhere applies to the size of Rion, who *auoit . . . xiiij pies de lonc, des pies qui lors estoient* (230, 11–12), though here the forms of LeM which I have seen say nothing about the size of Thoas.

4932 *þerof carf*: 'cut off from it . . .' But *þerof* may well have a partitive sense (as certainly in lines 7549 and 7869), with *of* then doing 'double duty': 'cut off (a quarter) of it'. Line 6176 is close to the present case; a simple *of* might be thought to be behaving similarly in lines 8190, 9357, and 9358. On the phenomenon of 'double duty' see above, note to line 885.

4936 *Aswon*: *MED* treats the case in line 7172 as *aswou*, and would doubtless so take this, and the other cases within the line (5810, 8469, 8535, 9073), and presumably of related words also (*swoned* 5819, *swoninge* 9850). Liedholm (p. 120) accepts without discussion that they are *n*-forms. The three rhymes (3294, 7132, 8444) are all on fricatives; on the other hand the regular spelling of the derivative of *ǒ3* is *ow*, and a whole series of *ou*-spellings would be surprising (though an occasional one would not be unexpected, since *ow/ou* are alternative spellings for *ū*). I assume that the scribe substituted his own usual form of these words within the line, intending *-on*, but retained his exemplar's where alteration would falsify a rhyme.

4945 *Sum*: all the other pronominal uses in AM are plural; probably this should be also, with *him* 4946 then an error for *hem*.

4989 *striif*: LeM's '*c'ales vous sermounant?*' (137, 18) provides the basis for this and for *speki and makeþ tale* in line 4991. The poet presumably sees Gawain's speeches in 4981–4 and 4986–8 (the latter expanded and modified from LeM) as sufficiently like arguing about the situation instead of getting on with the rescue to justify the word.

4991–2 *speki, lachi*: the appearance in these verbs of *i*-forms, elsewhere in AM found only (occasionally) in verbs derived from OE weak class II, or (twice) from OF (*graunti* 59, **gouerny* 89), is curious. In the case of *lachi* analogy with the verb of similar form and sense derived from OF *cachier* may be suspected (see Wallenberg's *Vocabulary of . . . Ayenbite*, p. 46); it is hard to see any basis for *speki* except mechanical influence from *lachi* in copying.

5013 *girt*: if the semantic development can be made to seem plausible, it is more attractive to identify *gird* 'strike' with *gird* 'put girdle on' than to invoke an unrecorded OE verb homonymous with the recorded *gyrdan* but related (obscurely) to *gierd*, which is *MED*'s principal suggestion. The suggestion in the 1911 edition of Webster's *Dictionary*, that the verb was 'first used of striking with a belt or whip, the lash circling round the one struck', would be more attractive if early (or indeed any) examples of its use of such an instrument could be found, but in fact the regular use is of striking with a rigid instrument, usually a sword. However, a colloquial, euphemistic, usage in the sense 'whip' might well have existed in OE, without finding its way into preserved texts until it had become a simple word for 'strike' generally. It seems possible, too, that the development has been assisted by semantic contamination (occurring first in the south-east) between the derivatives of **gerdan = gyrdan* and *grētan* 'attack'; see below, note to lines 5945–6.

5043 *No durst no abide*: use of *no* with both auxiliary and infinitive is highly unusual; the original was probably *no durst non . . .* 'none (of them) dared . . .', or perhaps *no durst þo* '(they) dared not then . . .'

5083–7 Rendering LeM . . . *et cil lor content que Gauainet . . . et si troi frere et Galescins . . . sont uenu a vij compaignons, si encontrerent iiij fouriers qui cest proie enmenerent, si se combatirent a els tant que tous les ont ocis* (138, 2–7)

5152 *þeroȝin*: probably a mere error for the regular *oȝain*, but the form may be genuine; see Cornelius . . . *Diphthongierung durch Palatale . . .*, p. 97 A.

5165 *donward*: this, and similarly in line 5248, may simply be errors (by omission of a mark of contraction) for *dounward*; Kölbing so emends in 5248, though not here. The form *donward* is quite well attested, however, reflecting a shortening demonstrated by Orrm's *dunnwarrd* (2056, etc.).

5167–8 'and had not Gawain (also) come down on foot he would there have killed the king (Gvinbating)'; anticipating the events described in lines 5169 ff., culminating in 5176—but awkwardly, since Gvinbating is remounted, and presumably removed from the risk of instant death at Gawain's hands, before Gawain's horse is killed. The phrase possibly arises from a misunderstanding of LeM *si trebuchent tout* [Guinemant and his horse] *en j mont ensemble* (138, 39–40) as implying that both knights fell together. Smithers's rendering of *ylawe* here as 'descended, got down' ('Notes on ME Texts', 212) would imply voluntary dismounting, presumably then at the moment to which the line would naturally refer. But why should Gawain voluntarily do what the poet tells us prevented him from killing his adversary; and if he did what reason had the Saracens then to kill his horse?

5230 *ford*: again in line 8948; also in KA 3810 (on the form see Smithers's note) and in *fordward* KA 4311. The sense in 8948 is 'cut off (head, so that it flies forth)'; here an extension from that sense gives simply 'cut through (neck)'.

5235–7 'and struck Agravain . . . under the arm, through the . . . hauberk (and through the shield)'. This renders LeM *si le fiert de la lance par desous l'aissele si grant cop que parmi les ij plois del hauberc* . . . (139, 22–3); the reference to the shield has been added, rather awkwardly, by the AM poet. If the lines are to be read with the words in a natural sequence, *ruhel* must signify some part of the body (or the clothes) under the arm; for discussion on this basis see Kölbing's 'nachträge und besserungen' (p. 503), Kaluza's review of Kölbing, col. 269, and Liedholm, p. 187, but none of the suggestions are satisfactory (note that the supposed *e* erased after *þe ru*, which Liedholm uses to support her suggestion of an original reading *þerne hel*, does not exist—the scribe wrote four minims after *þe r*, erased the third, and converted the fourth into *h*; he also clearly divides *þe* from the rest). Smithers's derivation ('Notes on ME Texts', 212–13) from OF *roële*, with inorganic *h* used to represent hiatus, is to be preferred, despite the combination of a unique sense for the word in English and an awkward construction.

5262 '(did not know) where Gawain had anywhere got to', an unusual but comprehensible expression, though the emendation *Hou* for *Whare* (with *nowhere* then treated as two words) suggested in Kölbing's note has a good deal to be said for it; compare line 4198.

5301–2 'Nobody was able to deprive that cursed foe of him', i.e. '. . . get him away from . . .'; for this construction compare line 7203.

5304 *tolling*: Kölbing glosses 'anreizen, aufhetzen', and *OED* understands it similarly, or else as 'incitement, instigation', but nobody is inciting or enticing anybody. The sense is rather literally 'dragging'; Medlan is dragging at Do's helmet to get it off. We should then take *hadde . . . bireued* 5299 as 'would have pulled off (had not Gawain come)'.

5353 The manuscript can be read unemended; the present statement then looks back to lines 4125 ff. But there Arthur, Ban, and Bohort arrived with some 120 men (4126), while here they have but thirty-nine, and those chosen by the advice of Merlin, who, as he reached Brekenho after they did (4133), could hardly have chosen the men with whom they were to arrive there. Moreover, the passage in LeM equivalent to 5353–62 reads . . . *quant li rois Artus se fu partis de Bedingran, entre lui et ses ij rois et lor compaignie il cheualcierent tant par lor iornees qu'il uindrent a Carohase* (141, 5–7). The emendation [*fr*]*o* seems certain (for another probable case of the same error, see above, note to line 4487).

5354 This line provides a unique exception to my statement in Volume I, p. xii, that the manuscripts have no punctuation; my commas here reflect manuscript points.

5355 *pritti and* [*n*]*i*[*ʒ*]*e*: the manuscript *fiue* makes neither sense nor rhyme. For *niʒe* rhyming on *compainie* compare lines 6840 and 9719; the number thirty-nine makes good sense on the basis that the forty-two of line 5357 includes Arthur, Ban, and Bohort, but that Merlin is the selector, not a member, of the company. When the company is named (lines 5409–94) the forty-two clearly includes Merlin, but the many references in and after the ensuing battle would all seem to permit the former understanding, and those in lines 5845 and 6031–3 to require it. It is probably the original understanding, for though the forms of LeM which I know agree in listing only forty-two names, including all the leaders, if we put them together we have a probable original list of forty-three. Number 21 is Amadans *li crispes* in W (f. 194ra, 2–3), but Iesmeladant in G^l (148, 12); the form of LeM which underlies AM had clearly both (though the second has been run together at some stage in transmission with the next knight, Placides *li gais*—on other peculiarities of the names in AM see below, note to lines 5427–9), but instead omitted the previous knight, Meleaudon de blois (unless this omission is the AM poet's own). It seems we have to do with different deletions from the original list by different reworkers, on the basis of a shared view as to the total number required, resting perhaps on an originally inconsistent earlier statement of the number when the party came before Leodegan (see above, Introduction, p. 15).

5373–4 *miʒt . . . to awreke*: so unusual, without an intervening simple infinitive (cf. lines 1729–30), that one suspects corruption by a scribe thinking of the proper construction after *miʒt* n.

5397 *ring*: the sense is that proper to *reng(e)* <OF *reng*. Smithers (KA, note to line 1110) uses the present case, among others, to demonstrate semantic contamination between this word and that from OE *hring*. This could easily occur since both the OF and the OE word can be used of a line of men (though the OE always, and the OF never, refers to a circular line), and because the existence of *-eng/-ing* variants in many other words would encourage the feeling that this was another such pair. The tendency for the two words to fall together is also demonstrated by *reng* in line 76 for a king's ring (whether it represents the form before or after correction), and in 6100 for a ring of men. The existence of the variants mentioned, and the possibility in any case that *-ing*:*-eng* rhymes would be only marginally imprecise in a period when the tendency to raise the *e* was

active, makes it impossible to distinguish between authorial and scribal contributions to the confused uses of the words in AM as we have it.

5406 *Tofor men*: if 'publicly', *ʒou* 5407 is awkward. Possibly the poet intended 'above (all other) men' (LeM could be so taken), or the awkwardness may simply result from compression; LeM has . . . *que li contes* vous *die lor nons* . . ., *car moult font bien a nomer deuant tous preudommes* (148, 1-2). In any case the suggestion in Kölbing's 'nachträge und besserungen', p. 503, to omit *ʒou* is inappropriate.

5427–9 *Erl Does sone, Grifles*: a division of the man from his parentage, which is here stated in LeM, *Gifles le fil Do de Carduel* (148, 6). Similarly AM's Gornain and Craddoc (5477, 9) represent a division of the person who in LeM is Gornains Cadrus (5477, 18–19), as they do again in lines 6187–8, 6299, and 9752 (see below, note to first of these). Both divisions may well go back to a variant form of LeM, as that discussed above in the note to line 3405 seems to do. The total number of the party is not changed by these divisions, because of the combination of two other names noted above (note to line 5355), and the omission of LeM's fortieth knight, Gales *li chaus* (148, 22).

5459 *of þe roche norþ*: LeM has *de la roche bise* (148, 14): *norþ* is a mistranslation of *bise* 'grey', presumably under the influence of usages like *vent de bise* 'north-east wind'. Kölbing, noting the imperfect rhyme, suggests in his note that the original was *bys:ywis*, corrupted in copying, but the misunderstanding of *bise*, with the attendant difficulty of finding a rhyme for *norþ*, seems more likely to have been the poet's than a copyist's.

5468 *wiʒtschip*: repetition of the element *wiʒt* from the previous line is clumsy if the sense is the same. The simplex generally seems to indicate physical prowess (see lines 2921, 3192, 9059, etc.; possibly not in line 8240), but 7652–3 *afong þe anour of wiʒtschippe* requires for the compound a sense rather of knightly quality, and the same is appropriate here. Of the other compounds *wiʒtlich* 3930 is answered by *wiʒt* 3935, and presumably contains the same sense; there is nothing to indicate just how the poet apprehended *wiʒtling*. Knightly quality and physical prowess would of course be intimately connected in his mind.

5471 *Gimires*: carelessly omitted in LeM (G¹), which numbers Kehedin xxxi and has no xxxii (148, 17–18), but he duly appears as the thirty-first in W (f. 194ʳᵃ, 14–15).

5545 *For*: rendering a *car* which makes good sense in LeM, where Leodegan is showing courteous anxiety lest, not knowing his guests' degree, he may treat them with less honour than their status calls for, '*car vous estes par auenture plus haut homme que ie ne soie*' (142, 12–15). Conversion of Leodegan's doubt to certainty makes the sense of *car* inappropriate.

5552 *biker*: clearly rests on an iterative formed on the root exemplified in MDu *bicken*. The root may derive from Gmc **bug-* (whose direct

derivative appears in pa. t. pl. and pp. of OE *būgan*), with the same consonant substitution as Smithers suggests for *tukke* ('Ideophones', 103–4),
expressing intensity, and in addition a similarly 'ideophonic' substitution
of a front vowel, expressing rapidity, giving the underlying sense then of
persistent sharp movement.

5555–6 'King Ban (pledged) his faith thereto, and thereto Leodegan
pledged (his faith)'; in effect Kaluza's suggestion in his review of Kölbing,
col. 269. Kölbing's *þer to*[*k*] in line 5555 would give the sense 'king Ban
there received his pledge' (a sense which does not absolutely need emendation, since *to* is a possible pa. t. form; see above, note to line 782), but
clearly Ban as spokesman for the party must give the pledge demanded in
lines 5551 ff. One is tempted to emend by deleting *to* in one or other line,
assuming dittographic error, giving 'and there king Ban pledged to
Leodegan his faith thereto' (with postponed *and*), but on the assumption
that pledges are being given on both sides the manuscript reading may
stand, though it is certainly rather awkward.

5580 *And him hing*: 'and (the king would) hang him'; the shift from
passive to active construction is also awkward, but to emend to [*be*]
h[*o*]*ng* as suggested in Kölbing's note would rather be to correct the poet's
style than restore what he probably wrote.

5585–6 LeM has *vn mardi au soir la ueille de May* (142, 38). *Seint
Philip in May* is the birth-feast of St. Philip the Apostle, 1 May (distinguished from the feast of St. Philip the Evangelist, 6 June), so this correctly represents LeM, but *Estre* is more puzzling. *In Estre on þe Tewisday*
cannot mean Easter Tuesday, for Easter day cannot fall later than 25
April; *Estre* must signify the whole season, extending from Palm Sunday
to Whitsun, and the couplet can be rendered 'During the Easter season,
on that Tuesday which was the eve . . .'. The use of the definite article in
þe Tewisday is then admittedly exceptional; for what may perhaps be a
parallel see below, note to line 6174.

5605–6 'loaded with (everything in the way of) food and drink which
anybody could think of'. The phrasing is loose but the sense is conveyed.

5635 *þer wer on*: *þer* probably to be seen as doing 'double duty' (see
above, note to line 885), 'there were thereon'.

5659 *a littel croume*: LeM describes the dragon as *j dragon petit, ne
gaires grant, qui auoit la keue longue vne toise et demie tortice* (143, 29–30).
If *croume* here is adjectival, *a litel croume* must render *demie tortice* (this
is in effect Kölbing's view in his note), and its use of the dragon as a whole
is awkward; besides, the description of the tail is separately translated in
lines 5665–6, *wiþþerhoked* rendering *tortice*. Moreover, this would represent an instance more than a century earlier than the next recorded cases
of *a litel* modifying an adjective ('somewhat'); and it would leave *petit,
ne gaires grant* untranslated. I therefore take *croume* here to be quasi-noun;
the dragon is 'a small curled (creature)'.

5700 *þai*: the slain Saracens.

5704–6 '. . . in as short a time as a man would go a mile's distance of his journey in', rendering, rather clumsily, LeM's *en mains d'eure . . . que on ne fust ales demie lieue de terre* (144, 7–8). The suggestion in Kölbing's note to understand lines 5705–6 'als wie wenn jemand in der zeit, die eine meile beansprucht, eine ganze tagesreise zurücklegen wollte' is not supported by LeM. This sort of phrase is clearly the basis for the use of *mile(-way)* as an expression of time which appears in lines 5860, 8525, etc., in the latter case rendering a phrase of LeM (204, 37–8) similar to the present one.

5713 *þre kinges*: presumably simply following the source form of LeM: G¹ has *les iij rois* (144, 9–10). This is an error, however, W has the correct *iiij* here (f. 192ʳᵃ, 42), and so has G¹ in 144, 27; these kings are identical with those earlier described as setting out plundering (AM 5587 ff.). The AM poet may have noticed the discrepancy, and for that reason refrained from naming any of the kings in the ensuing battle (as LeM does), so that a reader could take the groups as quite separate.

5748 *þridde half hundred*: the 250 referred to in line 5629. Compare KA 5168 *þrid half hundreþ*; Smithers's gloss of *þrid half* as 'one and a half' is presumably mere oversight.

5751 *þousandes to*: apparently a further force, which came with Leodegan but in a separate group from the Round Table knights, who as usual kept together and away from others. But it rests on nothing in LeM, where Leodegan comes with the Round Table knights only, and it is never referred to in the ensuing battle. Probably then a mere error here, perhaps a displaced reference to the force of 2,000 which emerges from the city in line 6027, though no reason for such a displacement appears.

5811 *To gret mile*: 'a full two miles', rendering LeM's *ij lieues et plus* (145, 12). Compare line 5997 (and my note, below).

5817 Kölbing's note suggests that the line should read *Sche totor þo hir smok*. But an extension of the sense of *(to)tere* (reflexive) from 'tear oneself' to 'tear one's clothes' is easy to understand; there is no need for emendation. For another probable case in this sense, again (if so) with the frequent pairing of tearing the hair and garments, see line 7716.

5825 *wolden*: perhaps another curious extension of the sense of habitual action (cf. above, note to line 2129); the line may be rendered 'they spoke for some time among themselves, (saying)'. But *wolden* may be merely dittographed from the following line for an original perhaps . . . *gan to speke* (cf. 6281). LeM reads *si dient entr'eus et afichent* . . . (145, 14).

5847 '(having) against them Sornegreons . . .', but *hem* is very possibly an error, perhaps for *king*.

5852 *to mede*: implying 'as the only reward they got for their fighting'.

5874 *singel*: On the probable etymology we would expect ME *schindel. On the s- cf. 2316 *senche* (see my note, above). The puzzling *g* may reflect folk-etymologizing (the word would be more used by craftsmen than scholars), on the basis that a shingle is a *single* element of a roof, whence *g* could invade the 'correct' forms. If so this probably occurred in French rather than in English, where the word is recorded (in the odd form *scincles*) nearly a century before the first record of *single* adj.

5896 *poine of man*: an adaptation of the OF phrase *poignee de gens* 'handful of men', though here *swiche* . . . *man* renders LeM's simple *si pau de gent* (146, 2); the further development in which the qualifying *of man* disappears is represented by *punay* 3233 (no equivalent in LeM). One cannot tell whether to the AM poet the word retained in itself the sense of a *small* company; in the only other use of the word known to me in English (Gavin Douglas's *Aeneid*, bk. IX, ch. viii, 129) there seems to be no implication of size. The semantic shift to 'company' simply may well be under the influence of the homonym meaning 'fight' (<OF *poigneis*, etc.; see *OED* s.v. Poygné), as though the sense were 'fighting force', a supposition perhaps encouraged by the existence of homonyms *bataile* in the senses 'fight' and 'fighting force'.

5911 *sett him vp*: combining the senses of literally raising him up (summarizing lines 5905–10) and restoring him to his royal status.

5942 'so that their lives were nearly at an end'; *þat* is postponed, a construction parallel to the common one with *and*.

5945–6 'that whoever encountered each of them quickly struck his head off'. To emend, as suggested in Kölbing's note, to *whom so he mett* would give a slightly easier flow of sense, but is not necessary (it would not in fact demand *whom*; cf. 4817). The use of *grett* here may be an extension of the sense 'attack (person)', though this seems likely already in AM to be thought of as an ironic application of the sense 'greet'; or may be a metathesized variant of *gert*; or may reflect the same semantic contamination between the two words which can be invoked to explain the sense 'strike' for the latter (see above, note to line 5013).

5971 Kölbing takes *þis* as in apposition to *he and anoþer* . . ., and suggests in his note that a copyist, mistakenly assuming it a singular, 'corrected' an original *her* to *his*. My treatment of lines 5069–70 as parenthetic, however, not only allows the manuscript to be read unemended, but more closely reflects LeM *li rois Artus encontra le roy Caelenc, qui moult se penoit des compaignons de la table roonde desconfire* (146, 39–40).

5977 *to him haue*: 'so as to overcome him', but the usage is curious and very probably corrupt. The original may have been *to him pare*, with *haue* either simple miscopying (cf. above, note to lines 1937–8), or an alteration by a scribe who did not realize that *fest* was a verb infinitive.

5979 LeM describes the blow as above the shield, *par desus l'escu, entre les ij espaules* (147, 1–2). AM's *vnder*, as though for *desuz, desous*, represents mistranslation, or translation of a corrupt exemplar, and lack of regard for the implausibility thus created.

5984 [*c*]*rudand*: Koeppel's emendation, in his review of Kölbing, p. 107. The unemended *arudand* can be construed, as 'forcing a way'; the verb would then be derived from ON *ryðja* with altered prefix, and would be a variant of the verb *rede* which occurs in line 3334, etc. The spelling *u* for a derivative of *ȳ* cannot be certainly demonstrated anywhere in our text, however (though for a possible case see below, note to line 7749, and Kölbing reads one in line 4676); also *rede* is elsewhere used of a knight clearing a way with his strokes, and its use of the panic-stricken flight of a horse would seem unlikely. Further, a sense 'hastening' is suggested by LeM *li cheuaus tourne en fuie parmi la bataille a tout le cors* (147, 3–4).

5989 *And* '*ȝeue* . . . : for *and* immediately introducing *oratio recta* compare line 8998; also probably the hypermetrical KA 1093 *And seide* '*Fader whan my moder is q[ue]ne*', in which *seide* only, rather than *And seide* as suggested in Smithers's note (though he compares the present instance), seems likely to be a copyist's insertion. For *ȝeue* (*þat*) 'would that' compare KA 413, and Smithers's note ad loc.

5992 *So were it me*: as though Guinevere had said '*It were me ioie ȝif he* . . .', or the like (cf. 8630 *þat were . . . ioie min*). Since this is implied by her speech, the usage here is understandable, though the awkwardness, coupled with the unexpected singular *me* (contrasting with *we* in the next line), makes one suspect corruption. *So wold it were*, for instance, would be an acceptable reading; dittography, followed by clumsy 'correction' (probably of *were* contracted), would give the manuscript form.

5997 *gret xiiii fet*: a full fourteen feet; compare line 5811, and KA 6808 *He had of lengþe ten grete feet*. The use of *gret* in successive lines in different senses (5998 'thick-set') is probably a deliberate stylistic trick.

6071 *þe buteler*: Lucan. But he is never elsewhere spoken of by his office only, and the suggestion in Kölbing's note to emend *Vlfin* to *Lucan* is supported by LeM *Keus li sensecaus et Gyfles et Lucans li boutelliers se desrengent et se fierent entre els* (149, 40–1). It is difficult to see, however, why a copyist should have made such an error.

6076 *flit*: unique use in the sense 'attack'; semantic extension from 'going' perhaps under the influence of MDu *flijt*, which has the sense 'hostile disposition' beside 'haste'. Smithers, however, suggests in 'Notes on ME Texts', 214, that the original was *flet* 'battlefield', with the imperfect rhyme 'corrected' by a copyist. This is plausible; an alternative emendation would be *fit*; the phrase *in þat fit* would be a parallel to the regular *in þat stounde* 'at once'; compare *in litel fit(t)* beside *in litel stounde*.

6087 *Were ouercomen*: '(who) had been defeated'; this is the force referred to as 8,000 strong in line 5745 and 7,000 strong in 5831; both figures come from LeM (144, 28 and 37; 145, 12). LeM explains that by the time this force turned to flee (= AM 6025–6) the 8,000 had been reduced to 5,000 (147, 9), and we should probably understand the intermediate figure of 7,000 as implying the first stage of their losses. At the point equivalent to the present one, however, they are again 'the 8,000' (150,

14); this in itself could be taken as a mere designation of the force, not an erroneous statement of its numbers at the time, but it seems to be this force which supplies Sornegrieu with 8,000 men a little later on (150, 41; AM 6142).

6125 *neiȝen þousand*: apparently the heathen division which has been fighting against Cleodalis since 5743–4, now commanded by Saphiran only; since it would seem that the remounted Sornigrex rallied the other division when its flight brought it in his direction (it is *þo Sarains* in line 6095), and took over its command, finding it leaderless (see 6021–4). This other division is *þe oþer* of 6128; the 2,000 men of the city (see 6027) who have pursued it now shift their attack to the division engaging Cleodalis. The two divisions continue to be described separately at this stage of the battle, though they are now in effect two wings of one more or less coalesced heathen army. Their stated numbers do not accord with what has gone before (see note above); one cannot always trace how such variations arise—scribal corruption of Roman numerals is of course very easy.

6131 'and struck down in their onset . . .' with postponed *and*. *In her coming* renders LeM *a lor uenir* (150, 34).

6152 *Ten geuantes*: LeM and EPM both quote the number as five, but both at once go on to speak of an attack on ten (respectively 151, 3 and 10; 216, 19 and 27), and in both the list of killings which follows adds up to ten. Whether the AM poet was working from a correct version of LeM or himself made the correction one cannot tell.

6167 *Þe Sarraȝins*: presumably those in the immediate vicinity, since the general flight does not develop until line 6195, but very probably this should be a singular, reflecting LeM *Et quant Sornegrieu se sent ensi atourne, si tourne en fuie, et iete j brait grant et orrible* (151, 17–18).

6174 *wiþ [an] amiral*: perhaps we should rather read *wiþ [þ]amiral* 'with the leader (who)', but this would be an abnormal way of defining a previously unspecified person (see however above, note to lines 5585–6).

6176 *þerof*: see above, note to line 4932.

6181 *Sabalant*: see above, Introduction, p. 71 n. 9.

6183 *dan Deriard*: LeM *Candenart* (151, 23), so possibly one should read *Danderiard*, with Kölbing, but it seems quite likely that the (erroneous) *dan* was apprehended as the title.

6187–8 As in 5477–9 (see above, note to 5427–9) the two British names reflect one person in LeM, *et Gornain Cadrus [ochist] Dorilas* (151, 24–5). Presumably after the division some reworker created Maupas to fill what he took to be a lacuna between the names, heedless that this brought the killings up to eleven.

6202 *xiiii þousand*: the two heathen divisions now definitively coalesce, adding the 5,000 survivors of Sornigrex's (6199) to the 9,000 with whom Saphiran was credited in line 6125 (see my note, above).

6229 *adden*: the scribe would probably have corrected to *hadden* had he noticed. In line 6269 he first wrote *adde* and then squeezed in *h*; in 8058 he evidently began to write *arnois* but realized his error before he had finished *a*, which he converted into *h* before continuing the word.

6230 [*þ*]*e*: compare line 6405.

6231 *soft and sarre*: rendering LeM (*cheualche*) *le petit pas sans desreer* (153, 2); compare the earlier *le petit pas estroit serre sans desreer* (150, 23).

6266 'how well they, their (the kings') companions did'; 6265–6 render LeM *et si font moult bien li proisie cheualier d'armes qui en lor compaignie furent venu* (153, 26–7, speaking of the support given to Arthur by all those about him).

6299 *Gor*[*n*]*ains and Craddoc*: see above, note to lines 5427–9.

6317 *heiʒe ferly*: LeM has *et il porta sa lance basse* (154, 4); by what confusion the sense has become reversed (producing an absurdity, since one cannot kill an adversary's horse by carrying the spear too high) I cannot suggest.

6343 *Wat abidestow*: the brief speeches of lines 6332–40 are hardly enough to justify an accusation of delay. In LeM (154, 11–17) the exchanges between Arthur and Ban are a good deal longer, and give some basis for the charge.

6370 *bi line*: or, of course, *biliue*, and similarly in line 9680, where Kölbing originally adopted that reading. The resultant rhymes are not of an impossible type (see above, note to lines 3447–8), but certainly rare, and it seems better not to postulate it unnecessarily.

6427 *xiiii þousand*: see above, note to line 6202.

6462 *þat*: an illogical blend of conjunction and relative pronoun, arising in the course of a change of syntax in rendering LeM . . . *douna a son oste et a sa femme . . . tant d'auoir que tous les iours de lor uies en furent puis riche et manant* (156, 30–2). For what may be a parallel structure, see line 8348 (and my note, below).

6485 *þer him hete þe king*: this vague phrase results from the poet's elimination of a digressive reference; LeM has *li rois auoit enuoiet Cleodalis en vne cheualchie contre les Yrois, qui le guerrooient en chelui tans* (148, 40–1).

6492 *bi wrongful lines*: compare KA 7259 *þe riʒttest lyne* 'the most proper course of conduct'; as Smithers points out in his note these are the only recorded instances of *line* in this sense up to the seventeenth century.

6509–10 Reflecting two passages in LeM:

. . .et li rois Bohors et li rois Bans assistrent le roy Artu entre els ij, car il li portoient ausi grant honor comme il plus pooient. Et li rois Leodegans s'en prinst garde, qui se sist coste a coste d'els a la table, si pensa bien en son corage a l'onor qu'il li portoient et al seruice qu'il li faisoient qu'il estoit sires d'eus (157, 9–13).

[Leodegan] regarda la ioie et la feste que li preudomme faisoient d'Artu (159, 14–15).

The manuscript *wiþ* must clearly be emended; the *wich* suggested in Kaluza's review of Kölbing, col. 269 (and similarly in Zupitza's, p. 93) is clearly better than the *oþ þe* suggested in Kölbing's own note.

6512 *Midelest at þe heiȝe table*: appropriate rather to Arthur's own hall than to his place as a guest, however honoured, in another. LeM, in the passage immediately preceding that quoted in the above note, describes how *li cheualier de la table roonde s'asistrent coste a coste des soldoiers a vne table qui estoit d'une part* (157, 8–9); it was at this table that Arthur had the principal seat.

6532 *gamen-gle*: compare OE *glīg-gamen*; the order of elements here is just as sensible. But Kölbing's *gamen [and] gle*, a regular phrase, may well represent the original; the scribe certainly omitted an ampersand in line 8869.

6547 *þou[s]and*: Kölbing glosses the unemended *þouand* 'sklavin' (p. 501). But even if we could accept the existence of this unrecorded word, in an unlikely form for a derivative of OE *þēowan*, the context clearly requires Guinevere to say that *nobody* could repay such service as Arthur has given, not that a poor wretch such as herself cannot. LeM is not close enough here to provide evidence on the point.

6557 *trumpes*: a ME extension of the OF sense, probably arising because *trumpet* could signify both instrument and player in OF (and hence in ME).

6569 *if were ner*: LeM (158, 40–2) is fuller; Leodegan explains that for seven years king Rion has constantly warred against him, so that in that time no suitable suitor has come into his land.

6578 *toforn hem pleyd*: it is not clear just what Merlin is conceived of as doing. Perhaps some sort of distracting exhibition, like the Norman before Hastings who *pleide tofore þe oostes* by tossing his sword in the air (Trevisa, rendering Higden's . . . *ensem iactando ludens coram exercitibus* . . ., Rolls series ed. of *Polychronicon*, VII, 242). Alternatively, it seems possible that the verb means no more than 'moved'; for senses of this sort see *OED* s.v. Play *v.*, 1, 2. On either interpretation there is no equivalent in LeM, but such touches of added circumstantial detail appear elsewhere in AM (see above, Introduction, pp. 19 and 34). Kölbing, however, understanding the phrase as meaning 'machte ihnen ein zeichen', suggests in his note that lines 6577 and 6578 should be interchanged, the couplet then rendering LeM *Merlins . . . regarda le roy Bohort, et li fist signe que ce auoit il* [Leodegan] *dit por le roy Artu* (159, 7–8). But this would be a quite unparalleled sense for the verb; and 6577 rather renders the direct statement which immediately follows the above in LeM, *et sans faille por li le disoit il*. If we seek to derive from something in LeM, a possibility would be to emend the verb to, say, *leiȝed* 'laughed', making it render LeM's statement that Merlin *commencha a rire* at Leodegan's pointed remark (159, 7), but it would be a unique weak past tense of the verb in AM.

6656 *deden wel*: can be construed unemended; it should refer to deeds in battle, as an equivalent of OF *faire bien*, but is here used ironically, 'did well—(as regards) gold and silver . . .' However, LeM has *saisirent la uiande dont il trouerent* . . . (161, 27), so Kölbing's [*ses*]*eden* very probably restores the original.

6660–2 In LeM Arundel is one of the cities which Arthur garrisoned (AM 6603 ff.), hence this initially detached interest in the battle between the rebel British barons and the Saxons. The AM poet, however, had earlier made it the rebel duke E(u)stas's city (see above, note to lines 3771–2), and he continues to treat it as a rebel refuge in lines 6726 and 7435 (in each case requiring a modification of LeM, which in 163, 3 ff. has the greeting and conferring all take place in the field, and in 188, 19–20 has the booty taken to Cambenic). This spoils the point of the present passage. Later the poet presumably forgets what he has done, and in the story beginning at line 8231 he follows LeM 198, 16 ff. fairly closely, with the men of Arundel clearly Arthur's supporters.

6693 *recoile*: on the source of the diphthong here and in (*de*)*foile* (and in other such cases) see Dobson's *English Pronunciation*, vol. II, § 260; also Liedholm, p. 141. *Recoile* seems best explained by contamination between *reculer* 'retreat' and *recueillir*, *recoillir* 'assemble'; one often retreats, and more often says that one does, in order to assemble one's forces. (*De*)*foile* may be similarly explained, by contamination between (*de*)*foler* 'trample down' and *foiller* 'dig'. Alternatively, *l mouillé* may have arisen in (*de*)*foler* on the analogy of verbs like *bolir* which regularly have it in stem-stressed forms. Liedholm's suggestion that the (rare) variant *defolier* might have been misinterpreted by an English ear, or eye, as containing *l mouillé* is less attractive.

6700 'than storm or thunder overhead'. For the form *vfer* compare Orrm's *uferr* (1715)—not in this sense. Careful examination of the initial letter suggests that the bottom part of the loop (which is all that is clear) is of a form which if continued would be open at the top left, whereas for *o* it would be closed there, hence my reading, but even if it be read *o*, *ofer* 'above' seems preferable to Kölbing's *o fer*. The phrase 'tempest of fire' for a storm with lightning would be as far as I am aware unparalleled, and to make lightning an alternative to thunder in a comparison with a fearful *noise* would be strange.

6713–16 Presumably 'for since the beginning (of the main battle) 15,000 had been killed there in a short time, and previously (i.e. in the attack on the sleeping men, lines 6627 ff.) 13,000 had been killed' (for *first* 'beginning of battle' cf. 8257; the word is commonly used to render OF *commencement*). Neither LeM, EPM, nor Louelich has any equivalent for the present passage, but if the AM poet constructed it himself he did so carelessly, for neither figure is consistent with earlier references. Different manuscripts of LeM, EPM, and Louelich offer variously differing figures for the numbers involved in, and killed in, the different stages of this battle. By *ad hoc* selection one could create a postulated form of LeM whence both the present totals could have been derived, but among so much numerical confusion it would not be worth doing. The figure of 15,000 may perhaps be compounded out of the 4,000 of line 6674 plus the 11,000 implied by 6705–6, although the latter should include the former.

6745 'and keep watch to detect them by the noise their armies will make'. The form *tropie* is probably an error under the influence of *aspie*, as suggested by Liedholm, p. 154. The original was most likely *tropeie* (OF *tropoie*, early *trepei*); for the rhyme compare those of lines 7079–80, 7225–6, and 7263–4. The emendation *troplie* (<OF *tropele(e)* 'troop') approved in Kölbing's 'nachträge und besserungen' (p. 503) is certainly not needed.

6747–8 The equivalent passages in LeM (163, 28–30 and 34–6) relate to his willingness to join in a general attack on the Saxons if the other barons recommend it, though his own advice (as in AM 6739–42) is against it. This agreement to join in a general attack has disappeared in AM's shorter version, and the present passage is something of a misfit with the brief defensive proposal which is substituted.

6757 *comen vp*: LeM has no new landing at this point; the ensuing battle is waged by Saxons already established in Britain.

6770 *fiften c þousinde*: does not directly reflect anything in LeM; the party seems meant to include three groups, with the stated total probably under the influence of the first of them: (i) the 15,000 of line 6784, who in LeM are riding to meet booty being conducted to the Saxon host by leaders with names equivalent to the first nine of lines 6759–68 (164, 9–11; Gondeffles not supported by G¹, but duly by A¹ f. 170ra, 25, and W f. 302rb, 23); (ii) the 40,000 of line 6820, who in LeM seem to represent the whole Saxon force after *li rois des Sesnes* joins the battle (165, 2–4); and (iii) the immense force of line 6836. This last in LeM appears to be the main Saxon host, which *les x rois que ie vous ai dit* thereafter bring upon the Britons (165, 7–8). It is not made clear who these ten kings are, but their identification with the leaders mentioned under (i) is reasonable; whether there were ten names in the source form of LeM, or whether Vargon is added in AM to make up the number, one cannot tell.

6783 *Lanernv*: *ner* represented by a mark of contraction over two minims. This normally represents *un*, but *Launnv* is hardly a possible form; it can represent *uer* in (*n*)*euer*, etc., so Kölbing's *Lauernv* is possible, but LeM evidence, though not wholly clear, suggests *n*.

6787 *socourep*: possibly plural by attraction to *hem*, but see above, note to line 1647.

6802 *bot*: conceivably from *bite* 'taste, experience', but it would be a unique usage of this verb; rather for *bod*, with the phrase then a well-established one—see for instance KA 1049–50. On the *t*-form compare Pearl 617 *abate* (which could, however, be merely an unnatural form for the sake of rhyme); here the *t* perhaps represents unvoicing under the influence of following *þ*.

6810 *Wan þat maiden*: according to LeM he did not capture her, merely *fist . . . maintes beles proeces . . . pour l'amour a la damoisele de Branlanc qu'il voloit auoir a feme a force . . . tant que Gaudin* [*sic*; Gawain should be meant] *le conquist par sa proece* (164, 32–5). A full story of Gaudin's attempt to win the lady, her seeking of help from Arthur, and Gawain's defeat of Gaudin, is developed in the unique set of adventures which in MS. Bibl. Nat. f. fr. 337 replaces the last part of LeM (Sommer, *Livre d'Artus*, pp. 77–8 and 95–106).

6816 *sex†*: manuscript *sexti* is an obvious error; LeM has *plus de $\overset{m}{vj}$* (165, 2).

6817 'as one may say, all for nothing' (because they lost no men in exchange). For this use of *for nouȝt* compare line 5702, where the phrase is linked with *gode chep* (5700); it could also be rendered 'effortlessly', as in line 2889. Kölbing's formidable emendation is quite unnecessary.

6818 *ydreyȝt*: a weak pp. from OE *dragan* (so *OED* s.v. Draw *v.*, A, 3γ); the original form was probably *ydrauȝt*, apprehended by a scribe as one of those which derive from Anglian *æh* and have an equivalent WSax. from *eah*. For the present phrase see *MED* s.v. Drauen *v.*, 1g (b). The line renders LeM *car il n'estoient mie conree, ains s'estoient espandu par toute la terre, li vns cha et li autres la* (164, 42–165, 1), which forbids Liedholm's derivation (p. 117) from OE *dreaht*, pp. of *drecc(e)an* 'afflict'.

6825 *deden forþ*: 'went forward'; this sense of the verb represents a modification of the reflexive application of the sense 'put'. Compare *Cursor Mundi* 6140 (Cotton MS.) *Dos now forth . . . in hi* (the Egyptians speaking to Moses); two other manuscripts have the verb reflexive.

6849 *his nevou Baldemagu*: LeM similarly describes him as accompanied by *Baudemagu son neueu* (165, 18–19), but it is not to him that Urien is said to have given *grant partie de sa terre* (165, 31 = AM 6851) but to Ywain *li auoutres*, Urien's son by his seneschal's wife. Later, however, when Ywain is seeking his mother's leave to go to Arthur, he is made to say '*et vous saues que mes peres a doune sa terre son neueu Baudemagu*' (167, 22). If this discrepancy was present in the form of LeM used by the AM poet, to resolve it in favour of Baudemagu was sensible. Since the loss of part of his inheritance is evidently a grievance which helps to make the legitimate Ywain willing to leave his father, his namesake and close companion on the expedition to seek Arthur is a less satisfactory recipient than Baudemagu, a supporter of the rebel kings.

But, perplexingly, at the later point in AM (7635–60) another of their supporters, Morganor, is substituted for Baudemagu. The relationship ascribed to him could have been extracted for Baudemagu from a careless reading (or corrupt text) of LeM 165, 22–3 *Avoec Yuonet fu Meleagant*

... *et fu fiex au roy Baudemagu de sa premiere feme*, taken to mean '... and Baudemagu was the son of the king by his first wife'; the term *neueu* could then have been understood in its familiar euphemistic sense to make him a bastard son, and he thus could have been associated with Morganor, introduced earlier (4032) as *Vriens sone o bast*. But it is hard to see how any likely variant on *de sa premiere feme* could suggest bastardy, AM 7635–6 is likewise phrased rather for legitimacy, and the earlier reference to Morganor itself appears to rest on nothing in LeM, where he was described (a little earlier yet) merely as *le senescal au roy des c cheualiers* (116, 32–3).

6879 *honteye*: MED compares OF *hontoiier*, and *honteye* can be simply explained as formed on a normal early (western) form **honteier* of that verb. Smithers, however (KA, note to line 3827) regards it as a corruption of *honteys*, itself 'an irregular formation (by the author of KA), with the OF suffix *-eiz*'. If the author was truly bilingual, as Smithers supposes, this would be an acceptable suggestion; but see above, Introduction, p. 71 n. 9.

6881–2 *his : weys*: Liedholm (p. 109) explains the rhyme as in the quality *i*, though imperfect in quantity. This is possible; compare *Sir Orfeo* 95–6 *cri : owy*, and see Bliss's discussion of *owy* on p. xx of his edition. Liedholm alternatively suggests (p. 109 n. 1) that the original may have been *his me(i)ney : wey*, but as all the nine instances of *meine* in rhyme in AM are on *e* (410, 2588, etc.) this is not attractive. It seems to me possible that line 6882 originally concluded *afer, iwys*.

6889 *of mende*: 'worthy of remembrance', and so again in line 8115. Alternatively *mende* can be derived from ON **mynd-*, a mutated form of **mund-* (see above, note to line 3091), but in view of 5288 *bataile of remembraunce* and 7764 *bataile of þincheing* this seems less satisfactory.

6896–7 'Neither could approach, or see, the other over the long distance'; *fele wayes* is equivalent to 6892 *fele mile-way*.

6913 *hem*: in ablative sense, though [*of*] *hem*, as suggested in Kölbing's note, would be much more usual.

6922 *to þe cite*: to Schorham, his city in line 6847; LeM *a sa cite de Sorham* (166, 16).

6930 'and they were besieging Wandlesbiri'; in LeM 166, 24 the party is described as going *al ost qui estoit deuant la cite de Uambieres* (EPM 239, 29 *Valdesbery*), and they reply to Urien's inquiry simply *qu'il estoient au roy Brangoire de Sessoigne*. The manuscript reading could be defended only if Wandlesbiri were a fellow-leader to Brangore (which is plainly nonsense, from line 8217 as well as from LeM), or if the first *And* were a unique survivor into ME, in the sense 'before', of the prepositional use of the word which even in OE is rare, and nowhere recorded in any such context as this. The suggestion in Kölbing's note to emend it to *At* or *In* (retaining *þore*) implies that Brangore was residing in Wandlesbiri, which one might indeed suppose from lines 8217–18 but which would not accord with LeM. The emendation I adopt requires only a slight scribal error to give *fore* (particularly easy as this use of *fore* simplex is comparatively rare in ME; metre would, however, be better with the regular *bifore*), and dittography to give the second *and* for an original pronoun (singular or plural).

6966 *noble biker*: by chivalric standards Urien's attack might rather be considered decidedly ignoble!

6977 Kölbing's note suggests emending *be* to *here* or the like, or we could simply delete the word. Compare lines 5347, 8327; *þis* then becomes a pronoun, as in line 8570. But for the line unemended compare 5131.

6979 *þis ich*: should imply that the number has been given earlier; the poet overlooks that although LeM did so (as 4000, in 166, 38), he did not. The present passage does not rest on LeM; see above, Introduction, p. 16.

6980 *him bihinde*: 'in his rear'; they were on their way to join him, as LeM makes clear (see above, note to line 6930).

7005 *þai*: if correct, Sagremor and his companions; but it is more probably a 'correction' of *he*, treated as though plural, as in line 401, etc. The suggestion in Kölbing's note to emend *him* 7006 to *hem* is less attractive.

7052 *him . . . deden red*: best understood as 'brought rescue to him', a construction paralleled in lines 6857–8 and 8557. *OED* does not record such a noun in this sense, but in formation from the verb represented in line 8596 it would be identical with Redd *sb.*[1] Alternatively *red* could be this verb, a very clumsy use of the periphrastic past tense; or could be the noun meaning 'counsel', but counsel would be of little help to Sagremor here. The phrase does not rest on LeM.

7060 *swiþe and ner*: 'swiftly and (to a spot) near (the battle)', but the construction is awkward and the original may perhaps have been *swiþe and fer*. LeM is not close enough to help.

7094 'If (it is) well begun, let us now do better'; there is no need to emend.

7114 A clumsy line. Even if there be some technical difference between a *helme* and an *ysen hat*, one can obviously not hit one man on both (though line 9727 perhaps refers to the hitting of some men on one, some on the other). Probably there is none, and the poet is just throwing together technical terms; LeM here speaks simply of *le hiaume* (182, 40 and 43).

7115 *plat*: here and in line 9072 Kölbing emends to *fel plat*, on the grounds, stated in his note to 9072, that the verb *plat* is recorded only transitively. Compare, however, *Havelok* 2282 *come plattinde*, with semantic development to 'hasten', probably by way of 'strike the earth with one's feet', a sense comparable with that required here 'fall heavily'. Kölbing does not emend in line 9913, where the verb is again intransitive, *plat on* 'fall upon'.

7121 *a kni3t*: LeM has *et li uilains qui ot amene Gauainet se fu changies de sa forme, et ot prins la fourme d'un cheualier arme* (183, 12–13).

7131 *his limes drou3*: compare KA 2262 *his lymes to him drawe*; there is, however, no need to emend, as proposed in Kölbing's note, to make the phrases identical.

7146 *hem*: Gawain and his *felawe* (7123), as named in lines 7155–7. But it may well be an error for *him*.

7147 *Wele an tventi*: compare KA 93 *Wel a pritty*.

7158 *teld*: 'gave the numbers of', referring to line 7147, but very possibly the original had the regular phrase *of teld* (as in line 360, etc.).

7162 Rather 'defended their people well, (fighting) in the front rank' than 'in the van of their people, fought well', in view of LeM *et quant il voient lor compaignons trop chargies de colps, si les deliurent* (184, 17–18).

7168–9 '. . . because of his great haste hit him with the flat of his sword'; LeM explains that Gawain allowed Oriel to pass him, then quickly turned his horse to get in his blow, *si le fiert parmi le hiaume, si fu du plat de l'espee, car trop se hasta de ferir, si qu'il ne sot comment il l'assenoit* (184, 26–8).

7204 *Ac Oriens slou3*: 'but (they) killed Oriens' men'; the use of *Oriens* in successive lines as first objective and then possessive is probably a deliberate trick of style, and it would be a pity to remove it, as Kölbing's note proposes, by emending *Oriens* here to *pai* or the like.

7250 *tronsoun*: LeM (186, 18–19) specifies this as a *tronchon de lanche* 'broken piece of a lance'; no doubt such broken lance-shafts were often used as staves.

7266 Probably 'in uncountable numbers', with the awkward introduction of *tong* by reminiscence of such a phrase as *swiche . . . pat no tong telle no mi3t pe haluendel* (2114–16; similarly 7975–6) 'such that nobody could recount the half of it'. But possibly we should here understand 'which (spectacle) nobody could describe'.

7286 *fresche*: Kölbing's *f[l]esche*, by comparison with line 3660, is quite unnecessary, as Kaluza points out in his review (col. 270). The circumstances are in fact entirely different in the two cases; here they are feasting on meat both fresh-killed and preserved, but there Merlin is laying in stocks, for which fresh meat would be useless but preserving-salt most necessary.

7279 *Ac*: very possibly dittographed for an original *And*, as Kölbing's note suggests.

7305 *fel on croice*: probably 'bowed down'. *Crouche* n. is regular in ME for 'cross' (<OE *crūc*); the homonym meaning 'bowing down' (from ME

crouche v., itself of disputed etymology but most probably from OE *crochir*) is not recorded till later, but may nevertheless have existed in ME. I suggest then that ME *croise*, a synonym of the former (<OF *croiz*), has been taken as a synonym also of the latter. Compare an extension of the sense of *hond* by a similar process (see above, note to line 190); in that case, however, in contrast to the present one, the normal sense could easily be apprehended as symbolic of the extended one, which would promote the general acceptance of the extension.

7342 *Brekenham*: LeM *Brekeham* (187, 21), but when the name reappears a little later (188, 7 as *Bresqueham*, but A¹ f. 179ᵛᵃ, 32 has *Brekeham*) AM 7391 has *Rokingham*, which the poet presumably identified with his earlier *Rokingham* (3640–3776), though there LeM has *Bedingran* (108, 9, etc.; W f. 172ʳᶜ, 21, etc. *Bredigan* and similar forms), a name which when it reappears is treated in AM as though a distinct place *Bedingham* (7684 = LeM 190, 7, etc.).

7354 'into fragments as small as vetch-seeds'. On uses of the word *tare* see *OED*. It was probably first used in English of wheat, the sense of its source, MDu *tarwe*, as the existence of *wiilde tare* 'vetch' implies (vetch is a common weed of corn); the use of *tare* unqualified in the same sense is presumably a simplification of this phrase. The word is commonly used with reference to small size. In later instances this will certainly be of vetch-seed, but the present case, considerably the earliest known to *OED*, may well antedate the shift of meaning, in which case we should understand here '. . . as small as grains of corn'.

7379 *schosen*: *sch-* as a variant of *ch-* is regular in various words of French origin (*chamelet, chartre, chauncell*, etc.), and is thence extended to native words, as in *schalk(e)* beside *chalk* (on all these see *MED*). Such forms are rare before late ME, however, and in the present case the initial *s* could easily be mere scribal error in copying *þo chosen*.

7381 *þe lord of þe toun sori*: rendering LeM *le segneur de la dolerouse tour* (188, 5); *toun* very probably represents a mere copying error. *Brandris* is his proper name; LeM does not give it here, but later refers to *Brandelias li sires de la dolerouse tor* (A¹ f. 219ʳᵇ, 34–5; G¹ 294, 39, has an obviously erroneous *et* after the name).

7458 *l[e]ft*: manuscript *laft* is hardly a possible form; it doubtless arises from regularising of the rhyme after an original *scheft* 7457 had been normalized (so Liedholm, p. 45).

7466 *made to deþ legge*: properly 'caused to be struck down dead'; the weakening of *make* to a mere auxiliary is similar to that familiar with *do*. *MED* (s.v. Leien v. (1), 12 (a)) instead sees *legge* as = 'lie'. It certainly seems to have that sense in line 9025, but 'lie to death' is strange phrase for 'fall down dead'.

7469–70 *þurth-þrest, of-smiten*: an editor is forced to choose between treating such forms as single word, hyphenated compound, or two words;

as in other cases (see above, note to line 915) there is no clear difference in ME. I use a hyphen where the affix element appears to be restricted to a position preceding the main one, and yet has the same sense as in contexts where it can be more freely disposed. So in these past-participial adjectives; compare on the one hand verbal groups such as 7950–1 *was . . . of koruen, smiten of* . . ., on the other cases where the prefix has a distinctive sense, as in *ofsend* 'send for'.

7476 *l[e]gge*: manuscript *ligge* results no doubt from regularizing of the rhyme after an original *regge* 7475 had been normalized; on the rhyme as emended compare 8441–2.

7484 *alenge*: if genuine, the form is influenced by OE *leng(u)* 'length', but the original may well have been *alange* (: *range*); see Liedholm, p. 8.

7500 *lord*: emendation to *god*, following Ellis's silent alteration in *Specimens of . . . Romances*, would give an acceptable rhyme (quantitative identity not being demanded).

7519 *[þer]wiþ*: for use, as here, to add a near-synonymous phrase, see the description of Nimrod in *Cursor Mundi* 2203–4 as . . . *stiif in stur* | *And þer-wit was he gret werrour*. Alternatively one might emend to *ywis*; the unusual (though possible) rhyme would then be the reason for the corruption. The manuscript unemended gives neither sense nor metre, though Kölbing retains it (without discussion).

7525 *smiten*: it is likely enough, as suggested in Kölbing's note, that this is dittographed from the previous line for an original *dede* or the like.

7546, 8 'On the next day our Christians were at once sought for'. The construction is awkward; possibly line 7546 originally ran *Amorwe souȝt* . . ., then with dittographic error *Amorwe we souȝt*, falsely 'corrected' to give the actual manuscript form. Kölbing's *Amorwe w[as] souȝt*, requiring an impersonal usage which would be as far as I am aware unparalleled, seems less attractive.

7581 The unemended reading is defended by Liedholm, p. 167. But apart from requiring a verbal form improbable in this text (see above, note to line 782), and an exceptional phrase *kniȝtes þousandes* 'thousands of knights', this also loses a specific numerical equivalence with LeM *et furent bien $\frac{m}{ij}$* (189, 22). Further, though this is a comparatively minor point, it offers a metrically doubtful line. I adopt Kölbing's straightforward *He [tok] kniȝtes*; the error might more easily have arisen had the original been *He kniȝtes þousandes tok to*, but there seems no reason why the poet should have used such a word-order.

7599 'If I hear you speak another word . . .'; on the conditional without either expressed *ȝif* or inversion compare lines 2481–2 (see my note, above). Kölbing's insertion of *if* gives a metrically unsatisfactory line.

7603 *þis lond*: presumably *þe lond of Canbernic* (7302), which they avoid because they have suffered in it severely from ambush in the forest.

7628 *Belisent*: should probably be seen not as morphologically un-inflected but as the idiomatically uninflected member of a split genitive group; similarly in L 1058 *Godes nome and seynte Marie*, and compare also A 1668–9 (see my note, above). This type would seem to be extended from the one usual with two nouns in apposition (as in 2571 *þe doukes man Tintagel*); see Jesperson, *Progress in Language*, p. 301. The extension will be by way of such cases as *kinges douhter and emperour* (Auchinleck *Guy of Warwick*, stanzaic section, 5, 8), in which the 'king and emperor' is one man. It is however noticeable that in many cases of such idioms the uninflected member is one which can also appear uninflected when single, which makes confident analysis difficult.

7637 *Morganor*: on his perplexing introduction here, and in line 7660, see above, note to line 6849.

7640 *h[i]m*: manuscript *hem* would represent Uriens and his *oþer quen* (7635), but in view of *his owen* 7659 the emendation seems reasonably certain.

7647–8 '... into any war where it befell me to be the victor'; lines 7646–8 render LeM '*et moult seroie recreans se ie chi demoroie em lieu ou ie ne puis nule proece faire*' (167, 34–5). My emendation seems the slightest that will serve. Kölbing reconstructs extensively, making the first part of line 7648 echo 7647 closely (*in werre* is to be understood after *come*, as he explains in his note); this is rather rewriting than emending.

7688 *iiii̇̇ m*: 80,000. Kölbing, in reading simply *XX m*, presumably assumes (though he nowhere says so) that the scribe meant to correct *iiii* to *xx*. But he clearly intended the complex form; he specially left space for the *xx* by making the last two minims of the *iiii* shorter than the first two. The poet, too, clearly intended the figure; it reappears as *four score m* in line 8212, and agrees with the total of advance-guard, main body, and rearguard in lines 7726–37, though it is larger than any figure which can be found in or inferred from LeM for this force.

7709 *vnder*: 'close to'; normally only of something which rises above one, as a town, wall, or wood (cf. line 5833 *vnder þe toun*). Extension to where there is no feeling of difference of level is unknown to *OED*; the present may be a unique instance.

7716 *tare*: perhaps 'lacerated with his nails', but I think rather 'rent his garments' (see above, note to line 5817).

7725 *þat soudan*: the leader responsible for the ravaging reported to Yder; this line is a rather clumsy reminder of 7690.

7741–2 'however, there were two or three miles between each division'; thus of the ten miles only four to six was actually occupied by men. Alternatively *naþeles* might be taken to imply 'moreover' (cf. line 5750), in which case the ten miles would be occupied by men and the length from van to rear would be 14–16 miles.

7749 *þrust*: if the form is correct this belongs to *þrest* (<ON *þrýsta*). There is no assured instance in our text of *u* for the vowel derived from *ȳ*, however (on two possible cases see above, note to line 5984), and as Liedholm suggests (p. 50) the original may well have been *þrast* (<OE *þrǣstan*), rhyming on *last* (for which form in rhyme cf. 8255 and 9263).

7754 *chon*: as far as I am aware, a unique transitive use of the verb *chine*; it could of course be avoided by inserting *in* before *deþ*.

7764 *bataile of þincheing*: compare line 6889, and see my note, above.

7785 The point of this line does not appear from AM; the equivalent in LeM is, however, appropriate to the situation as there described. See below, note to lines 7853–4.

7812 *Bedingram*: the reading *Bedingam* is legitimate, though this scribe cannot be shown to use the superscript to represent merely *a*, but the town ordinarily appears with *ra*, either spelt out or represented by the superscript, in the manuscripts of LeM which I have seen, at the point equivalent to this (191, 21) and elsewhere. See further above, note to line 3657.

7825 *Gaher[i]et*: so spelt everywhere else in AM; the manuscript form here is almost certainly an error under the influence of *Sagremoret* in the next line.

7848 *ratled*: the original and principal sense of the verb is certainly of sound (MDu *rotelen*, *ratelen*, from the noun *ratele* 'rattle', etc.). It occurs three times in KA, and is glossed by Smithers 'make a flapping sound', which would also be a suitable sense here. However, the verb *roten*, which seems to be derived from, if it is not a mere error for, the present verb, occurs in the phrase *se þe baners roten* (3867, see my note, above), which suggests extension to the appearance as well as the sound of a fluttering flag. Nothing in the present context, or those in KA, requires a sense of sound, and it seems quite likely that the verb came to mean simply 'flutter'.

7853–4: '. . . for they had previously, bravely, killed five (thousand)', referring to the killing described in lines 7801–3; they had been attacked by 15,000 (7789). The emendation *Þa[i]* seems essential; Kölbing's elaborate reconstruction is not attractive.

The details of the battle are obscure in AM, as a result of failure to adjust LeM's description to the rather different position assumed. In LeM (pp. 190 ff.) the Ywains have reached Arundel (on its loyalties see above, note to lines 6660–2), and wish to make for Bedingram, whither the way lies eastward across the *pons (de) Dian(n)e* (AM *þe brigge Drian*, reflecting the corrupted *Drianne* found in W, 196, footnote 2), but their way is blocked by heathens under Soriondes, who are encamped and resting near Bedingram and plundering the district as far as almost to Carduel. The heathens, however, then move west to plunder around

Arundel, in the territory of Yder of Cornwall, and the Ywains therefore suppose their way to Bedingram to be now clear (a supposition reflected in AM 7785, though the reasons for it are not given). They set out, but the bridge is guarded by a division of Soriondes' men under Bylas, 14,000 strong; this division is described as Soriondes' *auant-garde* because he has now turned back from Cornwall, bringing Bylas ahead of his new line of march. When the Ywains cross the bridge Bylas' men fall upon them, but they recross the bridge and are able to defend themselves at its western end, since Bylas' men now have to cross it to attack them. (This encounter appears in AM 7786–94. The difference in the numbers of Bylas' men is part of the numerical variations recorded above, note to line 7688; the AM poet is forced to eliminate the recrossing of the bridge because he has taken the Ywains to be going westwards towards Arundel instead of eastwards from it.)

Meanwhile Gawain has left Logres (= London), and is approaching the battle from the east by way of Carduel and Bedingram, while Soriondes, after a delay caused by his having to turn back against Yder, is approaching from the west, an approach which appears in AM 7805–10. His leading division arrives and takes the Ywains in the rear (AM 7866), but at the same time Gawain is seen approaching from the other side of the bridge, in Bylas' rear. The Ywains therefore suddenly cross the bridge, pursued over it by Soriondes' leading division (AM 7867; the Ywains' crossing does not appear), and, hard pressed by Bylas' men (now—193, 10—said to number 10,000, a discrepancy from which the AM poet seems to have inferred the killings of the present passage), turn and ride parallel with the river, but are trapped *en j pre entre ij riuieres* (this situation, and the sudden move which led to it, are reflected confusedly in AM 7895–8 and 7930–9). Then Agravain arrives, from what is now the Ywains' side of the main river (AM 7911 *on her side*), while Soriondes' main body is still approaching from the other side (AM 7901–2). Approaching, too, are carts of booty, which later arrive at the bridge but cannot pass while the battle continues, so their conductors encamp (195, 15–23). This is reflected rather confusedly in AM 8049 ff.; 8059–60 render Soriondes' instructions to the conductors '*Ore gardes que vous soies moult bien aparellie, et que vous aidies a nostre gent se mestier est*' (195, 25–7).

From the description in AM it would appear that the Ywains cross the bridge only once, in a westerly direction, and encounter Bilas just west of it; Soriandes is then either further west, which makes nonsense of 7866 ff., or (most improbably, since he has been plundering and fighting far west in Cornwall) he is approaching from the east, in which case Gawain's forces must come from the west, and Bedingham/Bedingram is west of Arundel, which conflicts with lines 7684–5 taken with 7783–4.

7894 *reke*: although ON *reki* is found only in the sense 'prosecution of a suit at law', the underlying sense was no doubt 'act of driving' (cf. *reka hesta* 'drive a horse'), and extension of sense to 'haste' is easy to understand.

7904 *þe tail*: 'the rear', here apparently used for the whole force except the vanguard (which had entered the battle already, 7865 ff.). *OED* does not know the word used of a force of men before the sixteenth century, but compare KA 3261 *Her tayl is kytt of, hundreþes fyue* (of the Macedonians).

7929 [*his*] *rede*: the line renders LeM *A chest conseil que Yuones li auoltres dist s'acordent bien tuit li autre compaignon* (193, 23–4). Some emendation is essential; there is little to choose between *his* and *þis*.

7945 *wiþ*: 'amid'; cf. KA 7976 *wiþ al þe fare* 'amidst all the commotion' (so Smithers, 'Notes on ME Texts', 215–16).

7970 *on steden sat*: line 7943 implies that they had been unhorsed; that they were remounted is left unstated. LeM is explicit, *Yuones li grans et Yuonet ses freres estoient abatu a terre moult laidement, mais il furent tost remis a cheual* (193, 42–194, 2).

7987 *þe oþer*: the Christians; the opposite side to that last mentioned (in lines 7985–6).

8012 *He asked h[i]m*: a scribe no doubt took *he* as singular and so 'corrected' the object to the plural (see above, Introduction, p. 61 and n. 4).

8019–20 An awkward rendering of LeM *les . . . a ces armeures miparties de blanc et de vermeil* (195, 4). One suspects corruption; perhaps the original had *. . . on riȝte half armes | And red on left half of her armes.*

8022 *him*: Ywain *þe hende*, but as Kölbing's note suggests the original was probably *hem*.

8039 *hadden born*: the object, exceptionally, is understood from the previous line, but the original was quite probably *had hem born; hadhē* could easily enough be misread as *haddē*.

8040 *Bedingha†m*: see above, note to line 3657.

8049 They were conducting the wagon-train, laden with plunder; see above, note to lines 7853–4.

8073 Metre would be improved if we read *. . . and [wiþ] battes.*

8077 *þe feld oȝain*: an unusual variant on *in(to) þe feld* 'to the ground'. One is tempted to identify here instead the regular phrase *bere oȝain* 'drive back' (cf. 8039 etc.); LeM makes it clear that the Christians were driven back before the arrival of Sagremor: *. . . trop estoient li enfant iouene et tendre; si les conuint ruser, et trop i eussent perdu quant Saigremoret vint poignant . . . si se fierent en els si durement que toute la cache en est arestee* (195, 30–3). This is possible if *þurth* is taken to be doing 'double duty' (see above, note to line 885); the sense would then be 'for which reason they drove back through the field . . .'—for *þurth* in this unusual sense of 'over the surface of' compare *Sir Gawain and the Green Knight* 2162 *Ridez þurȝ þe roȝe bonk ryȝt to þe dale.* If so, however, *Mani* in the next line would be odd; all rather than many would be driven back.

8086 '(who) were remounted'. The one word *bachelers* conceals a slight shift of attention; those who achieved the killing of line 8084 would be of Sagremor's newly arrived company (LeM 195, 35–6 *si y feri tant Saigremoret et li sien que maint Sesne i ot abatu*), while those remounted would be the ones referred to in lines 8077–8. Kölbing's suggested *o[f]* would avoid assuming this shift. Accepting a phrase with *of* opposite in sense to the regular *bring on hors*, etc., we would have for lines 8085–6 the sense '(who) were felled from their horses in the field by our squires'. But perfect logicality is not to be required of the poet; there is no need to emend.

8087 *to*: possibly an error for *so*, which would give a regular phrase, but the unemended text gives good sense.

8098 *f[om]en*: accepting the emendation put forward in Zupitza's review of Kölbing, p. 94.

Drein: originally probably *Drian*, as in line 7867, rhyming on *oȝan*, but altered following normalization of the latter.

8120 *fers*: in OF subject form not only of *fier* 'mighty, proud etc.', but also of *ferm* 'resolute', and both may have contributed to the ME sense. On such (exceptional) survivals of subject forms in English see Bliss, 'Imparisyllabic Nouns'; here the fact that the word would frequently be used of a man, in emotionally charged contexts, in nominative and vocative applications, may have encouraged the survival.

8131–2 *lift:smit*: on the rare pa. t. sg. *smit* see Bülbring's *Geschichte des Ablauts . . .*, pp. 116–17; it is to be regarded as weak, rather than strong with the vowel of pa. t. pl. and pp. On the rare type of rhyme (unique in AM) see Gadow's Introduction to his edition of *Owl and Nightingale*, § 18, 5. The combination of rare form with rare rhyme makes one suspect corruption, however; possibly the original was *left:reft*.

8150 *pruaunce*: from its form, should rest on the OF noun *pro* 'profit, advantage' (cf. *joiance* 'joyfulness', from *joie* by way of *joiant* 'joyful'), but its sense here is probably rather that of *proëce*, formed on *pro* adj. 'valiant'. Since deeds of prowess will also be deeds of advantage to one's own side, situations for a transfer of sense would easily arise; the process would be like that in later English in which *durance* takes on the sense of *duress*. Indeed, Wartburg's *Wörterbuch* (IX, 419) records *prouance*, once, in OF in the present sense (in an eastern dialect).

8218 *made hem ioie and miri*: a blended construction: *made ioie* and *made hem miri* would both be regular (cf. respectively 2007, etc., and 6559, etc.).

8241 They are in several places in LeM described as related to the king(s) of Strangore, but not in any form that would justify *erles sones* here. It may reflect confusedly LeM's description of the defenders of Arundel, the three Ywains and Gosonains *d'Estrangore* (see below, note to lines 8266–70) as *tout haut homme et poisant, comme fils de rois et de contes et de dus* (199, 27).

8250 *þe etenild*: an incomprehensible form, probably corrupt. Possibly the original was *þe etenisse*, and the alteration follows some corruption in the proper name *Daril*. As neither LeM nor EPM knows of any character with a name like *Daril*, nor does either attach any cognomen to its equivalent of *Bramagne*, there is no useful basis for taking speculation further.

8254–5 Rendering LeM *Et si tost comme li Sesne les virent venir si lieuent le hui et lor courent sus tout a desroi* (198, 39–40). *So†* for *Sone* (dittographed) seems certain.

8266–70 The first three Ywains come directly from the equivalent passage in LeM, *Yuonet as blances mains et Yuones de Lionel et Yuones li esclarois* (199, 23–5); the fourth probably replaced LeM's *Gosonains d'Estrangore* by dittographic error at some stage of transmission (not in the copying of AM itself, in view of 8297–8 *þis Ywains | Alle four*). Dedinet probably comes from a passage listing those who did well in the battle that now begins: *Daudinaus li souages et Yuonet as blances mains et Yuonet de Lyonel et Gosenain d'Estrangort et Kex Destraus et Kehedins li petis* (200, 26–8). One would naturally assume from this that he was with the Ywains, but for two other passages which place him instead with Kay Destran and Kehedin, both when they set out to seek Arthur (pp. 173–4) and when they finally achieve knighthood at Arthur's hands (252, 37–8, though there he is defined only by parentage, as *fils au roy Belinant de Norgales*). The first of these passages is not rendered in AM and may perhaps have been missing in the underlying version of LeM; the second is well beyond the point at which AM comes to an end.

8278 *Til what*: a rare, if not unique, phrase, probably a blend of regular *til þat* (as in line 1860, etc.) and *al what* (7704, 9732).

8337 [*grade*]: compare line 7306. We could alternatively emend *gun* to *gradden*, with Smithers (KA, note to line 1231); there seems little to choose.

8343 *his*: if this is correct, lines 8342–4 refer to Lot, to whom as leader the actions of his force are ascribed. But the transition to 8345 is awkward, and probably *He* 8342, 4 was intended as plural, *his* being a 'correction' of *her* on the assumption that *He* was singular.

8348 *Þat*: the construction resembles that in line 6462 (see my note, above), though here the easiest way to interpret it is perhaps with 'they' understood as subject of *astint*. There is at all events no need to follow the suggestion of Kölbing's note to read *Þa[i]*. LeM gives no help.

8350 *todrawe*: I take it 'drag off (to Hell)'; but it could be 'tear to pieces'.

8354 *duȝst*: on the spelling see reference in note to line 4472 above.

8361 *bad þe time mesauenture*: 'asked for misfortune on the time . . .', i.e. 'cursed the time . . .'. The phrase renders LeM *maldit l'eure et le iour* (201, 18); the same phrase was earlier rendered *acurssed . . . þe time* (7717; LeM 193, 1–2).

8369 LeM makes it clear that Lot was afraid of the imminent fall of the city, *car li mur estoient fendu en mains lieus et li rois Harans estoit tout entor logies, et si n'auoit mie gent en sa compaignie par coi il se puisse contretenir granment* (201, 21–3).

8385 *lene*: 'rest', reflecting LeM *il* [the disguised Merlin] . . . *voit les damoisiaus sor les murs en haut, qui moult grant ioie demenerent li vn as autres* (202, 9–11), with an understandable, though admittedly unparalleled, semantic extension to 'rest, take one's ease', without reference to posture. Alternatively, of course, the word can be read *leue*, with Kölbing. He presumably understands the verb from OE *lǣfan*, but a sense like 'remain' (so Liedholm, p. 61) would not fit very well. Or we could derive it from OF (*se*) *lever* (for the only recorded instance in English, not intransitive as here, see *OED* s.v. Leve *v.*³), in which case the line renders LeM *il* . . . *monterent as creniaus en haut* (201, 9–10), but the word in French is used of rising from a sitting or lying position, not mounting to a higher place. If *leue* is to be read, then either *rene* 8386 is in fact *reue* (see next note), or the rhyme is of a very rare type (but not impossible; see above, note to lines 3447–8).

8386 *wiþ gret rene*: 'at full gallop'; LeM has . . . *venoit par deuant le chastel les grans galos* (202, 8–9). Kölbing accepts *reue* (glossed 'eile'). So does Liedholm, suggesting that 'in all probability it goes back to OF *re(s)ver, raver* (= ramble, etc. . . . .; note also the OF adj. *reve* = violent) and rather means "great excitement" here' (p. 62). This sense, however, does not accord well with LeM.

8420 'if my friends should die . . .'.

8430–58 The details of this mistreatment are obscure in AM; several of the features are reproduced confusedly or out of order. In LeM (203, 24–39) the lady is first being pulled along by her hair by Taurus (W, f. 225ᵛᵇ, 42; A¹ and G¹ both corrupt) behind his horse, but is encumbered by her dress. She cries for help to Mary, and as often as she does so Taurus hits her in the face, until he knocks her down; then he puts her before him on his horse. She deliberately falls off (twice in EPM 299, 2–6), crying that she will never accept his love, and he then drags her along by the hair beside his horse, beating her, until she is all bloody and can no longer stand or cry out.

8449 *vpriȝt*: regularly in ME an equivalent of LeM *tout estendu* (so EPM, *passim*), though LeM has not, in fact, that phrase at the points equivalent to this line or 9098.

8459 *Wawain to*: in LeM (203, 40–1) the question is addressed to Gawain. As soon as it is put to him that he should recognize the lady he does so, and there is no equivalent of the declaration of AM 8463–4. Kölbing's [*to Wawain*] brings 8459 into accord with LeM but makes this declaration, which becomes a continuation of the speech, very awkward, whereas it is perfectly sensible in a reply. I prefer to see here a modification of LeM, whether deliberate or casual.

8477 *þou drawest amis*: if this means 'you are wrongfully dragging' it is a curiously weak way of putting it; in the equivalent passage in LeM Gawain speaks of *la dame que mar la batistes* (204, 5). I think it more likely that *drawe amis* is a hitherto unrecorded translation-borrowing of OF *mestraire* 'act wrongfully'.

8489 *wiþ main and schof*: 'with might and thrusting', i.e. 'with a mighty thrust'. The original, however, may well have been *wiþ main schof* (cf. line 8879).

8491 *hert-polk*: the image would seem to be of blood within the heart like water in a water-pit or well. It is possible that the same sort of image appears in KA 2246, 4450 *hert(e)-pyt(t)*, though Smithers's derivation (Glossary) from MDu *pit* 'kernel of fruit' is of course equally possible.

8493–4 This furious conduct is rather more fully described in LeM, and the reason given, *car il ne lor estoit mie encore asses de ce que Gauaine en auoit fait, ains en font petites pieces* (204, 15–16).

8536 *ablewe*: evidently a reference to 'mouth to mouth breathing', the most ancient method of artificial respiration, and now again in favour. LeM has merely *il le baise et pleure moult durement* (205, 4).

8548 *welcome*: see above, note to line 3546.

8553–4 'that she should never see his lord until Arthur and he (Lot) . . .'. This was done to put pressure on Lot to make peace, as is clear in LeM *et iurent bien li iiij frere que iamais ne raura li rois Loth sa feme lor mere en sa compaignie deuant che qu'il aura fait pais au roy Artu* (205, 17–19). Although Gawain's *lord* is of course his father Lot (cf. line 4622) one would rather expect here *hir lord*; this may well have been the original reading, 'corrected' by a scribe who took *he* for the masculine.

8558 *an eld vauasour*: In line 7053 he was an *eld cherl*, correctly representing LeM, which calls him *vilain* (181, 31) and gives a full description of his rough appearance (180, 15–18). At the present point (p. 205) LeM gives no description, and *vauasour* probably reflects simply failure of memory by the AM poet.

8653 *bi fe, for wining*: respectively 'hired for wages' and 'in the hope of booty or generous reward'. Compare Lot's 5,000 mercenaries (*of purchas*), and 3,000 attracted by his reputation for, among other things, *largesse*, in lines 4388–93. There is no need for the unusual derivation of *fe* here from AN *fee*, *fie* 'obligation, service', suggested by Liedholm (p. 90).

8660 *sour*: compare *Promptorium Parvulorum* (Mayhew's ed., cols. 416 and 423), in which *soore*, *sowre* appears as synonym of *fylþ*, glossing *limus*, *cenum*, *lutum*. Björkman ('Scandinavian Loan-Words', 72) derives it from ON *saurr* (OSw *sør*) 'dirt'; Liedholm accepts this, suggesting that the form was influenced by OE *sūr*, 'the association in meaning may easily be imagined: sour∼turbid∼dirty' (p.127). In fact *sūr* has a sense which could yield the present one directly, in the compound *sūr-ēagede*, ME **sur-eʒhedd* (Orrm, Burchfield's reconstructed form from Vliet's transcription;

see his 'Words copied by Van Vliet', 103). An extension from a bleary eye to a muddied river (in both cases opposed to a clear one) is easy to understand, and the word is then one with the well-established nominal use of *sour* adj.

8672 *Of beten gold*: the phrase directly reproduces OF *a or batu* (not here in LeM, however), in which *batu* qualifies the thing worked with gold; a logically sounder adoption appears in line 5643. For discussion and parallels see Smithers's note to KA 1032.

8672–3 '. . . of various styles, according to how (they) displayed their armorial bearings', or perhaps simply '. . . how (they) wore their armour'. A smoother reading would be given by the simple emendation [w]ar, 'according to what their armorial bearings were'.

8679 *ich armour*: 'each piece of armour', an unparalleled use of the word in English. The Tobler–Lommatsch *Wörterbuch* records for OF *armëure* the sense 'Rüstungsstück' beside usual 'Rüstung', but none of the instances quoted in support require as definitely singular a sense, 'one element of a full suit of armour' as the present case would. In LeM, moreover, there is only a single kiss at the end of the arming (219, 24–6). One is tempted to suggest that the AM poet originally wrote *at þis ich arming*, or the like, and that *armour* results from an attempt to correct the line after loss of *þis* in copying.

8680 *maden*: elsewhere in AM *maiden*, and this is very probably a simple error, but it is a legitimate form (cf. *sade*, etc. from *say*); the same scribe earlier in the manuscript wrote *madenes* (*Floris and Blancheflour*, Taylor's ed. 899).

8701–2 *nevou:retour*: apparently an isolated extension of the type of rhyming licence noticed above, note to line 1329.

8713 *Gremporemole*: in LeM *groing poire mele* (218, 19), apparently an epithet meaning 'muzzle like a soft pear'; the 'soft pear' may be descriptive, pejorative (*poir molle* can signify a valueless thing), or both. See full discussion in Ackerman's 'Wild Man Knight'.

8723–4 '(that) he had given you five towns (if this would secure that) he was . . .', admissible colloquial syntax; it is not necessary to regularize, as Kölbing's note suggests, by emending *He* 8724 to *And*. LeM has, straightforwardly, *anchois que li rois Rions vous escape il voldroit estre en son pais tous nus par ensi qu'il li eust couste tout le millor cite qu'il ait* (215, 31–3).

8760 *vnspa[n]d*: OE *spannan* is strong; the weak form here probably reflects influence from ON *spenna*, of which a derivative appears in *Ancrene Riwle* in a sense not unlike the present one, . . . *vnspende his fader tunge in to prophecie* (Titus, Mack's ed., 47, 9; other MSS. have the same or variants). What the mechanics of the 'unspanning' of the dragon, to let it start casting fire, may have been conceived to be one cannot tell.

8780 *þat þai nouȝt schrof*: '(of) which (arrival on the scene) they were unaware'; LeM has *la ot moult grant ochision ains que cil del ost s'en aperchusent quel gent ce estoient* (220, 12–13). The sense 'not concern oneself' for *nouȝt schriue* is well attested in OE and ME; the semantic development is presumably from the basic sense 'make no decree' through 'do nothing' (about something one knows of). An equally possible line of development would be 'make no provision' (because unaware of circumstances calling for action), and hence the sense suggested here. This sense would also suit KA 3892 *Alisaunder nouȝth of hym shroof*, making Alexander unaware of rather than aware of but unconcerned about the approach of a (disguised) assassin, though Smithers glosses in the latter sense.

8785 Smithers ('Notes on ME Texts', 216–17) proposes to read *And tohewen hem to deþ ond † gerten* 'and cut them in pieces and smote them to death', assuming that the (postponed) *and*, perhaps in the form *an, on*, was mistaken as part of a compound and a further ampersand then inserted. However, though *on gerten* (cf. 9777 *On a paien . . . he girt*) certainly seems an anticlimax after *tohewen . . . to deþ*, the manuscript can well enough be read unemended.

8797 *on of þe grest*: the original was quite probably *on þe grest*.

8802 On the line as emended, compare RCL 4643 *Trumpes blewen, tabours dasshen* (the verbs are finite, intransitive). The scribal substitution of *beten* for *blowen* would be either because of the proximity of *tabours*, which are regularly 'beaten', or because the phrase *trumpes beten* 'trumpets of hammered-out metal' was for some reason in the scribe's mind. An alternative emendation would be *Drummes* for *Trumpes*; *d* and *t* are not dissimilar (especially when *t* is formed with the cross-stroke sloping slightly downwards to the right), and an initial *d* obscured by rubrication could well be misread as *t*, with the resultant *trummes* then miscorrected. A line linking near-synonyms, however, is less satisfactory than one joining the usual pair of trumpet and drum. I retain the rather awkward syntax of the manuscript; an original *blowing* would make the error harder to understand.

8804 *Tireing togging*: referring no doubt to the method of felling an enemy in a close mêlée by seizing him and dragging him from his horse; similarly 8873 *wristling . . . togging*.

8842 *Hou manliche þat*: apparently a blend of *hou manliche* and *hou þat*.

8879 *main*: so Smithers ('Notes on ME Texts', 218 note 2), on the authority of Mr. Dobie, then Keeper of Manuscripts in the National Library of Scotland, against the *mani* read by Turnbull and Kölbing. He is certainly right; the stroke is made to the second of the final three minims. Displacement of stroke one minim to the right of an *i* is very common in this hand; displacement left would be an error (such as occurs, and is corrected, in 6054 *miȝt*.)

8884 ff. The obscurity of the family relationships here is carried over from LeM. They are clearer in other parts of the Vulgate cycle. The Grail story (see conveniently the *Aventures . . . del . . . Graal*, Sommer, pp. 96–8) explains that the first Nascien took that name on his baptism by Joseph of Arimathea. Because of his great love and faith God granted him a vision of the Grail, *dont onques cheualiers n'auoit gaires veu a celui tans se Ioseph non.* His son, Celidoine, the first king of Scotland, was also a faithful servant of Christ. Celidoine's son was king Narpus, and *his* son was the second Nascien (*de Betique, de Berique*, or *d'Orberique*), called so in remembrance of his great-grandfather. The royal line continued; king Ban was the seventh of the line after Celidoine. Ban's son was Lancelot, and *his* son Galahad. Further, in *Livre d'Artus* (see above, note to line 6810), the Nascien of the present story declares that he is *filz de la Dame de la Blanche Nue, qui fu du parente Ioseph, et sa cosine du tierz genoill*; he is also told '*tu apartiens de par ta mere au lignage Ioseph, et de par ton pere au lignage Celidoine, qui fu filz Nascien*' (246, 33–4; 261, 3–4).

The form in LeM reflects confusion between the three Nasciens, and a general telescoping of generations. Our Nascien was *fiex Hauingues* [properly *Haningnes?*], *qui fu de la seror Iosep* (221, 33–4), or according to W, *cousins germains Joseph d'Arimacie, car il fu fils aisnez de la sereur Joseph* (f. 233^{vc}, 7–10); and he was *parent prochain Celidoine, le fils al duc Nascien de Betique, qui la grant merueille del Graal vit premierement* (221, 35–7). AM goes with W in making Nascien's mother Joseph's sister rather than the daughter of his sister, but with G[1] in naming her, and in not specifying Joseph as of Arimathea (8891–2); lines 8899–8902 directly render LeM 221, 35–7, though taking the wrong antecedent for *qui . . . vit*. The other relationships in AM (8893, 8904–5) come straightforwardly from LeM and raise no difficulties.

8897–8 'In whose persons . . . England was glorious'; *ali3t* renders LeM *enluminee* (221, 35).

8908 Reflects a promise in LeM, *. . . dont li contes vous deuisera toutes les estoires les vns apres les autres si comme eles auendront de iour en iour* (221, 39–40). It is not clear where, if anywhere, the promise is fulfilled, unless perhaps the *preudomme* who supervises Galahad's upbringing in *Livre de Lancelot*, part iii, p. 408, and (probably the same man) brings him to the perilous seat in *Aventures . . . del . . . Graal* p. 7, is to be identified with Nascien, in which case the tradition which has Galahad instead of Lancelot in Nascien's guardianship (AM 8906–7; see above, Introduction, p. 6) is established as the original.

8909–12 *Livre d'Artus*, pp. 244–6, presents a full circumstantial story of how Nascien became a hermit. He saw a marvellous white hart, bearing a draped vessel on its back which he recognized as the Grail. While wandering, thinking on this, he met a hermit, who was astonished that a man of his holy lineage (see above, note to lines 8884 ff.) dared be a sinner, and urged him to the service of God so successfully that he *fist a Nascien cheualerie laisser, et deuint ilec renduz et uesti les dras de religion* (261, 12–13).

8911 *and al þing*: compare 2820 *Kerue stiel and iren and al þing*.

8912 Renders LeM *il deuint puis prestres messe cantant* (221, 43).

8914 *Godes*: retained as making acceptable sense, but the original was probably *gostes*, as Kölbing's note suggests. LeM has *icestui Nascien raui puis li Saint Espris et l'en porta ou tierch chiel* (222, 1–2).

8915 *þe þridde heuen*: following LeM, which appears to conceive of it as the supreme sphere. But LeM is merely referring in a very compressed way to a story told at length in the introduction to *L'estoire del Saint Graal*, which opens the Vulgate cycle, and the apparent treatment of the third sphere may result simply from thoughtless compression. In this *Saint Graal* (Sommer, pp. 5–7 and 12) the supposed author—never named but plainly identical with our Nascien—describes how he was first carried to the third heaven, *la ou saint Pols fu portes*, but then further to a yet more glorious level, where *iou . . . vi deuiseement le Pere et le Fil et le Saint Esperit, et si vi que ces iij persones repairoient a vne deite et a vne poissance*. The version of LeM underlying AM may in fact have been a little fuller than any I have seen, since AM 8918 seems to contain an echo of *a vne deite . . . a vne poissance* absent from these; *in on acost* is rather 'in one unity' (OF *acost* n.) than the theologically dubious 'side-by-side' of *MED* (s.v. Acōst *adv.*).

8919–26 Closely translated from LeM (222, 5–7), except perhaps for the description of Galahos as *þe geauntes sone*, which does not appear here in any version of LeM which I have seen; it does elsewhere, however. The story of Arthur's peril against Galahos is told in the *Livre de Lancelot* (Sommer, part i, pp. 201–49). Galahos demands tribute of Arthur; refused, he appears with a great force, *si mande de ses gens les xxx rois que il auoit conquis, et des autres tant comme lui plot* (210, 39–40). Arthur has the worst of it, and *moult a li rois grant paor de perdre sa terre et toute honor* (251, 21–2). There then appears *vns preudons plains de grant sauoir* (215, 31–2), not named in the *Lancelot* but clearly taking the part attributed in LeM to Nascien. His *riche conseil* is to advise Arthur that the reason for his lack of success against Galahos is that God is angry with him because, particularly, he is not ruling his realm with proper benevolence, but that if he will repent God will help him. He repents, does penance, and amends, and his 'peril' ends when Galahos is filled with such admiration for Lancelot's deeds that he agrees to a reconciliation with Arthur, after having defeated him on the field.

8922 *ben exil*: *MED* derives *exil* here from Lat. *exsul* 'banished person', influenced by ME (<OF) *exil* 'banishment'. It is notable, however, that all *MED*'s instances (s.v. Exīl *n.* (2)), except the last, which is of about 1500, have the same construction, with the verb 'to be' and no article, as the present one, so though the Latin word is certainly involved (because of cases in the form *exul*) OF *estre exilié* seems likely to have been the main source, with the participle however treated as a noun and so accommodated in form to *exsul* or *exil*.

8942–4 The function of a 'standard' is as a rallying-point in battle. It could be an elaborate structure; Richard of Hexham describes the standard at the 'Battle of the Standard' (1138) as consisting of a ship's mast with flags on top, mounted on a machine. But I cannot trace any other standard consisting of several parts, like the four banners, each on an elephant-borne 'castle', described here; it would not well serve its purpose since it could be dispersed. The original conception was probably of one elephant only. The manuscripts of LeM which I have seen all refer to four at the present point, but, oddly, to a singular banner carried by them (cf. AM 9034 *baner*), and Louelich's one banner on one elephant (23350–1) seems more likely to go back to a form of LeM than to be his correction. A clear case of the error 'four' for 'one' in a very similar context occurs in *Livre de Marco Polo* (Pauthier's ed., p. 244), where one manuscript has the Khan's ensign borne on *une grant bretesche sus quatre olifans*, but the other two have *un* for *quatre*—it is hardly possible that a single castle carried on four elephants represents the original. The error would arise by a misreading of the four minims of *un* as *iiii*.

One wonders, however, further, if a more fundamental error does not underlie the whole conception, with *olifaunt* 'horn', encountered in association with a standard, taken as the beast; the association would be a common one (as for instance in MS. Bibl. Nat. f. fr. 1449 of *Aliscans*, Guessard and de Montaiglon's ed. 6113, *a l'estandart sonent li olifant*). Conversion of 'horn' to 'elephant', interestingly, underlies KA at one point (see Smithers's Introduction, p. 27). If an error, it puzzles Smithers that an author so expert in French could make it, but if in fact it could be made in wholly French transmission (presumably because the sense 'horn' early became obsolete) there would be no reproach to a translator.

The manuscript reading *castels olifaunce* might perhaps be justified, with *olifaunce* quasi-adjectival and its position a Gallicism, giving the sense 'elephant-castles', but *castel olifant* would not be a natural French phrase. For the emendation I adopt compare KA 2027 *vpe vche olifaunt a castel*, which makes [*vp*] marginally preferable to the [*on*] suggested in Kölbing's note. *MED* (s.v. Castĕl 4. (b)) accepts the emendation in Kölbing's text, and the punctuation implied in his note, giving *Þat, on four castels, olifaunce* | *Bar . . .*, which would be the obvious reading if the manuscript actually read *. . . om four . . .*, as *MED* states, but *om* is a ghost; *om.* in Kölbing's apparatus is an abbreviation indicating that his *on* is not in the manuscript at all.

8988 *adiuel*: formed on *diueling* (AM 5024, 7752 *deueling*) as though the suffix were -*ing*, not -*ling*. The word is omitted in *MED*, though cross-referred to s.v. Divel.

8990 *gleft*: the relationship of the verb *gliff* with MDu *glippen* (mentioned by *OED*) is probably of 'ideophonic' type. The existence of *e* and *u* forms points to an OE **glyffan*; compare *abyffan*, *pyffan*, on which see Smithers, 'Ideophones', 85–7.

8998 *And 'Fiȝ . . .'*; compare line 5989 and see my note, above; emendation is not needed.

9003 *yhent*: in line 4982 the word implies 'in the enemy's grip and exposed to death'; here apparently by an extended implication simply 'killed': LeM has . . . *et encore aim ie miex a morir a honor que uiure a honte* (223, 25–6). But the form may represent merely a scribe's 'correction' of an original self-rhyme *yschent*; compare 2675–6, 3509–10, 3589–90, 3843–4, 8019–20, and 8493–4.

9013 In LeM Bohort deliberately avoids further combat with Rion, . . . *s'apense que moult seroit fols se plus l'atendoit, si se refiche es estriers et se refiert ariere en la prese* (223, 35–7). The alteration by which his horse carries him away is no doubt made for his greater glory.

9017 *code*: the established senses 'belly' and 'scrotum' are hardly possible here. *MED* gives 'larynx, throat', supported only by a fifteenth-century gloss *hoc frumen: code* from the Wright–Wülcker *Vocabularies* (vol. I, col. 635, line 20). The sense there is rather 'larynx' than 'throat' in general, for the preceding gloss is *hic ysofagus: waysande*, and *code* in any case could be a glossator's rather clumsy attempt at a rendering (chosen because of the hollowness of the larynx) rather than a genuine English usage; in the only other occurrence of *frumen* in the Wright–Wülcker collections (I, 676, 21; also fifteenth century) the gloss has simply *hoc frumen, i. summa pars gutturis*, which suggests that there was no generally accepted English equivalent of *frumen*. In this unsatisfactory situation I hazard 'cheeks' as a possible sense. It could develop from the literal 'bag'; and it accords well enough with LeM *tenoit Herui . . . parmi le hiaume* (223, 38), reflecting a reasonable way to hold an enemy while preparing to cut his head off, one which might well cause his mouth and nose to run with blood.

9021 In this case LeM establishes that this line goes with 9020, not 9022: . . . *Adragans . . . qui . . . le desfendoit encontre plus de xl cheualiers* (223, 40–1). In many other such cases there is no way of telling. Kölbing's note suggests that a couplet must have dropped out before this line, explicitly referring to his defending of Herui, but the sense is sufficiently implied as the text stands.

9026 *his*: Aroans'; LeM has *et quant Herui se voit si deliure si prent le cheual au roy et saut sus deliurement* (224, 2–3).

9027 *smiten hem*: presumably Adragenis, Bohort, and Herui. The abrupt change to plural does not occur in LeM, where Herui continues as the subject of the equivalent clause (224, 4). There is, however, no need to suppose a couplet omitted before this line, as Kölbing does in his note, and certainly not that it contained a reference to Leodegan's men. For similar abrupt plurals see lines 9085 and 9444; in each of these cases the change of number is supported by LeM (see my notes, below).

9031–2 *is . . . | Smiten on*: 'has galloped against'; an over-literal rendering of LeM *se furent flatis al* (224, 5; subject *les eschieles au roy Leodegan*).

9039 Renders LeM *et cil faut a lui et ataint le cheual* (224, 9–10).

9054 In LeM (224, 22–3) this blow damages the hauberk but not the body; it is hard to see how anyone would 'withsit' the stroke as described in AM.

9059 *eft wald*: 'wished (to turn) back;' the line renders LeM *et cil volt recourer comme cil qui estoit de grant force* (224, 26–7).

9078 *þat honged worþ*: 'may he be hanged!' *Pat* does 'double duty' (see above, note to line 885), as relative pronoun and jussive conjunction; *worþ* is to be taken as subjunctive.

9085 *wered*: the subject is 'they' understood, not Adragein. The change of numbers has become abrupt by the conversion of the 'companions' of line 9083 from the subject of the present action to the object of Adragein's help; LeM has . . . *mais tost resailli en pies. Quant li troi compaignon se voent si mal mener si se traient li vns vers l'autre et se desfendent si durement* . . . (224, 43–225, 1). For similar abrupt plurals in AM see lines 9027 and 9444, and notes ad loc.

9098 *vpriȝt*: see above, note to line 8449.

9117 *Agreuein*: probably a mere slip into a form familiar as Gawain's brother, and so again in line 9298, instead of the Adragein of 9082, etc.; LeM has no equivalent name at either point. There are so many variant forms of proper names, however, that I have been unwilling to admit to text any emendations beyond the most obvious running corrections.

9155 Perhaps meant ironically; despite the great heaps of slain, by comparison with what now follows the earlier fighting could not really be called a battle. But very probably this is simply clumsy rendering of the source; no form of LeM which I have seen has any equivalent at this point, but EPM reads *Ther be-gan the stour newe full hidouse and fell* (333, 30–1), probably reproducing a source which here more or less repeated an earlier phrase, *illuec ot estour merueilleus et felon* (225, 37).

9164 *sonne schineing*: see above, note to line 4718.

9168 *toteren*: quite probably 'tore (pieces of armour) off' rather than 'lacerated', and similarly in line 9289; compare note to line 5817 above.

9214 Implying 'what is the point of talking of honourable duty, when we must in any case fight to save our own skins?' In LeM Guiomair says simply '*nous sommes prest chascuns de nos testes desfendre*' (227, 20–1), but the equivalent of the present proverb-like phrase occurs earlier in LeM, where Merlin encourages Leodegan's forces in their attack on Rion's camp by saying '*il n'a point de teste qui hui ne la desfendra*' (220, 6).

9219–20 'Of those (whom) they encountered (they) thrust 10,000 pagans through—they fell to the ground.' The subject of *bar* is understood from the previous structures; *hem* is in apposition to *X m paiens*.

9227 *resten*: probably transitive (cf. line 7482); the line reflects LeM *lor fist lor cheuaus rechengler et restraindre* (227, 34).

9228–9 *oȝain þresten* . . . *oȝan*: 'once more thrust back'; Kölbing's deletion of *oȝain* is quite unnecessary.

9249 'because of the crowns and beards with which his armour was covered', i.e. his surcoat was so decorated. The historic present *were* is abrupt, but this is not unparalleled, and the possible alternative rendering '. . . which constituted his armorial bearings' goes less well with LeM . . . *puis choisi le roy Rion qui estoit couers de couertures toutes plaines de barbes et de courones* (228, 13–14). The nature of the beards appears from a later incident in LeM, in which Rion demands Arthur's beard to put the finishing touch to a mantle furred with the beards of conquered kings (412, 20–9); one supposes the crowns to be embroidered representations of the crowns of these or other such kings. Liedholm (p. 23) would explain *berdes* here as from OE *brid(d)* with lowering of the vowel; a curious suggestion and contradicted by LeM.

9250 *wiþ strengþe of armes*: 'by the power of his (use of his) weapons' (cf. line 9186), or perhaps 'by the strength of his two arms' (cf. KA 3481–2 *He swam . . . wiþ strengþe of armes*).

9256 *þe purpoint of o serpent*: 'his doublet, made of snake-skin', a close rendering of LeM *li porpoins d'un serpent*; LeM explains that *la pel fu si dure qu'il* [Arthur] *ne la pot mie rompre ne perchier* (228, 18–20).

9264 LeM has *li iaiant et li Sesne . . . le fierent et assaillent de toutes pars si qu'il le portent a terre, lui et le cheual tout en j mont* (228, 22–4). This supports Kölbing's *h[is] hors*. But the meaning as unemended, that Arthur's attackers used their horses to knock him down, is a quite possible one; compare a later incident in LeM, in which Arthur *hurte le cheual des esperons et se fiert encontre li si roidement de cors et de cheual qu'il s'entreportent a terre, les cheuals sor les cors* (230, 16–18). The emendation is not therefore essential.

9281 *Pat*: probably Ban, not Arthur; LeM has *Car il remonta le roy Artu . . . et fist si grant ochision . . .* (228, 28–9).

9289 *totore*: see above, note to line 9168.

9330 *Goionard*: this heathen is a ghost-character; in LeM the Christian Guiomar (cf. AM lines 9213 and 9670) appears here. See above, Introduction, p. 14.

9345 On the creation of *Troimadac* from *rois* plus proper name see above, Introduction, p. 71 n. 9. Forcoars may have been created in the same way, though hardly directly from LeM's *li quars Cooars* (in enumerating these kings, 232, 13). An English intermediate version *þe forþ Coars* would account for the form, but it is hard to see how a verse antecedent of AM could have fitted ordinals into the metre, and a prose one at so early a date would be most unlikely; also this would not account for EPM's *Heroars* (342, 11). I speculate that there was a version of LeM with *li quars li fors Coars*, of which a variant with *fers* underlies EPM. The names in the English versions may indicate translators imperfect in French, but need not—impeccably French transmission presumably underlies W's *li quars furicouais* (f. 238ᵛᶜ, 2).

9359 *swarf*: there appears to have been semantic contamination between derivatives of OE *sweorfan* 'file' and *hweorfan* 'turn aside', perhaps based on an image of a sword skidding off a helmet like a file which fails to bite. Cognates of *sweorfan* appear in various Germanic languages in senses like 'swerve', but not early; similar semantic contamination may well have occurred independently in more than one language.

9371 *on heiȝe*: 'loudly'. The only example of this sense in AM (Kölbing's Glossary gives 'laut' also for line 1633, but the commoner sense is more likely in context). One could render here '"Stop at once, traitor!"', but this would not accord so well with LeM . . . *si li escrie Kahanins: 'Cuuers, mal le cachastes . . .!' Quant li rois Artus entendi celui qui si haut li escrie . . .'* (232, 37–9).

9372 'It will prove to your misfortune that you ever saw Rion'; compare *Sir Otuel* 208 *Wroþer hele come þou her; I rede þou ȝeld op þi brand.* The manuscript could conceivably be construed unemended, with *hole* adjective and *wroþer* comparative, 'you have seen Rion more angry when uninjured', i.e. 'you would not dare to pursue Rion if he were fully fit', but in all probability an original *hale* has been mistaken for the adjective and 'normalized' into *hole*.

9407 *So driuen*: '(who) were similarly pursuing'. But probably the original was *So þai driuen* 'as they were pursuing'; or it is even possible that the poet intended this sense with the pronoun to be understood.

9411 *þritten*: but Minados, his *þre feren*, and the *ten kniȝtes* should make fourteen in all. This may be a mere casual error, Minados being overlooked. In LeM, however, Ban is chasing the three kings Gloriant, Minados, and Calufer, when they come on ten of their knights, and *si coururent sus al roy Ban si tost com il le uirent* (233, 21–2); the number 'thirteen' could well have been given in some manuscripts of LeM here, though not in those I have seen. Subsequently four other heathen kings, Pinoras, Sinagreus, Gardon, and Mengoras, arrive (W, 233 footnote 3, 3; not named in G¹ or A¹), pursued by Bohort. In AM Ban's and Bohort's pursuits have been combined, and the poet seems uncertain whether to take the number of the fleeing kings as the three or the four. See further the next two notes.

9433–4 Hardly appropriate to the situation in AM, even if the number ten were consistent with the earlier account. In LeM it is at this point that Bohort arrives, when Ban has disposed of three of the thirteen heathens who had attacked him, so that Bohort *uoit son frere qui se combat a x cheualiers* (233, 34).

9439 *Þo þre paiens*: in LeM Bohort is here attacked by *li roy qu'il auoit encauchie* (233, 37), and EPM's *the thre kynges that he hadde chaced* (344, 15–16) probably goes back to the same form of LeM as underlies AM here. We should therefore understand 'those three pagans', even though the transfer of preceding action from Bohort to Ban (including in lines 9431–2 the killing by which Bohort's four enemies are reduced to three, as well as the non-fatal felling of 9429–30) leaves the phrase inappropriate to its context, so that it would seem to mean 'then three pagans . . .'.

9444 *smiten*: the subject is 'Ban and Bohort'. The change of number rests firmly on LeM *Mais del releuer ne fu mie lens, ains tourne la teste du cheual encontre els er lor adrece l'espee el poing; si commenchent li doi frere j si grant capleis encontre les autres . . .* (234, 2–4). For similar abrupt plurals see lines 9027 and 9085, and notes ad loc.

9447 *his sw[erd ydrawe]*: LeM has *l'espee el poing* (234, 6), EPM *with swerde drawen* (344, 23).

9626 *Lectargis*: identical with *Blehartis* (line 5483) and *Beichardis* (9753), representing LeM's *li lais hardis*. On such formations see above, Introduction, p. 71 n. 9.

9641 *her king*: Arthur. According to LeM (237, 16–28) four fights continued into the night, maintained on the Christian side by (1) Leodegan and Cleodalis, (2) Guyomar and Synados (AM Salinas; see below, note to line 9670), (3) Antor, Kay, etc., and (4) Arthur, Ban, Bohort, Nacien, Adragein, and Herui. All the others returned to Daneblaise, but as they did not find the four kings there they would not enter, but encamped to await news. The AM poet misunderstood LeM to say that Antor's group (the last whose doings are described before the encamping outside Daneblaise) returned to Daneblaise; therefore when he later found this group engaged in the fighting he had to construct lines 9743–7 (for which LeM gives no warranty) to account for this.

9646 *Lord-ouer*: if the form is genuine, the order is presumably a Gallicism, reflecting such a phrase as *roi supereor*. It may, however, be just such an error as the scribe made in line 7153, where he (presumably) carelessly omitted *ouer*, realized what he had done after writing *token*, put *ouer* in after it, and marked the words for interchange; here he omitted so to mark them.

herdene lond: rendering LeM *la terre as pastures* (237, 33–4). One might speculate that such weak genitive plurals were commoner in 'Ur–AM'; this one uniquely retained in our text because taken for a proper name.

9647 *was*: compare line 4468, and see my note, above.

9655–6 LeM has *Et ce por coi Merlins fist cest enchantement vous deuisera bien li contes* (237, 40–1); there follows the story of how Merlin's enchantment delayed the Saxons until a certain Amans, bent on recovering a castle which Uterpendragon had taken from him, appeared, whereupon a battle developed. The description is then broken off, and resumed just after the 'rest' with which AM as we have it concludes. In all probability the AM poet, following his usual practice (see above, Introduction, pp. 14–15), intended to put the whole story together at the later point, and therefore adjusted LeM's phrasing so that the story was specifically promised soon but not immediately.

9670 *Salinas*: in lines 8808–9, as in the equivalent passage of LeM,

Salinas was a heathen king, Rion's *nevou*. Why the name should now replace LeM's *Synados* (239, 8) it is hard to guess, and harder still if the source had W's *le roy Ydier* (f. 242ra, 14). In some way Salinas and Goionar seem to have been linked in the poet's mind; the latter (as *Goionard*) was Rion's *nevou* in line 9330.

9673 *Pese four*: the number should be six; the error is probably mechanical miscopying of a Roman numeral. LeM has *li vj compaignon* (239, 10).

9680 *bi line*: see above, note to line 6370.

9698 'smote one . . . (making his way) through them (to do it)'; Kölbing's emendation, giving the regular *þurth smot*, is attractive but not essential.

9730 *d[r]ie*: LeM has *Lors . . . li rois Bans . . . dist . . . que toute nuit les conuendra deduire en bataille* (239, 23–4). It may be that the AM poet simply took over the French word, and that the manuscript form *duie* is either haplographed for *deduie* or is an aphetic development of it. But the word in either case would be unique in English; on the text as emended compare the Auchinleck *Reinbrun*, stanza 50, lines 10–12 . . . *wereþ him wel . . . | Whiles a miȝte driȝe*. Neither the emendation which Kölbing admits to his text, nor the rather elaborate reconstruction of lines 9729–30 suggested in his note, is satisfactory.

9731 *l[e]ueț*: the manuscript *loued* is certainly corrupt, and probably results from regularizing of the rhyme after the rhyme-word had been normalized. LeM has . . . *et il li dist que ce li est bel* (239, 24), and my emendation gives a good rendering of this sense. The phrase would be a positive equivalent of the regular comparative *haue leuer*, which occurs for instance in AM lines 167, 2359, and 7373, and would be parallel with MDu *lief hebben*; it is admittedly unrecorded in English. The original rhyme would have been *leue:preued*.

9744 *y nemd bifore*: in lines 9623–7.

9749–50 Line 9749 was first omitted, then supplied at the foot of the column and marked for insertion. One wonders if the error was not a telescoping of the two lines rather than simple omission, and followed by a botched correction. To interchange *mett* and *stett* would give a much easier reading, with line 9750 then a little smoother metrically as *Ich [on] oþer sone [st]ett*. The text, however, can be construed as it stands, approximately 'fell on a hundred "giants" (neither side wasted time in coming together)'.

9761 *anne*: 'number one', with the cardinal effectively in ordinal sense; LeM has . . . *et fiert si le premier qu'il encontre* . . . (239, 42).

9773–4 '. . . men who knew that the "giants" were being struck with this might well be delighted'; compare 7967–8 *delite . . . | On þe paiens to don it bite*. The present tense of *witeþ* may be taken to imply in effect a change to *oratio recta* in line 9774. Alternatively, *smite* may be taken as a noun. So *OED*, following Kölbing, who renders in his note 'Das wissen die riesen von diesen schlägen'; I think this less likely. LeM (240, 3–4) is not close enough to help.

9775 The line renders LeM *qu'il ont remonte les v compaignons qui estoient a pie* (240, 8), so although the division of LeM's Gornain Cadrus into two (see above, note to lines 5427–9) makes the number wrong relative to lines 9751–3, it would be inappropriate to emend *fiue* to *sex* as Kölbing's note suggests. It is possible that *he lift* is plural, as in LeM, but since there is no equivalent of LeM's *li vj compaignon qui sont uenu al secors* (= those named in AM 9657–68) as antecedent of *il*, singular is probably intended.

9825 *seuen and tventi*: there is no obvious basis for this number. In LeM Merlin tells Arthur that Leodegan and Cleodalis *se combatent a plus de xv iaians* (240, 20); in 236, 15–18 they had been described as pursuing four heathens, who encountered thirty-two of their fellows. The figure 32 in fact appears as xij, and should probably be *xij* only; W has a different corruption which could equally go back to this, *vij mille* (f. 240^{vc}, 5). But though that would make LeM's figures self-consistent it would not help with AM.

9829 *his*: Cleodalis'; the description referred to in line 9828 was no doubt on the lost f. 254A.

9837–8 'Because of the weakness resulting from (his) other wounds he lay (unable to rise) . . .'; Kölbing's *feblenis* † *oþer wounde* 'weakness or wounds' is unfortunate. LeM has *il ne se pouoit . . . soustenire sus membre, qu'il eust pour le trauail que il auoit sousfert des cops que il auoit donnez et receus* (W 240, footnote, 6–9).

9891 *made astert*: or *made a stert*, as Kölbing prints. The noun *stert* is well authenticated; *astert* is nowhere assured, but other occurrences of the present phrase may well contain it (e.g. *Generydes* 6699), its derivation from *asterte(n)* v. offers no difficulty, and it allows *make* here what is a common construction in AM (lines 4991, 8035, 9104, etc.)—use with the indefinite article is rarer.

9894 *lord-king*: an unusual formation, but compare RCL 3081 *oure lord kyng*; there is no reason to emend.

9913 *sextene*: the number should be twenty-one, consisting of the five named in lines 9666–8, the three whom they join in the fighting described in 9670 ff., and the thirteen whom they similarly join in 9757 ff. LeM has correctly *li xxi compaignon* (240, 25); doubtless *xxi* was simply misread as *xvi*.

9917 *her swerd*: the singular noun would be sound OE syntax, so I retain it as possible, but it would be abnormal here (cf. lines 5284, 5693, etc.), and *swerd[es]* would improve metre also.

baþen: perhaps intransitive, with *dede* causative, but it is harder so to see the case in line 6814, in view of *þurth* 6813; I treat both cases alike.

9925 *he*[*m*]: *he* is barely possible, in apposition to *Merlin* and with the object of *tauȝt* understood, but it would be a most unnatural usage.

9938 AM thus comes to an end, with no formula of conclusion; though we are at a pause in the action a good deal of the plot is left in the air. Kölbing (p. clii) has suggested that the poet was working from an imperfect transcript of LeM, which itself broke off here, but lines 9655–6 seem to imply that he intended to continue beyond the present point and knew of material which he would use (see my note, above). Ellis's suggestion, in his *Specimens of . . . Romances* (3rd ed., p. 142), that mere weariness caused a copyist to give up is a straightforward one, but if so this was rather a previous copyist than the actual scribe of our manuscript, for his insertion of the title of the next piece at the head of the column containing the last few lines of AM (see above, Introduction, p. 37) argues deliberation about the end of the latter. Perhaps the 'general editor' of the whole manuscript postulated by Loomis in 'The . . . MS. and a . . . London Bookshop', 609–13, decided that AM as he knew it was too long for his anthology, and so directed the scribe to stop at what seemed a convenient point; in this case (as also if the 'editor' knew that he was giving the scribe an exemplar which broke off rather than ended) one would have expected some formula of conclusion to be cobbled up. I cannot suggest any really satisfactory explanation.

GLOSSARY

The glossary is in principle complete for A and L, though to keep bulk within bounds devices such as bracketed letters are freely used to represent minor variants of form, and *etc.* to indicate incomplete citation (the references given being then chosen as convenient, characteristic, or interesting, not necessarily the earliest). Senses are not generally distinguished in a word which has retained the variety in modern English; the notation (mod. uses) draws attention to many applications thus put together.

The presentation in general follows that recommended by EETS, though I have indulged my belief that head-forms not, as it happens, occurring in the text (chiefly infinitives) can be useful when the glossary is used as a short-cut reference to the text, to the extent of printing such forms (bracketed), with cross-reference, where the entry might not otherwise be readily found. The letter *y* is universally treated as equivalent to *i*, and *u* and *v* as the same letter; ʒ is a separate letter after *g* (but where, very rarely, it represents [z] it is so placed), and þ after *t* (rare *th* is placed as for þ).

Forms cited occur in A unless otherwise indicated. Forms or variants specifically from L are placed in square brackets, and those from P in angle brackets (but here glossing is restricted to a few cases of interest or difficulty). A line-reference 1–2000 without prefix is to A and to the equivalent point of L (subject to arbitrary decision sometimes on what *is* the equivalent point), after 2000 to A only. Where a sense given under the head-form is supported by instances which are not in fact in that form, the line-references are italicized. Where a phrase as cited contains a form which does not in fact occur in that phrase, a small cross is prefixed.

Etymologies are not given. Where I would dissent from, or comment on, the received view (which normally means that of *MED* for A–L, of *OED* thereafter), I refer at the end of the entry to a note in the Commentary. The suffix ⁿ to a line-reference indicates a note dealing with the particular instance. The suffix ʳ indicates occurrence in rhyme, where the form appears to be distinctively so used (sometimes clearly for metrical rather than rhyming reasons); if to a form it means that at least three-quarters of such forms occur in rhyme. An asterisk indicates editorial emendation of restoration of illegible matter.

Cross-references exclude all the many cases which would be from an *eo* form in L to an *e* head-form, and similarly from *w* to *u*, but the variants are noticed within the entry. In three other cases I have been unable to exhibit significant variation: (i) While an *i/y* form is printed with the commoner variant, to show also what proportion of the occurrences, if any, have the other would take too much space; this conceals in particular a much greater prevalence of *y* in L in many (but not all) cases. (ii) There is in L a strong tendency for weak and plural adjectives to be distinguished by -*e*, but even in L casual -*e* is so frequent that it would be difficult to show this, and in A it hardly appears. (iii) Subjunctives are distinguished from indicatives only where this can be done with certainty; never then in the plural, although one might wish to know what proportion of present plurals in -*e(n)* or endingless are subjunctive, what indicative in opposition to -*(e)þ*, but in too many cases mood is uncertain. Similarly with imperatives; cases with vocative pronoun cannot be certainly distinguished from (hortative) subjunctives, and are included with these.

a *interj.* ah! A961, etc., L869.

a *indef. art.* (+ cons.) 32, etc., and see **ich** *adj.*; **an** (+vowel or aspirate) 685, 701, A957, etc., (+cons.) 2451, 7147, 9277, 9295; **o** A1527, 3224, 3574, 4922, 5000; **on** A1165, 4029, 4037, 4135, etc. Cf. **on** *num. adj.* (some instances uncertain).

a *prep.* see **on**.

[a] *v.* see **haue(n)**.

abade *n.* see **abod(e)**.

abandoun *adv.* easily 6006. Cf. **baundoun**.

abast *adj.* bastard 4444. Cf. **bast.**

abide *v.* wait for A1953, etc.; remain, wait A1507, *8476*, etc.; stand up to 2166, 3337, L24, *lif* ~ survive (infant) L1001. **abidest**ow *pr. 2 sg.* 6343. **abide** *pr. subj. sg.* 8421; *imp. sg.* 8476, 9371. **abod** *pa. t. 3 sg.* 3489. **abiden** *pa. t. pl.* A437; *pp.* 4133. Cf. **bide.**

abigge *v.* pay for (fig.) A826, etc., (absol.) 2388. **abou3t** *pa. t. 3 sg.* A238. Cf. **bou3t.**

[abyte] *n.* habit (nun's) L1260.

ablewe *pa. t. 3 sg.* breathed into 8536[n].

a-blod *adv.* with blood (see **erne**) 9018.

abobbed *pp.* (adj.) bewildered A1959.

abod(e) *n.* delay, *wiþouten* ~ 2879, 3423, etc.; **abade** 6421[r].

aboue(n) *adv.* in the sky, heaven A28, A1520, etc., *fro* ~ from the air A718; in high place (fig.) 367 [L **abowe**], 2257; on top 3293, 7960, as outer garment 8671. *prep.* above A651, etc., L1125. Cf. **heraboue.**

about(e, -en) [-wte] *adv.* around 3278, L298, etc.; in(to) all parts 1306, 1727, etc.; +*ben* ~ concern oneself (to . . .) A430, etc. *prep.* around 2070, 2137, etc.; in all parts

of 4087, L1455; about (of time) 7412, 7982, L1407; **abuten** 6309. Cf. **þeraboute.**

abreke *v.* break out 7893.

abrod(e) *adv.* about the place, widely 545, 7018, etc.

ac *conj.* but A20, A24, etc.

achesoun *n.* motive A132.

a-childbed *adv.* in child-bed 2709.

acomber [-bre] *v.* bring to ruin 673. Cf. **encombraunce, encumbrement.**

acontred *pa. t. pl.* met (in battle) 4777. Cf. **contre** *n.*

acord *n.* reconciliation 4081, 4646, etc., (iron.) A335; *bi on* ~ with one accord A1783, *wiþ fair* ~ lovingly 2536.

acord *v.* come to agreement 2779, 2787. **acord** *pp.* 8554.

acordement *n.* reconciliation 2594.

acording *n.* reconciliation 5116.

acost *n.* union 8918. *See* 8915*n.*

acost *prep.* skirting 7603.

acouerd *pa. t. 3 sg.* see **akeuered.**

acurssed *pa. t. 3 sg.* cursed (tr.) 7717.

acurssedliche *adv.* in accursed manner A787.

adden *pa. t. pl.* see **haue(n).**

adiuel *adv.* grovelling 8988. *See n.*

adoun *adv.* down 1526, A1820, 3353, etc.

adrad *pp.* (adj.) afraid A210, etc.; **adred** 2532, etc.

adreint *pa. t. pl.* drowned (intr.) 8127.

afeld *pa. t. pl.* struck down 7075.

afer(e) *adv.* on fire A1516, 7310. Cf. **fer(e).**

aferd *pp.* (adj.) afraid A856, L1217.

afie *v.* put one's trust 7359.

afin(e) *adv.* (intensive, modifying adj.) A50, 3852, etc., (modifying statement) 8168, L83; **afins** 6152[r].

afong v. receive A123, 4595, etc.
afeng(e) pa. t. 3 sg. 2536, 2703.
afong pp. 3390.
afor adv. previously 6716.
aforce v. compel 2350ⁿ. **aforced** pa. t. 3 sg. strove 3275ⁿ.
aforn prep. in the presence of A1388.
afot adv. on foot 3880, etc.; to one's feet 9042, 9265.
after adv. afterwards A63, A384, etc., L1242, etc., seþþen (. . .) ~ A 1179, 8564, þer sone ~ see þerafter; following (motion) ?1150ⁿ, 2527, etc.; behind one (after motion) 7254. prep. after (time) A87, 1030, L304, etc., (place, rank) 6519, 8151; following (motion) 1886, etc.; behind (one, after motion) 5680, 6057; in the fashion of A980, L613; in accordance with A1561, L1248, ~ þat according as, etc. A160, 8673ⁿ, (without þat) 6520; sende ~ send for 66, etc., (sim.) gon ~ 1080, loke ~ 8471, etc., ⁺seche ~ 7548, [⁺sende sonde ~] *L513, [⁺wende ~] L75. Cf. her-, þer-after.
afterclap n. stroke to come 499. See n.
afternone n. period beginning 3 p.m. 4789, 4791. Cf. none.
afterward adv. afterwards A292, etc., L1790, in the future 4483; next (place, rank) 6515. Cf. þerafter-ward.
after-ward n. rearguard 7736.
[agayn] ⟨against⟩ adv., prep. see oȝain, oȝain(e)s.
a-game adv. in (amorous) play A1106.
agan pa. t. 3 sg. began (intr.) 6720. Cf. biginne, ginneþ.
agast v. strike fear into A314, 8002. **agast** pp. (adj.) afraid 7914, L1053.
age n. (mature) age A10, 4616.
agile v. beguile A770. Cf. bygyle, gile.
ago v. obtain 4318.
ago(n) pp. (adj.) past A1058, etc.; gone away 7586.
[agramed] pp. (adj.) troubled L1013. Cf. grame v.
agreued pa. t. 3 sg. harassed 6300.

agrise v. be(come) afraid, dismayed (intr. or impers.) A889, 1504, 4093.
agros pa. t. 3 sg. A1005, etc. **agrisen** pa. t. pl. 5986; pp. 3288, L984.
[aȝeyn(s)] adv. prep. see oȝain, oȝain(e)s.
aȝeld imp. sg. yield (refl.) 9350.
ay adv. ever (after) A631, A1194, etc.
ay n. fear A255; **ayȝe** A465; **eiȝe** 6419. Cf. awe.
air [eyr] n. heir 1831, etc. **air(e)s** pl. A519, 1642, 6567; [heires] L1727, etc.
air(e) n. air A644, 8762, 9158; [eyr] L609, etc.
aise n. ease, at ~ A1294, 4233, etc., **ese** 1437, 3528, iuel at ~ 9640, take ~ 8209.
aiþer adj. each 6065, etc.; [*eyþir] L285. Cf. noiþer.
aketoun n. padded jacket worn under armour (see 2975–6n) 2976, 5957, etc. **aketouns** pl. 8665.
akeuered pa. t. 3 sg. recovered (intr.) 8540, 9443; **acouerd** 8509. Cf. keuer(en), recouerd.
aknawe pp., ben ~ admit A1081. Cf. biknawe.
a-knewes adv. on one's knees 2343; **a-knowe** 9871.
al(le) adj. all 107, 227, etc., on and ~ all A573, 3817; every, see þing, wise. (as pron.) everything 709, etc.; (constr. sg. or pl. [pl.]) everyone A337, A668, L518, etc., [~ and somme] everyone L494; in ~ in all (of numbers) 4531 etc., in every respect 7639. **alder** pl. gen. 3910ⁿ, (intensive, modifying superl.) A761, etc. Cf. oueral(le).
al(le) adv. altogether (and other intensive uses) A436, 545, A1106, etc.
alaine n. breath 8456.
alange adj. dreary 4199ⁿ.
alangeþ pr. 3 sg. makes dreary 4202.
[alas] interj. see allas.
alblast n. cross-bow A313, A456, etc.
alderman pl. leaders of ward of city 5095ʳ, 5121ʳ.
ale n. ale 4713, etc., to þe ~ = to the alehouse L810.

a-left *adv.* on the left 8139. Cf. **left** *adj*.
aleft *pp.* lifted, *vp* ~ = pushed up
  A552. Cf. **lift**.
alegaunce *n.* alleviation 6857.
alenge *prep.* see **along**.
algat *adv.* absolutely 2300ⁿ.
ali3t *pp.* (adj.) glorious 8898ⁿ.
ali3t *v.* descend (fig.) 4878; dismount.
  ali3t *pa. t. 3 sg.* 8450; *pl.* 5273; *pp.*
  (*adoun* ~) 6229.
allas [-l(l)-] *interj.* alas! 704, etc., ~
  þat A782, L866, etc.
almast [-ost] *adv.* almost 1725, etc.;
  almest A1523, etc.; almost 2568,
  etc. Cf. **mest** *s.v.* **miche(l)**.
almi3t *adj.* almighty, *God* ~ A713,
  etc.
aloge *v.* set up (camp) 8056.
alon(e) *adv.* only, alone A290, 9316,
  etc., L1158. Cf. **on** *adv*.¹
along *adv.* onward 7729; at full
  length 9885; *wexeþ* ~ becomes
  longer (day) A1710, *draweþ* ~
  6597. alenge *prep.* along the length
  of 7484ʳⁿ.
aloude *adv.* loudly 6281, 8475;
  [alowd] L1114.
als(o) *conj.* see **as**.
also *adv.* also A277, L7, etc., als
  9783; similarly 4183, 8561, etc.;
  as A673, L470, etc., als A549, as
  A108, 5680, L602, etc; as . . . as
  possible 7851; ~ skete at once A302,
  (sim.) A732ⁿ, L123, etc., als A1789,
  3240.
[altogedre] *adv.* completely L1633.
alway *adv.* continuously A414, with
  continuous labour A1476.
amay *imp. sg.* (refl.) be dismayed
  8721. amayd *pp.* 2294; [amayed]
  L1209, L1439.
amen *interj.* amen 2800, 5992.
amende *v.* remedy A191, 8465.
ami *n.* friend, comrade 7350, etc.,
  (iron.) L1165; lover 6916.
amid *prep.* in(to) the middle of 3253,
  4824, etc.; squarely upon 7200.
amidward *adv.* into the middle
  2873; *prep.* in(to) the middle of
  4930, 5166, etc.
amira(i)l *n.* heathen leader 6174,
  7553, etc. amirayls *pl.* A1749;
  amiraile 8162ʳ.

amis *adv.* wrongfully, unnaturally
  1205, 8477, L771. Cf. **mys**.
among(es) *prep.* among (motion or
  rest) 564, 2225, 6963, L615, etc.;
  hem alle ~ all working together
  3056ⁿ, L1565; omang 5772ʳ.
amorwe *adv.* next day 1291 etc.;
  amorn 8220.
amour *n.* love (sexual) 6538, 8822,
  par ~ with this 2479, 8662, 8677;
  (friendly) 4662; *par* ~ as you love
  me (formula of request) 2902, 4574,
  etc.
an *num. adj.* see **o**.
an *indef. art.* see **a**.
an *prep.* see **on**.
anclowe *n.* ankle 5196.
and *conj.* and 67, etc., (postponed
  construction) A179, etc., and yet
  A931, A1498, A1897; if 871, etc.,
  ~ *þat* 2799.
andwaiteing *n.* keeping watch 3652.
  Cf. **await(e)**.
[aneowe] *adv.* anew L488.
angels *pl. gen.* see **aungelis**.
anhong *v.* kill by hanging A469.
  [anhong] *imp. sg.* L1160.
ani *adj.* (+sg.) any 232, etc., [ony]
  L537, *or* ~ *day* before dawn 2502;
  (as pron.) 4256, 5728, etc., (+pl.)
  8792, either 4022. *adv.* any (modifying compar., of time) 101, etc.
ani3t *adv.* at night 2802, 4234.
anne *num. adj.* see **o**.
anoi(e) *n.* affliction, trouble A880,
  6282, 7264. Cf. **noi3e**.
anoie *v.* harass 4331. anoied *pa. t.
  pl.* 4533. anoid *pp.* (adj.) angry
  6398, 7225.
anoiing *n.* harm 4460.
anon *adv.* straightway 68, A1038, L96,
  etc., *sone* ~ A842, L59, etc., *swiþe*
  ~ 2028, L267, etc.; onanʳ A1036,
  etc.
anoþer [-ir] *adj.* another, a second
  2878, 8697, L254, etc.; (as pron.)
  A1721, 5033, etc., somebody else
  A248, 7659, L1375, something else
  3636, any other (child) A982.
anouenon *prep.* on from above 9420.
anour *n.* see **honour**.
anoward *prep.* on top of 3313.
answerd *pa. t. 3 sg.* see **onsvere**.

answere *n.* answer(ing) A182, A694[n], etc.

answering [on- -ȝ(e)] *n.* answer 1628, L1112.

a-paise *adv.* untroubled 2332.

ape *n.* = fool A813.

aperceiued *pp.* observed A774. Cf. **parceyued.**

aplat *adv.* flat (on ground) 9024, 9835, *wiþ his swerd* ~ with the flat of his sword 7169.

apliȝt *pp.* (adv.) assuredly (usually tag) A1426, 1615, etc.

[apon] *prep.* see **opon.**

apose *v.* question 5525. **aposed** [-(e)] *pa. t. 3 sg.* 573, 894 [L **apposede**], L755.

aposeing *n.* questioning 2461.

apostles *pl.* apostles 2225.

aqueiȝt *pa. t. 3 sg.* quivered 3250. Cf. **queiȝte.**

aquelle *pr. subj. sg.* kill A1162. **aqueld** *pa. t. 3 sg.* A400, 8842; *pl.* 7330; *pp.* 6432, 6682.

ar(e) *adv., prep., conj.* see **er.**

arawe *adv.* in sequence, one after the other A1278, etc.; **arowe** A148, 9702.

arere(n) *v.* lift up A1484, 7128, ?L1539; build up *A536*, L476; raise (cry, strife, etc.) 3044, 6192. **arereþ** *pr. 3 sg.* 6598. **arered** *pa. t. 3 sg.* (~ *miȝt* exerted his strength) A1531[n]; *pl.* 6699; *pp.* A536, 8997, L1539.

ariȝt *adv.* properly 6904, 9108, as is proper L480; at once A1846, 7373.

a-riȝt *adv.* on the right 8139. Cf. phr. s.v. **left.**

arise *v.* get up *2531, 3129,* 7132, *etc.*; rise up (dragons) 1503, *A1511*; arise (fame, strife, etc.) 4094, *4881, etc.* **arist** *pr. 3 sg.* 7399. **arise** *pr. subj. sg.* 2531; *imp. sg.* (~ *vp*) 2546. **aros** *pa. t. 3 sg.* 2685, etc. **arisen** *pa. t. pl.* A1511, 9134; *pp.* 3287.

ariue *v.* land (from sea) 2129. **ariue** *pp.* 7043.

arm(e) *n.* arm 745, 4934, etc. **armes** *pl.* A1126, etc.

arm(e) *v.* put armour on (refl.) 2498, 4767. **armed** *pa. t. 3 sg.* 8399,

(tr.) 8678; *pl.* 3792, etc., (tr.) 5907; *pp.* (adj.) in armour 3161, etc., **yarmed** 3448, etc. Cf. **vnarmed.**

armerie *n.* armour 7563.

armes *pl.* arms (esp. defensive = armour) A246, 3686, 9088, L110, L220, etc., = use of weapons 9186, 9250[n]; armorial bearings 8019[n], 8020[n], 8673[n], L1858. **arme** *sg.* piece of armour 4841[n].

arminge *n.* putting on of armour 9242.

armour *n.* armour 4684, etc.; piece of armour 8679[n].

arnand *pr. p.* galloping (man on horse) 8386, 8404. *See 1228n.*

arnemorwe *n.* early morning 4786, etc.

aroum(e) *adv., fer* ~ to a distance 5777, 8864.

arsoun *n.* saddle-bow 5218, etc. **arsouns** *pl.* 7235.

arst *adj., adv. superl.* see **er.**

ar(u)we *n.* arrow A313, 4136, etc. **aruwe** *pl.* 9159; [**arwes**] L287.

arwe *adj.* afraid 9637.

as *adv.* see **also.**

as *conj.* as A63, L64, etc., (of time) 1410, etc.; as if A1516, L182, etc.; also A467, A1909, etc.; als L205, L467, etc., 6817.

as *prep.,* ~ *armes* to arms! 4863, etc.

asay *v.* attempt (to . . .) 747. **aseyd** *pp.* tested 9734.

asayle *v.* attack 2093; **asaily** 7367; [**assaylle**] L285, L1626. **asailed** *pa. t. 3 sg.* 2428; *pl.* 5175, 9426; *pp.* 5092.

asailing *n.* attack 2503. Cf. **seylinge.**

asaut [-ȝt] *n.* attack 213, *9205.

ascape, -sk- *v.* escape (intr.) A339, etc., L1916, (tr.) 5776. **ascapeþ** *pr. pl.* 5867. **ascaped** [-sk-] *pa. t. 3 sg.* A396, 8528, L1929; *pl.* A236, etc., **aschaped** 6428. **ascaped** *pp.* 3229, etc.; **aschape** 9647[r]. Cf. **scape.**

aschamed *pp.* (adj.) ashamed 4020, 7225, L1207.

asent *n.* assent 2361, *bi on* ~ in unanimous agreement 3530, *at on* ~ 9217.

a-sex *adv.* into six parts 7833.

aside *adv.* aside 9776.

asise *n.* style 8672.

asit *v.* withstand (in saddle) 8140. Cf. **wiþsat.**

aske(n) *v.* ask 1557, 5523; (obj. person and thing requested) 364; (with *to*+person) 6563, L696; **asky** 5534; **axi** 2950. **aske** *pr. pl.* A196, 5519. **ask** *pr. subj. sg.* 5929. **asked** *pa. t. 3 sg.* A183, L996, etc.; **axed** 4147. **asked** *pa. t. pl.* A1608, etc.; **axed** 3802, L1409; [**askeden**] L1337, L1366.

asking *n.* asking A1301; **axing** 2956.

[**asoyled**] *pa. t. 3 sg.* gave absolution to L682.

asoine *n.* excuse, *wiþouten* ~ indeed (tag) A140, 4351; [**ensoyne**] L79.

aspie(n) *v.* observe A559, 7406, etc. **aspie** *pr. subj. sg.* 6745. **aspide** *pa. t. 3 sg.* A1165.

aspies *pl.* scouts (milit.) 3652.

[**assaylle**] *v.* see **asayle.**

Assensioun *n.* feast of the Ascension 5584, 6590.

astert *n.* jumping 9891[n]. Cf. **starte** *v.*

astint *pa. t. pl.* put stop to actions of 8348.

astond *v.* withstand 8880.

astoned *pp.* (adj.) knocked senseless 3271, etc.; **astuned** 6287.

astore *n.* provisions 8058.

astore *v.* provision 4104. **astored** *pp.* 2420.

astray *adj.* wandering 7525; *adv.* 6712.

astroie *v.* kill 6746. Cf. **destroie, stroi(e).**

astromiens *pl.* astrologers A585[n].

aswon *adv.* unconscious 4936, etc.; **aswowe** 3294[r]; **aswouȝ** 8444[r]. *See 4936n.* Cf. **swoned, swouȝ.**

at *prep.* (mod. uses) A5, 97, 229, 1437, 2798, 3995, 8825, etc.; in 2287, 2419, 4213, 7507, on L657; *take leue* ~ take leave of A1293; *wite* ~ learn from 1603, (sim.) 5376, 5377; [+*lete beon* ~] stop talking about L1263; [~ *his miȝt*] to the utmost of his power L52. **atte** (+*þe*) A235, (+ bare n.) 2567, 4965, 5575, L628. Cf. **þerat(e).**

at *conj.* (*wiþ þat* ~) see **þat.**

atake *v.* gain certain knowledge of A1363. **atok** *pa. t. 3 sg.* captured A468. **atoken** *pa. t. pl.* learned A1334.

atheld *pp.* held in custody A618.

atire *n.* knightly gear 4696; **ater** 3542[r].

atiren *v.* (refl.) put on (knightly) gear 3788. **atired** *pa. t. pl.* 3441, 3815; *pp.* (adj.) (*wel(e)* ~ in noble gear) 3434, etc.

at(v)o *adv.* into two parts 2091, etc.; apart 1482, etc.

atrauȝt *pa. t. 3 sg.* succeeded in striking 4817. Cf. **rawȝt.**

atsit *v.* rest on (fig.), *iuel* ~ bring woe on A1796.

atwot *pa. t. 3 sg.* teased about 3555. **atwite** *pp.* upbraided for 9240. Cf. **wite** *v.*[2]

auantages *pl.* advantages A17.

auberk *n.* see **hauberk.**

[**avenge**] *v.* (refl.) take vengeance L134, *L158.

auensong *n.* time of vespers (6 p.m.) 4783, 4791; [**euesong**] = bell for vespers L1614. Cf. **euen** *n.*

auentour [-ure] *n.* adventure 9665, event L1681, L1794; *par* ~ if it so fell out 6358, perhaps L961. **auentours** [-ures] *pl.* 9665, L1794. Cf. **misauentour.**

auentour *v.* risk (refl.) A217.

Auerille [-el] *n.* April 259.

averray *v.* assure of the truth A1184. *See n.*

auȝt *pron.* see **ouȝt.**

[**auȝht(e), auhȝt**] *pa. t. 3 sg.* see **owes.**

[**aungelis**] *pl.* angels L592. **angels** *pl. gen.* 8916.

avowe *v.* prove the truth of A945, L1316, exhibit the truth A1052, A1388, *ichil* ~ I declare (tag) 5195, etc.; uphold (person) 2962, 2968.

away *adv.* see **oway.**

away *interj.* alas! A997. Cf. **walewo.**

await(e) *v.* lay ambush on 4409; take by surprise 6990. Cf. **andwaiteing.**

awaked *pa. t. 3 sg.* awoke (intr.) A849; *pp.* L851.

awaped *pp.* (adj.) stunned 3230.

awe *adj.* see **ow(h)en.**

awe *n.* fear 6000. Cf. **ay.**

[awey(ȝe)] *adv.* see **oway.**

awerreþ *pr. 3 sg.* makes war on 4304. **awerred** *pp.* 4287, 4330.

awondred *pa. t. 3 sg.* was astonished A1925; *pl.* A1628; *pp.* (adj.) A1137, 1399.

awreke(n) *v.* avenge 2082, 4770, 6960, etc. **awreke** *imp. sg.* 7997. **awreke(n)** *pp.* (adj.) (*ben* ~ be avenged) A402, A960, etc., (+*worþ* ~) 4228.

ax *n.* battle-axe 4888, etc.; **ex** 4797, etc. **axes** *pl.* A336, etc.

axi *v.* see **aske(n).**

ax-helue *n.* axe-shaft 5203.

ax-lengþe *n.* axe's reach 5178.

*aȝur *n.* azure (herald.) 5642.

bacbiteing *n.* calumniation behind victim's back A808.

bacheler *n.* young (unmarried) man, esp. aspirant to knighthood 3587, 4547, 5994, 6571. **bachelers** *pl.* 5393, etc.

bachelrie *n.* company of *bachelers* 4089.

bacin(e) **[basyn]** *n.* round (metal) dish 1490; helmet 3484, etc.; head-piece worn inside helmet 6400, etc.

badde *adj.* bad (in quality) A1934, (in conduct) 4854.

baye *adj.* both A1528. Cf. **bo, boþe.**

bal *n.* ball, *þe* ~ *vp in þe hod* = the head A394[n].

balaunce *n.* uncertainty, *wiþouten* ~ certainly (tag) 8096, etc.

[baldely] *adv.* without hesitation L1246. Cf. **beld.**

bale *n.* harm 4992.

baneour *n.* banner-bearer 6023.

baner *n.* banner 5122, L281, etc.; company ranged under a banner 3849, etc. **baners** *pl.* 3841, 3867, etc.

[baptiȝed] *pa. t. 3 sg.* baptized L1008.

bar *n.* bar (securing door) 5678.

bard *n.* see **berd.**

bare *adj.* unprotected, ~ *of liif* exposed to death A1686.

bare *n.* see **bere** *n.*[1]

barm *n.* waist 7952.

barn *n.* child 2578.

barnage *n.* company of noblemen 2421.

baroun *n.* nobleman (general) 205, etc., (ranked below *erl*) A405, L107, etc. **barouns** *pl.* 66, 99, etc.; **[barons]** L212, etc.; **[barounes]** L149.

[barst] *pa. t. 3 sg.* see **brast.**

[basyn] *n.* see **bacin(e).**

bast *adj.* bastard 7633.

bast *n.* bastardy 7634, *sone o* ~ bastard son 4032.

bastard *n.*, (quasi-adj.) bastard 7681, 7780, 8015.

batayl(e) *n.* battle 130, 1518, etc., and see **ȝiue(n), smite(n).**

bataileinge *n.* battle (see **ȝiue(n)**) 8925.

bat *pa. t. 3 sg.* struck together A565[n]; **[beot]** beat (person) L826. **bete(n)** *pa. t. pl.* beat (person) A830, 5789; knocked (on gate) 2521. **ybete** *pp.* (adj.) worked (with gold) 5643; **beten** 8672[n]. Cf. **tobete.**

battes *pl.* maces 8073.

baþe *n.* bath 6466.

baþen *v.* plunge (tr., weapon in enemy) 6814, 9917[n].

baudekines *n.* brocades 7417.

baundoun *n.* restraint 3915.

be(n) **[beo(n)]** *v.* be (mod. uses) 78, A254, 380, etc.; ((plu)perf. auxil+ v. intr.) *133, 2384, etc.*; signify A1918; **[beone]**[r] L1092, etc. **am** *pr. 1 sg.* 73, etc., *ich***am** A915[n], etc., **nam** (neg.) A195, 2322; **be** 6547[r]. **art** *pr. 2 sg.* 367, etc., **[artow]** L1025, etc., **nart** (neg.) 7498. **is** *pr. 3 sg.* 224, etc., (impers.) it is A10 (and sim. other *3 sg.* forms), **nis** (neg.) A201, L178, etc. **be(n)** **[beon]** *pr. pl.* A635, 652, etc.; **beþ** A1239, A1453, etc.; **are** 4197[r]; **[buþ]** L905, etc.; **[arn]** L333, etc. **be** **[beo]** *pr. subj. sg.* 370, 516, etc. *imp. sg.* A1117, 2661, L1166. **beþ** *imp. pl.* 7914. **was** *pa. t. 1, 3 sg.* 92, 197, A1232, etc., **nas** (neg.) A164, L231, etc.; **wes**[r] A98, L590, etc. **were** *pa. t. 2 sg.* A211, etc.; **[weore]** L1199, L1217; **[ware]** L1172. **were(n)** **[weore(n)]** *pa. t.*

pl. 67, 282, 1485, etc., had social status 6520, wer 2145, etc., **ner(e)**, **-en** (neg.) A586, 3088, 6141, etc.; **ware(n)**[r][not L] A160, 7353, L150, L1334, etc., **[war]** L1895, **nar** (neg.) A253, etc. **wer(e) [weore]** *pa. t. subj. sg.* 168, A663, etc., = were active L908, **ner(e)** (neg.) A813, 6569, etc.; **war(e)** 165, A526, L1374, etc., **nar** (neg.) 3182. **be(n)** *pp.* A1412, 4659, etc.; **ybe(n)**[r] A1769, 7775, etc.; **[beo(n)]** L183, L1441, etc.

beaute *n.* beauty 2255.

bed(de) *n.* bed 755, 837, etc. Cf. **a-childbed.**

bede *v.* invite 2228. **boden** *pp.* 3007; **yboden** (+infin.) commanded (action to be performed) A498. Cf. **bidden, forboden.**

⟨**befall**⟩ *pp.* gone to P1965[n].

begger(e) *n.* beggar A1931, 2451, etc.

being(e) *n.* presence 3784, status and circumstances 8591, etc.

bek *v.* = make weapon-stroke (as if bird with beak) 5202.

bel *adj.* worthy, *þe* ~ (cognomen) 5389, *le* ~ 8268; ~ *ami* good friend 9872, (iron.) L1165. Cf. **bieu.**

beld *adj.* bold A1216, A1382, etc.; **bold** [-(e)] A1417, L260, L1249, etc., = shameless L814. Cf. **baldely.**

benche *n.* bench (in hall) 2315, 6533.

[benesoun] *n.* blessing L1006.

bent *pa. t. 3 sg.* bent (bow) 4137. **ybent** *pp.* (adj.) imprisoned 1486[n]. Cf. **tobent.**

berd *n.* beard A1932, ~ *and snout* over whole face = totally 2918; **bard** 3678[r]. **berdes** *pl.* 9249.

bere *n.*[1] bier 1318; **bare** A1326[r]. Cf. **hors-bere.**

bere *n.*[2] bear 7518.

bere *n.*[3] outcry 8529, 9322.

bere [beore] *v.* carry, wear A246, 2679, *3065, 8673*[n], L125, etc.; ~ *a spere to* attack with spear 3299, (sim.) 2062, 6692, etc.; thrust (with weapon) 5691, 7798, etc. **berþ** *pr. 3 sg.* (~ *þe priis* is esteemed the best)

3614 (and sim. with other forms). **ber** *imp. sg.* 2272. **berand** *pr. p.* 7250. **bar** *pa. t. 3 sg.* A1981, 2984, L1007, etc., ~ *witnes(se)* bore witness A1285, etc.; **bare** 7187. **bar(e)**, **-en** *pa. t. pl.* 5779, 6254, 7464, etc.; **bere(n)** 6439, 7948, L475; **born** 3602, ~ *honour* paid respect to 6510. **born** *pp.* born A22, L907, etc., given birth to L978; **yborn** carried 2643; **(y)bore**[r] born 594, 667, L536, etc., carried L1360.

bereing *n.* how one was born A1414.

bern(e) *v.* see **brenne(n).**

best *n.* beast A1494, 7335, L1974.

bet(t) *adv. comp.*, etc. see **wel(e).**

bete(n) *pa. t. pl.*, etc. see **bat.**

bewe *adj.* see **bieu.**

bi *adv.* by L1281. *prep.* by (mod. uses) 180, 375, 852, A979, 985, etc., and see **cas, day, niȝt, riȝt** *n.*; on, at (point of action) 3889, 6161, etc., L796, L1953, (living) to the (north, etc.) 3107, 3186, 7395, etc., in (direction) A615, 7294, along (track, etc.) 1416, 3648, 4519, etc., through (wood) 9316, (fig.) see **lin;** during, at (time) A675, A1275, 2083, etc.; by the advice of L965; concerning L1100, [~ *þan*] = in þis matter L1103; ~ *alle her miȝt* with all their might 4533; ~ *fe* for money 8653; ~ *seuen þousand* in groups of seven thousand 6775, (sim.) 7204, etc.; ~ *þat* by the time that A1224, etc.; [~ *his name*] as his name L1020; also see **acord, asent, half** *n.*, **hond, rawe, tale, t(v)o.** Cf. **þerbi.**

bibled *pp.* (adj.) covered in blood 7235.

bichaunte *v.* induce by deluding A725. Cf. **enchaunte.**

biches *pl. gen.* bitches' (abus.) 8726.

biche-sone *n.* son of a bitch (abus.) 8477.

bicleppe *v.* seize 9382. **biclept** *pa. t. 3 sg.* embraced A1998; protected (with shield) 7881. **biclept(en)** *pa. t. pl.* surrounded 6101, 6627, etc.

bicom(e) *pa. t. 3 sg.* had gone to (question where) A1956, etc., L1777, became 2852, 8912, etc.; **bicam**[r] 1544, 2050, L888, befell

bicom(e) (*cont.*):
8226. **bicome(n)** *pa. t. pl.* 3033, 4198, 5242; *pp.* A1688, 7249.
bicouȝt *pp.* (adj.) beguiled A296^n.
bidden [**bydde**] *v.* invite 3392; (+ various constructs.) ask, tell (person, to do thing) *180*, L1944, *etc.* [**bydde**] *pr. 1 sg.* L783. **bid** *pr. pl.* L1454; *imp. sg.* A1368, etc., L799. **biddeþ** *imp. pl.* A1951. **bad(de)** [**bad**] *pa. t. 3 sg.* 180, A416, etc.; asked for A1936, 2453, ~ . . . *mesauenture* = cursed 8361^n. **bad(e)** *pa. t. pl.* 376, A610, A1321; [**baden**] L156. Cf. **bede.**
bide *v.* wait 3811, L81, L1515. **bot** *pa. t. 1 sg.* lived to see 6802^n. Cf. **abide.**
bidelue *v.* bury A1026. **bidoluen** *pp.* (adj.) 4156.
[**bydene**] *adv.* at once L1529; ?completely L576, L1702, L1712.
bieu *adj.* worthy, ~ *seygnours* noble lords! 3607, 6147, **bewe** 5543. Cf. **bel.**
bifalle *v.* befall (intr.) 6662, L1681. **bifalle** *pr. subj. sg.* L870, (tr.) A1217. **bifel(le)** [**byfeol**] *pa. t. 3 sg.* 6594, etc., L9, (tr.) 5042, L1101, = was the duty of 7712. **bifalle** *pp.* L184, L675, (tr.) 3232.
bifor(e), **-rn** [**-e(n)**] *adv.* before (mod. uses) 3242, 5272, L121, L908, L1359, *etc.*; in one's path 7504; ~ *and hinde* all round 7558. *prep.* before (mod. uses) 775, A984, 2412, 7861, etc.; in attendance on 6555. Cf. **here-, þerbifore, tofor(e).**
bifornhand *adv.* previously 5496.
(**bigge** *v.*) see **bouȝt** *pa. t. 3 sg.*
[**bygyle**] *v.* beguile L746, L766^n. **bigiled** *pa. t. 3 sg.* 4448, L806; *pp.* 2576, L628, L1664. Cf. **agile, gile.**
bigining *n.* beginning = birth A4.
biginne *v.* (auxil.) begin, proceed (to) A27, *A884*, *2589*, *etc.*, L100, *L938*; begin (tr.) *A547*, *2196*, *L1550*, (absol.) L488, ~ *care* be troubled 2337. [**bygynnen**] *pr. pl.* L1550. **bigan** *pa. t. 3 sg.* A772, etc. L100, L938, *his wordes* ~ spoke 3508, began (intr.) 3866, etc.

bigonne *pa. t. pl.* A547. Cf. **agan, ginneþ.**
bigrauen *pp.* buried A98.
biȝete *n.* begetting A1414, etc.; child, A883; thing to be obtained 2488^n, 7655. **biȝate**^{r} A686, 1575, 2699.
biȝeteing *n.* begetting A595, A1178.
biȝeten [**-e**] *v.* beget 672. **biȝat** *pa. t. 3 sg.* 1053, etc., got . . . done 2697. **biȝete(n)** *pp.* 591, 628, etc., got (as wife) 2651^n. Cf. **ȝete, misbiȝeten.**
biȝo(u)nde *prep.* beyond A1651, 2841, 3443. [**byȝonden**] *adv.* overseas L1738.
bihef *adj.* needful 6146.
biheld *v.* look at 5500. **biheld** [**-uld**] *pa. t. 3 sg.* 996, ~ *on* looked at 2463, 6537; [**byheold**] L1362. **biheld** *pa. t. pl.* 5660, 6268, looked 7090; *pp.* 8841.
biheueded *pa. t. 3 sg.* beheaded 8182, etc. Cf. **heued(en).**
bihinde(n) *adv.* behind (mod. uses) A337, 4851, 5977, etc., *bifore and hinde* all round 7558. *prep.* behind (mod. uses) A331, 3860, 5714, 6848, etc.
bihonged *pp.* hung (with draperies) 3539.
bihot(e) *pr. 1 sg.* promise 3049, 4638. **bihete** *pa. t. 3 sg.* A723. **biheten** *pa. t. pl.* 3051, ~ *þat hast* made that vow 4642. **bihoten** *pp.* commanded A1234. Cf. **hot(e).**
bihoueþ *pr. 3 sg.* is necessary 4650.
bihouesum *adj.* of service 2794.
biker *n.* fight 5552, 6870, etc. *See* 5552^n.
bikering *n.* fighting 7945.
biknawe *pp.*, *be* ~ (*of*) acknowledge, confess A425, A948, etc., make known 8631; **biknowe** A764. Cf. **aknawe.**
bilay *pa. t. 3 sg.* besieged 2423, 7607. **bilay(n)** [**-eyn**] *pp.* 343, 5368, etc. Cf. **ylay.**
bileue(n) *v.* remain 6755, 6910; rest (honour with man) 3050; **bilaue** A1999^r. **bileuestow** *pr. 2 sg.* 7592. **bileueing** *pr. p.* (as n.) survivors 4358. **bileft** *pa. t. 3 sg.* A1595, A1973; **bileued** 4527, 5857. **bileft(en)** *pa.*

t. pl. A1290, 6590, etc.; **bileued(en)** A646, 2505, survived 4376, 4386, 4405, ~ *for* waited for 9641. **bileued** *pp.* 6226, 7159.

bileueing *n.* waiting 8601.

biliif, -iue *adv.* at once 3240, 5866, etc.; **bliue** A223, L1004, etc.

bilimeden *pa. t. pl.* cut off parts of body 5765.

biloke(n) *pp.* surrounded A1838, 9116.

biment *pa. t. 3 sg.* bemoaned 6959.

binde *v.* bind (person) 8753. **bounde** *pa. t. pl.* 5790; *pp.* 7942; **ybounden** 5863. Cf. **vnbynde**.

bineþen [**byneoþe(n)**] *adv.* underneath 3293, L1569; in a valley 4987. *prep.* underneath L1543, L1651. Cf. **herebineþe**.

binim(en) *v.* take away, cut off (from) 5301[n], 6684. **binam** *pa. t. 3 sg.* 3335, etc., ~ *her liif-dawe* killed 3904 (and sim. with *pa. t. pl.*). **binome(n)** *pa. t. pl.* 2130, 5696, 6950, etc.; **binam** 3217. **binome** *pp.* A186, etc.

bireue *v.* take away from 7661. **bireued** *pp.* cut, pulled off (from) 4814, 5299.

biri *v.* bury 6727. **ybiried** [**buryed**] *pp.* 96. Cf. **burying**.

bischet *pp.* (adj.) locked in A587, A970.

bischop *n.* bishop 2757, etc.

biseiȝe *pa. t. 3 sg.* dealt with 8831, 9770.

biseche *imp. pl.* beg (person for action, etc.) A203. **bisouȝt** [**-e**] *pa. t. 3 sg.* A53, 122, 2141, etc. **bisouȝt** *pa. t. pl.* A157, 7214, L1677; *pp.* 2349.

bisecheing(e) *n.* earnest request, prayer 2803, 2942.

bisege *v.* besiege A342, A1905. **biseged** *pa. t. 3 sg.* 8367. Cf. **segeing**.

bisett [**-e**] *v.* assail *A1825*, 2499; surround *L298*, *L1915*; lay on (blow) *4830, 6829, L1947*. **bisett** [**-e**] *pa. t. 3 sg.* 4830, L298; *pl.* A1825, 6829. **bisett** [**-t**] *pp.* L1947; employed (thing) 2718.

biside *adv.* nearby A701, L664, ~

a lite a little way off A435; to the side 9244. *prep.* beside, near 4463, 5269, etc., L1328. Cf. **here-, þerbiside**.

bismare *n.* shame A1938.

bispac, -k *pa. t. 3 sg.* spoke A205, A1039, etc., (refl.) A193, 1612, etc. **bispoken** *pa. t. pl.* planned A1240; **bispake** 2505; **bispeke** 5402. **bispoke** *pp.* 3720.

bistere *v.* (refl.) act with full power 4271[r], 9738[r]. **bistere** *pr. subj. sg.* A1719[r]. **bistir** *imp. sg.* 6238. **bistireþ** *imp. pl.* 6015. **bistired** *pa. t. 3 sg.* 2142. **bistirden** *pl. pt.* 8757.

bistrode *pa. t. 3 sg.* sat on (horse) 8485; **bistride** stood astride 9842. **bistriden** *pa. t. pl.* mounted 5129.

biswike *pp.* deceived A1582, A1587.

bitauȝt [**-ȝht**] *pa. t. 3 sg.* entrusted to 6750, consigned L649.

bite *n.* blade (of axe) 4798.

bite(n) *v.* bite (lit. and fig.) 7968, 8956, 9636. **biteand** *pr. p.* 2978; **biteing** 3358. **bot** *pa. t. 3 sg.* 1682, etc., ~ *þe gres* bit the dust 7107. **bite(n)** *pa. t. pl.* A1521, 5767, etc. **ybite** *pp.* 9328.

bitide *v.* befall (tr.) 4464, L1002.

bitimes *adv.* in good time 7061.

bitoke *pa. t. 3 sg.* entrusted (to) 7736. **bitake** *pp.* 2701.

bitokneþ [**-enyþ**] *pr. 3 sg.* signifies 1636, etc. **bitokned** *pa. t. 3 sg.* A1610.

bitowe *pp.* (adj.) bestowed 8618.

bitter *adj.* bitter (fig.) A1019, 7870, 7941.

bitven(e) [**bytweone**] between (mod. uses) *adv.* 3143, etc. *prep.* A389, A476, 4783, etc., L828, L1604, among 3011; between . . . and enemy, etc. 5171, 5210, 9150.

bitvix(en) *prep.* between A286, 2514.

biþenche *v.* (refl.) take thought, have thought come into mind A893. **biþenke** *pr. 1 sg.* (so *y* ~ as I suppose (tag)) 6971; *subj. sg.* 2631. **biþouȝt** [**-ȝ(h)te**] *pa. t 3 sg.* 495, A795, 9855, L443. **biþouȝt** [**-ȝhten**] *pa. t. pl.* 362. [**byþouȝt**] *pp.* *L457, *þey were* ~ it came into their minds L1283, (*sim.*) L1384.

biwepe *pa. t. 3 sg.* wept for A458 6916, etc.

biwray *v.* reveal secret of A1336. **biwray** [-ȝen] *pp.* 1154. Cf. **wray.**

blak(e) *adj.* black L598, L981, etc., þe (*letters*) ~ = my written source A1957, 2702. **blacker** comp. A981.

[blame] *n.,* wiþowte ~ = courteously L1019.

blamen *pr. pl.* blame 4634.

blast *n.* surge of (dragon's) breath A1461, etc.

blawe *v.* see **blowe(n).**

ble *pl.* appearances A1978ʳ.

blede *v.* bleed 3274, 9836. Cf. **bibled.**

blent *pa. t. 3 sg.* blinded 5722.

bleþeliche *adv.* gladly 2683, etc. *See n.*

blinde *adj.* blind 3820.

blinne *v.* cease (intr.) 4645, L127.

blis(se) *n.* joy A1330, 5929, etc., L1387, and see **king.** Cf. **heuenblis.**

blisse *pr. subj. sg.* bless (as by making sign of cross on) 5505; **[blesse]** L1980. **blisced** *pa. t. 3 sg.* 3178, 4689, 4698; *pl.* 4372, **[blessedyn]** L1054. **(y)blisced** *pp.* A637, A816, 4268. Cf. **vnblisced.**

blisseing *n.* blessing A841, 7678; **[blessyng]** L882.

bliþe *adj.* glad, happy 601, 1029, etc., and see **glad(e).** Cf. **vnbliþe.**

bliþeful *adj.* glad 8605.

bliue *adv.* see **biliif.**

blod(e) *n.* blood 598, *A633, A1568, etc., = kin 1675, etc., ?L252ⁿ, = passion 6539; *noble* ~ man of noble blood 2833.

blodi *adj.* covered in blood 4804, etc.

blounde *adj.* fair-haired, þe ~ (cognomen) 8707.

blowe(n) *v.* blow (horn) 3832, 4041, etc.; be blown (trumpet) *8802ⁿ; **blawe** 4037, 6069. **blewe** *pa. t. 3 sg.* was carried (as by the wind) 9392.

bo *adj.* both 3998, 4158, (quasi-adv.) A1057, (with three conjoined nouns) 4737; **[boo]** L218. Cf. **baye, boþe.**

bod [-e] *n.* message 2036, L1457.

bodi *n.* body 653, 1027, 2058ⁿ, etc., and see **bon;** (of sexuality) 747, A782ⁿ, L704; = trunk 2012, etc.; man 5452, 6813, etc. **bodis** *pl.* 2188, 3270, etc.

boies *pl.* men of common rank 7064.

bok(e) *n.* book A1187, 8573, L1785, = bible 1629; = my written source 63, A979, etc., þe, our ~ A467, 2581, etc., þis ~ 9822; to ~ ysett educated A9.

bold(e) *adj.* see **beld.**

bolt *n.* arrow 4139.

bon *n.* bone, flesche and ~ (implying totality) 4832, 5215, 5980, L1812, [*body and* ~] L874, *in euerich* ~ 2444. **bones** *pl.* = body 9439. Cf. **brest-, nek-bon.**

bonair(e) *adj.* well-conducted (person) A810, courteous (words) 4601.

bond *adj.,* (as n.) bondmen A303.

bond [-e] *n.* confinement A1260, 1618; leash 4612. **[bondes]** *pl.* fetters L1487.

bone *n.* boon 2949.

bo(u)nde *n.* husband A691, A1328. Cf. **husbounde.**

[boo] *adj.* see **bo.**

bord *n.* dining-table 2209, 2218, etc., L207; flat wood (of gate) 5614, *scheldes* ~ = shield 7450.

bore-heuedes *pl.* boars' heads (herald.) 5643.

borioun *n.* new growth A1711. **buriouns** *pl.* 5351.

bors *pl.* boars 3119.

borwe *n.*[1] surety A1632, L1700. **borwes** *pl.* A1623.

borwe *n.*[2] fortified town 2419. **borwes** *pl.* 2191.

bost *n.* ostentation 356, 5596; arrogance 3137. *See 356n.*

bot [bote] *adv.* only A206, A1070, etc. *conj.* unless 729, A747, L794, etc., ~ ȝif 251, A577, L691, etc.; except (often quasi-prep.) 290, 584, A928, 940, L138, etc., *no more* ~ no more than 5357, (sim.) L182, L258, L488, etc., *nas* ~ was only (and sim.) A164, 4784, L178, L1096, etc., *no ascaped* ~ þre only three escaped 6706, (sim.) 6427; but, except that A589, A1435, 8648, etc., but L53, L63, etc.; **boten** 6427; **[bot]** L1245.

bot *pa. t. 1 sg.* see **bide.**

bote *n.* remedy 3412, ~ *of liue* means of saving's one's life 4023.

boteler, but- *n.* cupbearer 2262, 3591, 6071, etc.

botors *pl.* bitterns 3120.

boþe *adj.* both A76, A1230[n], 1457, L30, etc.; *adv.* A422, L66, etc. Cf. baye, bo.

bouȝt *pa. t. 3 sg.* redeemed (of Christ) A158, etc. bouȝt *pp.* bought 1304. Cf. abigge.

b(o)uke *n.* body 4017, 7179, 7461.

bounde *n.* see bo(u)nde.

bour [-e] *n.* private room 7280, (woman's) 3062, L729. Cf. bur-maiden.

bowe *n.* bow A313, etc. Cf. sadel-bowe.

⟨brayd⟩ *n.* quick movement, *in, att a* ~ at once P2131, P2350.

[brayd] *pa. t. 3 sg.*, ~ *vp* raised (eyes) L1036.

brain *n.* brain 9432.

brast [barst] *pa. t. 3 sg.* break (intr.) 2875, 3461, (fig.) 786, 2334; break (tr.) 3474; [~ *owt*] burst out L1586. brust *pa. t. pl.* 3318; brosten 3310. Cf. tobrast.

bredden *pa. t. pl.* burned (men) 7295.

bred(e) *n.* bread 4713, 7415, etc.

bref *adj.* short (time) 5194.

breke(n) *v.* break (tr., lit. and fig.) A1824, 2323, 3478. brac, -k *pa. t. 3 sg.* 93, 3469, etc.; (intr.) 3258, etc.; ~ *fro* broke free from A1828. broken *pa. t. pl.* 5283, 9167; breken (~ *fro*) 7205; [brak] L1918. broken *pp.* A137, 5736; [brokyn] L867. Cf. tobrac.

brenne(n), bren [brenne] *v.* burn (tr.) 1664, 6962, 6982, etc.; (intr., lit. and fig.) A1457, 2310, etc., L1970; bern(e) 2310, 7291. brin-neþ *pr. pl.* A1457; brennen 6786. brenand *pr. p.* A1500, 6796; brent [-e] *pa. t. 3 sg.* 1539, etc.; *pl.* A1892, etc., L1812; brend A1890. (y)brent *pp.* A1894, 7312, 8321, L1193. Cf. forbren.

brest *n.* breast (man's) 4890, etc. brestes *pl.* 8867.

brest-bon *n.* breast-bone 7191, 9278.

brest-heiȝe [breost-hyȝh] *adv.* breast-high 536.

breþeling [broþ-] *n.* wretch 164, 5912.

bridel *n.* bridle A1319, 4937, 5701, 5891. bridels *pl.* 6052.

brigge [brugge] *n.* bridge 1158, etc.; drawbridge 7255; bregge 7793.

[bryȝes] *n.* brightness L1578[n].

briȝt *adj.* bright A440, 6113, etc., L281, L592, L1022; beautiful (woman) 2249, L910, L1427. *adv.* brightly 3204, 6877, L1609.

bring [-e] *v.* bring (change of place, incl. metaphys., or state) 880, 1554, etc.; take A287; ~ *in erþe, mold* bury 2160, 2734; ~ *it þerto* bring things to such a point 1050, L705; ~ *on* incite 2023; ~ *on hors* (and sim.) remount 3360, 3921, *etc.*; ~ *of dawe* (and sim.) kill A146, 3213, 7854, *etc.*, ~ *to grounde* A451, *etc.*, L1829; ~ *to nouȝt* bring to ruin A1445, A1902; [~ *in bonde*] imprison L1695. brouȝt [-(e)] *pa. t. 3 sg.* A121, L83, L807, etc.; drove (enemy back, etc.) 2134, etc. brouȝt(en) [-(e)] *pa. t. pl.* A326, A404, etc., L327, L1567. (y)brouȝt *pp.* A146, 674, L1199, etc. [ne þar it neuer forþer ~] it need go no further L732.

brini *n.* corslet 2975, etc.

brink *n.* bank (river) 7900.

brinneþ *pr. pl.* see brenne(n).

brod(e) *adj.* broad 1452, A1479, etc., *adv.*, [*wide and* ~] far and wide L1173.

broke *n.* brook 2582, 7746.

brond *n.* sword 4242. brondes *pl.* A1876.

brosten *pa. t. pl.* see brast.

[broþelyng] *n.* see breþeling.

broþer [-ir] *n.* brother 1722, etc. breþer [-e] *pl.* 270, etc.; breþern 4625, 4633.

broþer-kniȝt *n.* brother-knight 7632.

broun *adj.* bright A324, 9704.

broun(e) *adj.* brown A1190, 7416, þe ~ (cognomen) 5636, etc.

br(o)ut *n.* authoritative work on the kings of Britain A538, 3675, etc.; [bruyt] L32.

brust *pa. t. pl.* see **brast**.
buffeyt *pa. t. 3 sg.* struck with fist 8438; *pp.* 8440.
buke *n.* see **b(o)uke**.
buriays *n.* freeman of city 5562. **buriays [-ǥeys]** *pl.* A1737, 1770.
[burying] *n.* funeral L58. Cf. **biri**.
buriouns *pl.* see **borioun**.
burmaiden *n.* lady's maid 6476.
burre *n.* bur 8280.
busse *n.* bush 8422.
but *n.* blow, *ful* ~ with full force 5247.
buteler *n.* see **boteler**.
butten *v.* fall head-first 5165.

cabel *n.* rope A974.
calle *v.* address, greet (formally) 509, 3549, etc., ~ *to* 8388, L1164; ~ *o* summon (with horn) 4036. **[calliþ]** *pr. pl.* (*men heore names* ~ they are named) L31. **[calde]** *pa. t. 3 sg.* described as L818.
calu *adj.* bald, *þe* ~ (cognomen) 9752.
can *pr. sg.* see **conne**.
[can] *pa. t. sg., pl.* see **con(ne)**.
candel *n.* candle 3204.
[candel-lyȝt] *n.* candle-light L794.
Candelmesse *n.* Candlemas 2834.
care *n.* distress 166, etc., anxiety A499.
carf *pa. t. 3 sg.* see **kerue**.
cark *n.* woe 9181, *haue þe* ~ *of* bear the brunt of 3942.
carked *pp.* (adj.) harassed 4454ⁿ.
carking *n.* toil of battle 3945ⁿ.
carols [-es] *pl.* round dances 1714; **karols** 3544.
carpenter *n.* carpenter 8838. **carpenters** *pl.* 501, 6044.
carroy *n.* assembly of carts 4777; **charrois** 8057; **korray** 8544.
carters *pl.* cart-drivers 7427.
cartes *pl.* carts 4711, etc.
carting(e) *n.* train of carts 7412, 7421, 7568.
cas *n.* (set of) circumstances, state of affairs A240, 749, A1175, 5206, 5450, 7308, L630, L1205, etc., *in þat* ~ = then 2003; *bi* ~ as it fell out 1199, 7151, 9669.
cast *n.* range of shot 8986.
cast *v.* put 5152. **cast** *pa. t. 3 sg.* 2836; threw (lit. and fig.) 3816, 5923, etc.,

L1631, ~ *adoun* threw down A1537, A1657; **kest** 5210, 5240, etc.; **[kast]** L1734. **cast** [-en] *pa.t.pl.* 1521, etc.; **kest(en)** A1515, A1889, uttered (cry) 6167. **cast** *pp.* 8676, L496, L524; **ycast** A1462. *See 1515n.*
casteinge *n.* throwing 2430.
castel *n.* castle 329, etc.; **castil** A1974ʳ. **castels** *pl.* 148, etc.; fighting-towers (on elephants) 8943, 9306.
castel-ȝates *pl.* castle gates A1887. Cf. **ǥate**.
castel-wal *n.* castle wall 3173.
cat *n.* cat 8716.
catel *n.* money 4318; property 5088.
cauci *n.* raised way 7746.
celle *n.* (subordinate) monastery 2211.
cendel *n.* silken cloth 5634, etc.
cert *adv.* assuredly (tag) 3499, etc.
certain [-(e)] *adj.* reliable 7920, [*for* ~] assuredly (tag) L1806; **certeyns** unfailing 2616ʳⁿ. *adv.* assuredly (tag) 8206, L1506; **certein** 5243, 7632.
[certaynly] *adv.* assuredly L193.
certes *adv.* assuredly 753, etc.
chalanged *pa. t. 3 sg.* exhorted 3929ⁿ.
chapman *n.* pedlar A1981.
(y)charged *pp.* (adj.) loaded 4710, 4713, etc.
charging *n.* train of loaded carts 4717.
charite *n.* Christian love, *for* ~ (formula of request) A72, *par* (*seynt*) ~ 7371, L41, L1943.
charrois *n.* see **carroy**.
chasteleins *pl. gen.* castellans' 4761.
chaufed *pp.* (adj.) heated, *wiþ* ~ *blod* = with renewed energy 7135.
chaumber [-bre] *n.* private room 831, etc.; **[chaumbur]** L834.
chaumberlain [-burleyn] *n.* personal servant (to king, queen, etc.) 1392, etc.; **chaumberleyn** A1401; **chaumberlains**ʳ 2265, 2518.
[chaumbre-dore] *n.* door of private room L1215.
chaunce *n.* event befalling by fortune A779, A1701, L184, etc., (person's) fate A332; fortune (as a power) 1042, etc. **chaunces** *pl.* A799, etc.

chaunceler *n.* (king's) secretary A1732.

chaunged *pa. t. 3 sg.* changed (intr.) A1138, A1520; *pp.* 2250.

cheke *n.* cheek 6003, etc.

cheld *adj.* cold 8829; [**cold**] L1379.

chep(e) *n.* bargain, *gode* ~ as a good . . . (iron.) 5700, 9151.

chepeing *n.* conducting of a market A1297.

[**chepyng-toun**] *n.* market town L1332.

cher(e) *n.* expression of face, mood (esp. as expressed by this) A266, A374, 996, 1344, L92^n, L807, etc., and see **hong**.

cherl *n.* countryman 4136, etc.; bondman A1506. **cherl(e)s** *gen.* 7234, 7236.

chese(n) *v.* choose A248, 2796, etc. **ches(e)** *pa. t. 3 sg.* A632, 8687, 8751. **chosen** *pa. t. pl.* A173, A257; **schosen** 7379^n. **chosen** [-e(n)] *pp.* 275, L69, etc.; **ycorn** A635^r; [**ykore**] (as adv. intensive, modifying adj.) L1858^r.

chest *n.* contention, strife 3044, 3144, L642, L1762; trouble A762; disturbance 3778.

cheualrie *n.* chivalric status 4090, 7653; knightly deeds 2114.

[**chidde**] *pa. t. 3 sg.* railed L821. **chidde** *pp.* rebuked 7227.

chideing *n.* quarrelling A683.

child *v.* give birth A956. **childed** *pa. t. 3 sg.* gave birth to A978, 2698.

child(e) *n.* child, young man A604, 4828, L538, etc., (quasi-adj.) A1039, 1593, 4631, etc.; *wiþ* ~ with child 914, etc. **childes** *gen.* A1164, L1112, etc. **childer** [-dre] *pl.* A9, L218, etc., = offspring 74, etc.; **children** A294, etc., L644. **children** *pl. gen.* 4764; [**childre**] ?L1282. Cf. **a-childbed**.

chin(ne) *n.* chin A1860, 4812, etc.

chine *n.* spine 6369, etc.

chirche *n.* church (building) A658, etc.; *holy* ~ Holy Church A51, A710.

chirche-dore *n.* church-door 2807.

chircheȝerd [-ȝard] *n.* churchyard 1317.

chirche-hay *n.* churchyard 6728.

chirche-werd see **toward(e)**.

chon *pa. t. 3 sg.* split (tr., fig.) 7754.

chose(n) *pp.* see **chese(n)**.

cite *n.* city A56, A1643^n, etc. **cites** *gen.* 9188; *pl.* 2191, [**cytees**] L128.

cite-wal(le) *n.* city-wall 5813, 6375.

citisains *n.* inhabitants of city 5080, 5837; **citaisins** 6223; **citeseines** 6914.

[**yclad**] *pp.* (adj.) see **(y)cloþed**.

clay *n.* earth 73.

claim *pr. pl.* declare (selves) to be A519.

clappe *n.* blow 9142. [**clappes**] *pl.* L162. Cf. **afterclap**.

[**clapte**] *pa. t. 3 sg.* clapped (hands) L1600.

clare *n.* honeyed and spiced wine 3123.

clef, cleue *pa. t. 3 sg.* cut apart A1859, 3282, etc.; came in two 5212; **cleued** 6172, etc. **cleued** *pa. t. pl.* 5695, etc.; *pp.* A319, etc.; [**clowen**] L113. Cf. **tocleued**.

[**clene**] *adj.* free of sin L634, L682.

[**clepe**] *v.* name L1020; summon L558. **clepeþ** *pr. pl.* name A1380. **clept** *pa. t. 3 sg.* A987; **cleped** [-(e)] L1009, summoned A1145, etc., L1835, ~ *vp* 6579, called out (intr.) L995. **cleped** *pa. t. pl.* A104. [**clepid**] *pp.* L85; (y)**cleped** described as 2559, (adj.) named A48, 5560, L28, etc. Cf. **ofcleped**.

clepeing *n.* calling out (in welcome) 7259.

cler *adj.* bright 1490, 3204, 3350, etc.; clearly understandable A1552; flawless A475, 6295, 6572.

clerk *n.* learned man 2772, etc., *lewed no* ~ = nobody 561. **clerkes** *pl.* 568, etc.; clerics L1359; **clerk** A623^n.

cleued *pa. t. pl.* held fast (intr.) 8279.

clobbe *n.* mace 4542.

cloþ(e) *n.* cloth 4686, = tablecloth 3115, = caparison 2973^n, = ornamental hanging 3540; clothes A441, 2525, L825. **cloþes** *pl.* 2303, etc.; clothes A1396, etc.

(y)cloþed [**yclad**] *pp.* (adj.) with clothes on 838, 2371.

[cloþyng] n. clothes L1426, L1484.
cloude n. sky 4740.
clout [clowte] v. patch 1305.
clout-leþer n. leather for patching A1305.
[clowen] pp. see clef.
clowes pl. claws A1498, A1517.
code n. ?cheeks 9017[n].
cokin n. rogue 6371.
[cold] adj. see cheld.
colour n. colour 5641, 8659, L614.
com(e) n. arrival 3013, 4130, etc.
com(e), -en [come] v. come (mod. uses) 130, A1061, 8748, etc., ~ ride come riding 5270, (sim.) 3463, etc.; ~ þerin get in A1908, (sim.) 7282; ~ at on agree 2782; cum A416. com [-e] pr. 1 sg. 2004, L1935. comeþ pr. 3 sg. (me ~ comes upon me) A517, (3ou ~ is coming to you) 6240. come(n) [-en] pr. pl. 3423, 4087, L1289, etc.; comeþ A1219, 6615. com [-e] pr. subj. sg. 1310, etc. com imp. sg. 7501. comeþ imp. pl. A1272, wel ~ welcome! A1230[n]. comand pr. p. 3042, etc.; comend A1793; cominde 7078; coming(e)[r] 7851, 8576. com(e) pa. t. 1, 3 sg. 687, A977, 7647, etc.; (refl.) A722, 4265, L815; ~ to changed into A762; cam[r] [not L] A949, L453, etc., fro main ~ was delivered with force 9378. com(e), -en pa. t. pl. 265, A423, 3916, L569, L1269, etc.; cam[r] L495, L1332, etc., 6820. (y)comen pp. 67, A800, L1887, etc., þus fer ~ it is things have gone as far as this 4637; (y)come[r] [not L] A1753, 8022, L79, L109, etc., [hit was ~ to þe ny3t] night had come L479, etc.; com *8352. Cf. tocomen, welcome.
comand [-aunde] v. (+to and inf. [various in L]) order (person, to do thing) A1421, L274. [comaunde] pr. 1 sg. L1511. [comaunded] pa. t. 3 sg. L265, L563, L568, etc., [~ to horse and armes] = ordered to arm and mount L1888.
comandment [-aunde-] n. command(ment) L516, etc., A658.
combraunce n. harm 4324; malign influence L868. Cf. encombraunce.

[comburment] n. malign influence L678, L736. Cf. encumbrement.
comfort [coun-] n. consolation 4229; assistance 6252; pleasure L1433.
comfort v. hearten 9201.
[comyn] n. generality of the people L244.
coming(e) n. approach 5131, etc.; arrival 7328, L1518; togider ~ meeting 4655; in her ~ as they came 6131, (sim.) 5737, 7933, etc.
comonliche adv. all together 6447.
comoun adj. shared by all A734, etc.
[compacement] n. plot L261[n].
compa(i)nie, -ein- n. group (of fighting-men) 6515, 6839, 9720, etc., was þer no more ~ bot the group was no bigger than 5356; ~ of sexual union with A916.
compainoun n. comrade 9083.
[con(ne)] pr., pa. t. pl. (expletive auxil.) L1324, L1552, L1896; [can] L1813. [can] pa. t. 1, 3 sg. L462, L680, etc.
concentement n. consent 2825.
condue v. provide escort for 5608. condid pl. pt. 5714.
confusioun n. disaster A1698, 5778.
confussiouns ?pl. 6607[r].
conioun n. fool A680, A1110; (term of abuse, of child or unmanly man) A206, 1071, 1217; [konioun] L178.
[coniured] pa. t. 3 sg. conjured L1055.
conne v. know, understand A1032. can pr. 1, 3 sg. A24, 4315, etc., L1769; am, is able to [L kan] 1057, 1383, etc., (in pa. t. sequence) L1298; cun A1151; [con] L1201; [can] L1205; kan (gode ~ has sense) A1041 (and sim. with other forms, L and A). kanestow [canst] pr. 2 sg. 1049; [konst(ow)] L1098, L1313, L1505. conne [k-] pl. pr. A1191, L1799. can pr. subj. sg. A1407, L1167, L1532. couþe pa. t. 1, 3 sg. 1033, A1096, 8563, etc. [kouþe] L1178. couþe pa. t. pl. A588, L454, etc. couþe [couþ] pp. (adj.) 1078; ⟨sibb and couthe⟩ kinsmen and friends P339.
[conquerour] n. victor L18.
conquerre v. be the victor 7648[n].

conseil(e) [**counsail(e)**] *n.* (piece of) advice 1164, 1597, 6146, etc.; consultation, agreement A289, 6730, and see **nim(en)**, **take(n)**; council A189, ?A349, body of men in agreement A1674.

conseild *pa. t. 3 sg.*, ~ *him at* took counsel with 5375.

conseyler *n.* counsellor 2298, 2336.

conseiling *n.* advice A196, etc.

constable *n.* chief officer of city 4116, etc.

contein *pr. subj. sg.* conduct (self, in battle) 2097. **conteind** *pa. t. 3 sg.* 5289; **contend(e)** 2869, 4845. **conteined** *pa. t. pl.* 9153; **contend** *pp.* 8102.

contek *n.* battle A237, etc., L1926; **cuntek** 7775. Cf. **cunteked**.

contenaunce *n.* conduct (of men in battle) 5287; +*lese* ~ lose one's wits (from blow) 9442.

contre *n.* battle 6135.

[**contre, -ay**] *n.* see **cuntre.**

cop *n.* see **coupe.**

cord [**-e**] *n.* rope 1141, etc.

corn *n.* corn 4105, etc.

corner *n.* corner portion 9357.

coroning *n.* coronation 3058. Cf. **crouned.**

coro(u)nment [**-ounement**] *n.* coronation 281, 2051, 3068.

c(o)roun *n.* crown A276, etc., L68, = kingship 2049, 3136; **crone** [**corowne**] 76^r. **coroun(e)s** *pl.* 5370, 9249; **coroune** 5635^r.

cors *n.* body 6078, 7236, 9038, etc., (specif. dead) L1358, etc.; = man 5766, etc. **cors** *pl.* 6942, 7974.

[**corse**] *v.* curse (tr.) L644. **cors** *pr. 1 sg.* 3184. [**corsed**] *pa. t. 3 sg.* L648. **curs(s)ed** *pp.* (adj.) A482, A1112, etc. Cf. **acurssed** *pa. t. 3 sg.*

coruen *pa. t. pl.*, *pp.* see **kerue.**

cosyn *n.* cousin 6392, etc.

couaitise [**-et-**] *n.* covetousness A82, 807.

couched *pp.* (adj.) embroidered 5642.

coue *adv.* quickly 7145.

couenaunt *n.* agreement A425, etc., L307.

couered *pa. t. 3 sg.* protected (self) with shield 9356.

couered *pa. t. 3 sg.*, *pp.* see **keuer(en).**

[**counfort**] *n.* see **comfort.**

[**counsail(e)**] *n.* see **conseil(e).**

coupe *n.* drinking-cup 2269, etc.; **cop** 6944.

coure *n.* care (of child) 2856; heed (see **nim(en)**) A411, etc.

cours *n.* charge (in battle) 5147.

court *n.* court (king's) 3545, L1420, etc.

couþ(e) *pa. t. 3 sg.*, *etc.* see **conne.**

coward *adj.* cowardly 5109, etc.

cowardschippe *n.* cowardice 9200.

cradel *n.* ?harness supporting horse's caparison 2973^n.

craft *n.* power 6866.

crake *v.* break (intr.) 3268. **craked** *pa. t. 3 sg.* (tr.) 5762.

crane *n.* crane (bird) 3121.

(**crepe** *v.*) see **ycrope** *pp.*

cri(e) *n.* shout, cry 1212, 8427, etc., crying out A333, etc.; report 2544.

cri(e), -en [**cry(ȝ)e**] *v.* shout, cry (tr.) 6013, 8428, etc., L1275; cry out 9212, L1039, etc. **criinde** *pr. p.* 8454^r; **criand** 9390. **crid** *pa. t. 3 sg.* 8439; [**cryȝed**] L829. **criden** *pa. t. pl.* 4862.

criing *n.* crying out A334, 8966.

crispe *adj.* curly-haired, *þe* ~ (cognomen) 5451.

Cristen *adj.* Christian 6208, etc., L1000; (as n. pl.) 6100, etc.; **Cristiens** 6907^r.

cristen *v.* christen 2706. **cristned** *pa. t. 3 sg.* A986. **ycristned** [**cristened**] *pp.* 991.

[**Cristendam**] *n.* Christendom L848, L1128; christening L1009.

Cristenmesse-euen *n.* Christmas Eve 2783.

[**Cristiaunte**] *n.* Christendom L1134.

croice [**croys**] *n.* (sign of the) Cross L798, L846; bowing down (see **falle**) 7305^n.

crone, croun *n.* see **c(o)roun.**

ycrope *pp.* crept (iron.) 7219.

crouche *n.* sign of the Cross 9005.

croume *adj.* curled, (as n.) curled creature 5659^n.

crouned *pa. t. 3 sg.* crowned 3112. Cf. **coroning.**

croupe *n.* hindquarters 3273.
crowes *gen.* crow's 9174.
crud *n.* pushing 5500.
crudand *pr. p.* hastening *5984[n].
cum *v.* see com(e).
cun *pr. 3 sg.* see conne.
cuntasse *n.* noblewoman 2445[n].
cunteked *pa. t. 3 sg.* fought (intr.) 8362. Cf. contek *n.*
cuntre [con-] *n.* region A1516, 3196, L1256, etc., = inhabitants of . . . 7556, 7608; land L693, ?L725, ?L 1331; rural areas 4202; cuntray(e), -eie [contray][r] A696, 4543, 8312, etc., L1356; homeland 347, etc.; cuntreys 4368[r].
curagus *adj.* eager (to . . .) 8984.
curs(s)ed *pp.* (adj.) see corse.
curteys *adj.* noble-mannered 2721, 3070, etc.
curteyseliche *adv.* in noble manner 3376, 3549; curteyslich 2723; curtaisliche 6459.
curteisie *n.* noble manners 3382, 5468, 7654.

dade *pl.* see dede.
day *n.* day 494, A921, 1710, etc., *o ~* during the day A555, A1446, [*by ~*] L1213, *bi ~ and ni3t* = always, constantly (and sim.) A125, A559, A1970, etc., *li3t o ~* morning light 2363; (adverbial) *þat ~* (and sim.) 357, 550, 3430, 4206, L836, etc., *~ and ni3t* A877, 2263, L1126; = (life)time A87, A675, etc., *~ o liue* life 2130, 9702; dawe[r] 5103, = life (see bring, do(n), of *prep.*) A146, 4983, etc. days *gen.* (*sone ~* early in the day) 4236. day(e)s *pl.* A587, 4219; dawes 8326[r]; [dai3es] L601, *by ~ and by niyht* L66. Cf. liue-dawe, mid(d)ay, midmorwe-day, Mononday, today.
day *v.* see dye.
dayli3t *n.* morning light 2366, L1352, L1528.
dayspringing *n.* dawn 8799.
dale *n.* see del.
damage *n.* harm, injury 4182, 7275, 8847.
dame *n.* mother 1023, 1105, etc., *ma*

~ 4644, 7646; woman, lady 1117, 2279, 2580, L904, etc.; dam (quasi-adj.) 2284.
damisel(e) *n.* young unmarried woman A457, A912, etc. damisels [-es] *pl.* 1714 etc.; damisele 6599[r].
dan *adj.* Sir 6081, 6183[n], 7505.
da(u)nger [-aun-, -awn-] hesitation 280, A1560, 1611; menaces L1699.
dar *pr. 1, 3 sg.* dare 2462, 4977, 7352, [*y ~ sweore*] I can swear L1344. darst *pr. 2 sg.* A1088. durst [-e] *pa. t. 3 sg.* 256, etc.; [dorste] L1598. durst [-e] *pa. t. pl.* 2166, etc., L24.
dasse *pr. pl.* gallop fiercely 5118, 9125. dasseþ *imp. pl.* 5865. dasseand *pr. p.* 5146, 9669. dassed *pa. t. 3 sg.* 6074, etc., (refl.) 7582; struck fiercely 9041; dasched 8429; dast(e) 5687, 9700, etc. dassed *pa. t. pl.* 4994, etc., (refl.) 5870; dasched 6689, etc., (refl.) 7971; dast(en) 5060, 8256, 9264. (y)dast[r] *pp.* thrust or struck fiercely A455, 2111, 7950; dassed 2109. See 455*n.* Cf. dust, todaschen.
dassing *n.* beating (drum) 8802[n].
dawe *n.* see day.
dawe *v.* dawn 2589; dawy 2008.
daweing *n.* time of dawn 8777.
De *n.* see Dieu.
de *prep.*, *Herui ~ Riuel* prop. name 6529, etc.
decended *pa. t. 3 sg.* see dessenden.
decente *n.* inheritance 7642.
ded(e) *adj.* dead 73, 689, etc., and see ston. Cf. stan-ded.
ded(e) *n.* death A907, A1780, L253, L1099, etc., and see for.
dede *n.* deed 2629, L734; story A1270[n]; (number uncertain) deed(s) A764, A1382, L15, L947, etc., and see fleschly. dede *pl.* 2128; dade A1182[r]; [dedes] L1170. Cf. misdede.
ded(e)li *adj.* mortal (wounds) 8970, etc., (combat) 7944, (sin) L616; dedlich(e) 8158, 8950, (enemies) A306, A388.
defaut *n.* absence A214, *9206; [defau3t] fault L186. Cf. faut.

defende *v.* defend 2416, etc. **defende**
pr. subj. sg. forbid 2954. **defended**
pa. t. 3 sg. 9844, etc.; *pl.* 7855, 9754.
Cf. **fende**.

defense *n.* defence 9107.

defoil *n.* trampling down 9181.

defoile *v.* trample down 6694.
defuiland *pr. p.* doing shame to
5794. **defoiled** *pa. t. 3 sg.* 6078; *pl.*
6208, 8532; *pp.* 6942, etc.; **defoile**
7990ʳ. *See 6693n.*

[de3ed] *pa. t. 3 sg.* see **dye**.

deinte *n.* choice quality (*of gret* ~ and
sim.) 3118, 3583, 8646.

[deys] *n.* dais L152.

del *n.* party (of men) A327, 6621,
dale 3835ʳ; part, *eueri* ~ in every
particular 4096, [*vche* ~] L941.
Cf. **haluendel, sumdel**.

deled *pp.* shared out 5339; **delt** (fig.)
4876.

deleid *pp.*, ~ *it* delayed (intr.) 9733.

delite *n.* delight, *of* ~ delightful
A358.

delite *v.* have pleasure 9773, (+*to*
and inf.) 7967.

deliuerd *pa. t. 3 sg.* handed over
8549; *pl.* *A1789; ~ *fram* saved
from 5894; *pp.* 5901, 5928.

delue *v.* bury A1051. **[deluen]** *pr. pl.*
L932. **delue** *pr. subj. sg.* A933.
doluen [-e(n)] *pa. t. pl.* A732,
L770; dug A533, 1471; *pp.* buried
765, L726, etc.; **ydoluen** A1047,
A1093.

[deme] *v.* judge (= condemn) L1076.

demeyne *n.* king's personal land 2189.

den *n.*¹ lair 1511.

den *n.*² valley A1764, etc.

den(e) **[de(o)ne]** *n.* noise 9726, *wiþ
gret* [*loud*] ~ with a loud voice 1001,
wiþouten ~ quietly (fig.) 754; **din**
5735. Cf. **dined**.

[Denys] *adj.* Danish L88, etc.

dent *n.* blow A1852, etc.; **dint** 3307,
etc. **dintes** *pl.* A234, etc.; **dentes**
7882. Cf. **deþ-dentes**.

[deol] *n.* see **diol**.

[deo(ue)l] *n.* see **deuel**.

depart *n.* departure 4529.

[departen] *v.* divide (tr.) L559.
[departe] *pr. pl.* depart L1295.
departeþ *imp. pl.* divide 2091,

5336. **departed(e)** *pa. t. 3 sg.*
*3367; separated 2208. **departed**
pa. t. pl. 2102; *pp.* A603, 9339,
= dead 3516.

depe **[deop(e)]** *adj.* deep 1449 [L
obscure], etc., L1566; *adv.* A1453,
etc.

der(e) *n.* deer 6797, 7000, 7972.

[deray] *n.* see **desray**.

dere **[dure]** *adj.* well-loved A53,
L712, (iron.) 7517.

dere *adv.* at great price (fig.) A784,
A826.

dere *n.* harm A693, 2039.

dere *v.* do harm to A430, etc., L216;
deri(en) A656, A784, etc.

[derk] *adj.* obscure L1796.

derling *n.* well-loved man 7502.

derne *adj.* secret A1146, L1429.

descomfit *pp.* (adj.) defeated 3943,
4205; **[discomfy3t]** L118. Cf.
scomfite.

descomfite *n.* defeat A156. Cf.
scumfite.

desert *n.* deserted country 3500,
8324.

deserued *pp.* deserved (to . . .) 4277.
Cf. **serued**.

deshonour *n.* dishonour 3141, etc.

desire *n.* desire A1996, 4666.

desire *v.* desire 528. **desired** *pa. t. sg.*
(+(*for*)*to* and inf.) A181, 7993.

desirite *pp.* despoiled of possessions
9199.

desmay *n.* dismay 7909.

desmaied *pp.* discomfited 9758.

despite *n.* outrage 2397, 5773, etc.
Cf. **spite**.

desplayd *pa. t. 3 sg.* unfurled A1799.

despuled *pp.* stripped of clothes
A1403.

desray *n.* evil deeds 9861; **[deray]**
disturbance L816.

[dessenden] *pr. pl.* come down L615.
decended *pa. t. 3 sg.* continued
downwards 5213.

destaunce *n.* quarrel 4585.

destourbes [-eþ] *pr. 3 sg.* unsettles
1390.

destrer *n.* war-horse 1370, etc.
destrers *pl.* 3761, etc.

destroie *v.* kill 4332; **[distryen]**
L1753. **destroi(e)d** *pp.* 4039, 7262,

destroie (*cont.*):
7336; **destrued** destroyed and killed 4246. Cf. **astroie, stroi(e).**

[destruccioun] *n.* destruction and death L1787.

desturbing *n.* harassment 7057.

deþ(e) *n.* death A340, 2122, L272, L1110, etc., and see **for. deþes** *gen.* mortal (wounds etc.) 2098, 5959, etc. Cf. **ded(e)** *n.*

deþ-dentes *pl.* mortal blows 5220.

deþ-rentes *pl.* death as tribute (iron.) 7800.

deuel [**deouel**] *n.* devil 686, 1207, etc., (= fierce man) 6340, etc., *what* ~ what the Devil 2024; [**deol**] L1192. **deuels** *gen.* A706; *pl.* A640; **deuelen** A651, etc.

deueling *adv.* grovelling 5024, 7752. Cf. **adiuel.**

deuine *n.* astrologer 3553.

deuise *n.* plan A525.

deuise *v.* contrive 3003, 3126; describe in detail 6522.

devoided *pa. t. 3 sg.* deprived A471.

dewe *n.* dew 6596.

di *pr. 1 sg.*, *i(o)e vus* ~ I assure you 5913, 6546.

diche *n.* moat A524.

dye *v.* die 2359, 2399; **day** 2100^r; [**dyȝe**] L574. [**dyȝe**] *pr. subj. sg.* L1001. [**dyȝed**] *pa. t. 3 sg.* L771, L899; [**deȝed**] L661.

Dieu *n.* God, *a min* ~ (expletive) A961, *so* ~ *me saut* as may God save me (asseveration, tag) 3552, etc.; **De** (*par* ~ by God) 5191.

digne *adj.* worthy (to . . .) A1121, 2399; **dine**^{r} noble 3078, etc. **digner** *compar.* A1066.

diȝt(en) [**dyȝhte**] *v.* make ready 1423; give 4172, 6686, 7356. **diȝt** *pa. t. 3 sg.* (refl.) 2401, [~ *him to schip*] embarked L82. **diȝt** *pa. t. pl.* 3699, 5274, L1353; [**dyȝhte(n)**] L277, L1892. **diȝt** *pp.* A1654, etc., L279.

din *n.* see **den(e).**

dined *pa. t. 3 sg.* resounded 5740, 9158; [**donede**] L1605.

diner *n.* mid-day meal A1716, A1930.

dint *n.* see **dent.**

diol [**deol**] *n.* grief, distress A692,
A1124, etc., L1394; **dol** 6403; a grievous thing L189. *See 692n.*

diol-makeing *n.* lamentation 8507.

dische *n.* plate 2260; **disse** 6944.

[discomfyȝt] *pp.* (adj.) see **descomfit.**

diuers *adj.* different 8674.

do(n) *v.* do (mod. uses) *131*, A348, A610, *728*, 1049, *1580*, L652, L733, etc., work (suffering, etc.) on *4411*, *etc.*, bring (help, etc.) to 6857, *7052*^{n}, *8557*, ~ *strengþe* do one's utmost 5177, (sim.) A190, 5971, etc.; (+inf. or (*for*)*to* and inf.) cause (person) to . . . *A90*, *A602*, *1080*, *1081*, *etc.*; (+inf.) cause to be performed 597, *etc.*, [+*lete* ~] L1486, [+*to* and inf.] ?L1663; put 955, etc., (self under person's guidance) 8599, (sim.) *L933*; ~ (*op*)*on* put on 2370, *5048*, *etc.*, L1216, (sim.) ~ *of 4966*; ~ *opon* refer (question) to *A937*; ~ *oway* cause (infant) to be cared for by another *2716*; ~ *vp* open (gates) A1785; ~ *to deþ* kill A340, 2548, L1424, ~ *of dawe 6153*, [~ *to* (*þeo*) *ded*] *L253*, L954, L1099; ~ *to mirþe* make an occasion for pleasure 4220; (refl.) go *4776*, etc., (intr.) *6825*; **done**^{r} A817, etc., L133, *haue nouȝt of to* ~ have no concern with A1432. **do** *pr. 1 sg.* A1081. **dost** *pr. 2 sg.* 7499, 7593, L1102. **doþ** *pr. 3 sg.* 1620, etc., [auxil. forming periphrastic pr.] L1373. **doþ** *pr. pl.* 6044, etc.; **do(n)** 2211, 7094, 9114, etc. **do** *pr. subj. sg.* 2678, ?2679; *imp. sg.* A877, L953, etc. **doþ** *imp. pl.* 3198, L467, L553. **doinde** *pr. p.* 3133, etc., *wel(e)* ~ well performing of knightly deeds 2870, etc., ~ *wel* *3848, **doand** 5446. **dede** [**dude**] *pa. t. 1, 3 sg.* 381, 2026, etc., (auxil. forming periphrastic pa. t.) A708, L36, etc. (and sim. with *pa. t. pl.*); **ded** 8847. **dest** *pa. t. 2 sg.* 5054; [**dudest, -ust**] L734, L1216, L1722. **dede(n)** [**dude(n)**] *pa. t. pl.* 368, 550, L566, etc. **do(n)** *pp.* A570, 2629, L307, L527, etc., **ydo(n)**^{r} [not L] A274, 2627, L894, etc., [**doon**] (*hadden* ~ *and seid* had finished speaking) L683; (adj.) over A359, 2805, etc., accomplished 2749, 4294, made (agreement) L307. Cf. **misdo, vndudest.**

doke *n.* duck 4138.

dom(e) *n.* trial A888; sentence A1348; decision 2048; doom 9000, 9128.

donward *adv.* down (of motion) 5165, 5248. *See 5165n.*

dore *n.* door 832, etc. [dores] *pl.* L795. Cf. **chaumbre-dore, chirche-dore.**

dorren *pl.* bumble-bees 6418.

[dost] *n.* see **dust.**

d(o)uble *v.* double (intr.) 5190, 8130. **dubled** *pp.* 5221.

douhter [-ʒt-] *n.* daughter 871, etc.; **douster** 4472ⁿ; **dohter** 5803. **douhter** *gen.* 6526. **douhtren, -htern** [-ʒhtre(s)] *pl.* 678, 707.

douhti [-ʒ(h)ty] *adj.* doughty A244, L15, L84, etc.; **duʒst** 8354ʳⁿ.

douk(e), -c [duyk] *n.* duke 1422, 2306, 3769, 6934, etc.; commander (milit.) 3952. **doukes** *pl.* A302, etc.

doun *adv.* down 838, 4001, 6239, etc., = set A1459, = to death L 1975; *vp and* ~ to and fro 2372; *vp so* ~ upside down *A544ⁿ. Cf. **adoun.**

doun *n.* hill A1764, etc.

dounfalleing *n.* falling down 9905.

dour(e), -en *v.* last out A412, 5964, 6833, etc.

dout(e) *n.* fear A465, etc.; doubt (*wiþouten* ~ certainly (tag)) 2388, etc., L477, (*saun* ~) 5604.

dout(e) *v.* fear 3286; be afraid 4088, 8727. **[douted]** *pa. t. 3 sg.* (refl.) L448. **douted** *pa. t. pl.* 6606.

dradefullich [dredfully] *adv.* in a way expressing fear 1572.

drago(u)n *n.* dragon 1496, 5899, L1577, etc. **dragouns** [-o(u)ns] *pl.* 1454, 1604, etc.; *pl. gen.* 1678.

drawe(n) *v.* pull, drag *A444,* A975, *A1813,* 2827, *5891,* *6210,* *8443,* *9289, L1285,* etc., = drag to execution A383, *L1447,* = pull up L975; draw (sword etc.) *207,* *3279,* *L1918,* etc. **drawest** *pr. 2 sg.* (~

amis act wrongfully) 8477ⁿ. **draweþ** *pr. 3 sg.* (~ *along* becomes longer (day in spring)) 6597. **drawe** *pr. subj. sg.* 2822. **drawend** *pr. p.* 5891. **drawe** *pa. t. 1 sg.* made my way 8415ʳ. **drouʒ** *pa. t. 2 sg.* 2903ʳ. **drouʒ** [-ʒ(h)] *pa. t. 3 sg.* 2925, L825, L1018, etc., led (person) 2934, 3399, *his limes* ~ recovered control of self (after stunning) 7131. **drouʒ** *pa. t. pl.* A444, 7799, ~ *hem aroume* drew off 5777; **drowe(n)ʳ** 5693, etc., L1918, made their way 6111, closed (drawbridge, door-bolts) 7255. **(y)drawe** *pp.* A207, 763, L1447, etc., removed from table (cloth) 2303, *vp* ~ 6561, *forþ* ~ haled forth 763; **drawen** 9747, L287; **ydreyʒt** (*abrod* ~ scattered) 6818ⁿ. Cf. **to-, wiþdrawe.**

dred(e) *n.* fear A717, A1129, etc.

drede *v.* (refl.) be afraid 3197ⁿ. **drede** *imp. sg.* 2675, 4076; **[dred]** L731. **drede** *imp. pl.* 3627, 4334.

dreri [-e(o)-] *adj.* downcast 881, 9890, L1007, etc.

dresse *v.* cause (horse) to move under control 8855.

drie *adj.* (as n.) dry weather (see **for**) 3537.

***drie** *v.* last out 9730ⁿ.

Driʒt *n.,* *our* ~ Our Lord A645, etc.

drink *v.* drink 2273, 6533. **drinkeþ** *pr. 3 sg.* 2280, 2281. ***dronken** *pa. t. pl.* 6559. **dronken** [-kyn] *pp.* (adj.) drunk 8750, L812, L819.

drink(e) [dryng] *n.* drink, *mete and* ~ (and sim.) 4208, 6972, L530, etc.

driue *v.* drive (person back, etc.), pursue 1661, etc., (fig.) L272, (carts) *6449;* hasten *2534,* 9812, *etc.,* L1450, P374; strike, thrust (of weapon, intr.) A447, *8490.* **driue-and** *pr. p.* 7528, 9658. **drof** *pa. t. 3 sg.* 1526, etc. **driuen** *pa. t. pl.* 834, etc.; **[drof]** L1809. **(y)driuen** *pp.* 1869, 7857, etc. Cf. **todrof.**

dromouns *pl.* large ships A113.

drurie *n.* beloved one 8436.

dubbed *pp.* dubbed (knight) 4597.

dubbeing *n.* knighting 4650.

dubled *pp.* see **d(o)uble.**

duel(l)ing [dwell-] *n.* delay 101, 8091, etc.
duȝst *adj.* see douhti.
[duyk] *n.* see douk(e).
[dure] *adj. see* dere.
dust [dost] *n.* dust 1541, etc.
dust *pa. t. 3 sg.* struck fiercely (tr.) 9435; duȝste 9798. dusched *pa. t. pl.* (intr.) 5614. *See 455n.* Cf. dasse.
[dwelle] *v.* wait, remain L581, L1324, L1800. duellest *pr. 2 sg.* A1840. duelle *imp. sg.* A1832. [dwelled] *pa. t. pl.* L1351.

eft *adv.* afterwards, thereupon A1981, 8989; again 5710; (uncertain) A348, A1343, etc.; back again A551, 9059[n].
egge *n.* edge (of weapon) 2025, etc. Cf. swerde-egge.
[egre] *adj.* grim L330, etc.; eager L1624.
egreliche [-ly] *adv.* fiercely 8345, L1625; grimly L1090.
ey(e) *interj.* (of surprise) A911; (of anger) 2386.
eiȝe *n.* see ay.
eiȝen [eyȝne] *pl.* eyes 1490, etc.; eiȝe[r] 2756, etc.; eyin 8509[r].
eiȝt(e, -te) *num. adj.* eight 4925, 5745, 6199, etc.; heiȝte 6775. Cf. heiȝte *num. adj. ord.*
eiȝtte *n.* goods 7611.
[eyr] *n.* see air, air(e).
[*eyþir] *adj.* see aiþer.
ek(e) *adv.* also, and ~ A699, 6339, etc.
ek(e) *n.* addition, to ~ þat in addition 7279, 9737.
elbowe *n.* elbow A565, 9385.
eld *adj.* old A737, etc.; [elde] old [old(e)] 2701, L707, L1372, etc.; = old man 4159, 4174; ~ *and ȝing* = all of them (and sim.) A151, 257, L501, *L513, L692, etc. eldest [-st(e)] *sup.* 741, 759, etc.; *mi* neldest A75; heldest A725.
[elde] *n.* mature age, *so ȝonge wiþynne* ~ = so far below this L219.
elderlinges *pl.* parents A767.
eldfader *n.* father-in-law A1734, A1747.
ellen *n.* ell (45 in.) 3303, 7461.

elles *adv.* if it had been/is otherwise 9258, L1160; (quasi-adj.) other 2330, 6658.
elleswher(e) *adv.* elsewhere 2619, 3427, 8908.
em *n.* uncle 4661, etc.; *mi* nem (and sim.) 4573, etc.
emperour *n.* emperor 4472, etc.; [empere] ruler L225, [empour] L246.
empire *n.* empire 4481.
[enchaunte] *v.* induce by deluding L703. Cf. bichaunte.
enchaunteing *n.* magic spells 8778.
enchaunt(e)ment *n.* magic spells 3156, 3816, etc.; deluding persuasion L735.
encombraunce *n.* malign influence A864. Cf. combraunce.
encumbrement, -ber- *n.* malign influence A706; harm(ful thing) 3202, 3221, 6126. Cf. comburment.
ende *n.* end *1502, 4263, etc., *at side and at* ~ = in all parts 2871[n], ~ *and ord* = every detail A1177, 3023; *þe* nende *A1502, *at þe* nende in the end A1897, *þat o* nende 6893; hende coast A1728.
ende *v.* complete 2216. ended *pa. t. 3 sg.* = died A1899.
endeles *adj.* endless 5822.
ender *adj., þis* ~ *niȝt* some nights ago A917.
ending *n.* end A622, 2798, = death A2, A998, L3.
enemis *pl.* enemies A306, etc.
[Englysch(e)] *adj.* see Inglisse.
ensaumple *n.* example (see take(n)) 7964.
enserche *v.* search out (sin, in confession) A709.
[ensoyne] *n.* see asoine.
entent *n.* purpose 8790, *wiþ gode* ~ with good will 1194; attention (see take(n)) A1968.
enterement *n.* burial 2761.
enticement *n.* temptation A758.
entre *n.* entry A682; beginning 4675; ground by which one enters 8124, entres *pl.* 4356.
entre *v.* enter (intr.) 5610. entred *pa. t. pl.* A1757, 5383.

entring *n.* entry, *in þe* ~ as person enters (battle) 8834.

envie *n.* envy (sin) 808; resentment (justified) 1646.

[eode] *pa. t. 3 sg.* see **go(n).**

[eouel(e)] *adj., adv.* see **iuel.**

er *adv.* before A124, L607, etc.; *prep.* A274, etc., L1295; *conj.* A232, L540, etc., ~ *þan* *4079. **ere** 8766; **her** A1310, L1854; **ar(e)** A625, A815, A1125, etc.; **[or(e)]** L208, L1295, L1414. **arst** *sup.* before A1087, etc.; first (in sequence) 3636, 5551, 8487; *adj.* (quasi-n.) *þo at* ~ immediately 2333ⁿ, not until then 6720, 9155ⁿ.

erand *n.* message 4605.

⟨**ere**⟩ *adv.* see **euer.**

ere *n.* ear 6002, 8171.

erl [**eorl**] *n.* earl 1422, etc. **erls** [**eorles**] *pl.* 99, etc. **erl(e)s** *pl. gen.* 4685, 8021, 8241.

ermite *n.* see **hermite.**

erne *v.* run (lit. and fig.) A1228, 6844. **ran** *pa. t. 3 sg.* 2226, 2577, 3459, L1220, etc., ~ *a-blod* ran with blood 9018; (refl.) A831; **ernne** 5984, **vrn** *pa. t. pl.* 6999, etc.; **ourn(e)** A387, 8089; **run** A1815; **ron** 4865; [**ran**] L1904; [**rowned**] L206ⁿ, L209. Cf. **arnand, ouer-ran.**

errour *n.* wrongful deeds A1812.

erþe [**eo-**] *n.* earth (= human habitation, solid ground, surface) 1519, 1576, 9768, L640, etc.; ⁺*legge in* ~ bury 2760, and see **bring, reke** *v.*; soil A1481.

eschele *n.* company (of fighting-men) 7570.

ese *n.* see **aise.**

est *adj.* east 8747.

est *n.* the east 3107, 3186; **hest** 7395.

ester *n.* part (of room) A816.

Ester-tide *n.* Easter 2839.

Estre *n.* season of Easter 5585ⁿ.

-et *suffix* (on prop. name) the young 2717, 4610, 7009, etc.

eten *v.* eat (intr.) 3169, 6533. **at** *pa. t. 3 sg.* 2260, 2268, (tr.) 3468. **eten** *pa. t. pl.* 2212, 6559. **yeten** *pp.* 3127.

etenild *adj.* (cognomen, obscure) 8250ⁿ.

euen *adv.* smoothly (of weapon-stroke) 5163, 5955, 6370; in equal shares 4876. Cf. **vneuen** *adj.*

euen *n.* evening 685 [L *an* ~ in the . . .], 7527; eve (of feast-day) 5586. Cf. **auensong, Cristenmesse-euen, Palmesonnes-aue.**

[euenyng] *n.* evening L493.

euer [-(e)] *adv.* always, continually A198, 3813, L1402, etc., for ever 600, and see **more** s.v. **miche(l)**; at any time A950, 2969, 8419, 8798, L463, L1141, L1795; (intensive) *al(le) þat* ~ everything which (and sim.) A7, 1049, A1545, 4811, 4817, 7550, L1865, etc., *seþþen ich* ~ since ever I . . . 4635, *so ich* ~ *mot* as may I at all . . . (asseveration) A377, *woleway þat ich* ~ alas that I ever . . .! 6802, 6803, (sim.) 8418, [*or* ~] before L208; ⟨*whether soe* **ere** whicheuer⟩ P2284.

eueraywhar(e) *adv.* everywhere A18, 9340; **eueriwher** 9172.

euerich(e) *adj.* every A24, 6744, etc.; **eueri** 1459, 3024, L719, etc.; (as pron.) everybody A1594, etc., and see **oþer** *adj.*

euerichon *pron.* everybody 7818; every one (of them) 2800, 5996, 9266, (quasi-adj.) 99, etc.; [**euerilkon**] L37, etc.

[euesong] *n.* see **auensong.**

ex *n.* see **ax.**

exil *n., ben* ~ become an exile 8922. *See n.*

exile *v.* exile 8737.

fable *n.* falsehood, *wiþouten* ~ truly (tag) 2195, etc., *saun* ~ 5971, etc.

face *n.* see **fas.**

fader [-ir, -er] *n.* father A53, L771, L1661, etc., = God the Father 8917, = priest L869. **faders, -dres** *gen.* A930, 1769, 7656. **faders** *pl.* 8365.

fay *n., par (ma)* ~ by my faith (tag) A549, 4796, etc.

fail(e) *n.* error, *wiþouten* ~ certainly (tag) 135, etc., *saun* ~ A1163, etc.

fail(e) *v.* fail (intr.) 1619, etc., = weaken L100; fail to support 3052, etc. **faile** *pr. 1 sg.* 2969. **failed** *pa. t. 3 sg.* 7166, 9039.

[fayn] *adj.* pleased L72; *adv.* willingly L988.

faintise *adv.* lack of eagerness 5655, 7594; **feintis(e)** deceit (*wiþouten* ~) 2204, 9860.

fair [-(e)] *adj.* noble 410, *L49*, = noble men 3531, seemly L684, L1522; beautiful 743, 1351, etc.; (uncertain) A676, etc.; **[feir]** L49ʳ. **fairer** *comp.* 3603, etc., L1002. **fairest [-(e)]** *sup.* 2180, etc., L26, L636.

fair(e) *adv.* nobly, courteously, excellently A509, A534, 2256, 3133, 5559, L56, L155, etc.

faire *n.* fair 4602ⁿ.

[fairhed] *n.* beauty L593.

falle *v.* fall (lit. and fig.) *A793*, 3818, *4779, 6832*, etc., ~ *a-knewes* kneel *2343*, (sim.) L1464, ~ *on croice* bow down *7305*ⁿ; ~ *on* attack *6736*; ~ *to . . . hond* enter (person's) allegiance *4764*; ~ *to . . . honour* redound to (person's) credit 7664; [~ *to*] be appropriate to *L980*; befall (intr.) A1606, L1032, etc., (tr.) *3502*. **falle(n)** *pr. pl.* 4201, 6736. **fel** *pa. t. 3 sg.* 842, etc., *it* ~ *to þe niȝt* night fell 2153; **[feol]** L980, etc. **fel(le)** *pa. t. pl.* 642, 3872, etc.; **fellen** A1522, etc., L1599; **[felleon]** L608. **(y)falle** *pp.* 574, 7879, etc.; **fallen** A240, etc.

falling *n.* falling, *in his* ~ as he fell 3461.

fals [-(e)] *adj.* deceitful A82, L1428, etc.; untruthful L905; pretended A1367.

fame *n.* fame 4416.

fare *n.* to-do A739, etc.; proceeding L1696.

fare *v.* go (motion lit. and fig.) 70, 1424, etc.; fare (well) 6772. **[fareþ]** *pr. pl.* behave L1548. **ferd** *pa. t. 3 sg.* 7808, *þus it* ~ so things went on A554. **ferd(en)** *pa. t. pl.* A354, fared (in manner defined) 7072, etc.; **[ferdyn]** L498. **yfare** *pp.* 4206; **[fare]** L996. Cf. **forfare, misfare**.

fas *n.* facial appearance A1138, 2525; **face** A996.

fast [-(e)] *adv.* firmly A832, etc.,

L858; attentively 5660; close 2846, L1281; strongly (fight, etc.) A1522, 5074, etc., L1924, (call out, etc.) L1057, L1884, (run, etc.) A463, A1228, L296, L1852; quickly (see **also**) 7851.

fat *n.* vessel (fig. = woman) A1054.

fatt *adj.* well-fleshed 5851.

fauchoun *n.* large broadsword 8947, 9223. **fauchouns** *pl.* 8073, 9749.

faut *n.* absence 7824. Cf. **defaut**.

fawe *adj.* eager A208; pleased 2469.

fe [fee] *n.* wealth 723, etc.

feblenis *n.* weakness 9837.

feche *v.* fetch A381, A1035, etc.; **[fechche]** L266. **[feche]** *pr. subj. sg.* (= carry off, of Devil) L1192. **yfeched** *pp.* 6465. Cf. **fet(t)**.

feined *pa. t. 3 sg.* made pretence 3330, 6504; (refl.) A129.

feintis(e) *n.* see **faintise**.

[feir] *adj.* see **fair**.

fel *adj.* excellent (*fair and* ~) 6470ʳ; **fels** 3544ʳ.

fel(e) [feole] *adj.* many A153, L607, etc., (as pron.) 673, etc., ~ *and fewe* = everybody 6595.

fel(le) [fe(o)lle] *adj.* evil, formidable 162, 4724, 8023, 8710, L610, etc. **feller** *comp.* 7384.

felawe *n.* companion 3557, etc.; mate A492; *gode* ~ worthy man 8567. **felawes** *pl.* 1202, etc.; **felawe(n)ʳ** 4529, 5038, etc. Cf. **half-felawe**.

felawered *n.* body of companions 2127, etc. Cf. **ferred(e)**.

feld [-(e)] *n.* open country 1643, etc.; battlefield 2132, etc., L114, L1902, *in(to) þe* ~ to the earth (on battlefield) 5036, 9058, etc., *þe* ~ *oȝain* 8077ⁿ.

fele *v.* feel 2636. **feleþ** *pr. 2 sg.* 2637ⁿ. **fel(e)d** *pa. t. 3 sg.* A850, A851, 9365.

felefeld, -fold *adj.* made of several layers of material (*see 2975–6n*)3302, 5236, etc.; **felfeld [feolefold]** coiled in several layers 1487. Cf. **yfold**.

felle *n.* skin, *in flesche and* ~ = altogether A822.

felle *v.* strike down 9034. **felleþ** *pr. 3 sg.* causes to fall 6596. **fel(le)d** *pa. t. 3 sg.* A562, 2872, etc. **feld(en)**

pa. t. pl. 3971, 8940, etc. **fel(le)d**
pp. A320, 5936, etc., L114; **yfeld**ʳ
A138, etc.; **yfelled** A661. Cf. **afeld**.
feloun *n.* wicked man 8433.
fen *n.* fen 7547.
fende [feond(e)] *n.* devil 804, 843,
etc. **fendes [-eo-]** *gen.* 758, L678,
L868. **[feondes]** *pl.* L598, etc.;
?fende A988ⁿ. Cf. **helle-fende**.
fende *v.* defend (self) 3076.
fenel *n.* fennel 3060.
fenester *n.* window A815.
fer *adj.*¹ distant 5511, *a ~ weys* to a
distance 6882ⁿ.
[fer] *adj.*² valiant L1459. Cf. **fers**.
fer [fe(o)r] *adv.* far 1526, 3093, 3741,
etc.; far away 6499, 7710, L1033, ~
and ner = widely A200, L274, etc.,
~ *and neiȝe* 2165, 2413, (sim.) 7215,
~ *and wide* 4225, *fro* ~ from a
distance A1637; for a long time
2742ⁿ, *it was wel ~ in niȝt* night was
far advanced A1989; *as ~ forþ as*
to the extent that A108, *þus ~
comen it is* things have gone as far
as this 4637. **ferþere** *comp.* 3462.
fer(e) [fuyr] *n.* fire 995, 1489, 3208,
etc.; *wild(e)* ~ Greek fire 1888,
A1892, 4242, etc., *a ~ wilde* on fire
with this 7299; fire 6785. **feris
[fuyres]** *gen.* 1456. Cf. **afer(e),
helle-fer**.
ferd *n.* company (of fighting-men)
7839, 8341.
[ferd] *pp.* (adj.) afraid L1596; (quasi-
n.) *for* ~ because they were afraid
L1599.
ferd(en) etc. *pa. t. 3 sg., pl.* see **fare**.
[yfere] *adv., al(le)* ~ all together
L149, L687, etc.
fere *n.* companion A481, 3433.
feren *pl.* 3289, etc.; **fer(e)**ʳ A1343,
7087, etc.
ferly, -liche *adj.* extraordinary A1119,
5618, 9794.
ferly *adv.* extraordinarily 6317.
ferne *n.* bracken, *nouȝt a ~* = nothing
at all 8866.
ferred(e), -ade *n.* body of companions
A1680, A1787, 8211, etc.; com-
panionship *A1778; comradeship
3528ⁿ. Cf. **felawered**.
fers *adj.* valiant 8120. *See n.* Cf. **fer**.

ferst *adv.* see **first**.
ferþ(e) *num. adj. ord.* fourth 3785,
8703, etc.
fesaunce *pl.* pheasants 3121.
fest [-e] *n.*¹ feast 291, etc. **festes** *pl.*
A489.
fest *n.*² hand A565, 4815, etc.; **fist**
7470; **[fust]** L823.
fest *v.* land (blow) 5976.
fet(t) *pa. t. 3 sg.* fetched A994, 8621.
yfet *pp.* summoned 2763. Cf. **feche**.
feuer *n.* fever 4254.
fewe *adj.* few 4102, L1798, etc., (as
pron.) 4879, etc., *a(n)* ~ A1900,
9295, etc., and see **fel(e)**.
fi *n.* liver 7756.
fif *num. adj.* see **fiue**.
fift *num. adj. ord.* fifth 3851, etc.
fiften(e) *num. adj.* fifteen 2415, 7555,
L472, etc.
fiftend *num. adj. ord.* fifteenth 5440.
fifti *num. adj.* fifty 6140.
fiȝt *n.* battle, fighting A462, 683,
A1635, L1550, etc. **fiȝtes**ʳ *pl.*
3072ⁿ, 3748, 4432, etc.
fiȝt *v.* fight 126, etc.; **[fyȝhte]**
L1848. **fiȝteþ** *pr. 3 sg.* 5990, etc.
fiȝtand *pr. p.* 4508, etc.; **fiȝting**
7852ʳ. **fauȝt** *pa. t. 3 sg.* A1820, etc.
fouȝt(en) [-ȝhte(n)] *pa. t. pl.*
A407, A1609, L290, L1611, etc.;
yfouȝten 9923. **fouȝt** *pp.* 8411.
fiȝting(e) [fyȝ(h)tyng] *n.* fighting
1523, 7709, L1685, etc. **fiȝtinges**
pl. 3226ʳ.
[fyle] *v.* corrupt L764. **[fyled]** *pp.*
L627.
filled *pa. t. 3 sg.* filled A113; *pp.* 8741.
fin *adv.* exceedingly 5474, 8700.
fin *n.* end (of life) 2737, (of battle)
8069; **fins** (*no man þerof couþe þe ~*
there seemed no end of them)
8066ʳ. Cf. **afin(e)**.
fin(e) *adj.* of high or strong quality
A480, A1965, 4009, 4514, 4696,
5420, etc., ⁺*haue hert ~ to* love
strongly 2056, *wiþ hert ~* eagerly
6020, and see **wil(le)**; **fin(e)s**ʳ
6690, 7738, 8006.
finde(n) *v.* find (mod. uses) 295, *A871
1397*, 2894, *L859*, etc., (+ inf.)
A543, 5023, L852, **yfinde** 2645;
~ *me wiþ þe soþe* find I am telling

finde(n) (*cont.*):

the truth A1274; find in poet's source 8252, *in boke* ~ A1191; provide (with) 750, 1623, *2973*, *4426*, *etc.* **(y)finde** *pr. 1 sg.* A871, etc., L599, *as ich* ~ *in boke* as I learn from my source (and sim., tags) A63, 2730, etc., L1465 (and sim. with *pr. pl.*). **findeþ** *pr. 2 sg.* 2680ⁿ. **finde(n)** *pr. pl.* A467, A486, A1397, 2702, etc.; [*****fyndiþ**] L33. **fond(e)** *pa. t. 1, 3 sg.* 707, 853, 2898, L854, etc.; **fand** 5679. **founde(n)** *pa. t. pl.* A228, A295, 543, etc., ~ *bataile to* fought against 9672; **fond** [-(e)] 2590, 7517, L482, L1349, L1564. **founde** *pa. t. subj. sg.* (~ *wiþ hem lesing* found they were lying) A621. **(y)founde(n)** *pp.* A337, A1231, 1404, 1540, L1470, etc. Cf. **fondling**.

findeing *n.* finding A1198.

fined *pa. t. pl.* made an end of 5021.

fineliche *adv.* exceedingly 5907.

fire *n.* see **fer(e)**.

firmament *n.* heavens (astrol.) 590.

first [**furst(e)**] *adj.* first 3843, etc., L490, *at þe* ~ *word* = at once 2912; = (the) beginning 6713, 8257; [*þanne at* ~] immediately L270, L1861.

first *adv.* previously 3288, etc., **ferst** A351, 7776; first 2173, etc., *þo* ~ = as soon as 3869.

fische *n.* fish 4113, etc.

fit(t) *n.* (short) time A1598, 8963, etc.

fitlokes *pl.* fetlocks 5892.

fiþelers *pl.* viol-players 6557.

fiue *num. adj.* five A1215, etc., L535; **fif** A1189, etc., L1471.

fiȝ *n.*, ~ *a putain* son of a whore (abus.) 8998.

fist *n.* see **fest** *n.*²

flappes *pl.* blows 8074.

flat *n.* blow 1858, etc.

flatten *v.* strike 9728. **flattinge** *pr. p.* (*out* ~ darting out) 5662. **flat** *pa. t. 3 sg.* 9914.

flaunke *n.* side of the abdomen 9237.

fle(n) [**fleo**] *v.* flee A208, 328, etc., **fleiȝe** 4910; flee from *7894*, (fig.) 809; fly (fig. = hasten) 1158, 4043.

[**fleoþ**] *pr. 3 sg.* L182. **fle** *pr. pl.* 7894, 9194. **fleand** *pr. p.* 3812, etc.; **fleinde** 2572, etc. **flei(ȝe** [-ȝh] *pa. t. 3 sg.* fled A1870, etc., L293; flew (lit. and fig.) A1542, 5036, 5258, 5924, 9359, etc.; **flowe** 6221; [**fledde**] fled L827; (sim. distribution in *pa. t. pl.*). **flowe(n)** *pa. t. pl.* A141, 3344, 5664, 9161, etc.; **fleiȝe** 6168; [**fleyh**] L1961; [**fledde**] L118, L119. **(y)flowen** *pp.* 4197, 6088, 6882.

flegge *adj.* eager 3363ⁿ.

fleinge *n.* fleeing 8803.

flem(en) [**fleme**] *v.* put to flight, drive out A305, A498, 1641. [**flemed**] *pp.* L442, etc.

flesche [**flesch, -chs**] *n.* meat A484, 4104, etc.; (man's living) flesh 4253, 6397, and see **bon, felle, liche, nim(en)**; *mannes* ~ = male sexuality *A592, A901, A941, L788, L908. **flesches** *gen.* (~ *lire* butcher's meat) 8202; ?*pl.* store of meat 3660.

flesche-fleiȝen *pl.* blow-flies 6418.

flesche-hewer, -heweere *n.* butcher 4802, 8202.

flescheliche *adv.* carnally, ⁺*ligge* ~ have sexual intercourse A848.

[**fleschly**] *adj.* carnal, ~ *dede* sexual act L948.

[**flesch-lust**] *n.* carnal desire L901.

flet *n.* battlefield 7010.

[**flyȝt**] *n.* power of flying L1623, *L1731.

fling(e) *v.* gallop 5281, 7931, etc. **fling** *pr. pl.* 6423; *imp. sg.* 8824, 9216. **flingand** *pr. p.* 3916; **flinginde** 6108ʳ. **flang** *pa. t. 3 sg.* 5717; **flonge(n)** *pa. t. pl.* 5752, 7724, etc.

flit *n.* attack 6076ⁿ.

floc, -k *n.* company (of fighting-men) 3856, 5480, etc.

flod *n.* high stream (in river) 5758, 6708, 8090, 9302; water L1008.

floted *pa. t. pl.* wallowed 7109.

flour *n.* flower 8657, (fig. = woman) 2480, 2538. **floures** *pl.* A261, etc. Cf. **rose-flour**.

[**fo**] *n.* enemy L1824. **fon** *pl.* A8, A273, etc., L1848; [**fone**] L134; **foon** L158, etc.

fode *n.* child 1055, L1395.

foiled *pa. t. 3 sg.* trampled down 9430.
See 6693*n*.

yfold [-e] *pp.* (adj.) coiled 1454. Cf.
felefeld.

fole [fool] *n.* fool 218, L1393, L1435.

folye *n.* folly 4988; irresponsibility
4617; adultery A1076. folis *pl.* 1079.

foliliche *adv.* foolishly 5054.

folk *n.* (group of) people A110, A535,
A1627, 2554, 4543, 7499, L122,
L663, L1597, L1954, etc.; folc
company (of fighting-men) 3847ⁿ.

folwe *v.* pursue 9340. folweþ *imp.
pl.* follow (in support) 5918.
folwand *pr. p.* 4973. folwedest *pa.
t. 2 sg.* 5055. folwed *pa. t. 3 sg.*
4919, etc., ~ *after* pursued A1886.
folwed(en) *pa. t. pl.* 6128, 8932,
9628, ~ *on* pursued A1512, 9330.
Cf. tofolwed.

foman *n.* enemy A309, L1394.
fomen *pl.* 126, etc.; foman 5962ʳ.

fon etc. *pl.* see fo.

fond [-e] *v.* (+inf. or (*for*)to and inf.)
try 670, A770, 4591, etc.; test (*his
hert* ~ *why* find out his real reasons
why . . .) A174; = enjoy sexually
L714; yfond A521. fond(en) *pr. pl.*
A1460, 4271, 6737. fond *pr. subj.
sg.* A1720, 6746; *imp. sg.* 7669.

[fondement] *n.* see foundement.

fondling *n.* foundling, þe ~ (cognomen) 5469.

fong *v.* receive 2646. Cf. afong,
vndurfonge.

for *num. adj.* see four(e).

for *conj.* because 379, etc., ~ *þat*
A103, L1942.

for *prep.* for (mod. uses) A128, 131,
767, A999, 2789, 3930, 4544, 4667,
6443, L47, L450, L573, L1253,
L1942, etc.; as being A1395, etc.,
and see certain, siker; with reference to 6577; as defence/precaution
against 5126, 8376, etc.; despite
1049, etc.; *an* ~ *an* as in single
combat 2660ⁿ, 3264; ~ *deþ no pine*
for fear of death or torment = for
any cause 6748, (sim.) ~ *liif* ~ *dede
no* ~ *tene* A1780, ~ *liif no* ~ *deþe*
2837, ~ *drie no wete* 3537, ~ *wrong
no riȝt* A606; ~ *mi loue* tell me, as
you love me 7650; ~ *nouȝt þat*

despite everything which 7550; ~
þe nones for the time being 9848; ~
our Leudi for Our Lady's sake
(emphatic) 4975, (sim.) A1832,
5081, L1458, etc.; foreʳ A1167,
A1914, 8534, in front of *6930ⁿ. Cf.
forsoþe, þerfore, wher(e)fore.

forbi *adv.* so as to miss 3351, 9359.
prep. so as to miss 6318, 7167; past
7267, 9013. Cf. þerforbi.

forboden *pp.* forbidden 3647. Cf.
bede.

forbren *v.* burn to death (intr.) 7376.
forbrent *pp.* (adj.) 7714.

forced *pa. t. pl.* drove back 8941. Cf.
aforce.

ford *adv.* see forþ.

fordreinte *pp.* (adj.) drowned 7714.

forest *n.* forest A1954, etc.

forfare *v.* perish A500.

forfauȝt *pa. t. 3 sg.* had exhausted
(self) by fighting 9852. forfouȝten
pp. (adj.) 7885.

forgon *v.* abandon 8524.

[forgult] *pa. t. 3 sg.* lost through
guilt L595.

forȝeld *pr. subj. sg.* repay 2957.

forȝete *pr. subj. sg.* forget 2970.
forȝat *pa. t. 3 sg.* neglected L1089,
~ *vnblisced* neglected to protect with
sign of cross 839, *nouȝt* ~ *he leyd
on* [. . .*þat he no* . . .] did not neglect
to lay on 1857ⁿ. forȝeten [-ȝ-] *pp.*
6054, L1204.

forȝiue [-ȝ-] *pr. 1 sg.* forgive A1590,
2676; withdraw (anger from person)
L1667; *imp. sg.* 9867. forȝaf *pa. t.
3 sg.* 9878.

forlay *pa. t. 3 sg.* committed adultery
with 6494. forlain [-ey-] *pp.* 1360.

forlate [-lete] *v.* lose (life) 1309.
forlete *pa. t. 3 sg.* put out of his
mind A301.

forlese *v.* lose (life) 8524, (sim.)
A1558, etc. forles *pa. t. 3 sg.* A393.

forlorn *pa. t. pl.* were defeated
A213; *pp.* A636ⁿ, (adj.) doomed
6788, 9196; forloreʳ 5802, etc.,
damned A668, condemned A1168,
?doomed L54, destroyed L780.

[forlong] *n.* furlong L1350. forlong
pl. 5844, 6693.

form *adj.* first 4477.

[forme] *n.* see **fourm.**

formward *n.* vanguard 7787.

fors *n.* force, *par* ~ 8040, etc., *purth* ~ A1359; importance (+*make no* ~ = be unconcerned) *2089.

[**forsake**] *v.* give up, refrain from L785, L1431; *hit* ~ *þat þow neo* deny that you . . . L911. **forsoke** [-**sok**] *pa. t. 3 sg.* refused to do A127, refused (to . . .) 2061; denied L758.

forseyd *pp.* (adj.) spoken of before A679, 6835, 7865.

forsoþe *adv.* in truth A460, L14, etc.; ~ *to say* to tell the truth (and sim., tags) A299, A1541, 8930, L289, etc.; ~ *y wene* I verily believe (and sim., tags) 3937, 6171, 6905. **forsoþ**[r [not L] A941, 3539, 6171, etc., L117.

forswore *pp.* (adj.) forsworn 92, 9208.

fort *conj.* until 4293, *al* ~ A645; *prep.* 4786, 4789, until the coming of *4298[n].

forto *inf. particle* 126, A406, 726, 810, 2861, 4224, 8698, L714, L1138, L1483, L1624, etc.; in order to 112, etc.

forþ *adv.* out, on, forward, etc. (movement variously directed) A308, A763, 1294, A1339, 3251, Liii, L471, etc.; on (with story, etc.) A1100, A1707, 8571, L1210; *as fer* ~ *as* to the extent that A108, *no* ~ *nor* . . . either 6463, 8889; ford[r (*smite* ~ cut through, off) 5230[n], 8948. **forþer** *comp.* further (movement) 6291, (spread of knowledge, see **bring**) L732; *no* ~ *nor* . . . either 4295. Cf. **þerforþ.**

forþan *adv.* because of that 4002, *nouȝt* ~ nevertheless 6819.

forþi *adv.* therefore A53.

forwe *n.* see **furth.**

forwhi *adv.* for which reason A461; why L1377.

forwounded *pp.* (adj.) severely wounded 6430.

fot [-(**e**)] *n.* foot 743, etc., *o(n)* ~ on foot A312, 3998, etc., L78, *men o* ~ foot-soldiers 3340, ~ *hot* quickly 7934; foot-measure 6396, 8446. **fet(e)** [**feet**] *pl.* 382, 4886, etc., *o* ~ on foot 9102; hooves 3824, etc.;

fot (measure) 4798, 6065. Cf. **afot.**

fotmen *pl.* foot-soldiers 3193, 3762.

foule [-**l(e)**] *adj.* evil A694, 997, etc., *þe* ~ *wiȝt* the Devil A855; unpleasant (noise) 6417, (appearance) L1716.

foule *adv.* ignominiously 2557.

foule *n.* bird 2008. **foules** [-**ow**-] *pl.* 1713, etc.

founde *v.* lay foundations of A1443.

foundement [**fond**-] *n.* foundations 532, *543.

four(e) *num. adj.* four 614, A1180, etc.; *for* 2612.

fourm [**forme**] *n.* shape 980.

fourten(e) *num. adj.* fourteen 2625, 4886, 6673, etc.; **fourten**iȝt 3377[n].

fourti *num. adj.* forty 2980, 3685, etc.

[**frayne**] *v.* ask L1505.

fram *prep.* from (mod. uses) A14, A719, A1030, A1403, 2235, 4437, etc.; [**from**] L1610.

fre [**freo**] *adj.* noble A677, A716, 1073, etc., and see **wil(le), fri** 8885[r]; free L930, etc.; = freeman/ -men A303, A1506, *noiþer þral no* ~ = none of them 6262.

Freynsch *n.* the French language A18, etc.

frely *adv.* without hindrance 5889.

frem *adv.* forward 3915[rn].

frende *n.* friend 6920, 8421. **frende** *pl.* A1791[n], 8365, etc.; **frendes** [-**eo**-] A398, etc., L1296, L1832; ⟨ffreinds⟩ friends and kinsmen P339.

[**freodam**] *n.* privileges L1877.

fresche *adj.* not battle-weary 8038; (as n.) ~ *and selt* fresh and salt meat 7286[n].

fro *prep.* from (place) A223, A1123, 7882, L578, etc., acting from A1637, at a distance from A454, L989; (time) L491, L1261; (defence, etc.) A519, 5378, L1322; ~ *main* +*com* be delivered with might 9378.

frust *pa. t. 3 sg.* struck down 6286, 9436. **frusten** trampled 8784. **frust** *pp.* 8806. Cf. **tofrust.**

[**fuyr**] *n.* see **fer(e).**

ful *adj.* full A82, A113, etc., L592; delivered with full force 5247, 8197.

ful *adv.* (intensive, modifying adj. or

adv.) A312, A323, A398, L64, etc.; for the full period of 2053, 3582.

fulfille v. bring to completion 2220, 2222.

fulle n. completeness 8423.

fulliche [-ly] adv. completely 3217; for the full period of L1977.

fulrade v. describe fully 4258, etc.; **fulrede** 8149.

[furst(e)] adj. see **first**.

furth (see 249n) n. ditch 5020, 8174; **forwe** 3460.

[fust] n. see **fest** n.²

gabbe v. tell lies 1411. **gabbest** pr. 2 sg. A1071, L1074; lie to 2913. See 1071n.

gader pr pl. assemble (tr.) 6070; **geder** (refl.) 6735; **gadreþ** gather (flowers) 6600. **gadred** pa. t. 3 sg. 3366, 7066, ~ him assembled to himself A110. **gaderd, -red** pa t. pl. 3231, 3833, 6447.

⟨**gay**⟩ adj. gaily coloured (iron.) P2136.

game(n) n. amusement A1143, 7244, etc.; = amorous play L720, etc., 762. Cf. **a-game**.

gamen-gle n. pleasant entertainment 6532n.

garsoun n. young man not of noble birth 7249; ⟨**garrison**⟩ P1998. **garsouns** pl. 2156.

gastlich adj. terrifying A1494. See n.

gate n. gate 1310; (uncertainly sg. or pl.) 2521, etc.; pl. 5673, etc.; **gates** [ȝ-] 1738, etc. Cf. **castel-ȝates**.

gateward n. guards of gate 5611.

gauelokes pl. javelins 9161.

gaumbers pl. greaves 2976.

gea(u)nt n. gigantic man 4885, 7182, etc. **geauntes** gen. 8924. **geaunt(e)s** pl. *5587, 6152, etc.; **geaunce** 6274, 9774.

geder pr. pl. see **gader**.

genge n. (group of) fighting-men 3830, 6442, 8258; **ginge** 5497.

gent adj. noble 282, A291, etc.; beautiful A654.

gentil adj. noble A23, A1676, 2648, etc.; beautiful 744.

gert v. see **girten**.

gert(en) pa. t. 3 sg., pl. see **girt**.

gest n. story 7618, 8679.

gestening n. feast 2230, etc.

gestes pl. guests 6536.

[gete] pr. pl. obtain L176, L201. 3at **[gat]** pa. t. 3 sg. begot 8895, L1129.

[gete(n)] pp. begotten L6, L1172, etc. See 885n. Cf. **biȝeten**.

[getyng] n. begetting L928.

gette pr. 3 sg. (subj. impers. it) profits 4025. **gett** pa. t. 3 sg. A885n.

gie v. lead (armed force) 7834, 8694. **gied** pa. t. 3 sg. 7837.

gile v. beguile A820. Cf. **agile, bygyle**.

gilt adj. gold-adorned 7847.

gilt n. guilt 952, etc.; **[gult]** L1120. Cf. **gultles**.

gin n. skilful device (abstr.) 2501, etc., made bi ~ skilfully made A974; (concr.) 5678; **[gynne]** = siege-engine L1968.

ginge n. see **genge**.

ginneþ pr. 3 sg. (expletive auxil.) A1329; **gan** 2008, 4047. **gin** pr. pl. 7621, ~ to 2092. **gan** pa. t. 3 sg. 1409, etc., ~ to (some ?proceeded to) A328, 3255, L330, L647, etc. (and sim. in pa. t. pl.), ~ forto 2884; began (tr.) 2215; **[gon]** L70, L1464, etc. **gun** pa. t. pl. A463, A1528, etc.; began (tr.) A534, 8797; **gan** A226, etc., L1057; **[gon(ne)]** L296, L476, L1348, etc. **gunne** pp. begun 7094n. Cf. **agan, biginne**.

girdel n. girdle 6004, 9678.

girdel-stede n. waist 5216.

girt pa. t. 3 sg. struck 9764, 9777, 9930; **gert** 8133ʳ. **girt** pa. t. pl. ?5013; **gerten** 8785n. **ygirt** pp. 8972. Cf. **togert**. See 5013n.

girten v. adjust the girths of 9816; **gert** 9227. **girten** pa. t. pl. 3837, etc.; **gerten** 6034. **girt** pp. 6230.

gisharm n. halberd 6103. **gisarmes** pl. 8794.

gise n. guise A1350, A1991.

glad(e) adj. cheerful A266, 2495, 9124, etc., L803, and see **make(n)**; glad, pleased 8584, 9818, L707, L1003, L1518, [~ and blyþe (and sim.)] L72, L247, L545, etc.

glade v. gladden 8504. **[gladed]** pa. t. 3 sg. L1081.

gle *n.* pleasure 8210; **glewe** 3291ʳ.
Cf. **gamen-gle.**

glede *n.* glowing coal A1500.

[glem] *n.* light L1546.

glide *v.* gallop 3463; pass (weapon
through body, etc.) 6162, etc.; *of*
~ fly off (severed head) 9688.
glod(e) *pa. t. 3 sg.* 3251, etc.,
glanced off (weapon) 5160.

gliderand *pr. pl.* (adj.) glittering
A1768.

glift *pa. t. 3 sg.* turned aside (intr.)
9776; **gleft** 8990. *See 8990n.*

glorie *n.* glory (see **king**) 3369, 4268.

glosing *n.* specious statements 2478ⁿ.

glotonie *n.* gluttony A805.

gnattes *pl.* gnats 9162.

gnidded *pa. t. 3 sg.* rubbed 2514.
See n.

gnowe(n) *pa. t. pl.* bit, ~ *gras and
ston* bit the dust 7753, (sim.)
9175.

go(n) *v.* go (movement) A308, 1080,
6004, 8275, etc., ~ *quite* leave
custody, acquitted 1169, L930; =
run L296, = gallop A1829, etc.; walk
1033, 1530, etc., L1375; go about
2210, (fig.) A1896, = be actively
alive 1028, 2188, etc., and see **mot**;
be paid L573. **[go]** *pr. 1 sg.* (~ *wiþ
childe* am pregnant) L916. **goþ** *pr. 3
sg.* 1350, L1382, L1484, *how* ~ *þis*
what's the meaning of this? L1227.
go(þ) *pr. pl.* A202, 4975, 6599. **go**
pr. subj. sg. A1100, L1276; *imp. sg.*
875, etc., [~ *help ows*] come and
help us L1943. **goþ** *imp. pl.* A223,
2792, L467. **ȝede** *pa. t. 3 sg.* A792,
etc., ~ *astray* wandered about 6712;
[eode] (refl.) L1085. **ȝede(n)** [-eo-]
pa. t. pl. A1914, etc., L1398, (refl.)
9938. **go(n)** *pp.* 2254, 3215, L1350,
(to the Devil) A488, (adj.) past
A1385; **ygo** A496ʳ; **yganʳ** 7007,
7472. Cf. **ago, ago(n), forgon,
ouergon.**

God *n.* God 375, etc., ~ *it wot* God
is my witness 958, 8748, (tag) 2602,
etc.; (heathen) god 7498; **[Gode]**
(*for* ~) L1458, L1500. **Godes** *gen.*
1007, etc.; **[Godis]** L41.

god(e) *n.* good A209, 1056, 7499, etc.,
L1396, *so him were* ~ as if he were

all right 7136, and see **conne**; valuables 8316, = alms A1936, 2453, =
reward 2904; **[good]** L181, L1050,
etc., ~ *no harm* = anything L1093.
godes *pl.* valuables 7296.

gode [**god(e)**] *adj.* good (mod. uses)
A194, A310, 700, 1676, A1876,
2772, 6573, L451, L542, etc.,
~ *nevou* (polite address) 4986, (sim.)
5716, 7350, L869; = cheerful, un-
afraid (heart, etc.) 882, 2090, 6536,
8274, etc., and see **lete(n)**; ~ *time*
suitable time 2791; (intensive,
qualifying n.) 2118, *3944*, 8571,
L797, *L1317*, etc., and see
scour(e); **[good]** L3, L633, etc.
better [-t(t)-] *comp.* A491, etc.,
L487, L734. **best** [-(e)] *sup.* A569,
L133, L452, etc., *time* ~ most suitable time 3724, 7410; (quasi-n.)
wiþ þe ~ in the best style 6310, [*do
þy*] ~ do your best L1769.

godsone *n.* godson 5492.

gold *n.* gold 4054, L701, etc.,
= reward A1356, 3052, *siluer oþer*
~ 4350, (sim.) A128.

gomfa(y)noun *n.* banner A1759,
5657, etc.; **gonfaynoun** A440.

gomfanoun-bere *n.* banner-bearer
6008.

gore *n.* triangular piece 6395.

Gost *n.*, *Holy* ~ Holy Ghost 2224,
8917.

gouern *v.* rule 2778; ***gouerny**
exercise guardianship over A89ⁿ.
gouerned *pa. t. 3 sg.* commanded
(armed force) 3856.

[gouernour] *n.* general L94.

graal *n.* see **greal.**

grade *v.* cry out 7118, *8337. **gredeþ**
[-iþ] *pr. pl.* sing (birds) 1713.
gredeand *pr. p.* 9723; **gredinge**
8996ʳ. **grad(de)** *pa. t. 3 sg.* A833,
6790, etc.; **gred** 6095, etc. **grad(de)**
pa. t. pl. 3813, 4853, etc.; **gred(den)**
6666, 9323.

graiþeþ *pr. pl.* (refl.) get ready 9819.
graiþed *pa. t. 3 sg.* (tr.) equipped
4696. **graiþed** *pa. t. pl.* A304, A432.
ygraiþed *pp.* 4486.

grame *n.* anger A988, 9631.

[grame] *v.* be angry L647. Cf.
agramed.

gramerci *interj.* thank you A279, 6545; (as n.) 5914, *for* ~ = for nothing 5890.

gras, -ce *n.*[1] grace, mercy (God's) A920, 1043, 2540, 8892, etc., L1002; (judge's) L922; (woman's) 2320.

gras *n.*[2] grass 8970, 9830; **gres** 7972; and see **bite(n)**, **gnowe(n)**.

grauel *n.* gravel A1481.

graunt *n.* consent 2657.

graunt(i) *v.* grant 2949; consent A59. **graunt** *pr. 1 sg.* 2966. [**graunten**] *pr. pl.* L1666. **graunt** *pr. subj. sg.* A2, etc. **graunted** *pa. t. 3 sg.* A54[n], 1591. **graunt** [-ed] *pa. t. pl.* 78, L233.

greal *n.* Grail 2222, 4294; **graal** 8902. Cf. **sengreal**.

gred *pa. t. 3 sg.*, etc. see **grade**.

gref *n.* trouble A399.

grehound(e) *n.* greyhound 9028, 9126, 9760, L1697. **grehoundes** *pl.* 4611.

grene *adj.* green A262, etc., L1819; = greensward 6926, 9810.

greneþ *pr. 3 sg.* becomes green 5351.

[**gres**] *n.* dubbin L1342.

gret(e) *adj.* big A1480, L888, etc., thick A1493, etc.; great (of rank) A442, A1791, ~ *and smale* (and sim., implying unanimity, totality) A1723, 6446, etc., (as n.) A1708, A1752, 5075; (qualifying collect. n.) a large A781, A1674, A1680; (intensive, qualifying abstr. n.) 47, 230, A489, A723, A1518, A1652, 3908, 4976, 5724, L1618, etc., full (of length) 5811, 5997[n]. **grest** *sup.* 8797.

[**grete**] *v.*[1] greet L1522. **greteþ** *pr. 3 sg.* 3518. **gret(t)** [-tte] *pa. t. 3 sg.* A1428, L151, etc.; (iron). = struck 2106, etc.; *of* ~ struck off 5946[n]. **gret(ten)** *pa. t. pl.* A179, 3870, etc.

grete *v.*[2] increase in size A884. **greteþ** *pr. 3 sg.* 2635.

[**grete**] *v.*[3] weep L1069.

greteing *n.* greetings 5400.

gretliche *adv.* greatly A1137.

gretnesse *n.* large size 9001.

greuaunce *n.* injury 4399. Cf. **agreued**.

[**grylle**] *adj.* stern L1765.

grim *adj.* fierce A422, etc.; bitter (of abstracts) A332, 7133, 7717.

grininge *pr. p. (adj.)* with lips drawn back 5661.

griseli, -liche *adj.* such as might cause fear 4862, 5659, 5715, 7309; [**grysly**] L1584, etc.

griseliche *adv.* horribly 7108.

griþ *n.* amity 4604, *in* ~ undisturbed 600, 8224; [**gryth**] mercy L1975.

grof [-ff] *n.* grove of trees 1640, etc.

grom(e) *n.* boy-child A688, A978; male servant A1150, L1776; ⟨**groome**⟩ man P2015. **gromes** *pl.* horse-attendants 5398.

grop(e) *pa. t. 3 sg.* held firmly 6351, 8849. **gropen** *pa. t. pl.* 7797.

[**gropede**] *pa. t. 3 sg.* groped L853.

grot *n.* small bit, *eueri* ~ in its entirety A1250, 5954, 7195.

grounde [-d(e)] *n.* ground 544, A1444, 1471, A1894, L1635, etc., *to* ~ to the ground A338, L116, etc., *fram heued to* ~ from head to foot A1403, *fram þe top to þe* ~ *6824, [*by rof and* ~] at top and bottom L796; bottom (of water) 1477. Cf. **helle-grounde**.

grounden *pp. (adj.)* ground sharp A324, 8947.

[**gult**] *n.* see **gilt**.

[**gultles**] *adj.* guiltless L1132.

guttes *pl.* entrails 9170, etc.; **gutten** 5166[r].

ʒa *interj.* yes 2490, etc. Cf. **ʒis**.

ʒalle *n.* gall-bladder 7176, 9364.

ʒalu *adj.* blond A858.

[-**ʒard**] *see* **chircheʒerd**.

ʒare *adj.* (predicative) ready 2002, 3694; (see **make(n)**) 1423, etc.

ʒare *pl.* see **ʒer(e)**.

ʒat *pa. t. 3 sg.* see **ʒete**.

[**ʒates**] *pl.* see **ʒate**.

ʒe *pron.* you (plur.) 74, etc.; (sing. of respect) A272, L943, etc. **ʒou** [**ʒow**] *obj.* 161, A271, L1140, etc., (refl.) A526, etc.; **ʒo** A1234; [**ow**] L467, L1268. **ʒour** [-e] *gen.* 195, etc., and see **honour**, (partitive) 2085; [**ʒowre**] L200.

[**ʒef**] *conj.* see **ʒif**.

ʒeld(en) [-e] *v.* repay 5549, 6544, etc.;

ʒeld(en) (*cont.*):
  surrender (tr.) 2037, (refl.) 7887,
  etc., L1922, (? intr.) 3451ⁿ. ʒeld *pr.*
  1 sg. pay (tribute, iron.) 5219; *pr.*
  subj. sg. 4169; *imp. sg.* give (reward)
  L328. ʒalt *pa. t. 3 sg.* gave (thanks)
  5914. [ʒoldyn] *pa. t. pl.* L1874.
  ʒolden *pp.* 9241. Cf. a-, forʒeld.
[ʒelp] *n.* boasting, *wiþowte* ~ (formula
  of undertaking) L1842.
ʒelp *v.* speak with pride 8419.
ʒeme *n.* heed (see nim(en)) A497, etc.
ʒeme(n) *v.* guard A968, 4397, etc.
ʒem(e)ing *n.* care 2034, 6486.
ʒemers *pl.* protectors 8598.
ʒened *pa. t. 3 sg.* gaped open 7108;
  [ʒonede] L1585.
ʒep *adj.* swift in action 5699.
-ʒerd see chicheʒerd.
ʒerd(e) *n.* rod (length) A1449; staff
  of office 5494.
ʒer(e) *n.* year 554, etc.; ~ *and oþer*
  (*to*) for years 755, 1895ⁿ. ʒer(e) *pl.*
  (adj. precedes) A493, 957, 1900,
  etc., ʒare 6771ʳ; ʒeres (adj.
  follows) A1070, 2163, 4539.
ʒern(e) *adv.* diligently, eagerly,
  strongly, quickly A708, 2340, 2377,
  2509, 6057, etc.; ⟨yorne⟩ P1934.
ʒerne *v.* desire 2485, 2948.
ʒete [ʒet] *adv.* yet (mod. uses) A588,
  769, A1017, 1074, A1181, A1704,
  L805, etc.; *neuer* ~ never before
  6248, *I was neuer* ~ I have never
  been L167, L169.
ʒif [ʒef] *conj.* if 165, 370, etc., [~ *þat*]
  L722, etc., and *see* bot; ʒiue A251,
  A605, etc.; ʒeue (~ *þat* would that
  . . .) 5989ⁿ.
ʒift *n.* gift 2325. ʒiftes *pl.* A723, etc.
ʒimmes *pl.* jewels 8669.
ʒingþe *n.* youth 6269.
ʒis *interj.* yes (affirming course of
  action) A 1345, 7370, 8684. Cf. ʒa.
ʒiue(n) *v.* give (mod. uses) A1419,
  4080, etc., = give in marriage 6575,
  ~ *lest* listen 7617, ~ *souke* give suck
  2694; ʒeue(n) 4911, 7332, 9346,
  etc., L1509, [~ *batayle*] give battle
  to L112, L1893. ʒiue [ʒeue] *pr. 1 sg.*
  (*no* ~ *nouʒt* [*nothyng*] *of* care nothing
  for) 1622 (and sim. with other
  forms). ʒiueþ *pr. 3 sg.* (~ *listening*

listens) A1111 (and sim. other forms).
ʒiue *pr. subj. sg.* 2656, 2657; ʒeue
  ?5400, 5778, L3, L1768. ʒif *imp. sg.*
  A372, 6344; *imp. pl.* [ʒeueþ] 76.
ʒaue *pa. t. 1, 3 sg.* A86, 7239, etc.;
  ʒaf 2040, L1006, etc., ~ *his treuþe*
  pledged his good faith 5556ⁿ; ʒeue
  A612. ʒeue *pa. t. 2 sg.* 2632.
ʒaue(n) *pa. t. pl.* A234, 2825, etc.;
  ʒeue(n) A1602, 2361, etc.; ʒaf
  9128. (y)ʒouen *pp.* A276, 8629,
  etc.; ʒeue(n) 4170, 8723; yʒeueʳ
  6570, 8982. Cf. forʒiue.
ʒo(u) *pron. obj.*, etc. see ʒe.
ʒon *adj.* yonder 4972.
ʒond *adj.* the far 3589.
ʒond *adv.* yonder A1328, etc.;
  ʒounde 5395ʳ.
ʒonder *adv.* yonder 4972, 6239.
[ʒonede] *pa. t. 3 sg.* see ʒened.
ʒong [-(e)] *adj.* young 726, L218,
  etc.; ʒing [-(e)]ʳ 270, L1638, etc.;
  = young man 5990; and see eld.
ʒongling *n.* young man 5470. ʒong-
  linges *pl.* 8265.

hay *interj.* listen! 9859.
-hay see chirche-hay.
hayl(e) *adj.* safe 8304, *hole and* ~ safe
  and sound 350, ~ *þou be* hail!
  A1375.
hail(e) *n.* hail 5874, 7932, L602.
hale *n.* health, *soule* ~ salvation A30.
  Cf. wroþhale.
half *adj.* half 554, A957, 6806, etc.,
  þridde ~ *hundred* two hundred and
  fifty 5748, 5831.
half *adv.* half 2654, 4194, with half
  power 9738.
half *n.* side (of) 2841, 6513, 8054, etc.,
  and see left, (of battle) 8965, (of
  family) 8886; *bi* ~ aside 3399;
  behalf 7814, halue 2278, L782.
  half *pl.* A453, 5983, etc., *a four* ~
  [. . . *of*] to the four corners of 614;
  halue 7953.
half-felawe *n.* half-sharer A426.
halle *n.* hall (king's etc.) 228, etc.
hals *pr. 1 sg.* conjure A1007. halsed
  pa. t. 3 sg. A1009, A1173.
halue-broþer *n.* half-brother 7660.
haluendel *n.* half 2116, 6619, etc.,
  (adverbial) half way L1854.

hand *n.* see **hond.**

[hap] *n.* happening L447. [happes] *pl.* L8, etc.

happen *v.*, ~ *on* surround 3722[n].

haras *n.* (collect.) stud (iron., of vulgar men) 781.

hard [-(e)] *adj.* forcible A234, etc., L162; harsh A332, 3919, 5220, etc., L1604, L1791, (as n.) *in nesse in/and* ~ in good and evil times (= always) 2961, 2968; bad (news) A1718, (dream) 3801[n]; hardy 6688, etc., (as n.) ~ *and nesse* = every sort of adversary 8166.

hard [-e] *adv.* forcibly 2874; harshly L648; resolutely 2131, 2133, L1602.

hardi *adj.* hardy A194, A406, etc.; foolhardy L1166.

hardiliche *adv.* resolutely 3964, 6238.

[hare] *n.*[1] hare L1697.

hare *n.*[2] see **here.**

harlot *n.* low fellow 3145, L816; herlot 3139. harlotes *pl.* 792, L763, L832; herlotes A829, 8756.

harm *n.* A1174[n], 1630, etc., [*good no* ~] = anything L1093; = injury 5238, 5249, etc.; = loss 746, 3336. harmes *pl.* 5619, 9414.

harnois *n.* knightly gear 8058, harnais 4644; fighting-men 8329.

harou *interj.* help! 4854.

haspes *pl.* hasps 5677.

hast [-(e)] *n.* haste (see **haue(n)**) A1223; *on* [*in*] ~ quickly A432, A1569,1726, L1233, etc., hest 7409.

hast *v.* urge to speed A1847.

hastiliche [-ely] *adv.* at once, quickly A608, 2019, L539 etc.

hat *n.* helmet 3467, *ysen* ~ 7114[n], 7170. hatten *pl.* 9727.

[hate] *n.* emotion or sin of anger L646, L786, L1453. Cf. **hete.**

hat(e)rel *n.* neck 7174, 8190, 9236.

haþen *adj.* see **heþen.**

hauberioun *n.* coat of mail (*see 2975–6n*) 2975, 5442. hauberiouns *pl.* 8666.

hauberk *n.* coat of mail (*see 2975–6n*) A321, etc.; hauber 3302[n]; auberk 5957. hauberkes *pl.* 8666.

haue(n) *v.* have (mod. uses) 241, 376, A427, *558*, *676*, *743*, 1055, 9866, etc.; han A1221, etc., L760; [a]

(auxil.) L264, L627, L1906; = enjoy sexually 2486, *2489*, L760; = overcome 5977[n]; (+pp.) cause to be 514, A1558; ~ *age* be old enough *4616*; ~ *care* be distressed A156, *etc.*, (sim.) ~ *(de)spite 3135, 5773, etc.*, ~ *diol A1124, etc.*, ~ *game A1143, etc.*, ~ *grame A988*, ~ *meruail(e) A870*, etc., ~ *ond 669*, *A819*, ~ *wonder 801, etc.*; ~ *entre* gain entry *A682*; ~ *findeing of* find A1198, (sim.) ~ *meteing of 7057*; ~ *hast* be in a hurry *A1223*; ~ *herte fin to* love *2056*; ~ *non heued* have no sense 9214[n]; ~ *ful her hond* have their hands full (fig.) 4097; ~ **leue* be eager for 973[n]; ~ *liif of manne* be alive *4607*; ~ *nou3t of to done* have no concern with *A1433*; ~ *part of* have sexual intercourse with *A932*, *L912*; ~ *pite* be sorry *697*, have pity *7372, etc.*, ~ *reuþe A446*, *L252*, *etc.*, ~ *pite to* forbear to from pity *4738*; ~ *þe priis* be victorious *A341*; ~ *ri3t* be right *7378*; ~ *(a) si3t of* see *874*, *2740*, etc.; ~ *wrong* behave wrongly *4625*. haue *pr. 1 sg.* A25, L463, etc.; *ich*aue A1154, etc. hast *pr. 2 sg.* 743, etc.; hast*ow* 3697, L1174. haþ *pr. 3 sg.* 1304, etc., naþ (neg.) 9214; haueþ 7821. haue(n)*pr.pl.* A17, A275, L194, etc.; han 379, etc., ~ *leuer* would rather 7373; habben 5335; habbeþ 4225, 4312; haþ A1220, 7310. haue *pr. subj. sg.* A951, etc.; *imp. sg.* 876, etc. haueþ *imp. pl.* 4343. haddest *pa. t. 2 sg.* A932, L912, etc.; hadest*ow* 2896, L183. hadde *pa. t. 3 sg.* 79, etc., ~ *leuer* 2359, L1050, etc., nadde (neg.) 4790, etc.; had 674, etc.; hade A459, *2216*. hadde(n) *pa. t. pl.* 343, 669, etc., ~ *leuer* A167, nadde(n) (neg.) 6952, 7496, *8110; hadd 5848; haden 6888; adden 6229; [had(d)yn] L143, L263, etc. hadde *pp.* 1055, etc.; [had] L160, L161.

haunte *v.* resort to habitually 726.

hawe *n.* hawthorn berry, *nou3t worþ an* ~ = worth nothing 7224.

he *pron.*[1] he 65, etc.; it 5642, (of the Cross) L799. **him** *obj.* 76, etc.,

he (*cont.*):
  (refl.) A64, etc.; *ich*im 2022. **his**
  gen. 66, etc., = his men 5858, etc.,
  L1958; **is** A247; [hise] L1493. Cf.
  himselue(n).
he [heo] *pron.*[2] she 1351, 2656[n], etc.;
  hye A849; [he] L1423. **hir** [-e]
  obj. 723, etc., (refl.) A733, etc.; **hire**
  2664[r]; **her** A672, A767. **hir** [-e]
  gen. 689, etc.; **her** A410, etc.;
  [heore] L655. Cf. **hirselue, sche**.
he *pron.*[3] they A120, etc., L1357,
  L1358; **hye** A157, etc.; [heo] L62,
  etc. **hem** [heom] *obj.* 68, etc.,
  (refl.) 100, etc. **her** [heore] *gen.*
  163, etc., (partitive) A575, etc.;
  here 4203. Cf. **hemselue, hes,**
  þai.
⟨**heauye**⟩ *adj.* dejected P2142.
[**hed**] *n.* see **heued**.
hede *n.* heed (see **nim(en)**) 8405.
hede *v.* see **hide**.
hef *pa. t. 3 sg.* lifted up 5157, etc.;
  houe 5007.
heiȝe [hyȝh(e)] *adj.* high, tall 971,
  2696, 7900, etc., ~ *and lowe* (implying totality) 6604, *bi* ~ *sonne* at
  noon A1275, and see **pryme**; high
  (quality) 6478; noble (rank) A1072,
  etc., (as n.) 2993, ~ *and lowe* (and
  sim., implying unanimity, totality)
  L212, etc., 3190, (as n.) A277, A511,
  etc., principal 6512, 8063, 8217,
  8549; *on* ~ up 5720, L609, etc., in
  heaven, A794, 2814, loudly 9371[n].
  heiȝest *sup.* 3116.
heiȝe [hyȝh] *adv.* high 5007, etc.;
  shrilly, loudly 4739, 6192, L1288.
heiȝer *comp.* more nobly (born)
  8594. Cf. **brest-heiȝe**.
heiȝe *n.* haste 7168; *on* ~ at once,
  quickly A1152, 2356, 8208; **heye**
  A1633; **hy(e)** 3805, speed 6168.
h(e)iȝe *v.* hasten 3381, 5686, etc.,
  (refl.) 6793, L1236; **heye** 9729.
  heiȝe(n) *pr. pl.* A1844, 7242, 7821.
  heiȝeþ *imp. pl.* A526, 3438, heiȝed
  pa. t. 3 sg. A1797.
heiȝte *num. adj.* see **eiȝt(e)**.
heiȝte *num. adj. ord.* eighth 6766.
[**heires**] *pl.* see **air**.
held(en) [holde] *v.* hold (lit.) 4034,
  etc., (captive, etc.) *5041, 9856,*

L568, (under one's rule) *1647,*
2162, etc., L243; (refl.) remain (in
state or place) *3871, 7395,* [halde]
L1061, *etc.*; retain (fame) L1747;
conduct (battle, consultation, feast)
357, 5845, 6730, L1741, etc.;
adhere to (obligation, etc.) *A491,*
A863, A1739, *A1778;* consider to
be *A296,* 5868, *L18, etc.;* ~ *wiþ*
support *1644,* A1675, etc.; ~ *oȝain*
oppose *8044,* A1675, etc.; ***hold** 4594. hold *pr.*
1 sg. (~ *to* put my trust in) A920.
heldeþ [holdust] *pr. 2 sg.* 1647[n].
held *pr. subj. sg.* 3047, *þi þais þou*
~ be silent 2491; *imp. sg.* [hold]
L1195, ~ *þi þes* 7597, ~ *þi mouþe*
1077. **holdeþ** [-iþ] *imp. pl.* support
(as king) 77. **heldest** *pa. t. 2 sg.*
4588. **held** [heold] *pa. t. 3 sg.* 357,
etc., = forced back (enemy) 2131,
2133, no ~ *tale of* esteemed of no
account 5466. **held(en)** [heold] *pa.
t. pl.* 1644, 3341, L596, etc. **held-**
(en) *pp.* A359, 2161, 9856; **yhelden**
3968; **yholden** A700; [holde(n)]
L18, L568, L1190; [yholde] L259,
L317. Cf. **atheld**.
hele *n.* heel, *at her* ~ close behind
them 7569.
hele *v.* keep secret (from) 2690, 6147;
  heleþ *pr. pl.* 5544. Cf. **vnhele**.
helle *n.* hell 4834, L989, etc.
helle-fende *pl.* devils of hell (= wicked
  heathens) 8366[r].
helle-fer *n.* hell-fire A642.
helle-ȝrounde *n.* the abyss of hell
  9696.
helle-hounde *pl.* hell-hounds (=
  devils) 6374[r].
helle-pin(e) *n.* the torment of hell
  A326, A1878, 7516.
Helle-pouke *n.* Devil 7180.
[**helle-put**] *n.* the pit of hell L600.
helm(e) *n.* helmet A321, 5908, *L281.
  helmes *pl.* A447, etc.
help *n.* help A1821, L194, etc.
help(en) [-pe] *v.* help 87, A152, etc.,
  (+ inf. or (*for*)*to* and inf.) A125,
  A429, 2416, 2440, etc., L108; (refl.)
  wele ~ *in fiȝt* = fight effectively
  A1866; **helper** 4515, 8731. **helpeþ**
  pr. 3 sg. (see **w(h)at**) 3055, 4270.
  help(e) *pr. pl.* 4337, 9204, 9207,

L1941; *pr. subj. sg.* 3948, 9070, etc., L175. **help** *imp. sg.* 2484, etc. **helpeþ** [-iþ] *imp. pl.* 74. **halp** *pa. t. 3 sg.* A333, etc.; *pl.* 3356 6670; **holpe(n)** 4396, 5110, etc. **halp** *pp.* 6331; **holpen** 6110.

helping *n.* assistance 2069, 2748, 3053, L168.

-helue see **ax-helue.**

hem *pron. obj.* see **he** *pron.*³

hemselue, -self *pron.* themselves (refl.) A1790, (emphatic) 7804; *bi* ~ together and apart from others 2210, 2212, 5749.

hem-ward see **toward(e).**

hende *adj.* noble A385, L258, etc., = (the) legitimate (cognomen) 7814, 8015, etc.; nobly-minded 370. Cf. **vnhende.**

hende *adv.* near, ~ *bi* near to A434; *prep.* 6896.

hendelich(e) *adv.* courteously A1428, 3546, 8548, L151.

hendeschip(pe) *n.* nobility of character 4392, 8620.

heng *pa. t. 3 sg.* see **hong** *v.*

hennes *adv.* hence (motion) 2345; *fer* ~ far from here 2743, 5515.

[hente] *pa. t. 3 sg.* seized L1630. **yhent** *pp.* 4982, 9003ⁿ, captured 3653.

hepes *n.* quantities (of dead bodies) 5850, etc.

her *conj.* see **er.**

her(e) *adv.* here 1219, L1375, etc., = in this world A632, = (at this point) in my story 3339, 4025, etc.; ~ *is* here is (of proffered advice) 7920; ~ *and þere* all over the place (and sim.) 553, A648, 3928, etc., hither and thither 6999, 9389.

her(e) *pron. gen.* see **he** *pron.*² ³

heraboue *adv.* = in the heavens A1573.

herafter *adv.* in the future A956, later on (in my story) 9655; after that 3571.

herafterward *adv.* in the future 3429.

herberwe *n.* lodging 7222.

herbes *pl.* herbs 2513.

herbiȝonde *adv.* a little way from here 2897.

herd *n.* herdsman (see **hogges**) A1979. **herdene** *pl. gen.* 9646ⁿ.

yherd *pp.* praised, ~ *be Crist* (and sim.) 4665, 6551, etc.

here *n.* hair A858, etc.; **hare** 7715; [her] L825.

(y)here(n) *v.* hear 2184, 2460, 4552, 9074, L64, L1046, etc., **yher** 5518ʳ, (mass, etc.) 2376, 6490, listen to 2328; hear of, about 3565, L630, etc., ~ *of* A1244, L1472, etc., ~ *telle* (and sim.) *109, 6681, 8231,* etc., L1879; [~ *telle*] have news L960. **here** *pr. 1 sg.* 2681, 7599. **heren** *pr. pl.* 6993. **hereþ** *imp. pl.* 6593. **herd** [-e] *pa. t. 1, 3 sg.* 109, A928, etc.; **yherd** 7807. [**herdest**] *pa. t. 2 sg.* L1472. **herd(en)** [-de(n)] *pa. t. pl.* A1015, 1400, etc., L1414; [**herdyn**] L1282; **yherd** 4251. **herd** *pp.* 1155, A1244.

herebifore [her-] *adv.* earlier on (in my story) 6040; up to the present L169.

herebineþe *adv.* below here (in valley) 4859.

herebiside *adv.* near here A1954; **herbisiden** 5102.

here-gong *n.* ravaging invasion 4084.

her(e)of *adv.* about/of this A697, 3814, etc.

heretofore *adv.* facing this position 7489.

herken *imp. sg.* listen A1634. [**herk-(e)neþ**] *imp. pl.* L1417, listen concerning L1147.

herlot *n.* see **harlot.**

hermite [-r(e)-] *n.* hermit L671, etc., 801, 840; (þ)**ermite** A701, A795, etc.

herne *n.* corner (of room) A1145.

hern-panne *n.* skull 5762.

heron *adv.* onto this 5053.

herre *n.* hinge, *turned of* ~ = went into disorder 3568ⁿ.

hert [he(o)rte] *n.*¹ heart A393, etc., (as seat of emotions, etc.) 786, 882, etc., and see **fin(e), take(n). hertes** *pl.* 4252.

hert *n.*² hart 3119. **hertes** *pl.* 9674.

(y)hert *pa. t. 3 sg., pp.* see **hirt.**

hert-blod [heorte-] *n.* life-blood 1221.

herto *adv.* to this 2825.

hert-polk *n.* heart welling with blood 8491ⁿ.

hervnder *adv.* under here A1449.

hesʳ *pron. obj.* them A732, 5869, etc. *See 732n.*

hest *n.*¹ command A505, etc.; **hast** vow 4642ʳ.

hest *n.*² see **est**.

hest *n.*³ see **hast**.

het(e) *pa. t. 3 sg.*, etc. see **hiʒt**, **hot(e)**.

hete *n.* anger, hostility 230, 4207, 5147. Cf. **hate**.

heþen [-(e)] *adj.* heathen A479, L1789, L1923, etc., (as n.) 8100; **haþen** 6813, 7734, (as n.) A483, 2107, 6717, etc.

(heue *v.*) see **hef**.

heued [hed] *n.* head 231, etc., and see **grounde**, *haue non* ~ = have no sense 9214; = barbed tip 1502ⁿ, 1673; ruler 3158. **heuedes** *pl.* 8774, etc.; **heueden** 6937, 9171. Cf. **bore-heuedes**.

heued(en) *v.* behead 3350, 5202. **heueded** *pa. t. 3 sg.* 5184. Cf. **biheueded**.

heuedles *adj.* headless 8188, 8969.

heued-panne *n.* skull 9762.

heuen [heouene] *n.* heaven 640, etc., *þe þridde* ~ 8915ⁿ.

heuen-blis *n.* the joy of heaven 2088, 2746.

Heuen-king [Heouene-] *n.* the King of heaven A1, 3509, L571, etc., and see **vnder**.

Heuen-quen [Heouene-quene] *n.* the Queen of heaven 1038, 4664.

hewe [heowe] *n.*¹ complexion 1351, 4203.

hewe *n.*² servant A1165.

hewe *v.* hew (in battle) 9368, L1924, L1940. **hewe** *pa. t. 3 sg.* 5208, etc. **hewe(n)** [heo-] *pa. t. pl.* 5614, etc., hewed down 5727; shaped by hewing 531. Cf. **tohewe**, **flesche-hewer**.

heweing *n.* hewing 2429.

hy(e) *n.* see **heiʒe**.

[hyde] *n.* skin L985.

hide *v.* conceal 885; (refl.) 7343, hede find protection A518. **hide** *pr. subj. sg.* 8422. **hidden** *pa. t. pl.* 7402, 7405. **yhidde** *pp.* 3860.

hider *adv.* hither 4754, etc., L1935.

hiderward *adv.* (on way) hither A1653, 4979, etc.

hye *pron.* see **he** *pron.*², ³

hiʒe *v.* see **h(e)iʒe**.

[hyʒh(e)] *adj., adv.* see **heiʒe**.

[hyʒhte] *pa. t. 3 sg.* see **hot(e)**.

hiʒt *pa. t. 3 sg.* was named 32, 2262ⁿ, etc., **het(e)** A629, 4438, 6762, etc.; **[hyʒt(e)]** L778, L991, L1779. **hete(n)** *pa. t. pl.* 6064, 9335, 9343. **(y)hoten** *pp.* (adj.) A117, 3771, etc.; **(y)hot(e)** 2817, 4185, 5458, 7633, *hir name is* ~ 8464.

hille *n.* hill A1864, etc.

hilt *n.* hilt 2887.

himselue(n), **-self** [-seolue] *pron.* himself (emphatic) A171, 5961, etc., L67; (refl.) A1160, etc., ~ *here tere* tear his own hair 8360.

hinde see **bihinde(n)**.

hindeward *n.* rear (milit.) 7805.

hing *v.* see **hong**.

hir(e) *pron. obj., gen.* see **he** *pron.*²

hire [huyre] *n.* wages 527.

hire *pr. pl.* employ (for wages) 4317.

hir(r)itage *n.* inherited property A827, 6574; hereditary succession 8633.

hirselue, **-self** [hireseolue, -seolf] *pron.* herself (refl.) 690, A857, L769; (emphatic) L959.

hirt *pa. t. 3 sg.* wounded 3284, etc.; **hert** 8860ʳ. **hirt** *pa. t. pl.* 3479, ?5014; *pp.* 8872; **(y)hert**ʳ 7272, 9365, etc. Cf. **hurtinge**.

his *pron. gen.* see **he** *pron.*¹, **it**.

[hit] *pron.* see **it**.

hit(t) *v.* hit 4799, 5158, etc. **hit(t)** *pa. t. 3 sg.* 3254, 4140, etc., ~ *him a dint* struck him a blow 8987, 9061; **hitte** 4013. **hit(ten)** *pa. t. pl.* 3991, 6697, etc. **hit(t)** *pp.* A391, 5985.

ho *interj.* stop! A645.

hod *n.* hood (see **bal**) A394ⁿ.

hoge *adj.* huge 4892, etc.

hogges *pl. gen.*, ~ *herd* swineherd A1979.

hoked *adj.* barbed A1499. Cf. **wiþþerhoked**.

hold(e) *v.* see **held(en)**.

[holde] *adj.* firm L502.

hold-oþ *n.* oath of allegiance 3578.

hole [hol] *adj.* uninjured (see **hayl(e)**) 350, ~ *and sounde* 7804.

hole *n.* window A984.

holy *adj.* holy A51, A1054, L798, etc., and see **chirche, Gost, Þorsday, write** *n.*

hom *n.* one's abode (perm. or temp.), *at* ~ A1347, 2505, 4435; *adv.* to this 714, A1961, etc.

homward *adv.* homewards A1152, etc.

hond [-(e)] *n.* hand A1933, L853, etc., *bi* ~ in his hand 2887, (sim.) 2710, 5419, etc., L1694, (fig.) see **nim(en), take(n)**; = (armed) might (*see 190n*) 2648, 4428, etc., L1827, *wiþ* ~ A143, *don his* ~ do his utmost A190, *God saue and kepe þi miȝti* ~ (salutation to king) A1377; = power, lordship (over persons) A154, A488, A1660, 4764, etc., (over land) 1648, 6852, etc.; *an* ~ soon A577, L132; *an* ~ *go* be actively present A1896ⁿ; *deþes* ~ = the jaws of death 4423; **hand** 5495, etc. **honden** *pl.* A858, etc.; **hondes** 5815, 8442; **hond** [-(e)] 2514, etc., L713, L1600, *ful her* ~ *of* their hands full of (fig.) 4098, (and many number uncertain). Cf. **neiȝehond.**

hondling *n.* handling, + *haue in* ~ *hard* be giving rough handling to 4980.

hong [-e] *v.* kill by hanging 1393, etc.; hold hanging down 8448; be hanged A1781; **hing** 2324, 5580. **hongeþ** *pr. 3 sg.* ?grows 3060. **hong** *pa. t. 3 sg.* A384, L658, L769, ~ *his cher* made a long face A1682; **heng** A690; **hing** hung down 5983. **hong** *pa. t.* (or *pr.*) *pl.* [**honge** *pa. t.* (or *pr.*) *subj. sg.*] 1141. **honged** [-yd] *pp.* 380, 9078; [**honge**] L1447. Cᶠ. **tohong.**

honour *n.* honour A179, L17, etc., *þe* ~ = the highest esteem 2984, *ȝour* ~ (form of address) 3698; **onour** 6509; **anour** (*þe* ~ the honour (of knighthood)) 7652. Cf. **deshonour.**

honour *v.* honour A204. **onourd** *pp.* 2256.

honteye *n.* shouting of insults 6879. *See n.*

hope *n.* grounds for hope 7220. Cf. **wanhope.**

hope *pr. 1 sg.* (+ clause) trust 7363.

hopinges *pl.* dancing 3535.

hore *adj.* grey(-haired) 2701, 3678.

hore *n.* whore 791, etc. **hores** *gen.* 3157.

horn *n.* horn (for blowing) 3832, etc.

hors [-(e)] *n.* horse A138, etc., L116, and see **comand, lepe. hors** *gen.* 5162, etc.; *pl.* 1423, etc., [**horses**] L339. **hors** *pl. gen.* 3824, 6945, etc. (some may be *sg.*)

hors-bere *n.* horse-bier 8542.

[**hosol**] *n.* the Eucharist L662.

host *n.* see **ost** *n.*¹

hot *n.* heat 4867.

hot(e) *adj.* hot 3063, 8800, etc., *fot* ~ quickly 7934.

hot(e) *v.* (+inf.) order (person) to ... 4151; *þat hir* ~ ... *it be* order her that it be ... 2641. **hete** *pa. t. 3 sg.* A802, etc.; (+ inf.) ordered to be performed A501, etc., ~ *men schuld* A293, etc.; [**het(te)**] (*hire* ~ '*y bidde þe* ...') L782; (obj. person and thing) promised L706, **hyȝhte** L701. **hoten** *pp.* (~ *forto* ...) A1232. Cf. **bihot(e).**

(y)**hoten** etc. *pp.* (adj.) see **hiȝt.**

hou *adv.* [how] how (mod. uses) 120, A1067, 1245 [L **hou**], L1437, etc., ~ *þat* 3022, 6697, 8842ⁿ, L1172; = for what price 4148ⁿ; ~ *seistow* what do you say? A1135.

houe *v.* be present, remain, wait A1574, 7146. **houen** *pr. pl.* A651. **houed** *pa. t. 3 sg.* A1299, 9188; *pl.* 5644. *See 651n.*

houe *pa. t. 3 sg.* see **hef.**

hounde *n.* dog A492, 6985, (of heathen man) 6823, 8432, etc. **houndes** *pl.* 7883, etc., hunting dogs 7000; **houndeʳ** 5944, 7985. Cf. **helle-hounde.**

hous *n.* house 7292, etc., L654; [**hows**] L841. **houses** *pl.* 6983.

[**housbonde**] see **husbounde.**

howe *adj.* wise, ~ *wiif* wise-woman A994.

howe *n.*¹ distress A566, A1129, *of* ~ bitter (blow, etc.) 8147, etc.

howe *n.*² clamour 7268.

hucking *n.* bargaining 4150.
[huyre] *n.* see **hire**.
humilite *n.* humility 9876.
hundred *num. adj.* hundred 2353, etc., L77, ~ *of* A1877, etc.; = hundred men 4771, 5170, etc., L1972, **hunder** 7789[r]. **hundredes** *pl.* (as n.) 8520.
hunger *n.* famine 4084.
hunist *pp.* overthrown 9205.
hunting *n.* hunting 4610.
hunting *pr. p.* pursuing 5055.
hurtinge *n.* wounding 7275. Cf. **hirt**.
husbounde *n.* husband 4477; [**housbonde**] L1389. Cf. **bo(u)nde**.

y- *prefix* see next letter.
y *pron.* I 70, etc.; **ich** A25, etc., L1223, and (fused forms) see **be(n)**, **haue(n)**, **he** *pron.*[1], **wil**, **wite(n)**, **me** *obj.* 71, 196, etc., (refl.) A217, etc. **mi** *gen.* 74, etc.; **min(e)** 875, A961, 1066, A1221, 9872, etc., **mi** n*eldest* (and sim., see *58n*) A75, etc. Cf. **meself**.
ich [**vche**] *adj.*[1] every A816, L86, etc.; [~ *a*] L1945, [**ylk(e)**] L106, L1889, etc.; every sort of 3583; (as pron.) each A403, etc., and see **oþer** *adj.*
ich [**ilke**] *adj.*[2] very, same (often little meaning), *þat* ~ (and sim.) A191, 1133, L1221, etc., *þat* ~ *selue* 4667, (sim.) 6105; **iche** 9720; *þilke* A730, A971.
ichon [**vchon**] *pron.* each 8833, L1285, and see **oþer** *adj.*; every one A67, L229, etc.; [**ilkon**] L197, L1311.
i(o)e *pron.* I (see **di**) 5913, 6546. **ma** *gen.* (see **dame, fay**) A824, etc.
ille *adj.* harsh 6593, L153; bad (news) A184; wretched 4528, 6963.
in *adv.* in 845, etc.; *prep.* (mod. uses) 73, A147, 345, A822, 955, 4775, L12, L235, etc., ~ *his falling* as he fell 3461, (sim.) 5737, etc., ~ *her way* on their way (and sim.) A1339, etc., and see **al(le)**, **þing**; into (state, etc.) 683, etc., under (guidance) 8600; on (dogs on leash) 4612; to (attachment to rope) 993; on, in (of blow, etc.) 6389, etc., L824; at (time) A730, 4795, L237, etc.; **inne** set in (jewels) 8670[r]. Cf. **þerin**.
in *n.* lodging 1594, etc.

ynde *adj.* indigo 5634, 7848.
Inglisch(e) *n.* the English language *A20, A24, etc.; **Inglis** 2819.
Inglisse *adj.* English A119; [**Englysch(e)**] L117, L289, L1894; **Inglische** = Englishman A24.
Inglond-ward see **toward(e)**.
iniquite *n.* ignominy 6121; injustice 9857.
intil *prep.* onto 3831.
into *prep.* into 116, 2168, L626, etc.; *bren* ~ *þe grounde* burn to the ground (and sim.) A1894, 5600, 7756, etc. L1745.
ioie *n.* A750[n], 2007, L1387, etc.
ioifulliche *adv.* joyfully 4671.
ioinand *pr. p.,* ~ *bi hond* joining hand in hand 5416. **ioined** *pa. t. 3 sg.* put (hands) together 5913.
ioiouse *adj.* joyful 2600.
ioli(i)f *adj.* gay A263, 5562, etc.
iornaying *n.* travelling 3505. Cf. **iurnay**.
〈yorne〉 *adv.* see **ȝern(e)**.
ire *n.* anger A1815, 3269.
iren *n.* iron 7520, ~ *and stiel* (of armour) 2064, 3791, etc.; **ire** 8201[r]; **ysen** = spear-head 8829.
is *pron. gen.* see **he** *pron.*[1]
ysen *adj.* iron (see **hat**) 7114, etc.
it [**hit**] *pron.* it 109, etc.; (impers.) 539, etc., and see **bring. his** *gen.* A393, ?A492, ?A996.
iuel *adj.* evil A1055, ~ *lac* fault (of character) 2724, [+]*falle wiþ* ~ *rest* die and go to hell 5312, 6402; damaging (blow) 8982, 8987; [**eouel**] (~ *thryft* ill success) L1287. **wors** [-e] *comp.* = losing (side in battle) 327 (or adv.).
iuel *adv.* badly A296, A737, etc., and see **aise, atsit**; [**eouele**] L826. **wers** *comp.* (*him was* ~ he was in worse case, and sim.) 2580, 6212, 8468; **wors** 6290[r].
[iugged] *pa. t. 3 sg.* ([+] *to* and inf.) adjudge that (person) shall L896. **iugged** *pp.* 2597, 2599; [*yiugged*] (~ *ȝef* adjudged whether) L926.
iuggement *n.* judicial process A731, A765; sentence L753, L1087.
Iune *n.* June 3059, 8657.
iurnay, -eie [**ior-**] *n.* journey 4707,

5706, L1355; day's march (distance)
4736. **iurnes** *pl.* 3674; **iurneie**
7293; **iurne** 8322. Cf. **iornaying.**
iuste *v.* joust 3095.
iustes *pl.* jousts 2623.
iusting(e) *n.* jousting 6295, 6377,
7621.
iustise [-s(e), -ce] *n.* judge 775, 890,
893, etc.

kan *pr. 3 sg.*, etc., see **conne.**
karf *pa. t. 3 sg.* see **kerue.**
karols *pl.* see **carols.**
[**kast**] *pa. t. 3 sg.* see **cast.**
kedde(n) *pa. t. pl.*, etc. see **kiþe.**
ken(ne) *n.* see **kin.**
kende [ky-] *adj.* rightful A369, 4283,
L1932; noble 5110.
kende [ky-] *n.* kindred A386, etc.,
L1788; lineage L325, ?L586; natural
quality/function A1057, **kinde** 9275.
kene *adj.* warlike 4212, 7979, 8087,
etc., fierce L1685, etc.; eager A406;
sharp 3211.
keneþ *pr. 3 sg.* becomes eager 5352.
kepe *n.* heed (see **nim(en)**) A779,
9841, L791.
kepe(n) *v.* defend, guard A13, A1974,
3688, etc., look after L959; remain
in L958. **kepe** *pr. pl.* 4321ⁿ; *pr. subj.
sg.* A1377, 4576; *imp. pl.* watch out!
9324. **kept** *pa. t. 3 sg.* kept off 7882.
kerue *v.* cut 2063, 8732. **kerue** *pr. 1
sg.* 2820. **kerueinde** *pr.* 5978.
carf, k- *pa. t. 3 sg.* 3353, 4932, etc.
coruen, k- *pa. t. pl.* 531, 7884, etc.;
korwe(n) 3825, 8879. **coruen**, k-
pp. 5960, 7951, 9258. Cf. **tocarf.**
kest(en) *pa. t. 3 sg.*, *pl.* see **cast.**
keþe *v.* see **kiþe.**
keuer(en) *v.* get A1660; recover (tr.)
3909; rescue 3359, ~ *up to hors*
rescue and rehorse 9292, (sim.)9920,
9922; make one's way 7150, 8951.
keuer(e)d *pa. t. 3 sg.* 9922, recovered
(intr.) 8198; [**couered**] L1623;
[**kouorede**] L1731. **keuer(e)d** *pa.
t. pl.* 3359, 9920; **keuerden** 6115.
keuered *pp.* 8793; **couered** 9292.
Cf. **akeuered, recouerd.**
kin *n.* kindred A188, etc., L1026;
kind of 7264; **ken(ne)ʳ** A464, 8013;
kynne L1897.

kinde *n., adj.* see **kende.**
[**kyndom**] *n.* kingdom L243.
king *n.* king 32, A134, 7763, L14, etc.;
þe ~ *of glorie* = God 3369, 4268,
þe ~ *of blis* 4638, þe ~ *þat made
sonne* 9662; **kinge** 9032, L1639.
kinges *gen.* A62, 3677ⁿ, L566,
etc., ~ *ring* royal ring 3670; *pl.*
A114, etc. Cf. **Heuen-king, lord-
king.**
[**kynrade**] *n.* kindred L780, L1748.
kisse *v.* kiss 8680. **kist** [**kuste**] *pa. t.
1, 3 sg.* 910, 2474, etc.
kisseing(e) *n.* kissing 4656, 8682,
9241; **kissing** 8823.
kit(t) *pa. t. 3 sg.* cut 3482, 6178, etc.;
kitte 4014; **ykitt** 9254.
kiþ *n.* comrades 8204.
kiþe *v.* demonstrate (by actions) 2566,
4840, etc.; **keþe** act 2121ʳ. **kiþe**
imp. sg. 6246, **kid(de)** *pa. t. 3 sg.*
2512, 2784, etc. **kedde(n)** *pa. t. pl.*
3900, 7895, etc., showed (themselves) to be 9135. **yked** *pp.* 8595;
ykidde revealed 3859ⁿ.
knape *n.* male servant 7811ʳ.
knaue *n.* boy-child 2699; male
servant 7816, 7845; man of low
degree 4248 (*noiþer ~ no lord*,
implying totality), = abased 9865.
[**knawe-child, knaue-**] *n.* boy-
child L536, L548, L998.
knely *v.* sink on one's knees 9047.
knewe *n.* knee 2277. **knewes** *pl.* 6541;
[**kneos**] L1464. Cf. **a-knewes.**
kniȝt *n.* knight 138, etc., *com(e) to
~?* = be knighted 4484ⁿ. **kniȝtes**
[-ȝh-] *pl.* 564, etc.; **kniȝtʳ** 2365, etc.;
kniȝtenʳ 6249, 6685. **kniȝtes** *pl.
gen.* 8801. Cf. **broþer-kniȝt.**
kniȝtschippe *n.* knighthood 8911.
kniif *n.* dagger A336, etc. **kniues** *pl.*
3165, etc.
knitt *pa. t. 3 sg.* tied A993; **knett**
8451. Cf. **vnknett.**
knok(e) [-cke] *v.* knock (on door)
1127, (head on wall) 5818.
knowe *v.* recognize, know 4042, 4095,
8933; acknowledge as 4181; **knawe**
2470, 7999, 8568. **knowe** *pr. 1 sg.*
know about 2478; **knawe** know to
be 8619. **knowest** *pr. 2 sg.* A1064;
knawestow 8461. **knewe** [**kneow**]

knowe (*cont.*):

　pa. t. 3 sg. 2464, etc., L1899, had carnal knowledge of A950, *hir* ~ *for* acknowledged herself to be A733, *wiþ ded his dintes* ~ experienced death through his blows 8844; **iknewe** noticed 9049. **knewe** [kneow] *pa. t. pl.* 1771, etc. **yknawe** *pp.* A901; [(y)knowe] (*beo*(*n*)) ~ (*of*) confess! L742, L946, L1159, L1400. Cf. **biknawe.**

knoweing *n.* carnal knowledge A936.

knoweleche *n.* understanding, *conne* ~ possess this A1946.

[**konioun**] *n.* see **conioun.**

[**konst**] *pr. 2 sg.*, etc. see **conne.**

[**ykore**] *pp.* (adv.) see **chese**(n).

korray *n.* see **carroy.**

koruen etc. *pa. t. pl., pp.* see **kerue.**

[**kouorede**] *pa. t. 3 sg.* see **keuer**(en).

[**kuste**] *pa. t. 3 sg.* see **kisse.**

lac *n.* fault (of character), **iuel** ~ 2724.

lachi *v.* receive (injury) 4992. **lauȝt** *pa. t. pl.* 3358; seized 6374. *See 4991–2n.*

lade *v.*[1] see **lede**(n).

(**lade** *v.*[2]) see **loden** *pa. t. pl.*

lay *n.* law 906, *Cristen* ~ = Christian faith 8643. Cf. **lawe.**

lay *v.* see **legge**(n).

ylay *pp.* besieged 2441[n]. Cf. **bilay, ligge.**

laie *n.* lake 5296; **leye** 9652.

⟨**layne**⟩ *n.* concealment, *withouten* ~ openly P2282.

laist(e) *pa. t. 3 sg.* see **lasse.**

laite *n.* flames 6989. Cf. **leiȝe.**

land *n.* see **lond.**

lang(e) *adj.* see **long.**

larg(g)e *adj.* large A524, 7896.

largesse *n.* generosity 4392, 7702.

lark *n.* skylark 6598.

las *n.*[1] noose 9078. Cf. **loue-las.**

las *n.*[2] blow 9375.

las(se) *adj. comp.* see **litel.**

lasse *n.* see **les** *n.*[2]

lasse *v.* strike 9103. **laist**(e) *pa. t. 3 sg.* 7584, 9783. **last** *pa. t. pl.* 8255, 9263. *See 455n.* Cf. **luȝste.**

lassed *pa. t. pl.* became fewer A414.

last [-e] *adj. sup.* recent 8823; last, ~ *day* death-day 9862; (as n.) **atte** ~ in the end 4965, L628, at the latest 5575, *bi þe* ~ 4786.

last(ed) *pa. t. 3 sg.* continued A493, 2625, etc., (+ ind. obj.) 4785; extended 6892, etc.; **lest** 7421, etc. **ylast** *pp.* 8647.

late *adv.* recently A1576, etc.; late 685, 2568.

late(n) *v.* see **lete**(n).

Latin *n.* the Latin language A18, etc.

[**lauȝhyng**, **lawynȝg**] *n.* see **leiȝeing.**

[**lauhȝ**] *v.* see **leyȝe.**

launce *n.* lance A456, etc. **launces** *pl.* A1824, etc., L1918.

launce-schaft *n.* = lance 6865.

launde *n.* glade in forest 7403, 7484.

lawe *adj.* see **lowe.**

lawe *n.* law 902, etc., = (Christian) morality A491, 947, *in her* ~ within the framework of their law 2778, *it is* ~ = it is lawful A735, 2910; *it was* ~ = it was customary 2304, 6562. **lawes** *pl.* 3522. Cf. **lay.**

ylawe *pp.* come down 5167[n].

le *def. art.* (see **bel**) 8268.

le(a)**ute** *n.* loyalty A1739; *in* ~ honourably 2256; *bi mi* ~ = assuredly 4749, (tag) 4366, 5684.

lecherie *n.* lust 806, L901.

lede *n.* estate, *lond and* ~ A86.

lede(n) *v.* take, carry, convey, etc. A347, 4716, L968, L1847; lead (hounds on leash) *4611*; lead (armed force) *3845*, 8698, *etc.*; carry on (one's life) *4540*, L464; perform (dance) *1714, 3544*; **lade** 5792. **lede** *pr. 1 sg.* A1272. **ledeþ** [-iþ] *pr. pl.* 1714, 5862. **lede** *pr. subj. sg.* (or *pl.*) 9870. **lade** *imp. sg.* 9122. **led**(de) *pa. t. 3 sg.* 5412, 8703, etc.; **lad**(de) 4018, 8406, etc. **led**(den) *pa. t. pl.* 3544, 3962, etc.; **ladde**(n) 4540, 6973, etc.; (y)**ladde** *pp.* A888, 5077; **lade** 5800. Cf. **misled.**

lef *adj.* see **leue.**

left *adj.* left 5414, etc., *a* ~ *half and a riȝt* to left and right 4897, etc. Cf. **a-left.**

left *pa. t. 3 sg.* see **lift.**

legge *n.* leg 4815, 5956; gatepost 5673. **legges** *pl.* A850.

legge(n) [leyn] *v.* place, put in position *532*, *4030[n], *4867*, *6508*, *8541*, *L475*, L1017, (refl.) lie (down) *814*, ~ *hond(es) on* seize 8442, strike with weapon in hand 9086, and see **erþe**; strike 4046, 7011, 7466[n], etc., ~ *on* *7476, 8072, **lay** 8001; ~ *heued min* = pledge my life 4977; ~ *his liif* die 2026, 7188, (sim.) 6426; lie 9025. **leggeþ** *imp. pl.* 6016, 8738; **lay** 9323. **leyd** *pa. t. 3 sg.* A1858, etc., *in writt* ~ wrote down A1288; **laid(e)** [leyd(e)] 814, 8445, 9224, *L792*, ~ *penaunce on* 711; **legged** (~ *hir fore* pledged himself on her behalf) A1167[n]. **leyd(en)** [-de(n)] *pa. t. pl.* 5834, 6102, etc., *L474*, *L475*; **laiden** 5009, etc., *on him* ~ *al þe priis* esteemed him the best 6378. **(y)leyd** [-e] *pp.* A338, 8541, etc., [*in scripture* ~] written down L1793; **laid** 2760, 4867.
leye *n.* see **laie**.
leiȝe *n.* flames 6796. Cf. **laite**.
[**leyȝe**] *v.* (refl.) laugh L1061; [**lauhȝ**] (intr., and so all others) L1370. [**lawȝe**] *pr. 1 sg.* L1412. **lauȝh-wynge** *pr. p.* (adj.) L1410. **louȝ** [-ȝh] *pa. t. 3 sg.* 1214, etc.; [**lowȝ**] L1338, etc. **lowen** *pa. t. pl.* 7244.
leiȝe(þ) *pr. 3 sg., subj. sg.* see **lyȝe**.
leiȝeing *n.* laughing A1302; [**lawynȝg**] L1335; [**lauȝhyng**] L1363.
leiȝer *n.* liar 2559. **leiȝers** *pl.* A1239.
leke *pa. t. 3 sg.* closed (with lock, etc.) 5676; [**lowked**] L605. **loke(n)** [-yn] *pp.* (adj.) A853, 5679; [~ *in clay*] buried L43.
lel *adj.* faithful 3030, 5422.
lem *n.* light A1456.
leman [-mm-] *n.* lover 1353, *L748*.
lene *v.* rest 8385[n].
leng(er) etc. *adv. comp.* see **long**.
lengþe *n.* length 7448, 8846. Cf. **ax-lengþe**.
lenten *n.* Lent 4194.
lepe *v.* dance A1330, L1374. **lepe** *pa. t. 3 sg.* jumped 5046, etc.; ~ *vp his hors* mounted quickly 2891, (sim.) 4010, 5218, 9026, etc.; [**leop**] (~ *to hors*) L1516. **lopen** *pa. t. pl.* 5278, etc., pranced 7850; **lepen** 6665, etc.
ler(e) *n.* injury and slaughter 8338,

8359, 9632, *liues* ~ loss of life 8046; *it were to her* ~ it would be their death A611, (sim.) 3490. Cf. **lore** *n.*[2]
leren *v.* learn 7654. **lerd** *pa. t. 3 sg.* showed (the way) to A1980.
lern *v.* learn 4782. **lerne** *pr. 1 sg.* 3675.
les *n.*[1] untruth, *wiþout* ~ truly (tag) A97, L547, etc., ⟨**lesse**⟩ P2220.
les *n.*[2] leash 9028, 9760; **lasse** 9126.
lese *v.* release 2482.
lese(n) *v.* lose (person, as by death) *A410*, *8533*, etc., *L122*, ~ *lore and sleiȝst* lose men killed *6901*; (abstracts) *A1670*, *4203*, *5852*, *6322*, *L185*, *L240*, etc., ~ *winde and alaine* stop breathing *8456*, and see **contenaunce**; ~ ... *time* waste (one's) time *4615*, *4627*; ~ *his londes* be driven from his lands 8922, *to* ~ *and winne* though it made the difference between losing and winning ... 9903; ~ ... *sadel* be unseated *3272*, (sim.) *9442*. **les(es)t** *pr. 2 sg.* 3628, 4615. **lesen** *pr. pl.* 4200; **leseþ** 4203. **les(e)** *pa. t. 3 sg.* 2183, 3272, etc.; *pl.* A989, 5852, **lorn** 4627, [**lore**] L185. **(y)lorn** *pp.* 268, 6901, etc., (adj.) doomed 7334; **(y)lore**[r not L] L1174, etc., 8533, (adj.) 9194. Cf. **forlese**.
lesing [-(e)] *n.* lie, lack of truth 621, 1108, L1645, etc., *wiþouten* ~ truly (tag) A288, L28, etc. **lesinges** *pl.* A1115, *wiþouten* ~ 3617, 3712.
lesse *adj. comp.* see **litel**.
⟨**lesse**⟩ *n.*, see **les** *n.*[1]
lessoun *n.* lesson (iron.) 9675. **lessouns** *pl.* 6704.
lest *n.* listening 7617; ear 8438.
lest *v.* listen 8720. Cf. **listen**.
lest *pa. t. 3 sg.* see **last(ed)**.
let *n.* delay, *wiþouten* ~ A1755, etc.
lete(n) [let(e)] *v.* allow (person or thing) to ... 3663, L1841, (+*forto* and inf.) *2849*; ~ *out* let out (and sim.) *5668*, etc., ~ *(a)doun 985*, [~ *into*] L1866; cause (person) to ... *2693*; (+inf.) cause to be performed *A955*, *L261*, etc., [~ *do L1486*]; leave, give up, abandon A804, 4617, *5700*, 7656, *7808*, ~ *be 4989*, etc., L784, [*al hire wille*

lete(n) (*cont.*):
to him ~] =I et him have his will
of her *L749*; refrain from receiving
(person) 5540; leave (in place) *7338*,
etc., (alive) *7576*, *8519*; *no* ~
(+ clause) not fail to . . . *A503*,
A606, (+ neg. clause) *4927*; **late(n)**
5668, 7338. **lete** *pr. pl.*, ~ *we* let
us leave (persons of story) to . . .
6755, etc., (sim.) A623ⁿ, 5839, etc.; ~
we be(n) = let us turn our attention
from 5131, 6977ⁿ, L575, and see **at**.
lete *pr. subj. sg.* 6544; *imp. sg.* 6338,
etc., **late** 2693, [**let**] L959, L1486.
lete *imp. pl.* 9324; **leteþ** (~ *ben*
stop it!) 4223. **lete** [**lette**] *pa. t. 2
sg.* 1131. **let(e)** [-(te)]] *pa. t. 3 sg.*
350, A469, 760, etc., shed (tears)
A1019, lost (life) 6799, ~ *gode*
appeared pleased 2751, ~ *hem
blode* = made them bleed 9272.
lete(n) [**letten**] *pa. t. pl.* 1786,
3687, etc., ~ *þe rain* gave rein 7445;
let A985. **late(n)** *pp.* 2849, 6659, ~
me on hond bequeathed to me 7658;
[**leten**] L1881; [**ylaten**] (*in eorþe* ~
= born) L1653.

lett *v.* hinder A560.

letter *n.* missive 7813. **letters** *pl.*
A1733, 6439; writings constituting
one missive 7045, etc.; also see
blak(e); **leters** 8560.

letting *n.* delay, *wiþouten* ~ 3950,
etc.; hindrance 7590.

[**leþer**] *n.* leather L1341. Cf. **clout-
leþer**.

leue [-eo-] *adj.* dear A1995, L876;
haue(n) ~ be eager for *9731ⁿ*; ~ *to*
eager for 3072ⁿ; **lef** = mistress 2321,
as ~ *me were to* I would as soon . . .
4983. **leuer** [**leouere**] *comp.* 7823;
he hadde ~ he would rather (and
sim.) 2359, etc., L1050, ~ *hem were*
6826.

leue *n.* permission 2042, 5533, etc.;
leave (see **take(n)**) 1292, etc.

leue *v.*[1] remain (in place) 9308.
leueþ *pr. pl.* 7921. **left** *pa. t. 3 sg.*
left (in place) A331, 7324; **leued**
(*no* ~ *þat he no* did not fail to) 6409.
left *pa. t. pl.* 8224; remained alive
9719, 9809; [**laften**] lost (life)
L1927. **(y)leued** *pp.* 6601; left

alive 8104, (adj.) 6842, 8363; **left**
abandoned 4056.

leue *v.*[2] believe 4163. **leue** *pr. 1 sg.*
A925, L942, *y* ~ *wele* I can well
believe it A216, A869. [**leuen**] *pr.
pl.* L943. Cf. **misbileueand**.

leue *pr. subj. sg.* grant A6.

leu(e)di *n.* lady 1073, etc., = wife
2234, 4694, = mother 2877, etc.,
= (servant's) mistress 2272, etc., =
Our Lady 8436, *our* ~ 4975. **leuedis**
gen. 4419, etc.; *pl.* 2254, etc.

leues *pl.* leaves 4201.

leute *n.* see **le(a)ute**.

lewed *adj.* unlearned, (as n., see
clerk) 561.

lext *pr. 2 sg.* see **ly3e**.

[**ly**] *v.* see **ligge**.

libbe(n) *v.* see **liue(n)**.

libbeing *n.* livelihood A976.

licham *n.* body A950.

(y)liche *adj.* (quasi-prep.) like 2516,
5650, etc.; **like** 2517.

liche *n.* body, *viis and* ~ face and
body (implying totality) 2515, (sim.)
flesche and ~ 7248.

lickenisse *n.* appearance A721.

licour *n.* drink 2273, 2281.

lif *n.* see **liif**.

lift *v.* raise 8978. **lift** *pa. t. 3 sg.* 8131;
helped up (to horse) 9775, (to feet)
9877; left 4888, 9035. **lift** *pa. t. pl.*
A1759, 7880. Cf. **aleft**.

ligge [**ly**] *v.* lie 544, 5023, 7223,
L852; ~ *bi* lie sexually by A671,
852, etc., and see **flescheliche**. **liþ**
pr. 3 sg. A1326, etc. **ligge** [-en]
pr. pl. A1451, L1544. [**lyggand**]
pr. p. L484. **lay** *pa. t. 3 sg.* 918, etc.,
slept habitually 6488; was in residence A1295, etc., (refl.) A1340,
remained (in room) L834. **lay(en)**
pa. t. pl. A1486, etc., were encamped
A1909, 6930. **yleyen** [**ley3en**] *pp.*
852; **lay** 2639; **ylei3e** 4188. Cf.
bilay, forlay, ylay.

ly3e *v.* tell lies A1625. **lye** *pr. 1 sg.*
2113; [**ly3e**] L1223, **lext** [**ly(3)est**]
pr. 2 sg. 912, 1002, L1151.
lei3eþ [**ly-**] *pr. 3 sg.* 1142. **lei3e**
pr. subj. sg. (~ *lesinges* tell lies)
A1115. **lowe** [-en] *pa. t. pl.* A1387,
~ *lesing* L572, etc., 1556. **ylowe(n)**

[lowen] *pp.* 1108, A1261, L1452, L1645.

li3t *adj.*[1] agile 9060; undaunted (heart) 9443; ~ *woman* woman of easy virtue 733, 777.

[ly3t] *adj.*[2] bright L698.

li3t *n.* light (see **day**) 2363; ? sky L1125.

li3t *v.* come down A656; dismount 9815; ⟨**light** *on*⟩ come upon P2337. li3teþ *imp. pl.* 5396. li3t [ly3(h)te] *pa. t. 3 sg.* 679, 2473, L699. li3t(en) *pa. t. pl.* 3985, 7481, etc.

li3ted *pa. t. 3 sg.* shone 8762.

liif [lif] *n.* life A91, 700, L1045, etc., and see **abide, bare** *adj.*, **day, for, man, midel** *adj.*, **pain(e), periil, wiþ**; living being (= woman) 2243; lif 2180; liue[r] A482, L634, etc., adult life [*come to* ~ grow up] L271. liues *gen.* 8046; *pl.* 6998, 8734, *in her* ~ = totally (distressed) 8318. Cf. **liue-dawe, oliue(s)**.

like *adj.* see **(y)liche**.

likeþ *pr. 3 sg.* is acceptable to 5527. like *pr. subj. sg.* approve 5529. liked *pa. t. 3 sg.* pleased 3439, (A impers.) 761.

lilye *n.* lily 8659.

[lym] *n.* bodily member, *in* ~ *and lyth* = totally L1864, (sim.) L1974. limes *pl.* (see **drawe(n)**) 7131.

lime [lym] *n.* cement 515, etc.

limed *adj.*, *wele* ~ well built in body 3243.

lin *n.* lineage 5438, etc., kindred 8060; line[r] ⟨(*euen*) *bi* ~ straight (adv.)⟩ 6370[n], 9680. lins[r] ? *pl.* kindred 2068, *of biches* ~ = sons of bitches 8726; lines[r] (*bi wrongful* ~ behaving wrongfully) 6492.

linage *n.* lineage 6573.

lyoun *n.* lion A1768, etc. [lyouns] *pl.* L1949.

lippe *n.* lip 1682.

lire *n.* flesh (see **flesche**) 8202.

list *n.* ingenuity 2790.

listen *v.* listen A630; [listne] listen to L4. listen *imp. sg.* A1147, 2936, listen to A944; *pl.* A1345, 3403, ~ *meruaile* listen to (an account of) a ... 3041; listneþ [-tenyþ] A639, 1708, 5075, etc. Cf. **lest**.

listening *n.* listening A1111.

litel *adj.* small, little (mod. uses) A452, A1150, 2854, 3233, 4261, 7979, L1399, L1907, etc., (iron.) 3436, ~ *to* little toe 2057; *a* ~ = a little way A1800, etc.; lite[r] 6339, etc., *a* ~ = for a little while A944; low (of rank, see **gret(e)**) 6446. **las(se)** *comp.*, ~ *Breteyne* Brittany 2190, etc., *more and* ~ (implying numerosity, totality) 6710, 6456, (sim., neg.) = none 2446, *no* ~ no fewer 7027, *an hundred* ~ less a hundred 5141; (of rank) ~ *Ywain* = Ywain the bastard 7919, etc., ~ *and more* (implying totality) 69, etc., (as n.) 2801, etc., (sim., neg.) = nobody 3664; **lesse** A69, etc.

litel *adv.* little A588, 2367, etc., = a little way on/away 2569, 7327; lite (*miche no* ~ = not at all) 6903[r].

liter *n.* litter (carrying) 8541.

liþ *n.* bodily member 8494; [lyth] (see **lym**) L1864, L1974.

liþe *v.* ease (sorrow) A242.

liue *n.* see **liif**.

liue(n) *v.* live 1307, 6576, 9198, etc., and see **mot; libbe(n)** 3501, 8192, 9740. liueþ *pr. 3 sg.* 7889. **libbeing** *pr. p.* (adj.) alive 2729. liued *pa. t. 3 sg.* 2163, 2180. [lyued(e)] *pa. t. pl.* L439, L634, L1065. [lyued] *pp.* L670. Cf. **libbeing**.

liue-dawe *n.* life 3213, etc., **liif-dawe** 3904; **liif-day** lifetime 4458. **liif-days** *pl.* life 7428.

liuer *n.* liver 6006, 7176.

lo *interj.* see! A693, 5862, 9000.

lockes *pl.* locks 5677.

loden *pa. t. pl.*, *vp* ~ baled out A1475.

[lodly] *adj.*, *adv.* see **loþ(e)lich(e)**.

loged *pa. t. 3 sg.* caused to encamp 3692; encamped 8067; *pl.* (refl.) encamped 3777.

loges *pl.* tents 6925, 6938.

[lok] *n.* appearance L1584.

loke(n) *v.* look after (infant) A958, etc., guard 4427, etc.; look 5269, L1037, etc., [~ *3ef*] look to see if ... L1562, and see **after**; see to it 3047; *him harm* ~ contrive harm against him 1630[n]; lok 3662. **loke** *pr. subj. sg.* 6744, *God þe* ~ God

loke (*cont.*):
keep you 1376, A1994, (sim.) 3510; *imp. pl.* A523, 3434, consider 5101, **lokeþ** consider 4311. **loked** *pa. t. 3 sg.* 4367, etc., led (armed force) 3953, [∼ *as*] looked like L1582; *pl.* 2377 etc., [**lokid**] L532.

loke(n) [-yn] *pp.* see **leke**.

lokers *pl.* protectors 7429.

lond [-(e)] *n.* (the) land A153, 1419, 1831, L102, etc., = people of land 2045, etc.; (opposed to water) A643, A1765, L2, *vp on* ∼ ashore 6773; **land** 7657. **londes** *pl.* 2696, 3745, etc.; countryside 7901. Cf. **vplond(is)**.

lond-half *n.* landward side 2094.

long [-(e)] *adj.* long A663, 745, 1452, A1529, etc., tall 4886, 5997, 9261, etc.; **lang(e)**r 5968, 6065, 6779.

ylong *adj.* dependent, ∼ *on* because of 4626.

long [-e] *adv.* for a long time 343, A548, etc.; to a distance of 3303, 7461. **lenger** *comp.* any longer 6833, etc., L1598, *no* ∼ 5672, etc., L1515; **leng(e)** A1507, 5043, 6464; **longere** (*ani* ∼) 3489; [**lengur**] (*no* ∼) L81.

longeþ *pr. 3. sg.* is relevant (to . . .) A650, A1435. **longed** *pa. t. 3 sg.* belonged (to . . .) 2193.

lopen *pa. t. pl.* see **lepe**.

lord *n.* nobleman 3116, etc.; lord (= superior) 77, 2544, 3487, etc., *mi* ∼ *þe king* my royal lord A1358, 1717, etc.; = husband 1123, etc.; = father 4592, etc.; = god 7317, 7500, *our* ∼ 2658, L604, etc., and see **vnder**. **lordes** *gen.* A1347, etc.; *pl.* 8365.

lording *n.* nobleman A442. **lordinges** *pl.* 69, etc.; = my good men! L457; **lordinge** 9192r.

lord-king *n.* royal lord 9894n.

lord-ouer *n.* overlord 9646n.

lore *n.*1 teaching A710, 4284, L784. **lores** *pl.* A804.

lore *n.*2 losses (in battle) 6901, 7079. Cf. **ler(e)**.

(y)lorn, etc. *pa. t. pl.*, *pp.* see **lese(n)**.

los *adj.* separated (from . . .) 9418.

los *n.* fame 2686, 3620, etc., *þe* ∼ the highest esteem (see **bere**) 2984.

losten *pa. t. pl.* see **luȝste**.

loþ *adj.* unwilling to A59; hateful (*hir owen liif was hir* ∼ (effect of great anger)) A836, (*his* . . .) 5028, 7552.

loþ *n.* harm A352.

loþeliche *adv.* with cruel indignity 5800; [**lodly**] angrily L1037.

loþlich [**lodly**] *adj.* loathsome A1000, L1024; foul (weather) L1606.

loude *adj.* loud 3451, etc.; [**loud**] L1039.

loude *adv.* loudly A1203, etc.

loue *n.* love 72, A480, 1741, 7650, etc. *for her* ∼ for their sake A27, (sim.) 8823, [*for þy* ∼] because of you (and sim.) L1030, L1071, L1110, L1176, P405n; [*for* ∼] (formula in polite request) L1643.

loue *v.* love A1842, L747. **louest** *pr. 2 sg.* 2479. **loue** *pr. pl.* 8662; **louieþ** 4204. **loued** *pa. t. 3 sg.* A51, 2057; *pl.* 3029.

loued *pa. t. pl.* appraised A1300n.

loue-las *n.* love's snare 2251.

louely *adj.* amiable A1351.

(louk *v.*) see **leke** *pa. t. 3 sg.*

loureand *pr. p.* (adj.) scowling A374.

lowe *adj.* low-built (see **heiȝe**) 6604; low in rank, *þe* ∼ *folk* the common people 4543, and see **heiȝe**; **lawe**r A511, etc., L212; [**lowȝh**] L1776.

lowe *n.* small hill 3831, etc.

lower *n.* reward 364, 372; Atonement 375n.

luȝste *pa. t. 3 sg.* struck 9797. **lust(en)** *pa. t. pl.* 7750 (*see 7749n*), 8783; **losten** 8117. **ylust** *pp.* 6875. *See 455n.* Cf. **lasse** *v.*

lut *pa. t. 3 sg.* sank down 5248.

luxsorius *adj.* lustful A652.

ma *pron. gen.* see **i(o)e**.

mace *n.* mace (weapon) 6102, etc. **maces** *pl.* 8794.

[**mad**] *adj.* out of control with anger L835, L840.

may *n.*1 young woman 4185.

May *n.*2 May 1709, etc.

may *pr. 1, 3 sg.* (auxil. of ability, possibility, future contingency) 879,

935, 1028, 5116, L872, etc., (inf. understood) = can prevail A1042, [ʒef (þat) y ~] = if I can bring it about L335, L1294. miʒt *pr. 2 sg.* A754, 7504, etc., = should 2469, miʒtow [myʒht-] 2460, etc., L911, L960; may L728, etc., 2960ʳ. may *pr. pl.* 74, A867, L1315, etc., ʒe ~ here = I shall now tell you A79, 4782, L64, L630, etc.; mow(e) A946, A1464, etc., (inf. of motion understood) 7907; mo (~ witen) A11; mowen A272. mow *pr. subj. sg.* A1051. miʒt [-(e)] *pa. t. 1, 3 sg.* 749, 4258, etc., (inf. of motion understood) 845, etc., (as pr.) A278, etc., L717, (in indirect question) 4756, 8012, L1684, = had good reason to A889, (sim.) 8471, 9206, = was permitted to (*see 3859n*) 2201, ?2727; [myʒhte] L503, L528, etc. miʒtest *pa. t. 2 sg.* A1619, 2917, (as pr.) A1729. miʒt(en) [-t(e)] *pa. t. pl.* A250, A305, etc., L220, L492, (+ *to* and inf.) 5373ⁿ; miʒtten 5889, 7692; [myʒht(e)] L26, L125, etc.

maide(n) *n.* young unmarried woman A849, etc.; virgin L847, L935, etc., A666, A1404; girl-child 6495; (quasi-adj.) ~ *castel* 5435; maden 8680ⁿ. maidens *gen.* 3062; *pl.* [-enes] 715, etc.; maiden 6470. maidens *pl. gen.* A740.

maidenkin *n.* virgin A671.

main *adj.* mighty 8879.

main *n.* strength A1535, etc., *miʒt and* ~ 4632, etc.; = powerful support 4296.

maister *adj.* principal 5001, 5638.

maister *n.* teacher A1180, etc.; commander (milit.) 3843, etc. maisters *pl.* 5632; [maistres] learned men *L525, L575.

make *n.* wife 4556.

make(n) *v.* make (mod. uses) 522, 1078, 1192, 1420, 2862, 7483, 9649, *L643*, etc., [+ *to* and inf.] *L1400*, ~ . . . *at aise* make (person) comfortable *3528*, (refl.) *4233, etc.*, (sim. + *glade*, etc.) 6559, 6560, 7398, 8218ⁿ, ~ *me siker* give me assurances 5551; hold (feast, assembly, etc.)

2762, 8641, *L58*; bring about (reconciliation, etc.) 4591, 4662, etc.; express (emotion) *A768, 1344, 2007, L863, etc.*; ~ *wepeing* weep A1324, (sim. + other -*ing(es)*) A1706, 3535, etc., ~ *danger* hesitate *1611*, (sim. + other nouns of action) *4676*, 5500, 9182, etc., *L774*; ~ *song* sing 3064, 3535, (sim.) ~ *cri*, etc. 6224, 8529, etc., ~ *pleint A1357, 2397*; ~ *tale* (*long*) make a long story of it 3055, 4991; ~ *sleiʒt* (*of*) do slaughter (on) 4926, 5015, etc., ~ *biker* wage battle 7944, [~ *deray*] make a disturbance *L816*; ~ . . . *solas* entertain 5345, (sim.) 6532, [~ . . . *counfort*] L1433; ~ *ʒare* make ready 2357, (refl.) 1423, *L1353*, (sim.) *3838*, *L276*; (+inf.) cause to be performed A1641, 7466ⁿ; maki A57. makest *pr. 2 sg.* 2459, 2956. makeþ [-iþ] *pr. 3 sg.* 4974, L1394. make *pr. pl.* 3064, etc.; makeþ A653, etc. make *pr. subj. sg.* 5522; *imp. sg.* 6532, L797. makeþ *imp. pl.* (see fors) 2089; [makiþ] L46. mak(e)and *pr. p.* 8529, 9317. made *pa. t. 1, 3 sg.* 684, 4668, etc., wrote (letters) A415, A1733, composed L1797, ~ *his mon* spoke unhappily 3235, ~ . . . *semblaunt gode* put on a cheerful face for . . . 6536, ~ *it touʒ* fought toughly 9710, ~ *him way* forced a way for himself 9250, [~ *hir mong wiþ*] went in the company of L774; maked A1344. made(n) *pa. t. pl.* 102, 1474, etc., fought (battle) A1518, ~ *couenaunt* agreed 8035, ~ *reng about* encircled 6100, (sim.) 7117, ~ *solas* entertained themselves 2319, ~ *grete tasse* = laid low heaps of enemies 9104; maked swore (oath) 2046. (y)made [(y)mad] *pp.* 526, etc., = begotten 935, sworn 2047, established (institution) 5627, performed (ravaging) 6932, ~ *glad* behaved cheerfully 3386, ~ *it touʒ* behaved arrogantly 4077; maked A1598. Cf. diol-makeing.

malicious *adj.* wicked 8476.

man *n.* man 771, etc.; *fourm after a* ~ [L sim.] = the shape of a man-

man (*cont.*):
   child 980; **manne** (*liif of* ~ human life) 4607; **[mon]** L12, etc., (in negated sentences) = nobody L1242, L1637. **[monnes]** *gen.* = human (desires) L236. **men** *pl.* 139, etc., (as indef. pron.) A730, L770, etc., = liegemen L461; **man**[r] A23, etc.; **mene** A1663[r]. **mennes** *pl. gen.* 2596, 2598; **mannes** A726. Cf. **monkynne**.

maner(e) *n.* way (*on swiche* ~ and sim.) A629, A1008, L808, etc.; character 3001; nature 4781, 4793; custom 6489; *in his* ~ (little sense, *wroþ in his* ~ angry) A106; ich ~ every sort of 7414, (sim.) L1474, [*no* ~ *worde*] = not at all L1230.

mangunels *gen. pl.* seige-engines' 2430.

[manhod] *n.* manly honour L1174; **[monhed]** = male sexuality L928.

mani [mony] *adj.* (+ sg. or pl.) many A145, A148, L161, etc., ~ *a* A133, L20, etc., ~ *on* (following n. pl.) A1079, etc., (as pron.) A453, A1483, etc.; (as pron.) A155, A661, A1620, 3918, etc.; **[many]** L315; **[monye]** L1919. **mo** *comp.* 8159, *fourti . . . and* ~ (and sim.) 4833, etc., L77 **[moo]**, = further, in addition A1115, 4170, 4172, 4772, L8, etc.; (as pron.) 2143, 3228, 7066, L257, L1180, etc.; more 4549, etc. Cf. **namore**.

manliche *adv.* manfully 4000, etc.

manschip(e), -ppe *n.* manly honour, manly conduct 3634, 6827, 7374, 7654.

marais *n.* marshy land 4301.

marche *n.*[1] border district 2175, etc. **Marche** *n.*[2] March 5349.

marched *pa. t. 3 sg.*, ~ *on* had territory bordering on 4424.

mare, mast *adj. comp., sup.* see **michel**.

marked *pp.* observed to be . . . A1404.

maseline *n.* wooden drinking-bowl 6944.

masouns [-ons] *pl.* masons 503.

masse *n.* see **messe**.

mast *n.* mast A115.

mat *n.* doom 9346.

matery, *n.* material of story, A663.

matin(e)s *pl.* midnight office 6490, 6491.

maþen *pl.* maggots A484, *tofrust to* ~ = struck dead 8108.

maugre *prep.* despite 8959; **[mawgre(y)]** L1044, L1122, L1958.

maulard *n.* mallard 4140.

[mawgre] *n.* ?shame L1234.

meche *adj.* see **michel**.

mede *n.*[1] meadow A261, etc. **meden** *pl.* 8658.

mede *n.*[2] reward 2695, L322, etc., (iron.) 5852[n].

medicine *n.* means of cure 9210.

medlay *n.* fight 5576.

[medwif] *n.* see **midwiif**.

meine *n.* (body of) noble retainers A410, 3124, 5742, etc.

meynt *pa. t. 3 sg.* mixed A484.

meke *adj.* courteous 2852.

mele *n.* flour 3661, etc.

membre *n.* penis 3472.

mende [mynde] *n.* mind, *in* ~ 803; remembrance (*of* ~ worthy of this) 6889[n], 8115.

[mene] *v.* speak of L681; mean L1799. **ment** *pp.* (+inf. or *to* and inf.) intended 7089, 7887; **[mynt]** L1481[n], L1906.

merci *n.* mercy 9866, (as interj.) A334, etc., *God ~ God have mercy on us! 7349; thank you! A1592.

merk *n.* mark, ~ *of our Driȝt* = sign of the cross A846.

meruail(e) [-eille] *n.* marvel 924, 3041; astonishment (see **haue(n)**) A1014, etc. **meruails [-eyles]** *pl.* L1082; (religious) mysteries 2222, 2750; **meruail(e)**[r] 8580, 9186, etc. (some may be *sg.*).

meruailus *adj.* remarkably great 8706.

mes *n.* serving of food 6524.

mesauentour, etc. *n.* see **misauentour.**

meself *pron.* myself (emphatic) 4110; **[myseolf]** L1158, = I myself L913.

message *n.* message 3431, 7054, = action requested by this A420; errand L1468.

messanger *n.* messenger 1406, etc.

messangers [-(e)s] 1289, L1281,
etc.; [messangeris] L73, etc.

messe *n.* mass 2376, etc.; **masse**
2802; **misse** (*seyn Iones* ~ the
feast of St. John) 3391.

messel *n.* missal 3574.

mester *n.* occupation 3397, 3541;
mister (~ *to* need of) 3428, 4514.

mete *n.* food 584, L976; = (the) meal
229, 2267, 2304.

mete *v.* meet (tr.) A1494, L1521, (in
battle) 6366, 8080, *L115, etc.*; ~
wiþ 1426, 6174, etc. met(t)
[**mette**] *pa. t. 1, 3 sg.* 1426, 2021,
4884, etc. **met(t), metten** *pa. t. pl.*
A1318, etc., L115; = clashed together 3309, 8867, ~ *togider* 3269,
3311. **met(t)** *pp.* A1947, 5085,
L1946.

meteing *n.* dream 3796.

met(e)ing *n.* encounter 3810, 7058;
(in battle) 5754, etc., (see ʒiue(n))
6344, **meteinge** (*speres* ~ encounter with spears) 8344.

miche(l) [**muche**] *adv.* greatly,
much (modifying v.) 2268, 6527,
6959, L236, and see **litel** *adv.*,
(modifying compar.) A10; very
3742. **more** *comp.* A659, L1370,
etc.; (negated) = any more A19,
3337, L1064 [**mo**], *ani* ~ 8601, *no*
~ A1012, 2329, L103, L1208,
never again 3348, etc.; *euer* ~
(becoming one word) ever after
A104, 6828, L1876, [*for*] *euer* mo
77, A646, L706; *neuer* (*eft*) ~ never
after, again A1238[n], 2682, 9792,
neuer **mo** 6054, 9134, L990; **mo**
and **mo** to an ever greater extent
A413. **mest** *sup.* almost (~ *what*
euerich = until almost everyone
. . .) 8081. Cf. **almast**.

michel [**mukil**] *adj.* big A1190,
A1497, 8741, L1542 [**muchele**], ~
Breteyne Great Britain 118; ~ *ape*
great fool A813, (sim.) [**muche**]
L1393; much 2084, 5710, 5757,
etc., (qualifying abstr. n.) much,
great A746, L482, etc., **miche**
A166, etc., [**muche**] L89, etc.,
[**mukel**] L316, (as pron.) much 330,
A1386, etc., **miche** A12, 6461,
meche A1287; great (of rank, ~

Ywain = Ywain the legitimate)
7630, 7631. **more** *comp.* A1525,
4464, 5356, etc., (see **las(se)** s.v.
litel *adj.*) 2375, etc., L39, *Breteine*
þe~ Great Britain 3513; further 101,
4860, etc., (as pron.) more A625,
7566, 8306, *two ʒer and* ~ 4287,
(sim.) 6396, [**moo**] L130; **mare**
A69[r]. **mest** *sup.* 3820, 4620, 5626;
mast[r] 5335, = the greatest amount
4443.

mid *prep.* with (accompaniment)
A1468, 4835; ~ *ywis* with certainty
9196; **mid(d)e**[r] 3094, 4860, etc.,
(instrument) 7228.

mid(d)ay *n.* noon 4789, 5189, etc.,
þe ~ 4778, etc.

midde *n.* waist 9766[r].

midel *adj.* middle (in family) A770;
of ~ *liue* = in the prime of life
5392. **midelest** *adv. sup.* in the
middle position 6512.

midel *n.* waist 5013, etc.

midydone *adv.* immediately A1086,
etc.

midmorwe-day *n.* mid-morning (*c.*
9 a.m.) 7982.

midniʒt *n.* midnight 9898.

midward *n.* middle 9062.

midwiif [**medwif**] *n.* midwife L983,
etc., 967.

miʒt *n.* strength, power 89, 655,
2828, L196, etc., and see **main**.
miʒtes *pl.* A1736[rn].

miʒt(e) *pa. t. 1, 3 sg.*, etc. see **may**.

miʒti *adj.* mighty A1377, 3091, etc.

milce *n.* mercy A667.

mild(e) *adj.* courteous, gracious
1572, 2692, 2852, L604, etc.

mile *n.* mile 1530, etc.; = time it
takes to walk a mile (*see 5704–6n*)
5860, 7130. **mile** *pl.* 4437, 5860,
etc.; **miles** 2433.

mile-way *n.* mile's distance 5705[n];
= time it takes . . . *7802*, = for as
long as it takes . . . 8525. **mile-
way(e)s** *pl.* 7421, 7802, etc., = over
a distance of . . . miles 2147; **mile-
way**[r] 3793, 4511, etc., = over a . . .
6880, 7578.

milk(e) *n.* milk 2654, 2656, etc.
milkes *gen.* 1455.

[**mynde**] *n.* see **mende**.

mineinge *n.* mining (milit.) 2429.

[mynt] *pp.* see **mene.**

miri(e) [**mury**] *adj.* joyful 259, 1709, 8218[n], etc.; handsome (castle) L465, L1962.

miri(e) *adv.* joyfully A1713; gaily (flag waving) 7848.

mirþe *n.* pleasure 2496, 3605, 4220; [**murthe**] L720.

[mys] *adv.* wrongfully L811. Cf. **amis.**

[mysaide] *pa. t. 3 sg.* see **mysseide.**

misauentour *n.* misfortune 4384, 5814; **mesauentour** 6794; **mesauenture** (see **bidden**) 8361; **misantour** (*sterue(n) wiþ* ~ = die and go to Hell) 6180; [**mesanter**] L1060.

misbiȝeten [-te] *pp.* (adj.) misbegotten 1113, etc.

misbileueand *pr. p.* (adj.) holding false beliefs 5982. **misbileued** *pa. t. 3 sg.* A1900. Cf. **leue** *v.*[2]

mischef *n.* misfortune 6145.

miscreaunt *pr. p.* (adj.) holding false beliefs 5227.

misdede *n.* (number uncertain) evil deed(s) 9869, 9873.

misdo *v.* do injury to 3142.

[myseolf] *pron.* see **meself.**

misfare *v.* fare badly 6648.

misled *pp.,* [+]*be* ~ come to grief 4988; **mislad** 9123.

misse *n.* see **messe.**

[mysseide] *pa. t. 3 sg.* abused L817, L820; [*****mysaide**] L1274.

mist *n.* mist 7364.

misten *pa. t. pl.* discovered the absence of 7208, 8945.

mister *n.* see **mester.**

mo(o) *adj., adv. comp.* see **mani, miche(l), michel.**

mod(e) *n.* heart (as seat of emotions, etc.) A170, 881, L1292, etc.; [**mood**] L643.

moder [-ur] *n.* mother 787, etc. **moder** [-ur] *gen.* 2850, etc., L1148.

mold [-e] *n.* earth (deep layer) 1453, etc.

mon *n.*[1] unhappy speech (see **make(n)**) 3235.

[mon] *n.*[2] see **man.**

[mon] *n.*[3] sexual intercourse L537.

monay(e) *n.* money 4146, 6968.

mone *n.* moon 3238, 3567.

moneþ *n.* month A408.

[mong] *n.* assemblage (see **make(n)**) L774.

[monhed] *n.* see **manhod.**

[mony(e)] *adj.* see **mani.**

monke *n.* monk A55, etc. **monkes** *pl.* 2211.

[monkynne] *n.* mankind L615.

Mononday *n.* Monday 8663.

[mood] *n.* see **mod(e).**

more *adj. adv. comp.* see **mani, miche(l), michel.**

morne *adj.* see **murne.**

morning *n.* lamentation 4270.

morsel *n.* small piece 7356. **morsels** *pl.* 7354.

mort *n.* death 9066.

morter *n.* mortar A515.

morwe *n.* next morning 3826, L481, etc., [*on* ~] on the . . . L495, etc.; morning L491. Cf. **amorwe.**

mot [-(e)] *pr. 1, 3 sg.* must 957, A1181, 2634, 2671, *so* ~ *y þen* as may I prosper (asseveration) 1048, etc., (sim.) *so* ~ *y liue* 4154, etc., *so* ~ *y go* 5358. **most** *pr. 2 sg.* 1684, etc. **mot(en)** *pr. pl.* 4036, 7906, etc.; **mote** 3411[r]. **most** [-(e)] *pa. t. 1, 3 sg.* 65, 4147, etc., L1431, (as pr.) A70, L1767; (auxil. of permission, future contingency) A55, 345, A747, 9740, etc. **most(en)** *pa. t. pl.* 241, A248, 2038, etc.

moten *pl.* specks of dust 9160.

mounde *n.* power, strength 3091, 3307, 3354, etc., L1469; nobility 6495. *See* 3091n.

mountaunce [mon-] *n., þe* ~ *of* the value of 3629, a total of 7540, 8820, a period of 5860, 7130, L1621.

mounted *pa. t. pl.* mounted 9230. **mounted** *pp.* 3899.

mounteyn *n.* mountain 3446.

mouþe [mouþ, -th] *n.* mouth 1499, *****L902[n], etc., (see **held(en)**) 1077 [L mowþ]; **moþe** A1492[n].

mow(e) *pr. pl.,* etc. see **may.**

[muche, mukil] etc. *adj., adv.* see **miche(l), michel.**

[mury] *adj.* see **miri(e).**

murne *adj.* sorrowful 8213, etc.; morne 6978.

[murthe] *n.* see mirþe.

[na] *adv.* see no.

nay *interj.* no 223, 753, A1338, etc.

naying *n.* neighing 8768. Cf. neiȝed.

naked *adj.* naked 850, (sword) 7097.

nam, nart *pr. 1, 2 sg.*, etc. see be(n).

name *n.* name A45, L648, etc., *a Godes* ~ in God's name (and sim.) 987, 7677, etc., [nome] L1058. names *pl.* 5407, 5553, L31.

namlich(e) [name-] *adv.* especially 3563, 6337, L793.

namore *adj.* (as pron. sg.) no more (men) than that 5142, 6039; namo 3710.

nan(ne) *adj.* see no.

nArtour see no *conj.*

naturel *adj.* by right of birth 9202.

naþ, nadde *pr., pa. t. 3 sg.*, etc. see haue(n).

naþeles *adv.* nevertheless 2059, etc.; noþeles A60, L273; naþelas, no-ᵣ 4455, 9291.

nauel *n.* navel 4014; nouel 5981.

nauȝt *adv.* see nouȝt.

ne [ne(o)] *adv.* (before v.) not L24, L181, etc., 6903, 8041; *conj.* nor L306, L901, L902.

neb *n.* face 6163.

nede [ned(e)] *n.* critical situation A249, 517, 2963, etc., *at* ~ in critical situations A85, A312, in the present such L1846, (sim.) A5, L171 [neode]; need, *it is* ~ it is (urgently) necessary 1847, 7049, etc., ⁺*haue* ~ (*to*) be in need (of) 4312, 5335, 5513, L1833, *þat* ~ *was* of which there was need A976, *ȝou worþ* ~ *to* you will be in need of 3436; *þis* ~ = my present business A1435. nedes *pl.* business A1942, 2530.

[nede(s)] *adv.* of necessity L214, L1431, L1767.

nedel *n.* needle, = valueless thing 4012.

n(e)iȝen *num. adj.* nine 4687, 6777, etc.; niȝeᵣ 6840, etc.; neie 6516ᵣ.

neiȝd *num. adj. ord.* ninth 6767.

neiȝe [nyȝh] *adv.* almost 793, etc.;
near *A1802, 3782, 9364, L664, and see fer, (as prep.) 972, etc.; closely (pursuit) 1869; ~ *of Wawaines kende* = of Gawain's close kin 8272; nei 6356, 9441. next *sup.* most recently 2632, (quasi-prep.) next 2259, 6517, etc.

neiȝe [-ȝhe] *v.* approach 4949, etc., L621. [n(e)yȝhed] *pa. t. 3 sg.* L900, L948. neiȝed *pp.* A1802.

neiȝebours [-ȝh-] *pl.* neighbours 833, L810.

neiȝed *pa. t. pl.* neighed 7850. Cf. naying.

neiȝehond *adv.* near at hand 3695.

n(e)iȝen *num. adj.* nine 4687, 6777, etc.; niȝeᵣ 6840, etc.; neie 6516ᵣ.

neiȝer *adj. comp.* nearer (kinship) 3181.

[neyþir] *adv.* see noiþer.

nek *n.* neck 3260, etc.

nek-bon [nekke-] *n.* neck-bone 1862, etc.

neldest, nem, nende *see* eld, etc.

nemd(e) *pa. t. 1 sg.* gave the names of 9369, 9744.

ner(e) [ne(o)r] *adv.* almost 4581, etc., L1913; near 7060ⁿ, and see fer, (quasi-prep.) 2271, 4709.

ner(en) *pa. t. pl.*, etc. see be(n).

nesse *adj.* (as n., see hard) = good times 2961, 2968; = feeble men 8166.

nest *n.* nest 9174.

net *adj.* useful A1792. Cf. vnnet.

neuen *pr. 1 sg.* give names of 8161.

neuer [-(e)] *adv.* never 212, L732, etc., and see more s.v. miche(l); (strong neg., modifying negated v.) A919, L987, etc.; ~ *þe bet* none the better A1948, L1310; ~ *on* not one A339, etc.; ~ *a word* = not at all A1142, L1705.

nevou *n.* nephew 5232, 6849ⁿ, etc.; cousin 3262ⁿ, 4658, etc. nevou *gen.* 7814.

newe *adj.* A1304, 5900, 8822, etc.; *adv.* (modifying pp.) newly 8947, ~ *castel ymade* newly built castle A1871.

neweliche *adv.* soon A1984, 4648.

next *adv. sup.* (and quasi-prep.) see neiȝe.

nice *adj.* idle, negligent A1940ⁿ, etc.

nigramace *n.* necromancy 4442.

niȝe(n) *num. adj.* see **n(e)iȝen**.

[nyȝh] *adv.* see **neiȝe**.

[nyȝhed] *pa. t. 3 sg.* see **neiȝe**.

niȝt *n.* night 539, etc., *bi* ~ during the night 1125, etc., [*on* ~] L793, and see **day, fer**; (adverbial) *þat* ~ (and sim.) 1289, 3785, 9730, etc., and see **day**; [**niȝht**] L66. **niȝt** *pl.* (adverbial) L601, *seuen* ~ for a week 2053, etc., *fourten(e)* ~ 2625, etc., *fourteniȝt* 3377ⁿ, *a fewe* ~ 8656. **niȝtes** *pl. gen.* (*þe fourten* ~ *ende*) 4263. Cf. **aniȝt**.

niȝtingale *n.* nightingale 4679.

nil *pr. 1, 3 sg.*, etc. see **wil**.

nim(en) [-e] *v.* take (in various senses) *1888*, 2299, 6454, 7340, etc., ~ *coure* take heed *2945*, etc., ~ *ȝeme* A*1509*, etc., ~ *hede* 8405, ~ *kepe* A779, 9841, L791, ~ *sikernisse of* take a pledge from 5538, ~ *veniaunce of* take vengeance on 7140; capture, seize, arrest A763, 2443, *2562*, *7180*, etc.; take one's way, come *4610*, *7392*, L*1331*; **nimer** 2409, 9110. **nim** *imp. sg.* 2945. **nimeþ** *imp. pl.* 6150. **nam** *pa. t. 3 sg.* A721, etc., took in marriage 2602, etc., carried 5122, ~ *coroun* received the crown 2049, ~ *flesche and blod* = became incarnate A633, ~ *his pas* took his way 2526, ~ *him of his* . . . stopped his . . . 5304, [*a gret lauȝhyng vp* ~] burst out laughing L1335, L1363; **nome** 3987, etc. **nome(n)** *pa. t. pl.* *1888*, 5788, etc., seized hold of 6384, L830, ~ *comfort* took comfort 4229, *in* ~ received (into city) 5080, *vp* ~ picked up (fallen man) 5173, ~ *þe way* took their way 7703; **ynome** 2246; [**nam**] L1331. **(y)nome(n)** *pp.* 2251, 5808, etc., L110, = chosen A579, *þe, her conseil was* ~ = they agreed A178, A1754, ~ *an hond* undertaken A1617, [*heore armes haddyn* ~] had armed themselves L1851. Cf. **binim(en)**, **vndernam**.

nis *pr. 3 sg.* see **be(n)**.

nist(en) *pa. t. pl.* see **wite(n)**.

niþe *n.* envy 806, L101.

no *adj.* (+ cons.) no A26, L573, etc.; **non** (postposited) 225, A841, 2188, etc., (+ vowel or aspirate) 2724, 3336, L181, L1711, etc., (+ cons.) 1026 [L **none**], 4343, etc., (as pron. sg. or pl.) none (of men) A586, 5650, L1472, L1916, etc., (of help) L176 [**noon**], and see **oþer** *adj.*; no *noþer* A58ⁿ, 3984; **nan(ne)ʳ** 6263, 9354. Cf. **noþing**.

no *adv.* (before v.) not A16, L170, etc., (modifying comp.) no A192, A278, L81, L257, etc., [**na**] L1208, (as n.) *wiþouten* ~ = there is no denying it (tag) A118, etc. *conj.* nor 561, A1027, etc., and see **noiþer**; n*Artour* 2727. Cf. **namore, naþeles**.

nob(e)liche *adv.* in noble fashion 2760, 3163, etc.; **noblelich(e)** A1067, 4836, etc. **noblicher** *comp.* 4880.

noblay *n.* nobility 6526, *of* ~ noble, excellent 2391, 2810, 7403, etc., *wiþ* ~ in noble fashion 3110.

noble *adj.* noble, excellent A50, A291, A322, A1819, 2542, etc., L12, L1189, (as n.) such man/men A25, A497, 7835, etc. **nobler** *comp.* 3146, 3604. **noblest** *sup.* 2403, 2659.

noblesse *n.* precious things 4061.

noiȝe *n.* trouble 4464. Cf. **anoi(e)**.

noise *n.* noise 4976, etc.

noiþer [**neyþir**] *adj.* (as pron.) neither 3479; *adv.*, ~ . . . *no* neither . . . nor A128, etc., L231, ~ . . . *no* . . . *no* . . . *no* A333, (sim.) A1505; **noþer** A1970.

nold *pa. t. 1, 3 sg.*, etc., see **wil**.

no(u)mbre *n.* number 8252, *wiþouten* ~ innumerably *7297.

non *adj.* (and as pron.) see **no**.

none *n.* 3 p.m. 5189, etc. Cf. **after-none**.

nones *n., for þe* ~ on that occasion (weak sense) 9848.

nonne *n.* nun 1192, etc.

nonskinnes *adj.* no kind of 4278.

norice *n.* wet-nurse 2943. **norices** *gen.* 2856.

norice *v.* bring up (child) 3180.

norisement *n.* upbringing 2938.

nortour(e), -ture *n.* nursing (of infant) 2855; upbringing (*sone þurth* ~ = foster-son) 2946, good upbringing 8620.

norþ *adj.* north(ern) 3733, 5459ⁿ; *adv.* northwards 8402, *souþe and* ~ = everywhere 4572.

norþ *n.* the north 3186, 3741, etc.

norþþen-winde *n.* north wind 5934.

nose *n.* nose 8716, etc.

no(s)t *pr. 1, 2 sg.* see **wite(n)**.

[not] *adv.* see **nouȝt**.

noþeles, -las *adv.* see **naþeles**.

noþer see **oþer** *adj.*

noþer *adv.* see **noiþer**.

noþing *adv.* not at all A217, 4876, 6789, etc., L1579.

noþing [-þ-, -th-] *pron.* (doubtfully one word) nothing L1042, etc., A854, 8504, *of* ~ (*more*) in no (further) respect 6581, L529; *for* ~ (*for* ~ *he nold say* nothing would make him say) 2099, (sim.) 3139, 8394, L1922. Cf. phr. s.v. **þing**.

nouel *n.* see **nauel**.

ynouȝ *adj.* enough 4427; = ample 2904, (as pron.) 4078; *adv.* = amply, very 1420 [L ynowȝh], **ynowe** 2073ʳ, [ynouȝh] L1252.

nouȝt *adv.* not A253, 295, 1090, etc.; **nauȝtⁱ** 6894, 7976, *riȝt* ~ not at all A1136; [noȝ(h)t] L503, *riȝt* ~ L943; [not] L1479.

nouȝt *pron.* nothing A1432, A1937, etc., L138, L1224, = no effort 2889, = no cause 4544, and see **bring, for**.

noumbre *n.* see **no(u)mbre**.

nouþe *adv.* now 4226.

now *adv.* now 875, etc., = then 7683, 7811, ~ . . . ~ = sometimes . . . sometimes 3928, 6221; **nov** A119, etc.; **nowe** 2961ʳ.

nowhar, -er(e) *adv.* nowhere A1372, 5262ⁿ, 9308, etc.; **noure** 2135. Cf. **ow(h)ar**.

o *num. adj.* (+ cons.) one A581, A1978, 3453, 4784, etc. L1928; **on** (+ vowel or aspirate) A1783, 6440, 7873, etc., **o** n*ende* (*see 58n*) 6893, (+ cons.) 3673, etc., L1577, (post-posited) 5291, (as or approaching pron.) A460, 1202, A1489, etc.; *þat* ~ = the first (of two) 1455, 1489, 3453, etc., (of three) 3481; *at* ~ into agreement 2782, [*such* ~] such a one L1470; also see **al(le), mani, oþer**; **an(ne)ʳ** A928, 9761ⁿ, etc., and see **for**. Cf. **a** *indef. art.* (some instances uncertain), **on(n)es**.

o *prep.* see **of, on**.

o *interj.* (vocative) A895, 8565.

odour *n.* scent 8658.

of *adv.* off 231, etc. *prep.* from, off 111, A225, 2473, 3915, 5329, 6395, 7313, L55, L176, L1487, etc., + *bring* ~ *liue* (and sim.) = kill 6153, 7854, etc., [*blinne* ~] cease from L127; ~ *dawe* dead 4983, ~ *his witt* out of his wits 3322; of (mod. uses) 47, 289, A324, 330, 515, 666, 1104, A1382, 1678, 1833, 2190, 3040, 3587, 4398, 7653, L15, L968, etc., *a feste* ~ = a feast for 3375, 8642, *þe stouer* ~ *to ȝare* two years' provisions 6771, ~ *pite* pitiable 9858, (sim.) see **delite, howe** *n.*¹, **mende, remembraunce, sorwe, þincheing, wo** *n.*, **wonder**; some (of) 2506, 7011, a number of 2198ⁿ, 3081ⁿ; about, etc. (ask, feel emotion, etc.) A19, 499, A1608, 1622, etc.; on (pity) A446, A896, (vengeance) A402, etc., L134; for (vengeance) 6392, 7997; in respect of, *fail(e)* ~ fail in 1620, miss 9039, L1697, *feined* ~ *fiȝt* = pretended to fight 3330, and see **þing**, [*here me* ~ *a word or two*] = . . . to the extent of . . . L940; by, etc. (agent) A1157, 2081, 4039, 4805, L86, L262, L928, etc., (instrument) 9774ⁿ, and see **purchas** *n.*, ~ *gode conseyl* in accordance with . . . 2630, ~ *robberie* got by . . . 7564, *wreiȝen* ~ covered with 6836; ~ . . . (*eld*) = (. . . years) old A1070, A1215, L1380, (sim. of size) 4886; also see **bare, biknawe, compa(i)nie, do(n), knowe, riche**. Cf. **her(e)of, þerof, whereof**.

ofcleped *pa. t. 3 sg.* summoned A1732.

ofersett *pa. t. pl.* oppressed 7574.

office *n.* religious service 2758, 3112.

ofsende *v.* send for 2861, 3016.
  ofsent *pa. t. 3 sg.* A1401, etc.;
  osent 2686. **ofsent** *pp.* 2312.
of-smiten *pp.* (adj.) cut off 7470[n],
  7524, 9170.
oft [-e] *adv.* often 684, etc.
oftake *v.* overtake 6198. **oftakeþ** *imp.
  pl.* 5866. **oftok(e)** *pa. t. 3 sg.* 4922,
  7938, struck 3483, etc.; **otok** 9349.
  oftoke *pa. t. pl.* 9630. Cf. **ouertok.**
often *adv.* often 4399, etc.
oftsiþes *adv.* often A88.
(**ofþink** *v.*) see **oþouȝt** *pa. t. 3 sg.*
ofwoke *pa. t. 3 sg.* woke up 3800.
oȝain [aȝeyn] *adv.* back 541, A1533,
  5348, 9232, L1264, etc., as it was
  before 5676, L605, once more
  9228[n]; in reply (strike, etc.) 6952,
  9355, etc., L1921, (speak) L155,
  etc., 7217, (in recompense) *3630,*
  in opposition A256[n]. *prep.* against
  (opposed action) 126, 906, A1817,
  etc., (sim.) L800, (opposed forces)
  A460, etc., L1908, (hostile impact)
  3469, 3798, 8094; exposed to (wind)
  7072; to meet (in hostility) *A134,*
  etc., L147, (in friendship) A1424,
  etc.; in preparation for 3536;
  towards (duty owed) 2323, 6504; in
  comparison with *8853,* 8854; ~ *þe
  walle* against the wall 5828; *þe feld*
  ~ to the ground 8077[n]. **oȝan**[r] A134,
  etc.; **oȝen**[r] A150, etc.; **oȝein** 2861,
  6952; **ogain** A1986; [**agayn**]
  L1732, L1807. Cf. **þeroȝain.**
oȝain(e)s [aȝeyns] *prep.* against
  (opposed action) A902, 1654, etc.,
  (sim.) 2795, (opposed forces) 5770,
  7978, (hostile impact) 7070; to
  meet (in hostility) A309, etc., (in
  friendship) A1228; *þre ~ anne*
  three for every one 5761; ⟨against
  the night⟩ nearly night⟩ P2366. Cf.
  þeroȝaines.
oȝa(i)nward *adv.* back 2134, on his
  way back 3457; in reply (strike)
  9361, in opposition A233.
oke *n.* oak-tree 9821.
old(e) *adj.* see **eld.**
olifaunce *pl.* elephants 8943, 9305.
oliue(s) *adv.* (and quasi-adj.) alive
  224, A1004, 1074, etc.; = totally
  (distressed) 7580; **oliif** 7576.

omage *n.* homage 3579, etc.; **vmage**
  3131, etc.
omang *prep.* see **among(es).**
on *num. adj.* see **o.**
on *adv.*[1] (following n.) only 2998, 3236.
  Cf. **alon(e).**
on *adv.*[2] on, *þer . . . ~* = thereon
  5635[n], and see **do(n), legge(n);**
  prep. (mod. uses) A613, 711, 868,
  1370, A1815, 2094, 2783, L106,
  L1468, etc., *~ fer* on fire (and sim.)
  3208, 6796, etc., and see **calle,
  heiȝe** *adj.,* **marched;** onto 3839,
  etc., = under the judgement of
  L933; in 2551, etc., L1819, (grouping) A1508, etc., (manner) A629,
  7634, etc., L583, (language) A20,
  etc., (God's name) 4692, etc.; into
  (pieces) 3256, 9168; at (look, throw,
  shout, etc.) 1229, 2463, 4959,
  L1037, L1038, L1057, etc.; about
  (lie, think) 1556, 4619, etc.; at (time)
  L33, *~ a day* one day (and sim.)
  494, A685, etc., L919, and see **day,
  euen, morwe, niȝt;** *~ iustinge*
  a-jousting 7621, (sim.) L1271, [*~
  liue*] alive L679, L1973; also see
  falle, hond, ylong, slepe; an
  A116, L609, etc.; o A1026, 3340,
  4036, etc., *~ lengþe* in length (or =
  of) 7448; a, *~ boþe* half on both
  sides (and sim.) A453, 4897, 8745,
  etc., *it is ~ wel gode time* = the
  time is very suitable (or = indef.
  art.) 2791, and see **fer** *adj.*[1],
  fer(e), half *n.,* name. Cf. **heron,
  þeron.**
onan *adv.* see **anon.**
ond(e) *n.* hatred 669, A769, L101, etc.
  wiþouten ~ in friendship 6725.
on(n)es *adv.* once 5978; (negated) not
  at all 2832; (*al*) *at ~* all at the same
  time 3291, 7892, etc.
onest *adj.* as it should be 3394, 7707,
  etc.
onour(d) see **honour** *n., v.*
[**onswere**] *v.* answer L938. **answerd**
  pa. t. 3 sg. A1067; [**onswer(e)de**]
  L96, L1093, etc. [**onswer(e)de**]
  pa. t. pl. L155, L934.
[**onsweryng(e)**] *n.* see **answering.**
op *prep.* see **vp.**
[**open**] *adv.* open L1870, L1890.

openliche *adv.* without concealment A1983, 5939.

opon [a-] *adv.* on (clothes) A1396, and see **do(n)**. *prep.* (up)on (in various senses) A387, 520, A1629, A1889, 6933, L292, L481, *L561*, L1186, etc., and see **do(n)**, **pain(e)**; at (wink, etc.) 2466; about (lie) L1453; at (time) 2223, within A1314, ~ *a day* one day A823, L645, L809; ~ *al þing* above everything 8608. **vpon** L561, etc., 5057; **opan** A1396ʳ.

or(e) *n.* mercy 7258, 7308, etc.; *þi nore* = forgive my saying this 4614.

or *conj.* or A58, A427, L681, L692ⁿ, etc.

[or(e)] *adv.*, *conj.* see **er.**

ord *n.* point 7449; beginning (see **ende**) A1177, 3023.

ordeine *v.* range in order 8686. **ordeind** *pa. t. pl.* 3702; *pp.* 8766.

ordinaunce *n.* plan A1090.

orgulous *adj.* (postposited) proud 5485, 9334.

orible *adj.* terrible 5842.

orped *adj.* valiant 2156, etc.

orpedlich(e) *adv.* valiantly A1719, 2121, 9290; **orpedeliche** 9717.

osent *pa. t. 3 sg.* see **ofsende.**

ost *n.*¹ army, company of supporters 346, 3138, etc., *mani an* ~ = many men 2844; **host** L295, etc., 6463.

ost *n.*² host 5560, 6461. **hostes** *pl.* guests 6532.

otok *pa. t. 3 sg.* see **oftake.**

oþ(e) *n.* oath 1362, 3168, etc., [*wiþowte* ~] = without needing to swear to it (of reliable statement) L1415, L1756. Cf. **hold-oþ.**

oþer [oþir] *adj.* other 791, A1061, L181, etc., ~ *to* = two others 3463, ~ *ten* 4858, second A45, etc., L746; previous A550, 7080; (as or approaching pron.) other A674, 1456, 3483, etc., *non* ~, *no noþer* nobody else A58ⁿ, 6540, nothing else 3984, [~ *þan good*] = by no means good L818, (pl.) others A471, 2258, 3134, etc., L29, *þe* ~ = their enemies 3195, 3217, etc.; = the other (*on half* . . . ~) 7873; = another (*mani* (*kniȝt*) . . . ~) A443,

3874, etc., *þe burre wiþ* ~ one bur with another 8280; = the others (*ani* . . . ~) 5728, 6904, (*non* . . . ~) A446, 2205, etc., L560, *on and* ~ = all of them 8493, and see **ȝer(e)**; *ich* ~ each other 7261, (sim.) *ichon* . . . ~ 3047, *euerich* . . . ~ 3235, 3267, *ich tofore* ~ = each one faster than the next A1510, *ich* ~ *folk yseyȝe* the armies saw each other A1801, (sim.) [**eyþir ost* . . . ~] L285; (quasi-adv.) ~ *strongest* = second in strength 5996; [**oþre(o)**] L8, L29, L1272. **oþers** *gen.* (*ich* . . . ~) 7765, 9818.

oþer *adv.* either, ~ . . . *o(þe)r* 7010, 9286; *conj.* or A470, A1078, etc.

oþerwhile *adv.* from time to time A653.

oþerwise *adv.* in any other way 2327ⁿ.

oþouȝt *pa. t. 3 sg.* (impers.) displeased 8222.

ouer *adv.* over (cross over, etc.) A354, 7901, 8110, etc.; *þennes* ~ = at a distance from there of 2433, 4736, 6638. *prep.* over 287, 3273, 9099, etc., L1968, *þrewe armes* ~ embraced 8032; throughout L74, etc., A845; above A1574, 6002, Cf. **lord-ouer**, **ofersett.**

oueral(le) *adv.* everywhere A1000, 4322, etc., L845.

ouercarked *pp.* (adj.) severely harassed 5941. *See 3945n.*

ouercomen *v.* defeat A1924, 3371. **ouercom** *pa. t. 3 sg.* 2169, L22; **ouercam** 4369ʳ. **ouercome(n)** *pp.* A140, A185, etc., L1957.

ouergon *v.* traverse 5706.

ouerran *pa. t. 3 sg.* flowed all over 2151. Cf. **erne.**

ouerriden *pp.* ridden over (so as to trample) 9091.

ouersen *v.* keep watch over 4101.

ouertok *pa. t. 3 sg.* overtook 3349. **ouertoke(n)** *pa. t. pl.* 5869, 7153, 7745. Cf. **oftake.**

ouerþrewe *pa. t. 3 sg.* threw/struck down 3799, 8125; fell down 8535; *pa. t. pl.* 3473, 7521. **ouerþrowe** *pp.* A556.

ouerþroweinge *n.* throwing/striking down 8804.

ou3t *adv.* at all 8461, L1223; **au3t** A1233ʳ.

ou3t *pron.* anything 3628, 7588; **au3tʳ** A1135, = a man of worth 3480.

ourn(e) *pa. t. pl.* see **erne.**

out *adv.* out (mod. uses) 65, 880, 1131, 4134, 7791, 9170, *L1847*, etc., = out of the fight 9226, = aloud 833ⁿ, ~ ⁺*hit* = cut off (part of helmet) 9253, ⁺*seche* ~ seek out 2159, ~ *of wit(t)* out of one's wits (more or less hyperbolic) A1405, 1795, etc., unbelievably *L1970*; ⟨~ *off*⟩ as a result of P1946; [owt] L1285, etc. Cf. **þurthout(e).**

[outrage] *n.* see **vtrage.**

outward *adv.* outwards 2806.

[ow] *pron. obj.* see **3e.**

ow(e) *interj.* (surprise) A1581, A1841.

oway [awey] *adv.* away 834, 2716, 4735, etc., (fig.) 3215; gone A1692, *L1553*, etc., = dead *7336*; awayʳ L104, etc., 4735, 7336; [awey3e] L1774.

ow(h)ar *adv.* anywhere 6571, 7216, 7893; our A605.

ow(h)en [owne] *adj.* own A688, 1310, etc.; particular A60ⁿ; awe 2662ʳ.

[owes] *pr. 2 sg.* deserve L1198. [oweþ] *pr. 3 sg.* L1109. [owen] *pr. pl.* have as duty to give L42. ou3test *pa. t. 2 sg.* (as pr., +inf.) ought 8465. ou3t [au3ht(e)] *pa. t. 3 sg.* possessed L650; (as pr., + (*to* and) inf.) ought A1327, 1330, 9201, L1376; [auh3t] L1391.

pac *n.* (pedlar's) bundle of goods A1981

page *n.* servant-boy 8561.

paid *pa. t. pl.* paid (iron.) 7800. (y)paid *pp.* (adj.) pleased 2865, 7665.

paien *n.* pagan 6402, etc.; **paiem** 5200, etc. **paiens** *pl.* 4382, etc.; **paiems** 4805, etc. **paiems** *pl. gen.* 5808, 7152.

pain(e) *n.* punishment A1170, *opon* ~ *of her liue* on pain of death 3650; suffering 8455; effort(s) 4386, 8335, **peine** 8358, 8367.

painem *n.* pagan 5207, etc. **painem(e)s** *pl.* 4500, 4752, etc.; **panimes** 4470ⁿ.

pais(e) [pes] *n.* peace 4598, *5116*, L1981, *in* ~ untroubled 345, 5361, etc.; silence *A333*, and see **held(en)**; **pes** A333, 5116, etc. Cf. **a-paise.**

pal *n.* see **pelle.**

palays *n.* palace 8549.

palet *n.* leather head-piece worn inside helmet 4006, etc.; **pelet** 9353. *See 4006n.*

palfray *n.* saddle-horse A311, L1328.

Palmesonnes-aue *n.* Palm Sunday Eve 5381.

pani *n.* penny 3629, 4155, 6506.

panne *n.* skull 7977, 9353. Cf. **hern-panne, heued-panne.**

par *prep.* by (see **amour, auentour, charite, Dieu, fay, fors**) A549, L41, etc.

parage *n.* lineage 5434, 8269.

[parceyued] *pp.* observed L750, L890. Cf. **aperceiued.**

parlement *n.* formal council 293, etc.; what is said in discussion 3407, 3656.

part *n.* part 3820, 6752; also see **haue(n).**

part *v.* divide (tr.) 4054, etc. part *pr. pl.* 4316, parted *pa. t. 3 sg.* 6459; *pl.* 5742; *pp.* 7536. Cf. **departen.**

parti *n.* division (of men) 7339. **parties** *pl.* 4775.

parting *n.* dividing up 4067.

pas *n.* way (= route) 4420, 7338, 7712, (= course) see **nim(en), turne, wende(n),** (? = distance) L1317. pas *pl.* 4456, 6744.

[passage] *n.* crossing (of sea) L257.

passe(n) *v.* pass (intr., motion) 3663, 7267, etc., go (away) L301, *L544*, etc.; cross (tr.) *7794, 7867*, L305, (intr.) *L256*. pas *pr. pl.* 7333; passeþ 7603. pas(s)ed *pa. t. 3 sg.* 8830, L544, L850, *miday* ~ 5189. passed *pa. t. pl.* 7729, 7867, L256; [passeden] L312. ypassed *pp.* 7794; passed (adj.) over, past 6154, 8576, 8799, 9850, (quasi-prep., time) 4778, (motion) 7783.

paþ *n.* path 4525. paþes *pl.* 4381, etc.; **paþe** 7387ʳ.

pauement *n.* paved street A383.

pauiloun *n.* large tent 2494. **pauil-ouns** *pl.* 3208, etc.; **pauilounʳ** 3171, etc.

pautener *adj.* wicked A194.

pauteners *pl.* wicked men 7612.

peces *pl.* pieces 3256.

pecokes *pl.* peacocks 3120.

peine *n.* see pain(e).

pelet *n.* see palet.

pelle *n.* rich cloth 7417; pal 3540. pelles *pl.* 6657, 6968.

pelt *v.* thrust, put 2916. pelt *pa. t. 3 sg.* A1054, 4007, etc.; *pp.* A1044.

pena(u)nce *n.* penance 711, 863, A877.

pensel *n.* banner 5641, etc.

Pentecost *n.* Whitsun, 2843, þe ~ 2223, *Mononday in þe* ~ Whit Monday 8663.

per *n.* person of similar rank 8837. per(e)s [-is] *pl.* 215, 6734.

perced *pa. t. 3 sg.* pierced 5153; *pl.* 7936, 9413.

periil *n.* peril, ~ *of her liue* peril of death 7044, ~ *of mort* 9066, ~ *to lese* peril of losing 8921.

persone [-son] *n.* rector 1104, etc.

pertris *pl.* partridges 3121.

pes *n.* see pais(e).

pett *pa. t. 3 sg.* thrust 5256.

⟨pight⟩ *pp.* (adj.) pitched (tent) P2049.

piment *n.* honeyed and spiced wine 2316, 3123.

pin *n.* bolt, etc. (for securing gate) 5677, 7255.

pin(e) *n.* suffering 2335, 5836, etc.; effort 9291, 9831. pin(e)s *pl.* 4412, 8232. Cf. helle-pin(e).

pite *n.* pity 6028, 7377, etc., ~ *forto here* pitiable to hear 8530, *saun* ~ the pitiless (cognomen) 7383, and [incl. L666] see haue(n); grief 5367, 5822; pitiable state of affairs 3979, 4750, 6831, etc.

pitous *adj.* pitiable 7306.

pitouseliche *adv.* in a pitiable state 5023.

place, plas *n.* (open) place 6625, L1270, = battlefield 4917, etc.; = castle 2561, ?= town 4354.

play *n.* enjoyment 358, sport 4676, 4677.

play(en) *v.* play (child) *1201*, (refl.) amuse oneself 2450; ~ *wiþ* = have sexual intercourse with 748, 760. plaid *pa. t. 3 sg.* 2538; pleyd

A1201, ?made sport 6578[n]. [pley-ȝed] *pa. t. pl.* L1273. ypleyd *pp.* A1105.

[playȝyng] *n.* playing (child) L1271.

plain, plein(e) *n.* plain 520, 1391, 1656, 3446, etc. plein(e)s *pl.* 2191, 4353, L1608, L1618; plaines 5615.

plat *pa. t. 3 sg.* fell heavily 7115[n], 9072; *pl.* struck 9913.

plater *n.* plate 2260, 6944.

plates *pl.* plate-armour at bottom of mail-coat 8666.

pleint(e) *n.* formal complaint A1357; lamentation 2397, 7713.

plente *n.* plenty (of food, etc.) 3122, etc.

pliȝt *v.* pledge (faith) 90, 7352. pliȝt *pr. 1 sg., y ȝou* ~ I assure you (usually tag) A1907, 4334, etc., *y þe* ~ 2006. [plyȝt] *pa. t. 3 sg.* L51. ypliȝt *pp.* (adverbially) assuredly (tag) A684[n], etc. Cf. apliȝt.

pliȝt *pa. t. 3 sg.* snatched 8434, 9052.

plouȝ [plowȝ] *n.* plough 1419.

poine *n.* see punay.

point *n., at* ~ *of dede* at the point of death 8458.

-polk see hert-polk.

pomel *n.* pommel (of sword) 2816.

pople *n.* (*sg.*) people A1036, (of army) A1723, 4249, 5774, 7912, etc.

portcolice *n.* portcullis 8310.

porter *n.* gate-keeper 5668, 5669.

poruaid *pa. t. pl.* see puruay.

pouder [-ow-] *n.* dust 5285, L1736; poudre 4717.

pouer *adj.* poor (of men) 6858, 7369.

Pouke *n.* Devil 7462. Cf. Helle-pouke.

[pouste(e)] *n.* power L800, L1014, L1124.

po(u)wer [power(e)] *n.* strength, power 371, A783, A1622, 3592, 5240, L650, L1907, etc., +*haue* ~ (*for*)*to* A647, etc., = be able to 5783, 6952; military forces 8926, 8995; pouer 4273. powers[r] 4497, 4872, 6043; ?*pl.* 3910, dominions A502.

powe *n.* paw A1491, L1603.

pray *v.* (+ various constructs.) beg (person to . . .) A88, L103, pray (to God to . . .) *2793, L1192, L1978*. pray *pr. 1 sg.* A1588, 2789, etc.,

pray (*cont.*):
L1192; [prey3(e)] L1181, L1665; [pray3e] L1643. [prey3e] *pr. pl.* *L168, L1978; [praieþ] L1314. **pray** *imp. sg.* 2655; *pl.* 2793; [preyeþ] L174. [prey3ed] *pa. t. 3 sg.* L92, L1402.

pray(e) *n.* booty 5106, 6719, etc.

prayer, -ei- *n.* petition A54, 2327.

praise *v.* praise 9772. **ypraised** *pp.* esteemed 5338.

preche *v.* give exhortation 3174.

precheing *n.* exhorting 9215.

precious(e) *adj.* noble (of woman) 4474, etc.; *stones* ~ precious stones 8669.

[preoue] *v.* see **proue(n)**.

pres *n.* throng (in battle, etc.) 2086, 8050, etc.; **presse** 8856ʳ.

present *n.* gift 2280, etc.; *news* 2558ⁿ; *here in* ~ present here A1922, (sim.) [⁺*come in* ~] L1088, L1162. **presantes** *pl.* 4172.

prest *adj.* ready A507; *adv.* quickly 8188.

prest [-eo-] *n.* priest 1325. **prestes** *gen.* 1331. [preostes] *pl.* L1359.

pride *n.* pride 805 [L **pruyde**], L595, *in* ~ proudly 7622, [*wiþ* ~] L283; person looked to with pride A641ⁿ.

pri(i)s *n.* high quality, *of* ~ excellent, noble 310, A474, A1906, 2391, 5536, etc., L1939; fame 1670, 3620, 5802; *þe* ~ the highest esteem (see **bere, legge(n)**) 3602, etc., the victory A341; booty 5329, 5707; **priss** 2081, 3134; **prise** 6478, 6480.

prike(n) *v.* spur A1824, 5686; gallop 3450, 8983, L1460, L1885. **prike** *pr. pl.* 7892. **prikeþ** *imp. pl.* 5918. **priked** *pa. t. 3 sg.* spurred L1930, (refl.) galloped 2567; *pl.* A1846, 7830; [**prikyden, -edyn, -eden**] L111, L1852, L1965.

[pryme] *n.*, *hy3h* ~ mid-morning (*c.* 9 a.m.) L1407.

prince *n.*, prince (ranked below king) 3008, (king's son) A1962, 3012, etc., (= ruler) A165, L18. **princes** *gen.* 2042; *pl.* A162, 6190, etc.

priue *adj.* hidden A1549, 3569.

priueliche *adv.* secretly 3775, etc.; privately 2935.

priuete *n.* secret(s), private affairs A12, A649, 1247, 2689.

processioun *n.* procession 5328, 6452.

procoure *v.* obtain 3779. **procourd** *pp.* brought about A1637.

[procuryng] *n.* bringing about L1718.

profecies *pl.* prophecies 8575.

proferd *pa. t. 3 sg.* proffered 2033, 8623.

[profete] *n.* prophet L589.

proude *adj.* proud, glorious 8865, 9076, 9408; **prout** 4212.

proudeþ *pr. pl.* adorn themselves proudly A264ⁿ.

proue(n) [**preoue**] *v.* test A1368, 3001, 5222, 7649, 9664; prove A1239, L1121, L1167; aver 2671ⁿ. [**preoue**] *pr. 1 sg.* aver L1132, L1145. **proue** *pr. subj. sg.* 2914. **proued** *pa. t. 3 sg.* tried (to . . .) 2826; *pp.* 9732.

pruaunce *n.* prowess 8150. *See n.*

pruesse *n.* prowess 5292, etc.

[pruyde] *n.* see **pride**.

punay *n.* company (of fighting-men) 3233; **poine** 5896. *See 5896n.*

purchas *n.* plundering 6932, plunder 7536; obtaining for money (*of* ~ hired, = mercenaries) 4361, etc.

purchas *v.* procure (thing) for (person) A218. **purchast, -sced** *pa. t. 3 sg.* hired (mercenaries) 4433, 4498.

pure *adj.* sheer 3325; sinless 7514.

purpel *adj.* of rich red colour 6657, 7417.

purper *n.* cloth of *purpel* 6968.

purpoint *n.* quilted doublet worn under armour 9256.

puruay *v.* procure (thing) for (person) 3497, 3714. **puruay** *imp. sg.* (thing unstated) A1679. **purvaieþ** *imp. pl.* 4644. **puruaid** *pa. t. 3 sg.* 7671. **poruaid** *pa. t. pl.* 3056. **(y)puruayd** *pp.* 4682, 5558, (person unstated) A1348.

put *pa. t. 3 sg.* put, thrust A149, 5217; [**putte**] L849.

[-put] see **helle-put**.

putain *n.* whore (see **fi3**) 8998.

quake *v.* quake 4253, L1049. **quaked**
pa. t. 3 sg. A1519.

quarel *n.* bolt (shot from cross-bow)
318, etc.

quarre *adj.* with squared corners
2977.

quarter *n.* quarter 4932, etc.

quaþ *pa. t. 3 sg.* said A216, etc.
quaþ(e) *pa. t. pl.* A1592, 7370, etc.

qued *adj.* such as would do injury
A1498.

qued *n.* harm A1332, etc.; wicked
person 5231; evil L1100.

quei3te *pa. t. 3 sg.* quivered 9051. Cf.
aquei3t.

queint *adj.* cunning 4447; ⟨quante⟩
strange P2153.

queintise *n.* wisdom 4590; marvel-
lousness 3566; (knight's) surcoat
5649, 5656, 8671.

quelle(n) [qu-, qw-] *v.* kill 576, 1003,
5616, etc. **queld** *pa. t. 3 sg.* 7076.
Cf. **aquelle.**

quen [-e] *n.* beldam 753, etc. [qwenes]
gen. L735.

quen(e) *n.* queen 1347, 6475, etc.,
þe ~ Marie Mary, Queen of Heaven
A1075, etc.; lady A632, *2651ⁿ.
quenes *gen.* 6488, 6489. Cf.
Heuen-quen.

quic [qwyk] *adj.* alive 790, etc.;
[quuyk] L694. *adv.* quickly (see
also) A732ⁿ, A752.

quiclike *adv.* quickly 7809.

quiet *n.* tranquillity A1283.

quiked *pa. t. 3 sg.* revived (intr.)
2739.

quissers *pl.* thigh-pieces (armour)
2976.

quite [qwyt] *adj.* acquitted 1169,
L930.

rac *n.* speed, *gret ~* (adverbial) apace
3476.

raches *pl.* hunting-dogs (working by
scent) 4612.

rade *n.* see **red(e).**

rade *v.* see **rede** *v.¹*

rady *adj.* see **redi.**

rage *adj.* enraged 7276, 8433.

rage *n.* anger A828, 2422, 8848;
foolish behaviour 4618, P1946.

[ragged] *adj.* see **rugged.**

rain *n.¹* rain 3797; **rein** 4202.

rain *n.²* rein (see **lete(n)**) 7445; **rein**
5052.

rake *v.* run 8038.

rammed *pa. t. pl.* rammed (earth
firm) A533.

ran *pa. t. 3 sg., pl.* see **erne.**

rape *n.* haste 4850, etc.

rape *v.* hasten 7474.

ras *n.* onrush 3990, 7152; [res] (*in a
~* hastily) L822.

ratled *pa. t. 3 sg.* fluttered (banner)
7848ⁿ.

raþe *adv.* quickly A191, A1083, etc.
raþer *comp.* rather 2324, L1146.

rauist *pa. t. 3 sg.* carried away (in
spirit) 8915.

[raundoun] *n., wiþ gret ~* fiercely
(gallop) L1930.

[raunson] *n.* ransom L573.

rawe *n.* sequence, *on ~* (and sim.)
one after another 5408, 6887, 8632,
9770, one beside another 5850. Cf.
arawe.

[raw3t] *pp.* seized L1772. Cf.
atrau3t.

rebout *v.* attack with words 3000.

recoil *n.* retreat 9182.

recoile *v.* retreat 6693. *See n.*

recouerd *pa. t. 3 sg., ~ mi3t* recovered his strength A1650. **rekeuerd**
pa. t. pl. (*~ o3ain* brought back)
7987. Cf. **akeuered, keuer(en).**

recour *n.* recourse 4452ⁿ.

rect *pr. 3 sg.* cares, *who ~* who cares?
7241. **rou3t** *pa. t. 3 sg.* 6528,
(impers.) 4164. **rou3t(en)** *pa. t. pl.*
3736, 6854, 7886.

red *n.¹* red colour 8020.

red *n.²* rescue 7052ⁿ.

red *pp.* rescued 8596.

red(e) *adj.* red 1456, 1525, etc., (with
embarrassment) L1231; red-haired
(*þe ~*, cognomen) 5443; chestnut
(horse) 2565.

red(e) *n.* counsel (= advice) A1597,
L733, etc., (= wise planning, etc.)
A1242, L16, L160, L487, L1321;
agreement *A62, 2048, 2824,* consultation (see **take(n)**) A100, L213,
etc.; **radeʳ** A1602, etc.

rede *v.¹* describe 6265; = help (of
Christ) 9874; **rade** advise 1181ʳ.

rede (*cont.*):
  rede *pr. 1 sg.* advise A1679, etc.,
    L1832. reden *pr. pl.* 7369. rede *pr.
    subj. sg.* 9208. red(de) *pa. t. 3 sg.*
    read 7047, 7817. Cf. fulrade,
    wiþradden.
rede *v.²* clear a space 3334. ridde *pa.
    t. 3 sg.* cleared 5306. redde(n)
    pa. t. pl. 5259, 7896, etc., ~ hem
    cleared a way for themselves 8277.
    See 3334n.
redi *adj.* ready 308, 3057, etc., and
    see make(n); rady 3698.
regge *n.* see rigge.
regned [-ede] *pa. t. 3 sg.* reigned A33,
    L1976.
rein *n.* see rain *n.¹, n.²*
reke *n.* haste 7894. *See n.*
reke [wr-] *v., in erþe* ~ bury 1027ⁿ.
rekeuerd *pa. t. pl.* see recouerd.
rem *n.¹* cream 1455.
rem [rewme] *n.²* kingdom 1642.
remanant *n.* remainder 6210.
reme *v.* clear 4398.
remembraunce *n.* memory, *of* ~
    memorable 5288.
rene *n.* running, *wiþ gret* ~ = at full
    gallop 8386ⁿ.
reng(e) *n.* close body (of men) A1508,
    5044, 7483, ring 5397ⁿ; ring (of
    men) 6100.
renged *pa. t. pl.* ranged (themselves)
    5828.
renoun *n.* renown 47, 4390, L1190.
[rente] *pa. t. 3 sg.* tore L825.
    [yrent] *pp.* dragged (up) L1573. Cf.
    torent.
rentes *pl.* tribute (iron.) 5219. Cf.
    deþ-rentes.
[reouþfully] *adv.* piteously L1069.
rere [-en] *v.* raise (cry) 6417, (stones)
    L1572. [reryd] *pa. t. pl.* (banner)
    L1857. Cf. arere(n).
[res] *n.* see ras.
[resceyue] *v.* receive (judgement)
    L1087. ressaiued *pp.* (guests)
    3376.
resoun *n.* reasoned argument A1052.
rest [-(e)] *n.* rest A1315, 8209,
    9938, L494, L1768, and see iuel
    adj.
rest(en) *v.* rest A1528, 8570, (tr.)
    7482, 9227; wait 5669, 5672.

resteþ *pr. pl.* (refl.) 9819. rest(ed)
    pa. t. pl. (refl.) 5623, 7731, L1620.
resting *n.* taking of rest A1524.
retour *n.* return, *saunȝ* ~ whence
    none returns 8702.
reue(n) *v.* plunder 4541, ~ *her liif* =
    kill 9088, (sim.) 9394. reue *pr. pl.*
    7314. reften *pa. t. pl.* (~ . . . *o liif*)
    3210. yreued *pp.* = cut off (head
    from neck) A1862ⁿ, (body from
    head) 4967.
reuþe, rewþe *n.* pity 9854, (see
    haue(n)) A896, *L666*, etc., ~
    forto sen pitiable to see 4224; grief
    L1420, remorse 6828; pitiable
    state of affairs 6804, lamentable
    deeds 7693, *þat was* ~ that was
    lamentable A94, (sim.) A954, L1029;
    [reu(þ)the] L252, L666; [reouþe]
    L1420. Cf. reouþfully.
rewe *v.* (impers.) grieve (*see 284n*)
    1772, etc. reweþ *pr. 3 sg.* 3514.
    rewe *imp. sg.* have pity 7372, 9864.
    rewe *pa. t. 3 sg.* A284.
reweful *adj.* grievous 6232, 6782.
rewelich(e), -ly *adj.* piteous 4238,
    6224, 9322; reuly 8427, etc.
reweliche, reul- *adv.* pitiably, pit-
    eously A788, 8337.
ribaud *n.* scoundrel 7591. ribaudes
    pl. 7557, 7691; ribaus 7573, 7583.
ribaudye *n.* debauchery, loose be-
    haviour A781ⁿ, 4618; [rybawdy]
    amusement L1378.
ribbe *n.* (?*pl.*) rib(s) 8191ʳ. ribbes *pl.*
    5034, etc.
riche *adj.* powerful, rich A325, 1420,
    A1632, 4418, 6462, ~ *of* richly
    provided with 4492; excellent,
    sumptuous A523, 3378, 3540, 5558,
    5641, etc., L1858; valuable A598,
    2695, 4055, etc., (advice) 4058, 8919;
    rike 8899ʳ. richest *sup.* 3103.
richelich(e) *adv.* splendidly 2160,
    2734, 4486.
riches *n.* wealth 4062; splendid provi-
    sion 3583.
ridde *pa. t. 3 sg.* see rede *v.²*
ride(n) *v.* ride 1786, 2508, etc.
    rideinde *pr. p.* 7163, etc.; rideand
    9400. rod(e) *pa. t. 3 sg.* 2880, 6355,
    etc., L1328, (refl.) 3503. ride(n) *pa.
    t. pl.* A1211, 4421, etc., L1405;

rode^r 6196, 6936; [rod] L1365^r.
riden *pp.* 5859, 9112; yride 3093.
Cf. ouerriden.

rideing *n.* fight on horseback 3297,
etc. rideinges *pl.* 3908.

rigge *n.* back 3282, 5162, 5674, etc.,
at þe ~ close behind 7475; regge
5011.

riȝt *adj.* rightful, legitimate 1642,
A1808, 7642, etc., [~ . . . *of kynde*]
of rightful lineage L325; just (law)
L1489; accurate (story) 2116, exact
(truth) A445, A1258; right-hand,
etc. 5250, 6513, etc., and see left,
riȝte 8019^n; [ryȝhte] L1727. Cf.
a-riȝt, vnriȝt *adj.*

riȝt *adv.* straight (home, etc.), *ful* ~
A714, etc., *wel* ~ 2884; (intensive,
modifying adj., adv., adv. phr.) 838,
A1036, A1136, A1656, 2589, 5809,
L16, L96, L1250, L1502, etc.,
[modifying v., weak sense] L264,
L1520. Cf. vpriȝt.

riȝt *n.* right A540, 2795, *bi* ~ right-
(ful)ly A990, 3929, *to* ~ 2162, *wiþ* ~
A470, A1114, etc., L98, and see
for, haue(n); *it was* ~ (and sim.,
some perhaps *adj.*) A21, A735,
2264, 2947, 5406, etc., L1196;
territories (belonging to city) 2193,
(sim.) L239. riȝtes ?*pl.* (*bi* ~)
3738^{rn}. Cf. ariȝt, vnriȝt *n.*

riȝt(en) *v.* adjust 7482, 9816. riȝteþ
pr. pl. (refl.) adjust their gear 9819.
riȝt *pa. t. pl.* 3837, 9404; *pp.* 6230.

riȝtes *adv.* (intensive, modifying adv.)
2354, 5806, 7385, etc.

riȝtful *adj.* rightful 2804.

riȝtfulliche *adv.* rightfully 2948.

rike *adj.* see riche.

rime *n.* poem A1341.

ring *n.*^{1} ring (as royal token) A276,
3670, 3681; reng (*see 5397n*) A76.

ring *n.*^{2} see reng(e).

[rynge] *v.* ring (intr.) L1614.

riseing *pr. p.* rising 9163. ros *pa. t.
3 sg.* 9319, etc.; (from bed) A853,
[~ *vp*] L656, L857. risen *pa. t. pl.*
A1522, L1595. Cf. arise, vpriseing.

riue *v.* break (intr.) A448, 3255. Cf.
torof.

riued *pp.* landed A133.

riuer *n.* river 6708, etc.; land beside
this 8067.

robbe *v.* plunder 4541. robben *pr.
pl.* (obj. person and booty) 4323.
robbed(en) *pa. t. pl.* 4400, 5597,
7420. rob(b)ed *pp.* 4715, 5105,
8321.

robbeinges *pl.* booty 4730.

rob(be)rie *n.* plundering 3501, 4721,
etc.; booty 4720, 6684.

robours *pl.* plunderers 8320.

roche *n.* rocky height 5459, 6639;
castle on such *2435^n.

rode *n.*, *þe* ~ the Cross A634, etc.

rody *adj.* of healthy colour 654.

[rof] *n.* ceiling (see grounde) L796.

romaunce *n.* story A626, 8908, etc.;
romans 9405^r.

romende *pr. p.* wandering aimlessly
2372.

ron *pa. t. pl.* see erne.

rope *n.* rope A985, A993.

rose *n.* rose 8659.

rose-flour *n.* rose 3061.

roten *adj.* rotten A73.

roten *v.* flutter (banner) 3867^n.

roue *v.* cough A1935^n.

roum *adj.* extensive 6926.

roume *n.* space (cleared in battle)
7896, 9136; open place 8055.

roun [rown] *n.* speech 1218.

rounde *adj.* round (see table) 2196,
etc.

rout(e) *n.* (company of) people A330,
3277, 3739, etc.; [rowte] L297,
L1914.

rowe *adj.* hairy 7688; [rouȝh] L982,
[rowȝh] L985. rower *comp.* A982.

[rowned] *pa. t. pl.* see erne.

rugged [ra-] *adj.* shaggy 1501.

ruhel *n.* shield 5237^n.

run *pa. t. pl.* see erne.

⟨russett⟩ *n.* homespun cloth P2083.

sade *n.* semen A936.

sadel *n.* saddle 2112, etc. sadels, -les
pl. 3837, 3871, etc.

sadel-bowe *n.* saddle-bow 8148,
9676.

⟨sadlye⟩ *adv.* in plenty P2309.

say(n)^r *v.* say A344, A1153, A1415,
L71, L1401, etc.; speak A108, A256,
seye A26^r, and see forsoþe,

say(n) (*cont.*):
soþe *adv.*; tell (information, etc.)
A1335, A1409, 2640, *L156*; sig-
ge(n) A825, A1433, *hem ~ þat he
come* tell them to come 3421, (sim.)
4601; [seyn]ʳ L330, etc.; [seyʒe]
*L154, L523. sayʳ *pr. 1 sg.* A1183,
etc., L1245, *y ʒou ~* I assure you
(and sim., tags) A616, A1650, etc.,
saye A1541; sigge A445, A1718,
etc., *ich ʒou ~* I say to you (+
imperative) 4099 [and sim. with
pr. pl., L1485]; segge A1341;
[seyʒe] L1756. seyst *pr. 2 sg.*
A931; seistow A1135, etc., *what
conseil ~* what advice are you giving?
7350. seiþ *pr. 3 sg.* 8227, etc.,
L1482; seyt A1140, etc. siggeþ
pr. pl. A215, A277; seyt A1895,
2548; say (*þai ~* it is said (tag))
7086ʳ; [seiþ] L590; [seyn] L187;
[sayn] L1485; [say] L929, L931.
say *pr. subj. sg.* 2914; *imp. sg.*
A1087, 2287, sey 5401, L1451,
L1457. siggeþ *imp. pl.* A1953.
seyd [-(e)] *pa. t. 1, 3 sg.* 68, 5496,
etc., L1235; said [-(e)] A665, 915,
L1210, etc.; sadeʳ A1358, etc.;
sedeʳ 4344, etc. seydest *pa. t. 2
sg.* 1087, 4346. seyd(en) *pa. t. pl.*
163, 367, L551, etc.; sayd [-de(n)]
A670, L197, L222, L936; [seide]
L141, etc. (y)seyd *pp.* A620,
A1218, etc.; ysade A525ʳ. Cf.
mysseide.
(y)say(e) *pa. t. 1, 3 sg.*, etc. see
se(n).
[sayʒyng, sey-] *n.*, *my ~* what I say
L1715, (sim.) L1797.
sail *n.* sail A115.
*sailing *n.* see seylinge.
sake *n.* sake, *for . . . ~* A999, 4863,
L1253.
sank(e) *pa. t. 3 sg.* penetrated downwards (weapon (-stroke)) 5310, 9352.
Sarraʒin *n.* member of the heathen
race attacking Britain A325, etc.;
Sarrain 5692; [Sarsyn(e)] L20,
L84, etc. [Sarsynes] *gen.* (*sg.* or
pl.) L1952. Sar(r)aʒins *pl.* A474,
6099, etc.; Sarraʒin(e) 5169, 7515,
etc.; Sar(r)ains 4398, 6095, etc.;
[Sarsynes] L1951.

Sarraʒin(e) *adj.* of this race 4516,
9209.
sarre *adj.* closely packed (press of
battle) 5771; *adv.* holding closely
together 6231.
sarreliche *adv.* holding closely together 5279, 6047, etc.
sau(e)age *adj.* wild (forest) 5433;
fierce (*þe ~*, cognomen) 8270.
[saue] *prep.* except L909, L1101.
saue(n) *v.* save, protect 4753, 6998,
8369, L1045, L1763. saueþ *pr. 3
sg.* 5550. saue *pr. subj. sg.* A1377,
7034; saut (*see* Dieu) 6173, etc.
saued *pa. t. 3 sg.* 1280, L1148; *pp.*
L192.
Sau(e)our *n.* Saviour 2908, 7095, etc.
saun(ʒ) *prep.* without (*see* dout(e),
fable, fail(e), pite, retour) A869,
8702, etc.
sawe *n.* saying, *mi ~* what I say A512,
in ~ (tag, *tellen in ~* tell) 5407.
scape *v.* escape (intr.) 7473, etc.,
[*~ away*] = not be condemned
L761, [*~ freo*] L1034. scaped *pa. t.
3 sg.* 7772, 8356; [skapeode] *L761*.
scaped *pa. t. pl.* 8522, (tr.) 4924;
schaped 5887. scaped *pp.* 6845,
7496. Cf. ascape.
scapeing *n.* escape 7544.
scaþe *n.* harm A192, etc. scaþenʳ *pl.*
6718, etc.; scaþesʳ 4382, 4520.
scaþe *v.* harm 7388.
schad(de) *pa. t. 3 sg.* shed (blood)
5050, 6258. sched *pp.* 5757.
schaft *n.¹* (spear's) shaft 6363, =
spear A319, 8857, etc. schaftes *pl.*
A441, L1918.
[schaft] *n.²* nature (of a creature)
L1581.
(schake *v.*) see schoke *pa. t. 3 sg.*
schal *pr. 1, 3 sg.* (auxil. of futurity)
A631, A956, 1022, 2482ⁿ, L624,
etc., (of speaker's intention) 873,
964, etc.; schel 4293. schalt *pr. 2
sg.* 1624, etc., = must A1182, etc.,
L954, (and sim. in other forms),
schaltow A1050, etc., L930;
schald A1812; schal 2745, 2904.
schul(len) [-l(e)] *pr. pl.* 380, A521,
527, A1675, etc.; schulleþ 4226;
schal L465, L1753, etc., 2645ⁿ.
schuld [-e] *pa. t. 1, 3 sg.* A78,

A752, A1440, 1700, L140, L969, etc.,
= ought to A1323, A1324, L27
[schold], (forming equiv. of subjunct.) A123, A428, etc., L791, (do.
as pr.) 6803, 7661, L950 [scholde],
~ *haue* (impossible contingency)
A1332, A1569, ~ *to* would be needed
for 3058; schold [-(e)] r [not L] 2300,
L94, L993, etc. schust [schuldust]
pa. t. 2 sg. (as pr.) ought to 1114.
schuld(en) [-de] *pa. t. pl.* A182,
A352, 6441, etc., L1711, (forming
equiv. of subjunct.) A504, 1738,
etc., (as pr.) ought to A1398, etc.;
schold [-(e)] L253, L272, etc.,
A1781ʳ; [scholden] L694ⁿ.

schame *n.* shame 1144, A1174ⁿ,
L652, etc., +*say* . . . ~ = speak
shamingly to 7243, *me þenkeþ* ~ it
seems to me shaming 5543.
schame *v.* (impers.) shame 2918.
schameful *adj.* shameful A1157.
schandfulliche *adv.* in shame 9198.
schandliche *adj.* shameful, ~ *werk*
black arts 4276ⁿ. Cf. schond.
[schap] *n.* shape L980.
schaped *pa. t. pl.* see scape.
[schaped] *pp.* formed L1589.
schar(e) *pa. t. 3 sg.* cut 9687, 9779,
etc.; *pl.* 9800.
scharp(e) *adj.* sharp 2025, 3211, etc.;
scharppe 8072.
yschatred *pp.* (adj.) thrown about in
pieces A553.
sche *pron.* she A479, etc. Cf. he *pron.*²
sched *pp.* see schad(de).
scheld *n.* shield 137, etc., and see
vnder; schelde 3254. scheldes
gen. (see bord) 7450; *pl.* 7797.
scheld *v.* protect A1256. scheld *pr.*
subj. sg. A8. schilt *pp.* made safe
2013ʳⁿ.
schende *v.* disgrace, discomfit, destroy, etc. 2346, 4280, etc. schent
pa. t. 3 sg. 5774, 6068, (y)schent
pp. A322, A1337, 1836, 4674,
L1441, etc.; [schende] L1128ʳ.
schene *adj.* bright 5370; beautiful
6476.
schepe *pl.* sheep 9328; schip 4047.
schert *n.* shirt 8859, 9257.
schet [-utte] *v.* shut 1738. schet *pa.*
t. 2 sg. A1132. schett *pa. t. 3 sg.*

A832. schet(ten) *pa. t. pl.* 5611,
6660, etc.
schewe(n) *v.* show A1258, 3382,
5760, 8392, reveal A1550, 3384.
scheweþ [-iþ] *pr. 3 sg.* appears
[L allows to appear] 260, ~ *flour* =
is floriferous 8657. schewe(n) *pr.*
pl. A1711, = tell about 7615.
schewe *pr. subj. sg.* 2547. schewed
pa. t. 3 sg. 1575, etc.; *pl.* 5018, 5830,
L1858. yschewed *pp.* A1553.
scheweing *n.* revealing 5526; =
telling 7626.
schide *n.* hewn timber 8838. schides
pl. A531, 6044.
schift *pa. t. 3 sg.* divided (tr.) 6805.
schift *pa. t. pl.* 7833. schift(ed) *pp.*
2194, separated A1482. Cf. toschiften.
schille *adj.* resounding 6069; *adv.*
resoundingly A1320.
schilled *pa. t. 3 sg.* resounded 4740.
schilt *pp.* see scheld.
schining *n.* shining 8767.
schininge *pr. p.* shining 8800ʳ;
schin(e)ing (adj.) 4718ʳⁿ, 9164ʳ,
schineand 6877. [schon] *pa. t. pl.*
L1608.
[schip] *n.* ship L82. schippes *pl.* 2073.
schip *pl.* see schepe.
schire *n.* shire 2270.
schirt etc. *pa. t. pl.* see schriche.
[yschod] *pp.* (adj.) with shoes on
L839.
schode *n.* stratum that divides
A1480ⁿ.
schof *n.* thrusting 8489.
schoke [schok] *pa. t. 3 sg.* shook
(head) 1214, L1038, L1232.
scholder *n.* see schulder.
schon *pl.* shoes 1300, etc.
schond *n.* shame A1758, 4332, 6166,
etc., *is me* ~ is shaming to me
2386, 7646. Cf. schand(ful)liche.
[schort] *adj.* short L1434, L1437.
schortliche *adv.* briefly A1436.
schosen *pa. t. pl.* see chese(n).
schote *n.* range of shot 4920, 7949.
schoten *v.* rush 3868. schotest *pa.*
t. 2 sg. (*vp* ~ threw open A1130.
schoten *pa. t. pl.* A230, etc., flew
(arrows) 9159. yschote [schoten]
pp. shot (arrows) 317.

schouen *pa. t. pl.* thrust 8949.
schoue *pp.* 7959.
schourge *n.* scourge 8445.
schrede *n.* scrap 1540, L1737.
schrewe *n.* ill-disposed fellow 1204, L1659.
schriche *v.* shriek 5617. **schirsten** *pa. t. pl.* 4739[n]; **schirt** 6403.
[schryft] *n.* confession L662.
[schrylle] *adv.* loudly L1367.
schriue *v.* confess (obj. person, L do. and sins confessed) 708. **schrof** *pa. t. 3 sg.* (refl.) made confession A798; *nouȝt no* ~ did not concern himself 2533; *pl.* (*nouȝt* ~ were unaware) 8780[n]. **schriuen** *pp.* 947.
schul(len) *pr. pl.*, etc. see **schal.**
schulder *n.* shoulder 3934, etc.; **scholder** A1935, etc. **schulders** *pl.* 9081.
[schutte] *v.* see **schet.**
scippe [sk-] *v.* jump A1159, = dance L1374, L1392.
scomfite *pp.* (adj.) defeated 6664. Cf. **descomfit.**
score *pl.* score (numeral) 3194, 4126, etc., (as adj.) 3099, etc.
scorn *pr. pl.* treat with contempt A1941. *See n.*
Scottis *adj.* Scottish 3106.
scour(e) *n.* (adverbially), *gode* ~ with all speed 4970, 7164, etc.
[scripture] *n.* writing L1793.
scumfite *n.* defeat 6445. Cf. **descomfite.**
se [see] *n.* sea 287, etc., *ouer* ~ across the sea A464, 3691.
se(n) [seo] *v.* see (lit.) A1966, 3828, 3867, L286, etc., = meet, visit A1273, 3012, L665, etc.; (extended senses) A11, A946, 5138, etc., L1693; **yse(n)**[r] A182, A1262, etc.; **[yseo]** L877[r]; **[seon(e)]**[r] L1530, L1693, L1896. **se** *pr. 1 sg.* A871, etc.; **ise** A1089; **[seo]** L1372, L1375. **sest** *pr. 2 sg.* A1552. **seþ** *pr. 3 sg.* 4329; **[siþ]** L179. **se(n)** **[seo(n)]** *pl. pr.* 1303, 1328, etc.; **seþ** A1291, etc. **se** *pr. subj. sg.* 8389, 8423. **(y)say**[r] *pa. t. 1, 3 sg.* 3295, 4971, 8539; **saye** 7910[r]; **(y)seiȝe** A207, A691, etc.; **seye** 2366, etc. **seiȝe** *pa. t. 2 sg.* 9372;

[sawe] L1720; **[say]** L1730[r]. **(y)seiȝe(n)** *pa. t. pl.* A386, A666, 5169, *8502, etc.; **seye** 7902; **yseyn** 8510[r]; **saye** 7477[r]; **sayn** A1536[r]; **(y)sawe** 6327[r], 6914[r], L533, L1651; **sewe** 6696[r]. **sen(e)** *pp.* 370, 5769, etc.; **ysen(e)**[r] 7980, 9807; **yseiȝe**[r] A25, 4187; **ysaye** 8247[r]; **ysain** A1992[r]; **ysein** 9093; **[seyȝe]** L990. Cf. **ouersen.**
seche(n) *v.* seek A1379, 7040, etc.; **seke** L579, etc., 9665. **seche(n)** *pr. pl.* A1246, 8610. **souȝt** *pa. t. 3 sg.* 2513, etc.; *pl.* A1210, L267, etc., = sought and found L517 [sowȝt], (refl.) 2069, *out* ~ 2159. **(y)souȝt** *pp.* 1220, 7546[n], etc., = sought and found A571.
sechers *pl.* seekers A1196.
secounde *num. adj. ord.* second 3845, etc.
[see-stronde] *n.* coast L305.
sege *n.* siege A1909, A1968.
segeing *n.* besieging 7614. Cf. **bisege.**
seye *v.* see **say(n).**
seygnour *n.* lord 2523. **seygnours** *pl.* (see **bieu**) 5543, 6147, **sengours** 3607[n].
[seyȝyng] *n.* see **sayȝyng.**
seylinge *n.* attack 8257; *sailing 3969. Cf. **asailing.**
seyn(t) [-t(e)] *adj.* saint A3, 1103, L1058, etc., = (the) holy 2908, 7006, 7371. Cf. **sengreal.**
seke *adj.* see **sike.**
sekeling *n.* illness 2736.
[seknesse] *n.* see **sikenes.**
selcouþe [-couþ] *adj.* unheard-of, strange, marvellous A362, 918, 7408, 8392, L1469, etc.
sely *adj.* innocent, deserving pity A835, L1372, L1389. Cf. **vnsely.**
selle *v.* sell 1300, 4144.
selt *adj.* salted, (as n.) *fresche and* ~ fresh and salt meat 7286[n].
selt *n.* salt 3660.
selue [seo-] *adj.* same 7396, L477, and see **ich** *adj.*[2]; **self** 6105.
semblaunt *n.* (person's) appearance 2471, 5537; expression of face 2465, 6530, and see **make(n).**
semble *pr. pl.* seem to be 5547. **sembled** *pa. t. 3 sg.* 5536, 8853.

[semely] *adj.* attractive L280.
senche *v.* pour out (wine) 2316[n].
sende *v.* send 2794, 2878, 3418, =
send message(s) (to) *344, 2119,
8597, L1831,* and see after, =
send men 6778, 7290. sent *pr. 3
sg.* 2279; *pl.* 3514, sende 6733.
sende *pr. subj. sg.* A30, A1150,
L1981; *imp. sg.* [send] 1727,
L1235. sendeþ *imp. pl.* 4100. [sent]
pa. t. 2 sg. L1468. sent [-(e)]
pa. t. 3 sg. 344, L449, etc.; sant
7860. sent(en) [-te] *pa. t. pl.* 172,
A1945, etc. (y)sent *pp.* A1197,
2214, etc. Cf. ofsende.
sending *n.* sending 4668; = gifts (of
God) 4269.
sengours *pl.* see seygnour.
sengreal *n.* Holy Grail 2750. Cf.
seyn(t).
serche *imp. sg.* investigate A1463;
examine L1455. serchede *pa. t. 3
sg.* L1495.
seriaunce *pl.* servants 2522, 7265.
seriaunted *pa. t. 3 sg.* provided himself with servants 3396[n].
[seruaunt] *n.* servant L790.
[serpent] *n.* snake 9256[n].
serue(n) *v.* serve A378[n], 4630, etc.,
(at table) 6542, *6554*; treat *5037,*
L336, ?*L1781.* [serue] *pr. 1 sg.*
L1662. seruen *pr. pl.* 5529. serue
imp. sg. A878, 7668. serued
[-(e)] *pa. t. 3 sg.* 882, L803, etc.; *pl.*
[-edyn] 716, 3117. (y)serued *pp.*
A83, 2857, L1781, L1901.
serued *pp.* deserved 951. Cf. deserued.
seruise *n.* service 2980, 6503, etc.,
(at table) 3125, 6521; religious service 2805, 3113. seruise *gen.* 2798.
ses *n.* cessation 9178.
[sese] *v.* yield suzerainty of L1868.
set(t) *pa. t. 3 sg.* placed, put 2257,
5815, etc., ~ *on him þe crouche*
crossed himself 9005; [sette] L152.
set(t), setten *pa. t. pl.* appointed
(rendezvous) 4671, ~ *hem* sat down
A1930, 2319, ~ *oȝains* attacked
4874, ~ *on fer* set on fire 5602, (sim.)
6989, etc., ~ *on hors* mounted (tr.)
5174, (sim.) 5906, ~ *vp* hoisted
A115, raised up 5911[n], [~ *open*]

opened L1870. (y)set(t) *pp.* 4702,
6519, etc., founded, built 1238, *vp*
~ set up (as spectacle) 2012, and see
bok(e). Cf. ofersett.
seþþen [siþe(n), siþþe] *adv.* afterwards 1543, L682 [seothen], etc.,
and see after, hereafter 2184. *prep.*
since (time) 6713, L1413; *conj.*
2937, L159, L1199, ~ *þat* A926,
and see euer, (consequence) A239,
etc.
seuen [seo-] *num. adj.* seven 2053,
etc., L1977; [seoue] L601, L1257.
seuend *num. adj. ord.* seventh 3856,
etc.
seuenten(e) *num. adj.* seventeen
8895, 8975.
sewe *pa. t. pl.* see se(n).
sex *num. adj.* six 3043, etc.; [sixe]
L601. Cf. a-sex.
sext *num. adj. ord.* sixth 5421, etc.
sexten(e) *num. adj.* sixteen 3938,
7106, etc.
sexti *num. adj.* sixty 5590, etc.
sibbe ⟨sibb⟩ *adj.* related P339,
(quasi-prep.) related to 8904.
sibred *n.* kinship 6934.
side *adv.* widely, *wide and* ~ (from)
far and wide 6710, 8651, etc.
side *n.* side 6161, 7911, [*on ylk a* ~]
in all directions L106, etc., and see
ende *n.,* (of body) A455, etc., (in
battle) L292, L1954 [side *pl.*];
region 6610.
sigge(n) *v.* see say(n).
signe *n.* sign, ~ *of our Saueour* = of
the Cross 7916, [~ *of þe holy croys*]
L798.
signifieþ [-nefyȝeþ] *pr. 3 sg.* represents symbolically *1645[n], A1667,
A1674. signifie *pr. pl.* A1626.
siȝhing *n.* sigh A142.
siȝt *n.* sight (see haue(n)) 874, etc.,
⟨*before your* sight⟩ before I saw you
P2118; = thing seen A1962, L280,
etc.; appearance L1547, etc.
sike *adj.* ill 4292, etc., = wretched
2444; seke 4293. Cf. sekeling.
sikeende *pr. p.* sighing 2372.
sikenes [seknesse] *n.* illness 64.
siker *adj.* safe 7785, 8054; certain,
icham ~ (tag) 7740, *for soþe and* ~
in certain truth (tag) 6869, [~ *and*

siker (*cont.*):
soþ] certainly true L1757, and see
make(n); [sikir] (∼ ʒow beo you
may be certain) L193.
siker *adv.* certainly A871, etc.
sikerliche *adv.* certainly (usually tag)
A847, 2684, etc.; sikerlik(e) A1581,
7301; sikerly A1694, etc., L992.
sikernisse *n.* pledge 5538.
siluer *n.* silver 4054, etc., and see
gold.
sing [-e] *v.* sing 1324, etc., *messe* ∼
sing mass 8912. singeþ *pr. 3 sg.*
1325, 4679, L1387. sing(g)eþ *pr.
pl.* A262, 4677; sing(en) 5350,
7620. [syngynge] *pr. p.* L1359;
[syngand] crying out L120.
ysonge *pp.* 2379.
singel *n.* wooden tile 5874, 7932. *See
5874n.*
(sink *v.*) see sank(e) *pa. t. 3 sg.*
sinne *n.* sin 1327, etc.
sir [-(e)] *n.* sir (respectful address)
A206, L915, etc., (as adj.) ∼ *iustise*
sir judge A1089, L939, L1098; (of
knight, etc.) ∼ *Fortiger* (and sim.)
105, 1621, A1855, etc. sir *pl.* 4035ⁿ.
sire *n.* lord A1995, 2663.
sitt(e) *v.* sit 2200, 2201; distress
[*sowre* ∼ = have bitter consequences for] L1883; site A180ⁿ. sitt
pr. 3 sg. has his abode A28. sitten
pr. pl. A1941. sittand *pr. pl.* 5394.
sat *pa. t. 3 sg.* 229, etc., *a-knowe* ∼
knelt 9871. sete(n) *pa. t. pl.* 2302,
4019; sat 6518, 7970. sete *pa. t.
subj. sg.* A1434. ysiten *pp.* 2218.
Cf. atsit, wiþsat.
siþe *n.*, *mani* ∼ many times 4518,
9090.
[siþe(n)] etc. *adv.* see seþþen.
[sixe] *num. adj.* see sex.
[skapeode] *pa. t. 3 sg.* see scape.
skec *n.* seizing of plunder 4324,
4726. skekes *pl.* 4501.
skecken *v.* make a plundering-raid
7409.
sket(e) *adv.* without delay, quickly
381, 774, etc., and see also.
sky *n.* configuration of the heavens
(astrol). 1574, etc.; sky 7954.
skies *pl.* sky 5664, 5924.
[skil(e), -lle] *n.* cause L588; reason

L1121, *it were* ∼ = it would be
reasonable L1196.
[skippe] *v.* see scippe.
skirminge *n.* thrusting 8874.
slauʒter *n.* killing 3220, 3908.
sle(n) *v.* kill (A, esp. with weapons)
1223, A1393, A1826, etc.; ∼ *to
grounde* strike down (dead) A1839,
5223, etc., L116, (sim.) A1730,
etc.; slo(n)ʳ A866, A1924, etc.;
[slon(e)]ʳ L198, L1813, L1849.
sle *imp. sg.* 7504. sle(þ) *imp. pl.*
A1255, 3206, etc. slouʒ *pa. t. 3 sg.*
A1820, etc. slouʒ(wen) *pa. t. pl.*
A369, 4837, etc.; slo(u)weʳ [not L]
4027, 6051, L116, etc.; slowen
4734, L1919, etc. (y)slawe *pp.*
A145, 239, 903, etc.; slawen 7515,
8836; slain A1863, L264, etc.
sle(i)ʒster *n.* killing A143, 3981, etc.
sleiʒe *adj.* skilful, accomplished A535,
2318, etc.; [slyʒh] cunning L610.
sleiʒt *n.*¹ killing 4466, etc.; sleiʒst
(*see 4472n*) 5015, men killed (see
lese(n)) 6901.
sleiʒt *n.*² skill 8952.
slepe *n.* sleep, *falle on* ∼ fall asleep
842; slape [-e-] (*hir laid doun to* ∼)
814ʳ.
slepeand *pr. p.* 6626, 8749. slepe
[-pte] *pa. t. 1 sg.* 917. yslape *pp.*
2367ʳ.
sleuþe *n.* sloth (sin) A806.
slit *n.* front opening (doublet) A1406.
slit(t) *pa. t. 3 sg.* cut 4812, 4890, etc.;
pl. 8964.
slo *n.* sloe, = worthless thing 7498.
slod *pa. t. 3 sg.* fell (diverted blow)
6177.
slong *pa. t. 3 sg.* threw 5674.
[slowʒ] *n.* mire L1599.
smale *adj.* small 7354, [smal]
L1579; of low rank (see gret(e))
3836, etc., (as n.) A1752, etc.
⟨smart⟩ *adj.* sharp P2064.
smere *n.* dubbin A1306.
smere [-eo-] *v.* smear 1306. [smeore]
imp. sg. L555. smerd *pa. t. 3 sg.*
2515. [smeored] *pa. t. pl.* L541.
ysmerd *pp.* A599.
smite(n) *v.* strike, hit A608, 7347,
etc., ∼ *bataile* wage battle A436,
8649, *togider* ∼ attack each other

1513; spur *3266*, *3449*, etc., = gallop 7924, (refl.) *4824*. **smite** *imp. sg.* 7996, 9873. **smiteing** *pr. p.* 3970. **smot** *pa. t. 3 sg.* 4138, 6399, etc., L824; **smit** 8132ʳⁿ. **smite(n)** *pa. t. pl.* 231, A1604, etc. **smiten** *pp.* A136, etc., = struck down 7525; **(y)smite**ʳ 8047, 9327, etc. Cf. **of-smiten.**

smiteing *n.* striking 8874.

smiþ *n.* blacksmith 7520.

smok(e) *n.* smock (undergarment) 1128, 5817.

smoke *n.* smoke 7072.

snel(le) *adv.* vigorously A533, A1322; quickly (see **also**) A1789.

snelle *adj.* vigorous A1196.

snout(e) *n.* face 7688, and see **berd.**

so *adv.* so (mod. uses) 78, 1296, 1322, 6110, L1052, L1382, etc., = in this respect 6996, [~ *bold to*] bold enough to . . . L1166; similarly, things being thus (weak senses) A4, 2009, 3881, 5067, 5417, L237, etc.; as A548, A1529, 6258, L69, L1521, etc.; *vp* ~ *doun* upside-down *544ⁿ; *who* ~ whoever A233, etc., (sim.) 2001, 4809; [soo]ʳ L90, etc. *conj.* as A176, 377, 1455, 2308, etc., (of time) A917, 2153ⁿ, etc., [~ *þat*] when L55ⁿ; as if 5148, etc.; (as rel. pron.) who A155ⁿ; (quasi-prep.) like A1500, etc., as being 2410, 8598.

socour *n.* support, help 1652, etc., L529; = one who gives this 5820.

socour *v.* help, support 8813. **socoureþ** *pr. 2 sg.* 6787ⁿ. **socour** *pr. pl.* 9119; *pr. subj. sg.* A203. **socourd** *pa. t. pl.* 3920, 6310.

socouring(e) *n.* giving of help 8301, 8967.

sodanliche, -dein- *adv.* suddenly 3218, etc., [**sodeynly**] L661; without delay A597, A607.

soft *adv.* easily 2931; at an easy pace 6231.

soiour(ne) *n.* coming into/remaining in residence 3785, 6977ⁿ; delaying 2537.

soiour(ne) *v.* lodge, reside 5347, 6464, etc.; **soiurne** 8327. **soiour-(n)inge** *pr. p.* *7269, 7411. **soiurn-d(e)** *pa. t. pl.* 5342, 5566, etc.

soket *n.* spear-head (shaped like ploughshare) 7190.

solas *n.* comfort 750, 4231; help, support 4308, = person who gives this A267; hospitality 5345, 6556; taking of pleasure 2319, 8210, L316.

solausing *n.* taking of pleasure 5568.

solempne *adj.* solemn 2803.

som(e) etc. *adj.* see **sum.**

somers *gen.* summer 7619; [**som-ores**] L1612, L1817.

somers *pl.* pack-horses 4855, etc.; **somer** 4710ʳ.

[**somwhyle**] *adv.* see **sumwhyle.**

sond [-e] *n.* message (of summons) 4609, 5572, etc.; mission A570, 613; grace (God's) A744, etc.; envoy 1119, L1137.

sone *adv.* soon, straightway 92, A208, A867, A1702, L69, etc., ~ *þat* as soon as A849, and see **anon, day**; **son**ʳ A956, 2892. **soner** *comp.* 9119; = more willingly 4153.

sone *n.* son 75, etc., ~ *mine* (friendly address to child) A1442, and see **nortour(e). sones** *gen.* 6852, 8514; *pl.* 4566, etc., L25. Cf. **biche-sone.**

song *n.* song 3064, 3535, etc.

sonne *n.* sun A548, etc., and see **heiȝe** *adj.*, **vnder. sonnes** *gen.* 3865.

sonnebem *n.* sunbeam 9160.

soper *n.* supper 2495; **sopers** A1290ʳ.

sore *adj.* in pain 4292, (fig.) 8213.

sore *adv.* bitterly, grievously A780, A830, L1053, L1207, etc.

sore *pa. t. pl.* see **swere.**

[**sorewe**] *v.* sorrow L1386.

sori *adj.* distressed A862, etc.; grievous A1701, L160, etc.; sorrowful 7381ⁿ.

soriliche *adv.* grievously 4810.

sorwe *n.* distress A242, 690, L884, etc., = lamentation 7577, *of* ~ grievous 542, 9180. **sorwes** *pl.* afflictions 1624 [L *sg.*].

sorweful *adj.* expressing distress 6324, 7133; full of affliction 6779.

soster [**sus-**] *n.* sister 741, etc.; **suster** 3084, etc.; [***sustur**] L770, L773. **sostren** [**sustreon**] *pl.* 724, 738; **sustren** 2617.

soþ(e) *adj.* true L1879, (see þing) 8592, (predicative) A619, 1161, etc., and see **siker** *adj.*; ⟨*that* sooth *tyde*⟩ that very time P341. Cf. **forsoþe.**

soþe *adv.* truthfully A1140, A1148, A1550; [soþ], ~ *to say* to tell the truth (tag) L737, etc., ~ *to telle* L1565.

soþe *n.* truth A1122, A1258, L779, etc.; [soþ] L1506.

soudan *n.* heathen prince 4440, etc. soudans *pl.* 6758, 6835.

souders *pl.* professional soldiers 2414, 5511, etc.

souke(n)*v.*suck(infant)2717,2850,and see ȝiue(n). souke *pa. t. 2 sg.* 8466; soke 2944ʳ. seke *pa. t. 3 sg.* 2851.

soule [sowle] *n.* soul 1308, etc. soule *pl.* 7514; *gen.* (*sg.* or *pl.*) A30, 9210.

soun *n.* sound 3814.

sounde *n.* uninjured, *hole and* ~ 7804; in health 9792.

sour *n.* muddiness 8660. *See n.*

soure *adj.* trusty 7676; safe 7785.

soure *adv.* bitterly 4454ⁿ; [sowre] (see **sitt(e)**)) L1883. Cf. **sur.**

sout *n.* matching garb 4686ⁿ.

souþe *adj.* southern 8745; *adv.* in the south (see **norþ**) 4572.

souþe *n.* the south 3107, 3186.

souþe-west *adv.* south-westwards 7705.

ysowe *pp.* sown 4537.

span *n.* spread hand's breadth A1491.

sparc *n.* spark 2226. *sparkes *pl.* 5663.

[spare] *v.* spare pains L509. spareþ *imp. pl.* show mercy 8739. spar(e)d *pa. t. pl.* 6894, showed mercy to 4248, 6262; forbore (to . . .) 7476.

[sparklede] *pa. t. pl.* flashed L1609.

speche *n.* A1382, etc.

spede(n) *v.* be successful 250, 3922, etc., (+*to* and inf.) A1950; deal with A6, A1436. spede *pr. subj. sg.* (*so God me* ~ as may God prosper me) 3645, L172, (sim.) 5507; *imp. sg.* (~ *þe on* get on with) 2530. sped(den) [-ddyn] *pa. t. pl.* 549, 2842.

speke *v.* speak A609, 1012, 1028, etc.,

~ *hem bitven(e) þai wold(en)* = agree together to A1779, 5825; tell (one's trouble) 4227, *to hem* ~ *to* = tell them to . . . 6281. spekeþ *pr. 3 sg.* 7645. speke *pr. pl.* A1952, 5132, etc., L1265; speki 4991ⁿ. spac, -k *pa. t. 1, 3 sg.* spoke, said A720, 2027, 2380, 4267, etc., L208, said to (or refl., said) A1633; spake 4555ʳ. [spak] *pa. t. 2 sg.* L1288. spoken *pa. t. pl.* A1779, etc.; spac, -k [-ken] A1233, 2035, L1523; spake 8037ʳ; speken A162. [speke] *pa. t. subj. sg.* L540. yspeken *pp.* A401; [spoke] L143. Cf. **bispac.**

spending *n.* provisions 6443.

spere *n.*¹ spear A137, etc. speres *gen.* 6363, etc.; *pl.* A336, etc., speren 9167ʳ.

spere *n.*² celestial sphere (astrol.) 3566.

[sper(re)d] *pp.* barred (door, etc.) L796, L858.

speruer *n.* sparrow-hawk 5258.

spie *n.* scout (milit.) 8758, observer L1235, L1249. spies *pl.* 3806, etc. Cf. **aspies.**

spille(n) [spil(le)] *v.* kill 964, etc., destroy L1244; shed (or be shed, blood) L1663; perish A16, 2394. spilt *pp.* 951, 2014, shed (blood) A285.

spite *n.* contempt 3135. Cf. **despite.**

spor(e)s *pl.* spurs 3246, 8473, 9435; spurs 7228.

spouse *n.* wedlock 2773ⁿ.

spouse *v.* marry 2599, 3611. spoused *pa. t. 3 sg.* 2182, etc. (y)spoused *pp.* 2242, 3077, etc.; (y)spouseʳ 8893, given in marriage 6566.

spouseing [-syng] *n.* marrying 2621; wedlock L691, L723.

spredden *pa. t. pl.* spread out (intr.) 6988; [sprad] (~ *owt*) L1945. sprad *pp.* scattered A545, 7018, *L497; spred 7361.

[spryng(e)] *v.* spread (intr., news, etc.) L70, L1173. [spryngyþ] *pr. 3 sg.* dawns L1817. springeþ *pr. pl.* bloom A261, etc. sprong *pa. t. 3 sg.* spread 7623, L87; was born A638, 2770; leapt, etc. A1492, 9886. ysprongen *pp.* = come up (from Hell) 8024.

squiers *n.* squires (= not (yet) of knight's rank) 2156, 8253, etc.

staf *n.* staff (support) A1933. staues *pl.* (weapons) 3343, 4961.

[stak] *pa. t. 3 sg.* barred (door) L828.

stalworþ *adj.* stalwart 6688, etc.

stamered *pa. t. 3 sg.* stammered 2854.

stand *v.* see stond(en).

standard *n.* standard (milit.) 8942[n], etc.

stan-ded *adj.* stone-dead 7116.

[stark] *adj.* see sterk.

[starte] *v.* jump L1243. stirt [start(e)] *pa. t. 1, 3 sg.* A1997, 2021, etc., L822, (refl.) 1731, 4221, moved quickly 8474 (and do. in other forms); stert [-e] 9896, L937; strit 2549, 3891. stirtest *pa. t. 2 sg.* A1128. stirt(en) *pa. t. pl.* 3328, 3882, etc.; stert(en) 3137, 7281, 8786. stirt *pp.* 6330. Cf. astert.

stat *n.* bodily form 2584, 2586; condition 8458, 8465.

statout *n.* decree 2387, 2389.

staues *pl.* see staf.

[staunchen] *v.* put out (fire) L1971.

stede *n.*[1] war-horse 1829, etc. stedes *pl.* A1824, etc.; stede(n) 2696, 3362, etc.

stede [-e(o)-] *n.*[2] place 1439, etc., *L1273; [stude] L854. stedes *pl.* 2962.

sted(e)fast *adj.* firm A1570, +*make* ~ confirm A431.

stedfastliche *adv.* steadfastly A390.

stef *adj.* strong 2978, 3465, etc., firm 3855, 7970, [styf] L1308; taut 6352, rigid in death 7116, stif stretched out 7172. *See 2978n.*

steiȝen *pa. t. pl.* see stowen.

stel *n.* see stiel.

step(pe) *v.* step. 2148, 9381. steped *pa. t. 3 sg.* 2150.

stepe [steop] *adj.* running high (river) 1450[n], 7900.

ster *n.* star (astrol.) 3567. sterres *pl.* 3553.

stere(n) *v.* see stir(en).

sterk [-a-] *adj.* firm A1236, L542, unyielding [*stout and* ~] L20, etc.; severe (battle) L286, L1550, great (lie) L1188.

stern(e) [-eo-] *adj.* redoubtable 2170, 8865, L1584; severe (battle) 6870.

stert(e) *pa. t. 3 sg.*, etc. see starte.

sterue(n) *v.* die 3159, 5827, etc. sterue *pr. pl.* 8420. starf *pa. t. 3 sg.* A692, etc. storuen *pa. t. pl.* 9175.

stet(t) *pa. t. 1, 3 sg.* struck 2022, 6360, etc.; *doun* ~ dismounted hastily 8479. stet(t), -tten *pa. t. pl.* 8289, etc.; fell heavily 3312, etc.; hastened 3807, etc.; *togider* ~ crashed together 3270. stet *pp.* = trampled 6941; stite hastened 9020[r]. *See 2022n.* Cf. wiþstette.

steuen [-e] *n.* voice A639, 8916, L604.

steward [sty-] *n.* king's principal officer 80, etc.

sticke *pl.* sticks 9174[r].

stiel *n.* steel A324, etc., and see iren; stel 8141. steles *gen.* = sword's 9085. *See 324n.*

stif *adj.* see stef.

stille *adj.* (predicative) quiet A1117, L605 (or *adv.* quietly), L1061, L1195; *adj.* or *adv.* unmoved 1466, 3871, still (stand, etc.) L1094, L1224, L1758, L1764, +(*bi*)*leue* ~ remain where one is A1973, 4527, 8224, (sim.) 4195; *adv.* quietly A1299, 3778.

stilly *adj.* quiet 3781; *adv.* quietly 8769.

sting *pr. pl.* thrust through 6424. stong(en) *pa. t. pl.* 3825, 6630.

[stynte] *v.* cease efforts L1828. [stynt(en)] *pa. t. pl.* L563, ~ *of* ceased from L1613.

stir(en) *v.* move (negated = not even slightly) (tr.) 2832, 2838, 2997, (intr.) 5156; stere(n) 8980, (refl.) 3827, (refl.) be active 3323, *in blod* ~ = bathe (sword) in blood 5882. stireþ *pr. 3 sg.* moves (child in womb) 2636. stired *pa. t. 3 sg.* 5156.

stirop(e) *n.* stirrup 3250[n], 3986, 6352. stiropes *pl.* 3249.

stirt *pa. t. 1, 3 sg.*, etc. see starte.

stite *pp.* see stet(t).

stiuours *pl.* bagpipers 6558.

stok *n.* tree-trunk (*stef so* ~) 3855 7970.

ston *n.* stone 515, 2808, etc., *ded so*
~ stone-dead 3456, (sim.) L1349, *on
þe* ~ = to the earth 4963, (sim., *pl.*)
3992, and see **gnowe(n). stones** *pl.*
1451, 4960, etc., ~ *precious* 8669;
stonnes A1484. Cf. **stan-ded.**
stond(en) [-de] *v.* stand (mod. uses,
lit. and fig.) 600, 2207, 6796, etc.,
withstand 9282, ~ *oӡain* withstand
A150, 4842; **stand** [-e] L1764, etc.,
5680. **stont** *pr. 3 sg.* 2031; **stondeþ**
(*hem no* ~ *no doute of* they have no
fear of) 4341. **stode** *pa. t. 3 sg.*
2834, 4420, 5658, etc., ~ *at* =
reached (weapon-stroke through
body) 5216, 8134; [**stod**] L1224,
L1758 (refl.), stood still L1686.
stode(n) *pa. t. pl.* A389, 3208,
5937, etc. Cf. **astond, wiþstond.**
stong(en) *pa. t. pl.* see **sting.**
store *n.* provisions 3661, 6605, etc.
Cf. **astore** *n.*
stored *pa. t. 3 sg.* provisioned 4112.
Cf. **astore** *v.*
stouer *n.* provisions 6771. **stouers**
pl. 7611ʳ.
stounde *n.* (short) time A452, 2401,
L581, etc., moment A1692; time
(when something occurs) L1032; *in
þat* ~ at once 4935, 6132, etc., L1495,
at that moment, time 5747, L795,
(sim.) 5375, 6105, L115, L1533,
L1941.
stoupe *v.* bend, *on knewes* ~ kneel
6541.
stour *n.* battle 8932.
stout *adj.* resolute A422, L20, etc.;
[**stowt**] L1459, brazen L814.
stoutelich *adv.* resolutely 7227.
stowen *pa. t. pl.* climbed 6660
steiӡen 8311.
strait *adj.* narrow 4321, 4410.
strang *adj.* see **strong(e).**
strangled *pa. t. 3 sg.* strangled 688;
pp. L772.
streiӡt *pa. t. 3 sg.* thrust out 3249ⁿ;
stretched 6352; *pp.* (adj.) stretched
out 9838, 9885.
strem *n.* stream 7900. **stremes** *pl.*
8089. Cf. **wel-streme.**
stren [-eone] *n.* offspring, child
A1021, A1774, etc.; progeny A1667,
etc.; lineage 4298, 8243; begetting

L549; [~ *of a child*] = sperm L849ⁿ.
strengþe[streynthe,-þe]n. strength,
power 1461, 4781, L100, etc., *wiþ* ~
by main force 2132, 9314, L1444.
strete *n.* main road in town 3538,
5379, etc.
strewed *pp.* (adj.) scattered 9172.
stri(i)f *n.* fighting A237, 6085, etc.,
L1926, **striue** 5128ʳ; *bi* ~ by force
6493; arguing 4989ⁿ, L1147ʳ
[**stryue**], contention L1762, [*nay
wiþoutyn* ~] = certainly not L199.
stroi(e) *v.* kill, destroy 5972, *7690.
ystroied *pp.* 4244; **strued** 4241.
Cf. **astroie, destroie.**
[**strok**] *pa. t. 3 sg.* cut L1953.
stroke *n.* (weapon-)stroke 3338.
strokes *pl.* A1938, 4911, L1947.
strond *n.* shore A353.
strong *adv.* severely 4962, 9899,
fiercely 5175.
strong(e) *adj.* strong, 329, 1305,
3748, L1540, L1920, etc.; fierce
(battle, etc.) 2080, etc., L1607,
L1791; (pejorative intensive) L1306,
etc., A664, 791, 4262, 7044
strangʳ 5974, etc. **strongest**
sup. 3263, 5996; **strangest** 4320;
strengest 5969.
struted *pa. t. pl.*, ~ *oӡainward* opposed
(absol.) A233.
[**stude**] *n.* see **stede** *n.*²
substaunce *n.* substance (theol.) 8918.
[**such**] *adj.* see **swiche.**
sue, suwe(n) *v.* follow (leader) 4769,
5654; pursue 7777, ~ *after* 9367.
suweþ *imp. pl.* 5716, 5854. **suwed**
pa. t. pl. 4774, etc.; **sueden** 9813.
suffre *v.* allow to continue 4750.
sum *adj.* some A1269, 4997, etc.,
L861; (as pron.) A310, etc., L1524,
one 4945ⁿ; **som(e)** [**som(me)**]
748, A1062, L475, etc.
sumdel *adv.* somewhat 4272, 4782,
8129, L130; *pron.* 4780; (quasi-adj.)
a degree of A1611.
sumw(h)at *pron.* something A1610,
2330.
[**sumwhyle, som-**] *adv.* formerly
L9, L1897.
sur *adj.* bitter (fig.) 3945ⁿ. Cf. **soure**
adv.
surname *n.* cognomen 5488.

susten *v.* withstand 7152. **sustend** *pa. t. pl.* kept (battle) going 9926.

sustenaunce *n.* provisions 4323, 4400.

suster etc. *n.* see **soster**.

suwe(n) *v.* see **sue**.

swain [**sweyn**] *n.* squire (= not (yet) of knight's rank) A146, etc., L231, L1776, (= knight's attendant) 2862. **swaines, -ei-** *pl.* 4349, 8243, etc.

swannes *pl.* swans 3120.

swarf *pa. t. 3 sg.* glanced off 9359ⁿ.

swerd [**-eo-**] *n.* sword A1813, 9917 (or *pl.*), etc., L179, L1285; **sword**ʳ A231, etc.; **sward** 9349ʳ. **swerdes** *gen.* 3325, etc.; *pl.* [-eo] A207, etc., L287; **swordes** 8117, 9728.

swerde-egge *n.* sword's edge 7465.

swere *n.* neck 9073, 9383, etc.; [**swyre**] L715.

swere [**-eo**] *v.* swear, declare (that thing is true, etc.) 8395, L1344, (refl.) 2560. **swer(e)** *pr. 1 sg.* A1024, 3357, 4801. **swore** [**swor**] *pa. t. 3 sg.* 1037, etc., (obj. oath) 1362, L1114; [**swar**] L571, etc. **swore(n)** *pa. t. pl.* 3238, etc., L226, L1710, (obj. oath) A351, 3578, etc., *Mahoun þai ~ to* they swore to M. to ... 5066; **sore** (*~ þe dede of* = swore to kill) 3982 (and sim. with *pp.*). i [**sweore**] L229. **(y)swore** *pp.*; 3716, 4586, *þei þai it hadde* = though they had sworn the contrary A1011, (adj.) bound by oath (to person) 197, 3608; **(y)sworn** 3406, (adj.) 3417.

swete *adj.* dear, beloved A3, 742, L1979, etc.; fragrant 8658.

sweuen *n.* dream 3801, 3803.

swiche [**such**] *adj.* 809, etc., *~ ten þan* ten times as many as 6906, [*~ on*] such a one L1470, (as pron.) A516, etc.; what A629, etc. *rel. pron.* which A673, etc.

swift *adj.* quick(-working) A535, (-flowing) A1450.

swiftlich(e) *adv.* quickly, at once A1370, 6435, etc.; **suiftli** 8408ʳ.

[**swyn**] *n.* pig L982.

swiþe *adv.* very 971, etc.; greatly L652, L844, ⟨**swithe**⟩ strongly P2010; quickly, at once A602, A1744, 3579, L1508, etc., and see **anon**.

swoned *pa. t. 3 sg.* (*see 4936n*) fainted 5819. Cf. **aswon**.

swoninge *n.* period of unconsciousness 9850.

sword *n.* see **swerd**.

swouȝ *n.* period of unconsciousness 7132. Cf. **aswouȝ** etc. s.v. **aswon**.

table *n.* table 2200, 2201, 6512, = institution of the Round Table 2215, 2220; *þe rounde ~, ~ rounde* (institution) 2196, 2402, etc., = knights of this 5749; **tabel** 3092. **tables** *pl.* 6508, 6943.

tabourers *pl.* drummers 6558.

tabouringe *n.* drumming 9165.

tabours *pl. gen.* of drums 8802.

tail(e) *n.* tail 1493, 1501, etc.; *fram þe top to þe* = from top to bottom (man) 5952, *top and ~* neck and crop 8126; rear (milit.) 7904ⁿ.

take(n) *v.* take (mod. uses) 346, 2269, 2287, L1432, *etc., ~ aise* take one's ease *8209, ~ conseil* discuss, resolve *7480, 8373,* (sim.) L309, *~ rede* A286, (sim.) *L254, ~ensaumple* take example *7964, ~ leue* get permission *5533,* take one's leave *2552,* L202, (sim.) *1292,* L104, *of loue ~* = get sexual intercourse 2506, *~ rest* rest A*1315, 8209, ~þe way to* go to *8543, ~ þe winde* recover one's breath 9226, [*~ on honde*] undertake L163, [*~ veniaunce*] take vengeance L597; choose (persons) *3397, etc., ~ to wiue* take in marriage *A481, 4476;* assume (nun's habit) L1260; fetch L1254, etc.; seize and/or kill, capture, arrest *A147,* A227, A730, 7809, 8753, L525, etc.; strike 3267, 7098; give (to) *2710, 3179, etc.,* L999, *~ entent to* give attention to A1968; (refl.) apply self, *~ to rede* discuss together A100, L213, [*~ to-gedre*] L60, L132. **take** *pr. 1 sg.* (*our Lord y ~ to waraunt* I take God to witness) 2658; *pr.subj.sg.*L1694; *imp. sg.* 9872, [**tak**] L554, L999. [**takeþ**] *pr. pl.* L611; **takeþ** [-iþ] *imp. pl.* 75, *gode hert to ȝou ~* = be of good courage 2090. **tok(e)** *pa. t. 1, 3 sg.* 2943, 5047, L313, etc., accepted as

take(n) (*cont.*):
lover L722, (refl.) caught (disease) A64; *pl.* 7829, etc., L60, L202, *vp* ~ raised up (fallen man) 7119, **token** 2318, etc., L1326, **[tokyn]** L255, etc. **ytake** *pp.* 4476, 4864, seized on (fig., disease) 4254; **[take(n)]** L741, L1454, etc. Cf. **bitoke, oftake, ouertok.**

[takil] *n.* tool (euphemism) L1432, L1434.

tale *n.* what is said A601, L1210, 2692, etc., story, account A29, etc., L1264, L1316, and see **make(n)**, **tel(le)** ; enumeration, *bi* ~ 5472, = in total A1751, *wiþouten* ~ innumerable A1724, 6051; esteem (see **held(en)**) 5466. **tales** *pl.* A962, A1146, 3734.

[talkyng] *n.* story L4.

talent *n.* desire A1225, etc., what one wishes to do 1580, A1620, eagerness 2125, 5872; *gode* ~ affection 2118.

talle *v.* cut 5072, 6948.

tar(e) *adv.* see **þer(e).**

taren *pl.* vetch-seeds 7354ⁿ.

targeing, -ginge [-gyng] *n.* delaying (intr.) 1372, 7594.

tasse *n.* heap (of slain) 6709, 9104; close group 7507.

tat(e) *n.* breast 2850, 2944, 8466. *See 2850n.*

te(n) *v.* make one's way A1439, 5530, etc.

teche *v.* inform A1389. **tauʒt** *pa. t. 3 sg.* 6156, taught 713, etc., (iron.) 4818, 9675, showed (the way) 7055, 7845, directed 9925; consigned to A686; *pl.* 6704; *pp.* 947 [L **tawʒt**], A1234, L757, L801. Cf. **bitauʒt.**

teyed *pa. t. 3 sg.* tied A382. **[tyʒed]** *pp.* L974.

tel(le, -len) *v.* tell A19, 575, 1058, 1346, 4025, etc., ~ *tale(s)* speak *A1146, 3348,* [~ *counsaile*] give advice L1761, and see **(y)here(n)**, **soþe** *adv.*, say L1042, ?L1705; explain L1702, describe L1581; count 7266ⁿ. **tel(le)** *pr. 1 sg.* A31, L1171, etc., (*as*) *y ʒou telle* (and sim.) I tell you (usually tag) 161, A821, 2055, 2095, 2212, L1323, etc.; account A1065, A1110, 7224.

telleþ *pr. 3 sg.* 7271, 9657; *pl.* A1957, **telle** 4196, etc., L577.

telle *pr. subj. sg.* 1613, L1770.

tel(le) *imp. sg.* 1248, A1366, etc.

teld *pa. t. 1, 3 sg.* A360, A799, etc., enumerated 7158ⁿ; **telt** A1091; **told** [-(e)] 1694, L1250, L1268, etc., counted 3190. **told** *pa. t. 2 sg.* A1418. **teld(en)** *pa. t. pl.* A399, 7696, etc., counted 3702; **[tolde]** L1305. **(y)teld** *pp.* A1488, etc., *þat were* ~ ? = by count 3685; **told** A1794, L941, accounted L695.

telling *n.* telling A1706.

telt *pa. t. 3 sg.* pitched (tents) 3659. **telt(en)** *pa. t. pl.* 3171, 6909, etc. **telt** *pp.* 6926.

tempest *n.* storm 6700; **tempast** 5934ʳ.

tempred *pa. t. 3 sg.* restrained 6539.

[tempteþ] *pr. 3 sg.* tempts L1126. **[tempted]** *pa. t. 3 sg.* L639.

ten(e) *num. adj.* ten A579, 3649, etc., L1380.

ten(e) *n.* harm A1780, etc., **[teone]** L1280; anger 9634.

tene *v.* vex A1208.

tent *n.* tent 8789.

tenþ *num. adj. ord.* tenth 6768. Cf. **tiþe.**

ter(e) *adv.* see **þer(e).**

tere *v.* tear A1307, (hair) A857, 8360, *of* ~ tear off 5026. **tare** *pa. t. 3 sg.* (*himself* ~ ? rent his garments) 7716ⁿ. Cf. **totar.**

ter(e)s *pl.* tears (wept) A458, A1019, 6918.

terme *n.* end of prescribed time 8648.

terne *v.* turn (intr.) A1227, (tr.) 7930. Cf. **turne.**

Tewisday *n.* Tuesday 5585; **Tiwesday** 8777.

tide *n.* time, *in þat* ~ (and sim.) then, at once L73, L82, L291, etc., 2845, *seyn Ion* ~ the feast of St. John 3010, *somers* ~ summertime 7619, and see **time.**

tiding(e) *n.* news 2681, 3514, etc., L1879, piece of information 1718, L1305. **tidinges** *pl.* A184, 6439.

tiffen *pr. pl.* adorn themselves 7622.

[tyʒed] *pp.* see **teyed.**

[ty3t] *pp.* intended L263.

til *prep.* until 2839, etc.; to L700. *conj.* until 874, etc., ~ *þat* A1860, etc., L1829, ~ *þan* A1371, ~ *what* 8278ⁿ. Cf. intil, þertil(le), vntil.

[tymber] *n.* timber L459, L473.

time *n.* time (when something occurs) 2224, 6497, L1212, etc., *in þis* ~ at that time (and sim.) A730, 3795, 4211, 4473, 6779, L237, etc.; = season 1709, 4678, etc.; = appropriate time 3947, 5554, *at tide and* ~ at this 8059, and see **gode**, opportunity 5138, time for childbirth 977; *þe þridde* ~ for the third time 1342; also see **lese(n)**.

tireing *n.* dragging 8804ⁿ.

[tyse] *v.* entice L616.

tiþe *num. adj. ord.* tenth 5429. Cf. tenþ.

Tiwesday *n.* see Tewisday.

to *adv.* too 270, 4854, etc.; also (see 3er(e)) 1895ⁿ; thither 3725ⁿ. *prep.* to (mod. uses) 68, 141, 197, 382, 762, A2153, L653, etc., as far as 2175, until 2834, 4787, etc.; at (of striking) 1859ⁿ, 5200, etc.; for (in various senses) A598, A635, 3853, 5520, etc., L469, so as to bring (help, harm) 6252, 8352, ~ *no gode* of no profit A209, ~ *his wil(le)* = to do his will A1585, 2002, [~ *his counsail*] = to give him advice L1673, [~ *his cristendam*] = as his Christian name L1009, and see ler(e); as 676, A1632, 2189, 2658, etc., and see ek(e) *n.*; of (need) 5513, etc.; *diuers* ~ different from 8674; ~ *ri3t* rightly 2162, ~ *wille* as one would wish 9736; to . . . *ward* see toward(e). *inf. particle* to A13, 89, A681, 724, 1298, 1424, A1494, 2034, L133, L1590, etc., and see lese(n). Cf. forto, herto, into, þerto, vnto, whereto.

to *n.* toe 2057.

t(v)o [two] *num. adj.* two 282, 957, etc., (*bi*) ~ *and* ~ two by two A1476, 5416, [*in* ~] in two (break) L768; tvay 3308, 4788; [tweye] L1620ʳ. Cf. at(v)o.

tobent *pa. t. 3 sg.* stretched taut 3250ⁿ.

tobete *pa. t. 3 sg.* beat (severely) 7716. tobeten *pa. t. pl.* 8532.

tobrac *pa. t. 3 sg.* broke (intr.) 3475. tobroke(n) *pp.* A319, 5958, etc., (adj.) broken open A854.

tobrast *pa. t. 3 sg.* broke (intr.) 3256, 3260, 9008, etc.

tobrussed *pp.* battered 6092.

tocarf, -k- *pa. t. 3 sg.* cut through, down 5163, 8843. tokoruen, -c- *pa. t. pl.* 7766, 7802, 8005.

tocleued *pa. t. pl.* cut through, down 8118.

tocomen *pa. t. pl.* arrived 2840.

today *adv.* today 964, etc., = during the whole of today 4258.

todaschen *v.* strike apart 9038. todaiste *pa. t. 3 sg.* 9784. *See 455n.*

todrawe *v.* drag about (causing injury or death) A1082, drag to execution A469, L1481; dismember L1490. todrawe *pr. subj. sg.* drax off 8350ⁿ; *imp. sg.* dismember L1160. todrawe *pa. t. pl.* 8532; *pp.* A1364, dismembered A380ⁿ, 2012.

todrof *pa. t. 3 sg.* struck off 9780. todriuen *pa. t. pl.* drove back, pursued 9334, 9638; *pp.* 5703.

*tofolwed *pa. t. 3 sg.* (or *pl.*) pursued A782ⁿ.

tofor(e), -rn *adv.* previously A176; in front A1365, 7162ⁿ, 9233, 9244, 9270. *prep.* in front of, before 2343, 2807, 6351, 7148, 9650, etc., = in(to) the presence of A720, A1607, 2993, 3574, L564, L1086, ~ *men* ?publicly 5406ⁿ, = as a protector to A198, = in attendance on 6553; above (at table) 2258; before (time) 5324.

tofrust *pa. t. 3 sg.* burned up A1658. tofrusten *pa. t. pl.* struck down 8118. tofrust *pp.* 8108.

togert *pa. t. pl.* struck through, down 8929. *See 5013n.*

togging *n.* dragging 8804ⁿ, 8873.

togider [togedre] *adv.* together A1753, L229, etc., and see take(n), = against each other 1458, etc.

to3ain *prep.* against (person's will) A60.

tohewe *pa. t. 3 sg.* cut through, down 4801, etc. tohewe(n) *pa. t. pl.*

tohewe (*cont.*):
5835, 6951, etc.; *pp.* 9327, cut up 7353.

tohong *pp.* hanged A1364.

toil(e) *n.* heavy fighting 7989, 8079, 8973.

toiling(e) *n.* heavy fighting 6083, 8869, 9445. Cf. **totoiled**.

tokarf *pa. t. 3 sg.*, etc. see **tocarf**.

token *pr. pl.* signify A1641ⁿ. Cf. **bitokneþ**.

tokening *n.* signification 1677, L1684; sign 2797, L1315, L1680; ?remarkable event A1606ⁿ.

[tol] *n.* tool (euphemism) L1436. **tole** *pl.* (lit.) A507.

tolling *n.* dragging 5304ⁿ.

tombel *v.* fall to the ground 4818. **tombled, tum-** *pa. t. 3 sg.* 7171, 7511.

tomorwe *adv.* tomorrow 2798, (as n.) 2481.

tong(e) *n.* tongue A1500, 2380, etc., L594.

toniȝt *adv.* last night 2017, 2384, 8750; tonight 2635, 2792.

top *n.* top 5658, and see **grounde, tail(e)**.

topped *pa. t. 3 sg.*, ~ *of* tore out (hair) 7715.

torent *pp.* torn A321, etc.

torof *pa. t. 3 sg.* cut through, down 4843; broke (intr.) 6363.

toschiften *pa. t. pl.* drove apart 5010.

totar *pa. t. 3 sg.* (refl.) rent her garments 5817ⁿ; **totere** (tr.) tore (hair) 5816ʳ. **toteren** *pa. t. pl.* ?lacerated 9168ⁿ. **totore** *pp.* 9289; **[totorn]** (adj.) shattered L485.

totoiled *pa. t. pl.* trampled in the earth 8531; *pp.* 6945.

toþ *n.* tooth, *to þe* ~ to the teeth (cut open) 2108, 4006, etc. **teþ** *pl.* (*in her* ~ right in their faces) 3798.

touȝ *adj.* (see **make(n)**) arrogant 4077, hardy 9710.

toun(e) *n.* town 1104, 5660, etc.; **[town(e)]** L552, L1351, etc. **tounes** *gen.* 6321; *pl.* A148, etc., **touns** 6982. Cf. **chepyng-toun**.

tour *n.* tower, fortress 965, 4732, 6267, L1874, etc. **tours** *pl.* 6604.

toward(e) *prep.* towards 1295, 5085,

7233, etc., to A398, 7056, *beþ* ~ have gone to 4336; **to hem-ward** towards them 3450, (sim.) **to** *Inglond*-**ward** 4488; **to** *chirche*-**werd** going towards the church A1318ʳ.

tprut *interj.* (of derision) 3187.

trace *n.* way person has gone 4918.

tray(e) *n.* harm A348, etc., **[treyȝe]** L1280; vexation 2442, 9634.

trayd *pa. t. 3 sg.* gave away (person, to those seeking him) A1202.

ytrayd *pp.* grieved (tr.) A712.

[traysed] *pa. t. 3 sg.* attached with a (horse's) trace L340ⁿ.

traitour *n.* worker of treachery 92, 4864, etc. **traitours** *pl.* A360, 8738.

trauail(e) *n.* labour 2744, 6544, 6549.

tre [treo] *n.* tree 4201; the Cross 907; **trewe** timber A523, A1599.

trecherie [trich-] *n.* deceitfulness A807, L806.

trede *pa. t. pl.* trampled 3824.

tresoun [-son] *n.* treachery A93, etc., L67, treacherous action 283; **traisoun** A131, etc., revealing (to enemy) (~, ~! = the enemy knows of us!) 3813.

treso(u)r, -ore *n.* treasure (single) A598, 2818; store of valuables 2274, 4160, 8219, etc.

trespas *n.* offence 9867.

tresse *n.* braided hair 8434, etc. **tresses** *pl.* 5816.

trest *adj.* trusty A271, 2863.

treuþe, -ew- [treowþe, tr(e)owthe] *n.* good faith 90, 93, L1294, etc.; truth, *riȝt* ~ truly (tag) A445, *in* ~ 7694.

treuþed *pa. t. 3 sg.* plighted his troth to 8639.

trewe [-eo-] *adj.* loyal, faithful 2204, 4204, etc., L1752; true A1166, L1416. Cf. **vntrewe**.

trewe *n.* see **tre**.

trewes *pl.* truce 5581.

[tricherye] *n.* see **trecherie**.

Trinite *n.* feast of the Trinity 4079.

trist *n.* place of concealment 6499.

[tro] *pr. 1 sg.* believe, *y* ~ *wel* I can well believe it L188.

trom(e) *n.* company (of fighting-men) 5098, 7092. Cf. **þrome**.

tronsoun *n.* stave 7250ⁿ.

tropie *n.* noise made by throng of men 6745ⁿ.

trosse *v.* pack up 2357. trussed *pa. t. 3 sg.* 8215. trossed *pa. t. pl.* 2362.

trumpeing *n.* trumpeting 9165.

trumpes *pl.* trumpets 8802ⁿ; trumpeters 6557ⁿ.

trust *n.* trust A85.

[trusty] *adj.* fit to put trust in L468.

tvay, tvo, etc. *num. adj.* see t(v)o.

tvelue, -lf [twol(f)ue, -lf] *num. adj.* twelve 934, 3914, L144, L238, L318, etc., = twelve men A172, A177.

tventi [tw-] *num. adj.* twenty 3212, etc., L1909; (as pron.) 7076, *an ~* a score 7147ⁿ.

tvii(e)s *num. adv.* twice 3169, 4963, etc.

tumbled *pa. t. 3 sg.* see tombel.

turnay *n.* tournament 2868, 2892.

turnaien *v.* compete in tournament 2845.

turnament *n.* tournament 2886, etc. turnamens *pl.* 2623.

[turne] *pr. pl.* turn (intr.) L1264. turned *pa. t. 3 sg.* A1807, 6884, and see herre; *~ oӡain his pas* = came back A992, (sim.) 7185 (and with *pa. t. pl.*), *~ his bridel* = turned his horse 4937; changed (tr.) 2471, (refl.) 7248; [turnde] (*hit ~ hire to* it turned into . . . for her) L740. turned *pa. t. pl.* 3114, 3355, 6871, turned up (eyes, in unconsciousness) 8457; *~ hem to* = changed allegiance to A1783, *~ opon* turned on (in hostility) A1810; *pp.* 1056. Cf. terne.

þai *pron.* they 141, etc.; [þey] L24, etc.; ⟨the⟩ P330ⁿ, etc. þair *gen.* 2556, 7847; þer A1962. Cf. he *pron.³*, hes.

þan [þan(ne)] *adv.* then 79, A204, 205, L721, etc., (quasi-pron.) *after ~* = after that A1030, 6508, L748, L876, etc., *by ~* by then L960; *conj.* than A167, L818, etc., and see swiche; when 4360, and see er, til. þen(ne) L767, L1146, etc., A463ʳ, 7154ʳ.

þan *def. art. obj.* see þe.

þank(e) *n.* grace (God's) A1791ⁿ; thanks 5914, L1877. þonkes *gen.* (*our ~* willingly) 7890.

þar(e) *adv.* see þer(e).

þarf [þar] *pr. 3 sg.* (impers.) *hem no ~* they need not A16, (sim.) 4088, [*ne ~ hit*] it need not be L732; (pers.) ?cares to L730ⁿ.

þarmes *pl.* intestines 8972.

þat *demonst. adj.* that 536, etc., (*pl.*) 6644, L318, ?L1553; (as def. art.) 2564, 9796, L993, (uncertainly) 5969 (*pl.*), 6388, L1878, etc., *~ on, oþer* 1455–6, etc.; þo *pl.* 1196, etc. *pron.* 1583, etc., (*pl.*) 6430; (rel., *sg.* or *pl.*) 80, 283, A331, A976, A1186, 8576, etc., = when, etc. 2670, etc., L1413, L1622; (= demonst. + rel.) A7, A22, A784, etc., L941, = in (respect of) what A74, A427; [þan] *obj.* (see bi) L1103; þo *pl.* A331, etc., L609, þos 5041, etc. *conj.* that 163, 1296, etc., so that 65, 1269, etc.; = such that, *neuer on ~ he nas* = not one: all were . . . A339, *masouns ~ þai* = masons who were to . . . A503; = I wish that 2345, (sim.) 2690ⁿ, *~ sche* = may she . . .! A737, (sim.) 5778, 9078ⁿ; (as conjunctive particle) see after, and, bi, for *conj.*, ӡif, hou, seþþen, so, sone *adv.*, til, þo, w(h)at *adj.*, when, wher(e), wher(e)fore, whi, w(h)iche, while(s), who; *wiþ þat* at 2677. Cf. forþan, forþi.

þe [þe(o)] *adv.* the (with compar.) A10, 1238ⁿ, etc., L1002. Cf. naþeles.

þe [þe(o)] *def. art.* 361, 759, etc., *tventi . . . of wiche ~ ten* 4851, (sim.) 7768, 8212, and see while. þermite (and sim.) A795, 4149, 4472, etc., and see ich. *adj.²* þan *obj.* A1539, 7055; þe *nende* (*see 58n*) *A1502, A1897. Cf. atte *s.v.* at.

þede *n.* nation 5514, 8582.

þef *n.* evil-doer 2322, 2387, 8476. þeues *pl.* 8107, 8786; *pl. gen.* 9078.

þei [þauӡ(h), -hӡ, þouӡh] *conj.* although 1011, 1141, 1617, L1412, etc.

þei *n.* see þi.

[þey] *pron.* see þai.

(y)þen, ythe(n) [theo(n)] *v.* be successful 6996, thrive 9740, (see mot) 377, 1048, etc. the *pr. 1 sg.* (and y ~ ?asseveration) 2671ⁿ. þe *pr. subj. sg.* (iuel ~ not prosper) A737. yþei *pa. t. 3 sg.* (wele ~ throve) 2719.

þenche *v.* think (mod. uses) *368, 855*, 6534, 8682, *etc.*, þink 5606; (+inf. or (for)to and inf.) intend *A1839, 2330, 3141, L67, L102, L1292, etc.* þink *pr. 1 sg.* (me ~ (illogical) it seems to me) 5406, 6740. þenkeþ *pr. 3 sg.* 4280, me ~ 4974, etc. þenke [-yn] *pr. pl.* A1839, 8736, L1292; *imp. sg.* [þenk] 368, 4619, 8822; *pl.* 8733. þou3t [-(e)] *pa. t. 3 sg.* 855, etc., hem ~ it seemed to them (and sim.) A786, A1610, etc., L1252, it ~ hem 6719; *pl.* 6857, 8062, þou3ten (illogical hem ~) 6194. yþou3t *pp.* decided A513.

þen(ne) *adv., conj.* see þan.

þennes *adv.* from there A226, 2433, etc., L314.

þer *pron. gen.* see þai.

þer(e) *adv.* there 1528, 1531, etc., and see her(e), ((also) of time or circumstance) *A17, A103,* A252, L761, (and other cases less certain); (proclitic to v., sense weak if any) A282, 506, L11, etc.; where 229, 1200, etc. þar(e)ʳ A17, A1286, L995, etc.; þore A103ʳ; *and* ter(e) 7160, 9629, etc.; *and* tar 9339ʳ, 9781, 9799ʳ, *was* tare 3928ʳ.

þeraboute *adv.* around there 8322.

þerafter *adv.* after that 1606ⁿ, 2543, etc., L1067, þer sone after A887; in accordance therewith A963.

þerafterward *adv.* after that A1017, etc.

[þera3eyn] *adv.* see þero3ain.

þerat(e) *adv.* thereat 2644, 5732, etc.

þerbi *adv.* near there, a litel ~ = a little way away 7405.

[þerbyfore] *adv.* before that L535.

þerbiside *adv.* beside, near there 2846, L671.

þerforbi *adv.* past there A1211.

þerfore *adv.* for this reason, cause, etc.

A20, A71, 3628, 9360, L172, L1370, L1936, etc.; concerning that L1435.

þerforþ *adv.* in that direction 8743.

þerin *adv.* therein A149, L464, etc., thereon 3986. þerinne 1742ʳ, L1973.

þerof *adv.* thereof, etc. (with various senses of *of*) 874, 988, A1448, 7549, L1302, L1524, L1608, etc.; off from it 4932ⁿ, 6176.

þero3ain [-a3eyn] *adv.* in opposition 107, etc.; thereon 5612, L797; þero3en A253ʳ; þero3in = to withstand it 5152ⁿ.

þero3aines *adv.* in exchange 7076.

þeron *adv.* thereon 5258, L1309.

þertil(le) *adv.* to it (consent) A59; in addition 7454.

þerto *adv.* thereto, etc. (with various senses of *to*) 669, 1050, 3436, 4865, L974, L1710, etc., [~ gult] = guilt so as to deserve that L1120; in addition A1252, 8346, 9689, etc.

[þerþoru3] *adv.* because of it L1014.

þerwhile(s) *adv.* meanwhile 7852, etc., = at that time 6587; *conj.* while A1028; (could be treated as either) 3319, 3499, 7127, etc.

þerwiþ *adv.* with it (instrument) 599, 6772, L975, (accompaniment) L1361; moreover *7519ⁿ.

þeself *pron.* yourself (refl.) 9902; þiseluen A900; [þyseolue] (emphatic) L1717.

þester *adj.* dark (fig.) A1705.

þi *n.* thigh A851, = whole leg 7755, etc.; þei 5956. þies *pl.* 9100.

þicke *adj.* thick A1474, A1478; *adv.* thickly 9159, etc.

þider *adv.* thither A135, L815, etc.; [þydir] L79; [þidre] L665.

þiderward *adv.* thither (motion towards) 3805, 4990, going thither L1358; towards where A1340.

þilke *adj.* see ich *adj.*²

þincheing *n.* calling to mind, of ~ worthy of remembrance 7764ⁿ.

þing [th-, þ-] *n.* thing(s) 362, 542, A1061, A1298, A1567, L1536, etc., al(le) ~ everything 975, 1059, 3057, etc., [al maner ~] L1474, [al þe ~] L1504, *and* al ~ = and all such things 2820, 8911, *in al* ~ in all respects L12, etc., 3632, *of al* ~ 5363, *þurth al* ~ 6144, and see **opon**, *no selcouþe* ~ nothing strange A1448; *soþ* ~ truly 8592; (of person, etc.) 997, A1576, 5352, L861, etc., = maiden, etc. A3, A835, 6482, L1979; wealth, treasure 2033, 5082, etc. **þinges** *pl.* A809, etc. Cf. **noþing**.

þink *v.* see **þenche**.

þis *demonst. adj.* this 65, etc., (*pl.*) 623, etc.; ~ *gentil man* gentlemen A23, (sim.) 6044, etc., (vocative) 7369. *pron.* 557, etc., (*pl.*) A702, = the present time (*er* ~ previously) A274. **þisse** 8679ʳ. **þes(e)** *pl.* A585, 2617, 3961, 6755; **þise** 5595.

þiseluen etc. *pron.* see **þeself**.

þo *adj., pron. pl.* see **þat**.

þo *adv.* then 529, 727, 865, etc.; when A207, A1033, L149, etc., ~ *þat* A691; **þoo** L686.

þoly *v.* suffer (tr.) A776, etc. **þoleþ** *pr. 3 sg.* 8462. **þoled** *pa. t. 3 sg.* A907; *pl.* 5836.

þonder *n.* thunder 3799, etc.

þondred *pp.* thundered (*it hadde* ~) 9320.

[þondur-ly3t] *n.* ? = thunderstorm L602ⁿ, L1610.

þonked *pa. t. 3 sg.* thanked 2032, etc.; *pl.* 3150.

þonkeinge *n.* giving of thanks 7260.

þonkes *gen.* see **þank(e)**.

þore *adv.* see **þer(e)**.

þorsday *n.* Thursday, *Holy* ~ Ascension Day 5575.

[þoru3(h)] *prep.* see **þurth**.

þos *pron. pl.* see **þat**.

þou [þow] *pron.* you (sg.) 367, etc.; (fused forms) *wiltow* (and sim.) 222, A1049, 2485, L183, etc. **þe** *obj.* 749, etc., (refl.) A1719, etc. **þi** *gen.* 368, etc.; **þin(e)** A925, 1065, 1648, 1671, etc., **þi** *n.em* (*see 58n*) 7667. Cf. **þeself**.

[þou3h] *conj.* see **þei**.

[þou3t] *n.* (troubled) thoughts 2577, 6531, L775; = intention 2350, L1090, L1301.

þousand *num. adj.* thousand 530, etc., ~ *of* 3228, etc.; = thousand men

A421, 2143, etc.; **þousend(e)** 2146, 3687, 3747, etc.; **þousind(e)ʳ** 3743, 3962, 7863, etc.; **[þowsand]** L1900. **þousandes** *pl.* (as pron.) A506, A1809, etc.; **þousendes** 4507, 7542; **þousindes** 6673.

þral *n.* bondman (see **fre**) 6262.

þrang *n.* throng (in battle) 5771; **[þrong]** L1929. Cf. **þring**.

þrawe *n.* (short) time 2543, 6713, etc., L1399, (long) 6976; time (when something occurs) 2669; *in þat* ~ at once 7124; **þrowe** A147, L1399.

þre [þreo] *num. adj.* three 678, A1101, etc., = three men A1210, etc., ~ *and* ~ in(to) threes A603, A615, *on* ~ into three pieces 9168.

þrest *v.* force one's way 6309. **þrest** *pa. t. 3 sg.* (of weapon-stroke) 5031, thrust (with weapon-stroke) 7460. **þrest(en)** *pa. t. pl.* 3143, etc., ~ *o3an* forced back 9228; **þrust** 7749ⁿ. Cf. **þurth-þrest**.

þrete *v.* afflict 5148.

þrewe *pa. t. 3 sg.* struck (down) 3308, 6289; fell (down) 9024, 9391; ~ *armes ouer* embraced 8032; *pl.* 3292, 6303, etc.; threw at (with weapons, etc.) 5179, etc., **þrewen** threw (weapons, etc.) 4959. **yþrawe** *pp.* 9306. Cf. **ouerþrewe**.

þridde *num. adj. ord.* third 785, etc., and see **half** *adj.*, **heuen**.

þrie(s) *num. adv.* thrice 8430, 8440, 9099.

[thryft] *n.* success (see **iuel** *adj.*) L1287.

þring *n.* throng (in battle) 5066, 5984; **þreng** 6099. Cf. **þrang**.

þritten(e) *num. adj.* thirteen 6716, 8104, 9411; **þrettene** 5321.

þritti *num. adj.* thirty 2143, 6742, etc.

þriue *v.* thrive 3178.

þrome *n.* company (of fighting-men) A211, 5145, etc., group A580. Cf. **trom(e)**.

[þrong] *n.* see **þrang**.

þrong *pa. t. 3 sg.* fell violently 3304.

þrote *n.* throat 318, etc.

þrowe *n.* see **þrawe**.

þrust *pa. t. pl.* see **þrest**.

þurth (*see 249n*) **[þoru3(h)]** *adv.* through 4933, 5019, etc.; *prep.* 318, 1297, 9247, etc., ~ *and* ~ right

þurth (*cont.*):
through 7450; (of causation) 757,
A765, 1043, 1057, 6225, 8560,
L240, L588, etc.; in accordance
with 3395, etc., L1837, ~ *riȝt
decente* by legitimate inheritance
7642, ~ *iniquite* unjustly 9857, [~
skyl] = by reasoned argument L1121,
and see **nortour(e)**, **þing**. Cf.
þerþoruȝ, **wher(e)þurth**.
þurthout(e) *adv.* right through A455,
etc.; everywhere 2199. *prep.* right
through 3301, 7687, etc., **þurth**
armes out 4831.
þurth-þrest *pp.* (adj.) thrust through
7469ⁿ.
þus *adv.* thus A341, A510, L31, etc.;
as . . . as this 4637, 6804, 7027, etc.

valay(e) [-ay, -eye] valley 1527,
A1640, 1649, etc.
valour *n.* worth, *of* ~ 3265, 3402,
3534ⁿ, 4179, 6353, etc.
vauasour *n.* minor feudal tenant
8558ⁿ, 8661.vauasours *pl.gen.*4761.
[vche] *adj.* see ich *adj.*¹
[vchon] *pron.* see ichon.
veir(es) *adv.* truly (tag) 7640, 9139,
etc.; vair(s) 6568, 8761.
veniaunce *n.* vengeance 7140, L597.
venisoun *n.* meat of noble game 3119,
7415. venisouns ?*pl.* 4104ʳ.
ver(r)ament *adv.* truly (often tag)
589, 705, 6840, etc.; [verrayment]
L56.
verray *adj.* true L1315; *adv.* truly
(tag) 9005.
vert(o)uous *adj.* (postposited) mighty
4310, 5486, etc.
vertu *n.* power, might A1568, 4016,
4222, 7074, etc.
vfer *adv.* above 6700ⁿ.
victorie *n.* victory 3370.
vigour *n.* might (in arms) 3926, 5830,
etc.; vigour (of words) L93.
vigrous *adj.* mighty (in arms) 6572,
9060.
viis *n.* face A744, etc.
vila(i)nie [-en] *n.* shaming/evil
deed(s), etc. 2349, 2355, 3502,
4951, 8462, *in* [*wiþ*] ~ shamefully
910; vilaine 4441ʳ.
vila(i)nliche *adv.* with shameful ill-

treatment 5794, 9289.
vile *adj.* vile 5804, etc.; [vyl] shameful L272.
violet *n.* violet 3061.
virgine *adj.* chaste 8913.
[vyroun] *n.* circling course L1618.
[visage] *n.* face L824.
visite *v.* pay pastoral visit to A702,
A796, A1172.
vmage *n.* see omage.
vnarmed *pp.* (adj.) unarmed 6947.
[vnbynde] *imp. sg.* release (from
bonds) L1487. vnbounde *pa. t. pl.*
5905.
vnblisced [-essed] *pp.* (adj.) unbles-
sed with sign of cross 839.
vnbliþe *adj.* unhappy 8382.
vnder [-ur] *prep.* under 1451, etc.,
al ~ *sonne* = all on earth A1031, *al*
~ *Heuen-king* A1384, (sim.) 2217,
7601; (of subordination, etc.) A154,
2034, 3414, 5588, etc.; behind
(shield) 9006, ~ *scheld* = carrying
one's shield 3096, 3924, etc., ~
hauberioun = in armour 5442; close
beside 5833, 7396, 7700ⁿ, etc.; ~
hem alle (and sim.) all taken/acting
together A946, A1473, 5067. Cf.
hervnder.
vnderfong *pr. 1 sg.*, etc. see **vndurfonge**.
vndernam *pa. t. 3 sg.* perceived 6530.
[vndurnomen] *pp.* learned L1886.
vnderstond(e) [vndur-] *v.* know
(about), learn of 297, 627, 3339,
L10, etc., ~ *of* 3521, *don . . . to*
~ = inform 5512; realize, assume
A1209, A1567, 6540, 7917, L446,
etc.; understand (language) A21,
(meaning) 4167, L1799, hear (with
understanding) A1095, 2351, 6535;
give heed to A897, L1715, ~ *to*
A512, L1933. vnderstond(e)
[vndur-] *pr. 1 sg.* 5545, 7917, *ich*
~ I know on good authority (tag)
A1529, 6166, L631, etc.; *pl.* A627,
A1187; *subj. sg.* A21, L1933; *imp.
sg.* L1715; *imp. pl.* A512. vnder-
stode [vndurstod] *pa. t. 3 sg.* 297,
etc., ~ *þe douke ywent* learned that the
duke was gone 2395; *pl.* A169, etc.
⟨vndertooke⟩ *pa. t. 3 sg.* took (in
marriage) P414.

vndren *n.* 9 a.m. 7412, 7467.

[vndudest] *pa. t. 2 sg.* opened (tr.) L1218. **vndede** *pa. t. 3 sg.* 8509, 8512; *pl.* unfurled A1767. **vndon** *pp.* (*vp* ~ opened) 5731.

[vndurfonge] *v.* receive (judgement) L753. **vnderfong** *pr. 1 sg.* accept (gift) 2289. **vnderfenge** *pa. t. 3 sg.* received (person) 6957. **vnderfong** *pp.* A902.

vneuen *adj.* unequal (battle) 5832, 9756.

vnhele *v.* reveal 2689.

vnhende *adj.* ignoble 5109.

vnknett *pa. t. 3 sg.* untied 8480.

vnnet *adj.* foolish A1254.

vnneþ(e) [**-es**] *adv.* barely A395, 584, 2299, 2697, 4437, 6706, 8980, etc., (modifying negated v.) 2838, 5888.

vnplie *v.* unfurl 5063.

vnrede [**vnruyde**] *adj.* massive A1666, 8482, L1580; violent 9040; **vnride** large A886.

vnriȝt *adj.* unjust A1616.

vnriȝt *n.* unrighteous conduct A1902, 2326, 2360, L1811, *wiþ* ~ unright-(ful)ly 3626, 4615, 8735.

vnsely *adj.* accursed 5302, etc.

***vnspand** *pa. t. 3 sg.* released 8760ⁿ.

[*vntil] *prep.* until L510.

vnto *prep.* to A1594, A1734, 5981, 6030; for 2818.

vntrewe [**-eo-**] *adj.* unfaithful 1352.

vnwrast *adj.* wicked 8432; **vnwrest** = wicked man 6964.

voice *n.* voice 4853; [**voys**] ? = words of prayer L797.

volunte *n.* will A681.

vp *adv.* up (mod. uses) A115, A552, A975, A1731, 2546, 6661, L656, L822, L1018, L1036, etc., = mounted 9283, ~ *to* onto (horse) 9026, 9292, and see **clepe, doun**; towards head of table 3116; open A1130, A1785, 5731; ashore 2074, 6773, etc.; ~ ⁺*com* arrive 8288; also see **drawe(n), loden**.

vp *prep.* upon *8943ⁿ, = onto (horse) 2891, ⁺*com* ~ come upon (event/ person upon person) 2066, 2080, 6680; to meet A771, (in hostility) 3755; in (death and life) 3034, ~ *a chaunce* = by chance 9014; **op** A544.

vplond *adv.* in rural areas A698.

vplond *n.* rural areas 7015, 7311.

vplondis *adj.,* ~ *men* countrymen 5077, etc.

vpon *prep.* see **opon**.

vpriȝt *adv.* erect (sitting) 5156, 6365, ~ ⁺*stonde aswouȝ* = be unconscious as one stands 8444, (sim., sitting) 8469, 9011; at full length (falling) 8449ⁿ, 9098.

vpriseing *n.* rising (sun) 3865, (from ground) 9906.

[vpward] *adv.* upwards L995.

vrn *pa. t. pl.* see **erne**.

vs(s)age *n.* established practice 727, 3132, 3580.

vse *pr. pl.* use A23.

vterliche *adv.* frankly 8615.

vtrage [**out-**] *n.* sinful conduct 728; anger L823.

vus *pron. obj.* you (pl.) (see **di**) 5913, 6546.

(**wade** *v.*) see **woden** *pa. t. pl.*

way *n.* way (= route one follows) 1339, A1980, etc., (forced through enemy) 5306, 9095, etc.; (= track, etc.) 3648; (*bi*) *ich* ~ in every direction 7085, 7294, (sim.) *A615*; (= means) 2501; **weiȝe** 6420ʳ; [**wey(ȝ)e**] L1354, L1404. **way(e)s** *pl.* (= tracks, etc.) 4321, 4367, etc.; distance 6897ⁿ, **weys** (see **fer** *adj.*¹) 6882ⁿ; way A615, 7404, 7413. Cf. **mile-way**.

waile *v.* cry in lamentation 2563. *See 739n.*

wailing *n.* lamentation A739, 4257, 7773.

waines *pl.* waggons 4712, etc.

wait(e) *v.* contrive (injury, etc.) against (*see 1630n*) A1624, 3624, etc. **waiten** *pr. pl.* 4325. **waited** *pa. t. 3 sg.* 4726.

wal(le) *n.* wall 5818, 5828, etc., L1968. **walles** *pl.* A1474ⁿ, etc.

wald *pa. t. 1, 3 sg.*, etc. see **wil**.

walewo, wo- [**weylawo, -way**] *interj.* alas 142, A742, L668; **waile-way, wo-** 4262, 6801. Cf. **away**.

walled *pp.* walled (selves in) 8742, 8745.

wane *n.* lack 3122.

wanhope *n.* despair 793.

wante *pa. t. 3 sg.* see wende(n).

war *adj.* prudent 8696, L13.

war *adv.* see wher(e).

waraunt [-ant] *n.* authoritative witness/evidence 2658, 5228; defence L799, defensive strength 4210.

ward [-e] *n.* guardianship 4291, 4480, 8907, custody 955; ward of a city (= men from this) 5096.

ware *v.* see wer(e), were.

warfore *adv.* see wher(e)fore.

warld *n.* world A65, 3554, etc.; world 95, etc. warldes *gen.* worldly A14, A490; [worldes] (= intensive), ~ schame L1056.

[warmed] *pa. t. 3 sg.* warmed L1023.

[warne] *v.* warn L1698. warned *pa. t. 3 sg.* 2019.

warnise *v.* stock up, garrison 6605. warnisen *pr. pl.* 4338. ywarnist *pp.* 4732.

was *pron. gen.* see who.

(wasche *v.*) see wesche *pa. t. 3 sg.*

w(h)at *adj.* what (mod. uses) A693, 1102, 4756, 7331, L583, L1026, etc., [~ . . . þat] L586, ~ . . . so whatever 4809; *pron.* 183, 368, A1139, etc.; whom *obj.* which (rel.) A1872. *conj.* until 4646, 7704, 8081, etc., and see til. *adv.*, ~ *for* . . . ~ *for* (and sim.) between (of alternative forces efficacious 'between them') A255, A1791[n], 2579, 6866, 8873, 8874; how (~ *helpeþ it make* = what's the use of making . . . ?) 3055, (sim.) 4025, 4270.

water *n.* water A643, 1159, L2, etc.; = stream 1450, etc. [watres] *gen.* L1569.

wawe *v.* move 2637.

[wax(en)] *pa. t. 3 sg., pp.* see wexeþ.

we *pron.* we 213, etc.; whe A1378. ous [ows] *obj.* 1204, etc., (refl.) 4271, etc.; vs L181, etc., A273; [ous] L140. our [-e] *gen.* 206, etc., = British A162, 4769, etc., = 'our' men, army A460, 5069, 7532, etc.

wedde *v.* marry A483, 756. wedded *pa. t. 3 sg.* 6482.

wed(de)loc *n.* wedlock A485, A729.

wede *n.* armour 6652.

weder *n.* weather 1520.

wei(ȝ)e *n.* see way.

[weylaway, -wo] *interj.* see walewo.

weys *pl.* see way.

wel(e) *adv.* well (mod. uses) A174, 216, 323, 1578, 2718, 7033, 7232, L992, L1698; (other intensive uses, modifying v.) 2338, 2577, 2815, L845, L1440, L1441; in good order 2038, 4683, wel wele 5079; ~ comeþ welcome! A1230[n]; *him is nouȝt* ~ he is not well 2382, *Wawain was* ~ things were well for W. 8467 (and sim. with *comp.*); (intensive, modifying adj. or adv.) very, etc. A110, A328, A982, L151, L1370, etc., fully A554, L1621, etc. bet(t)[r] comp. A10, 1238, 4828, 6940, etc.; better 2057, 3922, 6743, etc.; [betre] (*þe weore* ~ you would do better to) L1208, (sim.) L1374, L1376. best *sup.* A272, 761, etc., L1763.

welcome [-com] *adj.* (predicative) welcome 5548, 7609, L1299; *interj.* A1831.

welcomed *pa. t. 3 sg.* welcomed A424, etc.; *pl.* A1788, etc. welcome *pp.* 3546[n], 8548.

welcoming(e) *n.* welcoming 2248, 7259, 7707.

weld [-e] *v.* have at one's (sexual) will 2492; [armes ~] bear arms L220. welt *pr. 3 sg.* rules (*He þat* ~ *al* = God) 5550.

wele [weole] *n.* prosperity A490, 2164, = salvation 674; valuables 7298.

welken *n.* (uppermost) celestial sphere (astrol.) 3568; [weolkyn, -ene] L533, L1651. *See* 3568n.

[welles] *pl.* wells L1566.

welp *n.* whelp (abus.) A415. welpe *pl.* 4516; welpes 8732.

wel-streme *n.* spring 6058.

wenche *n.* girl A830, A894.

wen(e) *pr. 1 sg.* (+ clause, also other constructs. with other forms) believe, suppose A1075, (poet's asseveration) 8007, 8300, *as ich* ~ (and sim.) as I believe (tag) 1207, 3710, 4211, 6674, etc., and see forsoþe. wenes [-yþ] *pr. 3 sg.* (+*to* and inf., also inf. with other forms) expects 1307, L180. wene

pr. pl. 4320. **wend(e)** *pa. t. 1, 3 sg.*
A1055, A1816, 2672, etc., L855,
L1128. **wende(n)** *pa. t. pl.* A611,
1579, L627, etc.
wende(n) *v.* go (away) 65, A345,
A604, 2038, L303, L321, etc.,
(refl.) *A288, 7341, L91, etc.,* = pass
away A1898; turn (back) *3227,* (to,
against, of allegiance) *A1817, 1835,*
(of attention) *5348.* **wende** *pr. pl.*
4669, etc. **[wend]** *pr. subj. sg.*
L1449. **wende** *imp. sg.* 6372.
wendeþ **[-ip]** *imp. pl.* A1365,
A1949, L173. **went** **[-(e)]** *pa. t. 3
sg.* 714, A818, L104, etc., ~ *oʒain
his pas* turned back 3488; **wante**
4364ʳⁿ. **went(en)** *pa. t. pl.* 227,
1438, L1266, etc., *her way* ~ took
their way A1316, ~ *her pas* 2806;
wente 5609ʳ; **[wenton]** L578;
[wentyn] L1329. **(y)went** *pp.*
A899, A1378, etc., gone through
(tr.) L1467.
wene *n.* supposition, *wiþouten* ~
certainly (tag) L1071, etc., 9808.
[weore] *v.* wear (shoes) L1343.
wepe **[weope]** *v.* weep 1323, etc.
wepe *pa. t. 3 sg.* A780, etc.; **[weop]**
L668; **[wepte]** L836. **wepe(n)** *pa.
t. pl.* 2755, 3980, etc. Cf. **biwepe.**
wepeing *n.* weeping A1324, 4262,
etc. **wepeinges** *pl.* A768.
[wepne] *pl.* weapons L125.
wer(e, -re) *n.* war 2213, 6569, 7647,
etc.; **[weorre]** L13. **werres** *pl.*
7615.
werche *v.* see **wirche(n).**
wer(e, -re) **[weorre]** *v.* wage war,
fight (not always distinguishable
from next) 112, A429ⁿ, 4106, 9907,
etc., drive by warfare *L164; **ware**
A1685ʳ. **werreþ** *pr. 3 sg.* 3618, is
making war on 4309. **werred** *pp.*
3493, made war on 3625. Cf.
awerreþ.
were **[weore]** *v.* defend A243, L126,
etc., (refl.) A518, etc.; **ware** A13ʳ.
were *pr. pl.* cover 9249ⁿ. **wer(e)d**
pr. p. 7927. **wer(e)d** *pa. t. 1, 3 sg.*
A199, 3886, etc.; *pl.* 5937, 7097, etc.
were *adv., conj.* see **wher(e).**
weri *adj.* exhausted 9889.
werk *n.* labour, product of labour

A547, A552, (sense passing into)
castle 536, 562, 599, etc.; = deed(s)
L743, L1200; *priue* ~ secret art
3569, (sim.) *schandliche* ~ 4276ⁿ.
werkes *pl.* = deeds 811, L789,
holy ~ A52.
werk(e)men *pl.* workmen 529, 1464,
1469. **werkmennes** *pl. gen.* A540.
[werne] *v.* refuse (obj. person) L1430.
wern(e) *pr. subj. sg.* (obj. person
and thing) 2947, 2955 (*1 sg.*).
werning *n.* refusing 5522.
wers *adv. comp.* see **iuel.**
wesche *pa. t. 3 sg.* washed (tr.) 2583,
etc. **weschen** *pa. t. pl.* 6471, 6507,
(intr.) 6562.
west *n.* the west 3186, 8742. Cf.
souþe-west.
wete *adj.* (as n.) wet weather (see **for**
prep.) 3537.
weued *pa. t. 3 sg.* struck (head off)
9708; *pp.* 5698, 6873.
wexeþ *pr. 3 sg.,* ~ *along* becomes
longer (day) A1710; *pl.* become
A263. **wex** **[wax]** *pa. t. 3 sg.*
became 298, A1029, etc., developed
(storm) L1606. **wexen** *pa. t. pl.*
increased in numbers A413.
[waxen] *pp.* grown up L1739.
whal *n.* whale A1495.
wham *pron. obj.,* etc. see **who.**
what *adj.,* etc. see **w(h)at.**
whe *pron.* see **we.**
when *adv.* when A120, 1459, etc., =
since (consequence) L906, *L1107;*
[whan] L37, etc., ~ *þat* L1573;
[whenne] L1206.
whennes *adv.* whence 5082;
[whenne] L1131.
wher(e) *adv.* where A330, 1688, 2213,
2381, L1637, etc., ~ *þat* A1977,
9248, [~ *he beo*] wherever he may
be L552; **were** 2252, ~ *so* wherever
2001; **whar(e), war** 2255, 4198,
6349, etc.
[wherby] *adv., heo fonde* ~ she found
that by means of which . . . L855.
whereof *adv.* for which reason 4514,
wharof to which (witness) 3025;
wereof of what (fear) 7488.
whereto *adv.* for what purpose? 6522.
wher(e)fore *adv.* why 4299, 4758,
L756, [~ *þat*] L1338; for which

wher(e)fore (*cont.*):
reason 7979, L1401; whar(e)fore,
war- A1557, etc., *whi and* ~ 4585,
9193.

wher(e)þurth *adv.* for which cause,
by which means A249, A409,
3653, etc.; whar(e)þurth A635,
A1065, etc.

[wheþen] *adv.* whence? L1026.

wheþer [-ir] *conj.* whether 9012,
L1001; ⟨whether⟩ *pron.* which (of
two) P2284 (see euer), P2287.

whi *adv.* why 196, 574, 1322, etc., ~
þat A578, L146, L1679.

w(h)iche [wych] *adj.* which (rel.)
293, 4923, 8809, etc.; what (in
various senses) A1415, A1567,
7655, 8424,*wich 6509. *pron.* which
2100, 6155; (rel.) A634, A1473,
4869, 5627, etc., who(m) A1380,
A1637ⁿ, 3691, 4772, ~ þat A772. Cf.
swiche.

whider *adv.* whither 4132, 7650, to
the place to which 7988.

whiderward(es) *adv.* whither A1544,
3802, 6500, 7219.

while *n.* space of time 4846, (adverbial) 1529, 4133, 5724, 5859, 7129;
time (when something occurs)
L765, (adverbial) L745. [whiles]
gen., þeo ~ while (conj.) L1077, (*or
meanwhile*) L730ⁿ.

while(s) [-l(es)] *adv.* formerly A32;
conj. while A211, 224, etc., ~ þat
1004. Cf. þerwhile(s).

whilom *adv.* formerly A659.

white *n.* white colour 8019.

white [-t(e)] *adj.* white 745, 1526,
etc. [whytes] *gen.* = white dragon's
L1750.

who *pron.* who 1206, 4160, 7241,
L1027, etc.; whoever (*sg.* or *pl.*)
2822, ~ þat 4022, ~ so A233,
2087, etc.; anyone (*als*~ *seyt* as one
may say) 6817; wo 5524. whom
obj. whom 6928, (rel.) A617, 8893,
etc., = him whom 2644, 4799;
wham 6851; wom (~ *euer þat*
whomever) 4811; who (~ *so euer*
whomever) 4817. w(h)os *gen.* 4757,
6928, (rel.) A1597, etc.; w(h)as
A1187, A1577, 2310.

whom *pron. obj.* see also w(h)at.

wich(e) *adj., pron.* see w(h)iche.

wiche *n.* witch 4438, 4463.

wichecraft *n.* witchcraft 4441.

wich(e)ing *n.* wizardry 3154, witchcraft 4459.

wicke *adj.* wicked A1667, etc.

wicked *adj.* wicked A268, L1135;
[wikkyd] L861. *See 268n.*

wide *adj.* wide A1499; *adv.* wide
(open) 1785, L1218, L1585, L1890;
widely, (from) far and wide 1078,
2840, 6609, L74, etc., and see
brod(e), fer *adv.*, side *adv.*

wiȝt *n.* being 918, (of unborn child)
2636, þe Foule ~ = the Devil A855,
[*no* ~] nobody L969; bit, *a litel* ~
a little (adverbial) 2854, 7731.

wiȝt *adj.* doughty A81, 2921, etc.,
L1920; [wyȝht] L13. wiȝtest *sup.*
5360.

wiȝtlich(e) *adv.* doughtily 3930,
6899, etc.

wiȝtling *pl.* doughty men 8093;
wiȝtlinges 8116.

wiȝtschip(pe) *n.* knightly quality
5468ⁿ, knighthood 7653.

wiif [wif] *n.* wife 689, etc., woman
A737, etc. (many instances uncertain); wif A1005, 6408, 9195; wiue
1662ʳ, 2708ʳ, *to* ~ 676, etc. wiif *gen.*
2715; wiues 2944. wiues *pl.* 934,
etc.

wiis *adj.* see wise.

wil [wol] *pr. 1 sg.* (auxil. of volition
or intention) 1625, etc. (and so in all
other forms); wish (+ clause, see
wite(n)) A626, etc.; [wil] L965ʳ;
*ich*il(le) A20, A963, etc., (inf. of
'motion' understood) A1707; nil
(neg.) A19, etc. wilt [wolt] *pr. 2
sg.* 1623, etc., wish L1119; wilt*ow*
[wo-] 2481, 2487, do you wish 222.

wil(le) [wol] *pr. 3 sg.* A1388,
A1842, 7617, etc., L1506, (of
futurity) 1159, etc. (and so in other
2 and 3 pers. forms), (inf. of motion
understood) A1152 (and so with
other forms), (of habitual action)
A1896; demands A904; nil (neg.)
9214. wil(le, -len) [wol(en)] *pr.
pl.* A15, 528, 3412, 3425, 5530,
L1122, etc.; wish A1266; [wolon]
L4, L581; nil(len) (neg.) A657,

4750, etc. **wold** [-(e)] *pa. t. 1, 3 sg.*
346, A600, 8392, L99, L146, L196,
etc., (as pr.) 4153; wished L988, (as
pr.) L1033; wald A769, 6575, 9059[n],
etc.; **nold** (neg.) A127, 3624, etc.
wost *pa. t. 2 sg.* (as pr.) 2345;
wostow (as pr.) 7650, 8607, 8628,
(+ obj. and also inf.) do you want
7656; **waldest**ow (as pr.) 7332;
noldestow(neg., as pr.) A897.**wold-
(en)** [-d(e), -dyn] *pa. t. pl.* 670,
1741, L1905, etc.; proceeded to
5825[n]; wished L142, L1647, wan-
ted(+obj.) L230; wald A402, 5148,
etc., ~ *ariue* landed (over a period)
2129[n]; **nold** (neg.) 5322, 8394, etc.
wil(le) *n.* will 183, 879, 1465, 2966,
etc., [*al heore* ~] as much as they
wanted to L1062, and see **to** prep.,
= eagerness A1965, *wiþ gode* ~
eagerly 6020, 6690, *wiþ* ~ *fin(s)*
8006, 9813, *wiþ* ~ *fre* 9789, [*wiþ* ~]
L1937. **willes** *gen.* (*ȝour* ~ in
accordance with your will) A1263.
wild(e) *adj.* wild (animals) A1082,
7000, (words) L905, and see **fer(e)**,
frenzied A1046, A1944, 6356;
desolate 8324.
wildernisse, -nesse *n.* wilderness
3444, 8324.
wiman [**womman, -on**] *n.* woman
676, 1035, etc.; **woman** A733, etc.
win(e) *n.* wine 2316, 6943, etc.
win(ne, -nen) *v.* conquer, capture
A1766, 2502, 8736, 9846, etc.,
L128; gain (tr.) 1741, 4350, etc.,
and see **lese(n)**. **wan** *pa. t. 3 sg.*
3368, 6810; = overcame and made
his liegeman 2171, ~ *vnder his hond*
A154, (sim.) 3414 (and sim. with
pp.). **wonnen** *pa. t. pl.* A1792.
wonne(n) *pp.* 2186, 2406, 3237,
9661; **ywonne** 7537.
winde *n.* wind 3797, 4844, etc.,
[**wynd**] air L2; breath 8456, and
see **take(n)**; windpipe A1398,
5580. Cf. **norþþen-winde**.
winde *v.* (of forcible movement) =
charge 5734, 7956, = fall 6320.
wond *pa. t. 3 sg.* = fell 9388.
wounde *pa. t. pl.* = jumped 9152.
windowe [-**ow**] *n.* window 973, 1130.
[**wyndowes**] *pl.* L795.

wining *n.* booty 8393, 8653; <win-
inge> profit P2091[n].
winking *n.* winking 2465.
winter *n.* winter 4199. **winter** *pl.* =
years (age, etc.) A1189, etc., L535,
L1471.
wiped *pa. t. 3 sg.* wiped 8499.
wirche(n) [**worche**] *v.* do A52, A657,
A1116, L89, = act A963, *L337*,
etc.; work in (material) L454;
werche build A1464. **wirche** *pr.
subj. sg.* 2098. **wircheþ** *imp. pl.*
2790. **wrouȝt** [-e] *pa. t. 1, 3 sg.*
A1188, 2167, L895, L898; *pl.*
built A555, **wrouȝten** exerted
themselves 8875. **(y)wrouȝt** *pp.*
L1200, etc., 1412; built, made
L944, L1437, etc., 514, 1446, 4841.
ywis *adv.* certainly (usually tag) 558,
A703, L201, etc.
ywis *n.* certainty, *mid* ~ certainly
9196.
wische *v.* wish 8722.
[**wisdam**] *n.* wisdom L1321, L1674.
[**wisdoms**] *pl.* L7.
wise [**wys(e)**] *adj.* wise, learned A50,
1090, A1382, L16, *L517, etc., þe*
~ = wise men 7593; skilled (in war)
?2203[n], 3244, etc.; **wiis**[r] 4587,
5484. **wiser** *comp.* A586. **wisest** *sup.*
A173, A580.
wise *n.* manner 6477, *þis* ~ in this
manner 2786; *in al* ~ = without
fail A776, 3004, 5528, L785, *o* [*in*]
non ~ = certainly not 1026, 5540.
<**wishe**> *v.* teach P1904, P1943.
ywissed [**wi**-] *pp.* 840.
wit(t) *n.* sagacity A1597; wits 3215,
3217, *in her* ~ in their mind (they
realized . . .) A169, (sim.) A513,
A1016, and [incl. L1882, L1970]
see **of, out.**
wite *v.*[1] protect self 3045.
wite *v.*[2], ~ *it* blame it on . . . 9200,
9206. **wite** *pl. pr.* A214. Cf. **atwot.**
wite(n) *v.* know (inf. often = find out,
learn) A11, 619, 867, 2727, 3521,
etc.; know of *2987, etc.* **wot** *pr. 1,
3 sg.* A921, A1041, etc., L1197,
L1278, and see **forsoþe, God,**
ichot 6171; **not** (neg.) 2023, 2668,
8613. [**wost**] *pr. 2 sg.* L1100,
L1143, **wost**ow A1245; **nost** (neg.)

wite(n) (*cont.*):
  A1206. **wite** *pr. pl.* (*y wil* (*þat*) *ʒe*
  ~ I want you to know) A627, 2815,
  3021, etc.; **witeþ** know that (person)
  is . . . A271, 9774ⁿ. **wist** [-(e)] *pa.*
  t. 1, 3 sg. A289, 6571, L921, L992,
  etc.; **nist** (neg.) A856, etc. **wist(en)**
  [-te] *pa. t. pl.* 3181, 3214, L257,
  etc., knew to be 2198; **nist(en)**
  (neg.) A1688, A1960, etc. **wist** *pp.*
  7602, L1436.
[witerly] *adv.* assuredly L534, etc.
witles *adj.* foolish A1944.
witnesseing *n.* testimony A1269.
wittnes *n.*, ⁺*bere* ~ bear witness A1285,
  3025; **witnesse, -nisse** 3027, 5537.
[wittnessiþ] *pr. 3 sg.* testifies to L32.
[witnesse] *pr. pl.* L590.
wiþ *prep.* with (mod. uses) A201, 230,
  A238, 748, 1424, 1538, 1572, 1580,
  1644, A1707, A1768, 3540, 7850,
  L595, L1578, etc., ~ *þis word he tok*
  with these words, he gave . . . 4157,
  (sim.) [~ *þis*] L202, ~ *þe, his liif*
  with his life 7432, 8724, etc., and
  see **child(e)**; ~ *lawe* lawfully 2989,
  L1489, ~ *tresoun* treacherously
  A93, A366, L67, (sim.) A731, 1648,
  2116, 2125, L245, L1691, etc., and
  see **best** s.v. **gode, iuel** *adj.*,
  (vn)riʒt *n.*, **wil(le)**; by (the action
  of) 2251, 8366, etc., L1133, ~ *þe*
  winde = in the wind (flutter) 7847,
  and see **strengþe**, with the help of
  4171, ~ *to liue* to live on 6576; in
  (fault in person) 2724, upon (God's
  power on . . .) 4878, and see **finde(n)**;
  towards 1935ⁿ; amid 7945; ~ *þat*
  (*at*) on condition that A428, 2677,
  etc., L1034. Cf. **þerwiþ**.
[wiþal] *adv.* moreover L1580.
wiþbraid *pa. t. 3 sg.* held back (intr.)
  8449.
wiþdrawe *v.* withdraw (milit., tr.)
  4052, (refl.) 5061. **wiþdrouʒ** *pa. t.*
  3 sg. 5265, *his hors* ~ reined in his
  horse A1213, *his bridel* ~ A1319; *pl.*
  7479, 8295, **wiþdrowe** 4028.
wiþin(ne) *adv.* inside A1457, L1969;
  prep. 7280, *wele* ~ *niʒt* fully night
  A1425, and see **elde**.
wiþouten [-oute(n), -owte(n)] *prep.*
  without 97, 595, 754, 3986, L662,

etc.; except for 3554, etc., besides
3762, etc.; outside A1800, 4446ⁿ,
etc.; **[wiþoutyn, -owt-]** L61, L199,
L537.
wiþradden *pa. t. pl.* opposed 3136.
wiþsat *pa. t. 3 sg.* failed (voice) 8457;
  withstood (in saddle, tr.) 9055. Cf.
  asit.
wiþstette *pa. t. pl.* made a counter-
  charge 7747.
wiþstond *v.* resist A462, 4752, 4880;
  stop (intr.) A644. **wiþstonde** *imp.*
  sg. stop! 8998. **wiþstode** *pa. t. 3 sg.*
  6221; stopped (tr.) 9815; *pl.* made
  a pause 6033; ~ *oʒain* resisted (tr.)
  3225, **wiþstonden** 3163.
wiþstonding *n.* resisting 8803, 8967.
wiþþerhoked *adj.* barbed 5666.
wiþþerwin(e), -nne *n.* enemy 2410,
  5302, 9109, etc. **wiþþerwins** *pl.*
  6908.
wiue *n.* see **wiif**.
wo *adv.* [*adj.*], ~ *was him* he was
  distressed 4002, 7580, [*heo was* ~]
  L860, (sim.) 785, 2448, 6211, 8534,
  etc., L1149, L1225; ~ *worþ me* woe
  on me! 5334, [*schal worþ* ~] shall be
  afflicted L624ⁿ. *n.* distress A1690,
  2458, etc., harm A1170, 1672, 2098,
  etc., L89 [woo], *of* ~ = deadly 3471,
  [*wiþ* ~] grievously L1031.
wo(m) *pron.* see **who**.
wode [wod(e)] *adj.* frenzied 298,
  9390, raging (lion) 1856, etc.; [wood]
  L293, L836.
wode *n.* wood (trees) 1713, etc.,
  (material) A515.
wodeliche *adv.* in a frenzied manner
  9426.
woden *pa. t. pl.* waded 9106.
wodenesse *n.* frenzy 8433.
[wol] *pr. 1, 3 sg.*, etc. see **wil**.
wolewo *interj.* see **walewo**.
wolf *n.* wolf 4047. **wolues** *pl.* 9328.
wom(m)an etc. *n.* see **wiman**.
wombe *n.* belly A455, etc., = womb
  884, etc.
won *n.* custom 2231.
won *v.* dwell 8589. **[wonyþ]** *pr. 3 sg.*
  L1125. **[wonen]** *pl. pr.* L609;
  woneþ are to be found 3062.
  woned [-e] *pa. t. 3 sg.* dwelt 701,
  etc.; *pl.* 696.

wonded *pp.* (+ clause) neglected 3537.

wonder [-ur] *adj.* astonishing L320, etc., 2302, 9186; *adv.* exceedingly L1445.

wonder [-ur] *n.* astonishment 546, and see haue(n); astonishing thing A1244, L1414, *it was no* ~ it was not surprising A299, (sim.) 7247, L1412; terrible happening 5739, *of* ~ terrible 6699, 7790.

wonderliche *adv.* exceedingly 7610.

wondred, -erd *pa. t. pl.* were astonished 7963, 8230, 9245. wondred *pp.* A1405, A1467.

ywone *adj.* accustomed A176.

[worche] *v.* see wirche(n).

word(e) *n.* word 232, 7599, L947, etc., [*a* ~ *or two*] L940, and see maner(e), neuer; (short) speech 6342, 8825, etc., *at o(n)* ~ in a word 2287, 4213, *at þe first* ~ in immediate reply 2912; news L70, L87, *sende* ~ send word 3418. wordes *pl.* 1430, etc.

world *n.* see warld.

wors(e) *adj., adv. comp.* see iuel.

worþ *adj.* distinguished 3742; (quasi-prep.) worth 2270, etc.

worþ *n.* value 4152; distinction 6758.

worþ [-þe, -the] *v.* (auxil.) be (in the future) A1843, L542, L624ⁿ. worþ *pr. 1 sg.* shall be A1180, 9124 (and sim. in all indic. forms); *2 sg.* 2532; *3 sg.* A1364, 2086, 9078ⁿ, 9742, etc.; ~ *ydo* = comes to pass A1251; ~ *ʒou* you will get, have A225, 3428, 3436, (sim.) A1225, 4290, etc., (impers.) A1237ⁿ, and see wo; *pl.* 4228, etc.; *imp. sg.* (~ *heron* = mount on this!) 5053. worþ *pa. t. 3 sg.* 9246, 9742.

worþi *adj.* worthy A160.

worþschip(e) *n.* honour 2347; personal merit 8619.

worþschipliche *adv.* honourably 9197.

wos *pron. gen.* see who.

wost(ow) *pa. t. 2 sg.* see wil.

wot *pr. 1, 3 sg.*, etc. see wite(n).

wouʒ [-ʒh] *n.* wrong 4806; [*wiþowte* ~] truly L1417.

wounde *n.* wound 6294. woundes *pl.*

3358, etc.; woundeʳ 7870, 7941, 9837, (and many number uncertain).

wounded *pa. t. 3 sg.* wounded 4948; *pl.* 4962, 9089; *pp.* 7274, etc., ywounded 8358.

wowen *v.* solicit to love A772.

wray *v.* reveal (secret) 3656. [wryed] *pp.* (*beo* ~ have secret revealed) L1440. Cf. biwray.

wraþfulliche, wretþe- *adv.* angrily A567, A1362.

wreche *adj.* wretched A1309.

[wreche] *n.* wretch L1191. wreches *pl.* A834.

[wreched] *adj.* wretched L1345.

wreien *v.* cover 7478. wray *pa. t. 3 sg.* = protected (behind shield) 9006. wreʒen *pa. t. pl.* covered A1764; wreiʒe 3196. wrei(ʒ)en *pp.* (adj.) 6836; armoured 7555.

wreke(n) *v.* avenge 3477, etc., (self) 3498, etc. wrake *pa. t. 3 sg.* 5962. wroken *pa. t. pl.* A1875.

wre(t)þe *n.* anger, hostility A298, 2125, etc.; wratþe [-thþe, -þþe] L1667, L1691, etc., A805, 6346.

[wrynge] *v.* wring (hands) L1376, etc.

wristling *n.* grappling 8873.

write, writt [wryt] *n.* (written) work 9655, [*holy* ~] scripture L599; *in* ~ ⁺*legge* put in writing A1288, ⁺*do ... in* ~ A1696.

write *v.* write A1182, A1183, L1785. write *pr. 1 sg.* 8909. writen *pp.* (adj.) A486, 8560, etc.; ywrite 2816.

writeing *n.* (written) words 2819, ⁺*make* ~ *of* put in writing A1186.

wrong *adj.* (morally) wrong 2290.

wrong [-(e)-] *n.* wrong A94, 1648, etc., and see for, haue(n); offence(s) A1363, L1811; [*wiþowte* ~] truly L1307, L1782.

wrongful *adj.* wrongful A1348, and see lin.

wroþ(e) *adj.* angry 106, 1458, etc., quick to anger (~ *and grim*) 3755, etc.; *adv.* angrily L826, ⟨wrath⟩ P2032.

*wroþerhale *adv.* to your misfortune 9372ⁿ.

wrouʒt(e) *pa. t. 1, 3 sg.*, etc. see wirche(n).

INDEX OF PROPER NAMES

This index seeks to record for **A** and **L** all distinct persons, places, etc. (occasionally, however, one can make only a plausible guess whether distinction is in fact intended), variant forms of their names, and their significant involvements in the action, if any, but with no attempt to notice every occurrence of a name; record from **P** is selective. Presentation is similar to that of the Glossary, but use of *etc.* to mark incomplete citation has not always been practicable. The following abbreviations are used for events often referred to:

b. 1 Aru.   Battle outside Arundel, by Cradelman and others against heathens; lines 6611–6728.

b. 2 Aru.   do. by 'young bachelors' against heathens under Harans and Daril; 8231–8310.

b. br. Dr.   Battle about the bridge called Drian, between Bedingham and Arundel, by Yder and young bachelors against heathens under Soriandes; 7709–8225.

b. Bris.   Battle by Uter Pendragon against heathens landing *at Bristowe*; 2065–2157.

b. Cam.   Battle near Camelot, by young bachelors against heathens under Oriens; 6981–7262.

b. Card.   Battle outside Cardoil, by Arthur against the six British kings who oppose his coronation; 3201–3371.

b. 1 Caro.   Battle outside Carohaise, by Leodegan, with Arthur and his companions, incognito, against heathens under kings subordinate to Rion; 5585–6430.

b. 2 Caro.   do. (Arthur, etc., now revealed) against heathens under Rion himself; 8685–9935.

b. Cor.   Battle near Coranges, by Angvisaunt and Uriens against heathens under Oriens; 6757–6920.

b. Lond.   Battle near London, by young bachelors, with Do, against heathens under Leodebron etc.; 4709–5324.

b. 1 Rok.   Battle in the forest of Rokingham, by Arthur, with Ban and Bohort, against opposing British kings; 3701–4066.

b. 2 Rok.   Battle by Clarion and E(u)stas against heathens under Oriens; 7287–7550.

b. Win.   Battle outside Winchester, by Uter Pendragon and Aurilis Brosias against Vortigern and Angys; 1715–1890.

c. Aru.   Council of British kings in Arundel, following b. 1 Aru.; 6729–51.

c. Nor.   do. in Norham, following b. 1 Rok.; 4205–4346.

t. Lond.   Tournament in London, held by Arthur as part of festivities for Ban and Bohort; 3585–3604.

Blehartis one of the 42 companions 5483; deeds in b. 2 Caro. 9626[n] (**Lectargis**), 9753 (**Beichardis**).

Bleherris godson of Bohort, one of the 42 companions 5491.

Bleoberi(i)s distinguishes himself in t. Lond. 3601 (*****Breoberiis**); leads one of Ban's and Bohort's companies at b. 1 Rok. 3957; one of the 42 companions 5447; overthrown in b. 1 Caro. 6301; deeds in b. 2 Caro. 9625, 9753 (**Blioberis**).

Blias lord of Bliodas, leader of one of Leodegan's companies at b. 2 Caro. 8703.

Bliobel one of the 42 companions 5445.

Bliodas town, seat of Blias 8704.

Bohort 2187, etc.; **Bohors**[r] 5879, 9037; king of Gaines, in Brittany, associated throughout with his brother **Ban**, q.v., though given rather less importance. **Bohortes** *gen.* 3680, etc.

Boloyne Boulogne, possession of king Harinan, acquired by Uter Pendragon 2174.

Bordogabron see **Hardogabran**.

Bramagnes *gen.* of heathen surnamed *þe etenild*, father of Harans and Daril 8250[n].

Brandris Christian knight, lord of *þe toun sori*, a leader of defence force left by E(u)stas and Clarion before b. 2 Rok. 7382[n].

Brangore heathen, high king of Saxony 6929.

Brangore(s), **-gors**; **Brangori** 4267[r]; king, lord of Strangore (*see 3405n*); against Arthur in b. 1 Rok. 3729–3910; speaks in c. Nor. 4263–4312; fights against heathens near Strangore 4461–70; married to Sagremor's mother 4471.

Branland duke 6810.

Brehus *saun pite* Christian knight, a leader of defence force left by E(u)stas and Clarion before b. 2 Rok. 7383.

Brekenham see **Rok(e)ingham**.

Brekenho town between England and Carmelide where Arthur and others meet Merlin and plan expedition to Carohaise, and Arthur lies with Li-anor 4107–94, 5353 (**Brekingho**), 5402.

Bremeins king 4305.

Breteine[1] [**Breotaine**] Britain 9741; *Michel [Mukyl]* ~ 118; ~ *þe more* 3513.

Breteyne[2] Brittany 3445; *lasse* ~ 2190, 3419, 3672.

Bretel Tintagel's cupbearer, carries Uter Pendragon's gift to Ygerne 2262–92; with Tintagel in his defence against Uter 2437; Ulfin given his form 2519; becomes supporter of Arthur 3017–34; deeds in b. Card. 3296, 3317; with Ulfin on embassy to Ban and Bohort 3433–3506; vouches to them for Arthur's parentage 3573; leads one of Arthur's companies at b. 1 Rok. 3847, deeds 3940; recognizes Merlin at Brekenho 4167; one of the 42 companions 5390, 5421; deeds in b. 1 Caro. 5904–6182.

Bretouns *pl.* Britons A119; *pl. gen.* A1672.

Brice bishop; officiates at funeral of Uter Pendragon and choosing of Arthur 2757–3112; speaks in his favour to opponents 3173–86.

Briollo heathen king, killed in b. br. Dr. 8179.

Bristowe Bristol, scene of b. Bris., 2074.

Brocklond site of *þe newe faire*, where Gawain and Galathin meet to plan their expedition to seek Arthur 4603, 4652.

Brosias see **Aurilis Brosias**.

Cay see **Kay**.

Calogreuand one of the 42 companions 5463; deeds in b. 2 Caro. 9627 (**Kalogreuant**).

Calufer heathen king, in b. 2 Caro. 9336, killed 9415.

Camal(ah)ot Camelot, city presumably in Sussex, scene of b. Cam., 7123, 7206, etc.

Cambernic, Can- (earlier name for **Arundel**, q.v.) 3770, 3772[n]; ?region containing Arundel 7302.

Fortiger (*cont.*):
why castle falls and what dragons that caused this signify 1375–1691; prepares for b. Win. 1715–97, defeated after many supporters abandon him 1810–72; death 1891. **[Fortageres]** *gen.* L1788.

Fraidons heathen leader in force which fights b. Cor. 6765.

Fraunce France 3445.

Frelent heathen in b. 1 Caro 6277, deeds 6383–97, killed 6402.

Fulgin heathen king, killed in b. br. Dr. 8175.

Gaheriet brother of Gawain 2611; goes with him to seek knighthood of Arthur 4641–92; deeds in b. Lond. 4827–5254; in b. Cam. 7157–7211, rebuked by Merlin 7217–44; in b. br. Dr. 7825–8183.

Gaidon heathen, in b. 2 Caro. 9424.

Gaines city in Brittany, seat of king Bohort 2192.

Galaous *þe geauntes sone* 4304[n]; later to be an adversary of Arthur 8923[n] **(Galahos)**.

Galat heathen king, overlord of *herdene lond*, escapes from b. 2 Caro. but stopped by Merlin's arts 9645, 9653 **(Galaþ)**.

Galathin son of Nanters and Blasine 2605[n] **(Galaas)**, 4563; one of the 'young bachelors', goes to seek knighthood of Arthur 4569–4706; deeds in b. Lond. 4807–5267; in b. Cam. 7155–7206; in b. br. Dr. 7841–8176.

Galence city, seat of king Carodas 4491[n].

Galescounde one of the 42 companions 5489; deeds in b. 2 Caro. 9626, 9752 **(Gales þe calu)**.

Galeus king 4309.

Galeway Galloway 4356.

Galoine region of Britain 4352.

⟨Gamor⟩ leader of heathens landing at Bristol P2256–62.

Garlot region of Britain, territory of king Nanters 2601, 3074, etc.

Gascoyne Gascony, possession of king Harinan, acquired by Uter Pendragon 2173.

Gaudin leader under Anguisaunt in b. Cor. 6807.

Gaw(a)inet see **Wawain**.

Gimires *of Lambale* one of the 42 companions 5471.

⟨Glasenburye⟩ Glastonbury, Pendragon (= A Aurilis Brosias) buried there P2373.

Glocedoine castle belonging to king Lot 8374.

Gloiant heathen king, in b. 2 Caro. 9335, killed 9419 **(Glorion)**.

Goionar nephew of Leodegan, leads one of his companies at b. 2 Caro. 8695 **(Gogenar)**, exhortations and deeds 9213, 9670, 9713 **(Goiomar)**.

Goionard heathen, nephew of Rion, in b. 2 Caro. 9330[n].

Gondeffles heathen leader in force which fights b. Cor. 6762.

Gornain(s) one of the 42 companions 5477; deed in b. 1 Caro. 6187 **(Gornenis)**, overthrown *6299; deeds in b. 2 Caro. 9624 **(Gernan)**, 9752.

Gorre region of Britain, territory of king Urien 3085, 4355.

Goweir heathen, killed in b. br. Dr. 8191.

Gracien(s), -an distinguishes himself in t. Lond. 3598; leads one of Ban's and Bohort's companies at b. 1 Rok. 3959; returns home with their men 4122.

Gremporemole leader of one of Leodegan's companies at b. 2 Caro. 8713[n].

Grifles distinguishes himself in t. Lond. 3595 **(Grimfles)**; leads one of Arthur's companies at b. 1 Rok. 3845, deeds 3887–3942; one of the 42 companions 5429[n]; deeds in b. 1 Caro. 6072, 6185, overthrown 6292; deeds in b. 2 Caro. **(Griflet)** 9299, 9623.

Gveheres brother of Gawain 2610 **(Guerehes)**, 4567; goes with him to seek knighthood of Arthur 4641–92; deeds in b. Lond. 4823–5267; in b. Cam. 7156–7211, rebuked by Merlin 7217–44; in b. br. Dr. 7826–8192.

Gven(e)our(e); Gwenore, Guen- 8639, 8678; Guinevere, daughter of

Nante city, seat of king Yder 4363.

Nanters; Nanter 3241; king of Garlot, lord of Hussidan, husband of Blasine, father of Galathin 2601, 4559–63; tries sword in stone 2829; at Arthur's coronation 3073, rejects him 3134; one of the six kings in b. Card., twice overthrown 3241–60, 3309–12; against Arthur again in b. 1 Rok.' 3753–3992; fights against heathens near Hussidan 4373–84. **Nanters** *gen.* 4551, 4694.

Napin heathen under Oriens, ravages leading to sortie by E(u)stas from Arundel 7554–7602.

Niniame properly sorceress, apparently treated as town near which Morgan le fay lives 4446^n.

Nohaut ?town 7380.

Norhant, -ham city, seat of king Urien, scene of c. Nor., 4209^n, 4211, 4528.

Normaga king of *þe Marais*, lord of Sorailes 4302^n.

Normondye Normandy, possession of king Harinan, acquired by Uter Pendragon 2174.

Norþhumberlond Northumberland, territory of king Clarion, 2235, 3727, 4402.

Norþlond ?region of Britain, territory of Yder^2 8709.

Orian Russel heathen, killed in b. Cam. 7173.

Oriens heathen king, chief of force which fights b. Cor. 6759; ravages leading to b. Cam. 6957–6990; leader in b. Cam., twice overthrown 7021–7204; further ravages leading to b. 2 Rok. 7271–7300; leader in b. 2 Rok. 7477–7550; further ravages leading to sortie by E(u)stas from Arundel 7551–7612. **Oriens** *gen.* 7200, 7204.

Orlende city, seat of king Clarion 4403.

Osoman surnamed *hardi of hert* one of the 42 companions 5487.

Owains *gen.* see Ywain(s)^1.

Paerne ?town, ?birthplace of Leonce 3676, 4119, seat of *þe lord of* ~ 7321, etc.

Paito Poitiers, possession of king Harinan, acquired by Uter Pendragon 2175.

Pamadas heathen, killed in b. br. Dr. 8183.

Pelleore brother of Pelles 4291.

Pelles king of Listonei 4289, 8904.

Pendrago(u)n see **Vter Pendrago(u)n**; P2337 ff. see **Aurilis Brosias.**

Perciuales *gen.* of Christian, cousin of Nacien(s) 8885.

Pharien see **Farien.**

Philip, St. 5586.

Pincenars heathen leader in force which fights b. Cor. 6764.

Pinnas heathen, killed in b. br. Dr. 8181.

Pin(n)ogras heathen, in b. 2 Caro. 9423, overthrown 9429.

Pinogres heathen king, with Morgalant in b. br. Dr. 8049, 8109, killed 8143–8.

Placidan heathen, killed in b. Cam. 7177.

Placides distinguishes himself in t. Lond. 3597 (*and see 5355n*).

Pollidamas nephew of Cradelman, leader in b. 1 Aru. 6619.

Pongerrens heathen leader in force which fights b. Cor. 6760.

Portesmouþe Portsmouth, Ban and Bohort land there 3533.

Rando(i)l, -del heathen, standardbearer at b. 1 Caro. 6280, 6404–8, killed 6411–15.

Rapas heathen king, in charge of Oriens' plunder 7567.

Ridras heathen king, killed in b. 2 Caro. 9930.

Rion; Riouns, -3^r 5588, 8944; heathen king from Ireland, leader of those warring on Leodegan 3617, 4286; besieges Carohaise 5369; subordinate kings fight b. 1 Caro. 5587–6432; summons more forces 6433–44; leader in b. 2 Caro. 8721–8944, personal deeds 8973–9110, overthrown 9247–60, renewed deeds 9287–9312, flees 9315–73, 9446, probably escapes 9448 ff. **Riones** *gen.* 8942, *etc.*; **Rion** 9077, 9304.

advances to Ygerne, and defends himself against him 2351–2440; king lies with Ygerne in his form 2516–42; death 2543–90.

Troimadac heathen king, in b. 2 Caro. 9345[n].

Vargon heathen duke, leader in force which fights b. Cor. 6768[n].

Vlfin counsellor and chamberlain of Uter Pendragon; encourages his love for Ygerne and assists in the consequent manœuvres 2297–2522; vouches for Arthur's begetting to Iurdains and Bretel 3025; deeds in b. Card. 3296–3314; with Bretel on embassy to Ban and Bohort, spokesman to Ban 3431–3522; vouches for Arthur's parentage to Ban and Bohort 3572; in charge of preparations for b. 1 Rok. 3658–92; leads one of Arthur's companies at b. 1 Rok. 3851, deeds 3893, 3940; recognizes Merlin at Brekenho 4167–74; one of the 42 companions *5389 (~ þe bel), 5419; deeds in b. 1 Caro. 5904–6181; in b. 2 Caro. 9299. **Vlfines** gen. 3475.

Vrien(s) king of Gorre, lord of Schorham and/or Norham (see 4209n), husband of Hermesent, father of Ywain, Ywain the bastard, and Morganor 2613, 4214, 7625, 7635, 8014; at Arthur's coronation 3083; one of the six kings in b. Card. 3317; against Arthur again in b. 1 Rok. 3759–4000; fights against heathens near Norham 4527–34; again in b. Cor. 6847–94; attacks heathens near Schorham 6921–76. **Vriens** gen. 4032.

[Vter] ⟨Vther⟩ see **Aurilis Brosias**; P2319 ff. see also below.

Vter Pendrago(u)n [Pendrago(u)n] ⟨Pendragon to P2300 = A2103, and in P2328 = A2131; **Vther** otherwise from P2319 = A2120⟩; **Pendragoun** A58; **Vter** 2215, etc.; **[Pendragouns]** L 1948[r]; third son of the old king Costaunce 48; taken with his brother Aurilis Brosias to safety from Vortigern 287; returns

with him 1721; [in L jointly with him] raises banner against Vortigern, welcomed into Winchester 1761–92; many of Vortigern's supporters change allegiance to him A1798–1808; hailed as heir 1830; fights (in A clearly leader in) b. Win. 1841–90; besieges Angys A1903; news of Merlin brought to him ⟨in P, and to his brother⟩ A1910–28; seeks and finds Merlin A1967–2000; becomes king 2049; deeds in b. Bris. 2093–2157; subjects Claudas, Harinan, Ban and Bohort (see 2185–7n) 2169–88; founds Round Table 2195–2222; falls in love with Ygerne and by Merlin's arts lies with her and begets Arthur 2249–2542; marries her 2593–9; at Merlin's behest has Arthur fostered 2663–96; death 2735–54. **Vter Pendrago(u)n(e)s** gen. A1808, 3152, 4579, 8888; **Vter** 3575.

Wales 2236, 3733[n], etc.

Wandlesbiri town in Britain, besieged by heathens 6930[n], 8217.

Wawain; **Gaw(a)inet** 4610, 4689, etc.; Gawain, son of Lot and Belisent 2609 (**Wawein**), greatest of the 'young bachelors' 4546; goes to seek knighthood of Arthur 4613–92; leader at b. Lond. 4741–77, nature of his superhuman strength 4778–94[n], deeds 4795–5037; leader at b. Cam. 7030–66, deeds 7101–7206, seeks messenger who had brought him news of Sagremor 7237–52; leader at b. br. Dr. 7695–7850, deeds 8122–8210; deeds in b. 2 Aru. 8234–8308; rescues Belisent and Mordred from Taurus 8383–8554. **Wawain(e)s** gen. 4819, 8371, etc.; **Wawain** 4895, etc.

Winchester [-ter, -tre]; **Vinchester** A56; the old king Costaunce buried there 97; Moyne flees there *141, murdered there L203; first city to receive Uter Pendragon 1725–92; scene of b. Win., 1760, etc.; Uter Pendragon crowned there 2052.

BIBLIOGRAPHY

This is primarily intended to provide full reference to works mentioned above, which in general are cited summarily. Omitted are only a few works, little related to the matter of my edition outside the special points on which I have referred to them, which it seemed more convenient to detail where cited.

ABBREVIATED REFERENCES

In addition to abbreviations recommended in the EETS *Notes for Editors*, certain frequently cited works are abbreviated thus: AM: *Of Arthour and of Merlin*. AM2: later version of AM. EPM: the English prose *Merlin*. *ESt*: *Englische Studien*. GM: Geoffrey of Monmouth's *Historia*. KA: *Kyng Alisaunder*. LeM: *Lestoire de Merlin* in the 'Vulgate' cycle. RCL: *Richard Cœur de Lion*. SS: *The Seven Sages of Rome*.

Ackerman, R. W., 'Arthur's Wild Man Knight', *Romance Philology*, ix (1955–6), 115–9.

Alexander, Flora, 'Late Medieval Scottish Attitudes to the Figure of King Arthur: a Reassessment', *Anglia*, xciii (1975), 17–34.

Aliscans, ed. F. Guessard and A. de Montaiglon (Les Anciens Poëtes de la France, x, Paris, 1870).

Amis and Amiloun, ed. MacE. Leach. EETS 203 (1937).

Ancrene Riwle, Cotton MS. Titus D. xviii, ed. F. Mack. EETS 252 (1963).

Ancrene Wisse, ed. J. R. R. Tokien. EETS 249 (1962).

Arnold, I. D. O., and M. H. Phelan, *La Partie Arthurienne du roman de Brut* (Paris, 1962).

Arthour and Merlin see *Of* . . .

Auchinleck Manuscript, The (facsimile), intro. D. Pearsall and I. C. Cunningham (London, 1977).

Aventures ou la queste del saint Graal, Les: *The Vulgate Version of the Arthurian Romances*, ed. H. O. Sommer, VI, 1 (Washington, 1912).

Ælfric, *Catholic Homilies*, ed. B. Thorpe (London, 1844–6).

Behrens, D., *Beiträge zur Geschichte der französischen Sprache in England*. I, *Zur Lautlehre der französischen Lehnwörter im Mittelenglischen* (Französische Studien, ed. G. Körting and E. Koschwitz, v, Hft. 2, Heilbronn, 1886).

Bennett, J. A. W., and G. V. Smithers, *Early Middle English Verse and Prose* (Oxford, 1966, 2nd. ed. 1968).

Benson, L. D., 'Sir Thomas Malory's *Le Morte Darthur*', in *Critical Approaches to Six Major English Works*, Beowulf *through* Paradise Lost, ed. R. M. Lumiansky and H. Baker (Philadelphia, 1968), 81–131.

—— *Malory's Morte Darthur* (Cambridge, Mass. and London, 1976).

Björkman, C. G., *Scandinavian Loan-Words in Middle English* (Studien zur englischen Philologie, vii, Halle, 1900).

Bliss, A. J., 'Imparisyllabic Nouns in English', *English Philological Studies* (*Birmingham*), viii (1963), 1–5.

—— 'Notes on the Auchinleck Manuscript', *Speculum*, xxvi (1951), 652–8.

Bohman, H., *Studies in the ME Dialects of Devon and London* (Göteborg, 1944).

Boron, Robert de, fragment of *Merlin* poem, in Robert de Borron, *Le Roman de l'Estoire dou Graal*, ed. W. A. Nitze (Paris, 1927), Appendix (126–30).

Brunner, K., *Die Englische Sprache* (Halle, 1951; 2nd ed. Tübingen, 1962).

—— 'Middle English Metrical Romances and their Audience', in *Studies in Medieval Literature in Honor of Albert Croll Baugh*, ed. MacE. Leach (Philadelphia, 1961), 219–27.

—— 'Die Reimsprache der sog. kentischen Fassung der *Sieben weisen Meister*', *Archiv für das Studium der neueren Sprachen und Literaturen*, cxl (1920), 199–205.

Bülbring, K. D., *Geschichte des Ablauts der starken Zeitwörter innerhalb des Südenglischen* (Quellen und Forschungen zur Sprach- und Kulturgeschichte der germanischen Völker, lxiii, Strassburg, 1889).

—— Review of Kölbing's AM, *ESt*, xvi (1892), 251–68.

—— *Über Erhaltung des altenglischen kurzen und langen œ-Lautes im Mittelenglischen* (Bonner Beiträge zur Anglistik, xv, Bonn, 1904, 101–40)

Burchfield, R. W., 'The Language of the Ormulum', *TPS*, (1956), 56–87.

—— 'Ormulum: Words Copied by Jan Van Vliet from Parts now Lost', in *English and Medieval Studies Presented to J. R. R Tolkien*, ed. N. Davis and C. L. Wrenn (London, 1962), 94–111.

Capgrave, John, *Þe Solace of Pilgrimes*, ed. C. A. Mills (London, 1911).

Chaucer, Geoffrey, *The Complete Works*, ed. F. N. Robinson (Boston and London, 1933, 2nd ed., London, 1957).

Childhood of Jesus, The (couplet version), in *Altenglische Legenden*, ed. C. Horstmann (Paderborn, 1875), 3–61.

Cleasby, R., and G. Vigfusson, *Icelandic-English Dictionary* (2nd ed., Oxford, 1957).

Cornelius, H., *Die altenglische Diphthongierung durch Palatale im Spiegel der mittelenglischen Dialekte* (Studien zur englischen Philologie, xxx, Halle, 1907).

Cunningham, I. C., 'Notes on the Auchinleck Manuscript', *Speculum*, xlvii (1972), 96–8.

Cursor Mundi, ed. R. Morris. EETS, os 57, etc. (1874, etc.).

Davis, N., 'Another Fragment of "Richard Coer de Lyon"', *N&Q*, ns xvi (1969), 447–52.

Dobson, E. J., *English Pronunciation 1500–1700* (Oxford, 1957, 2nd ed., 1968).

Douglas, Gavin, *Virgil's* Aeneid *translated into Scottish verse by Gavin Douglas, Bishop of Dunkeld*, ed. D. F. C. Coldwell. STS, 3rd Series, 30, 25, 27, 28 (1964, 57, 59, 60).

Duncan, T. G., 'Notes on the Language of the Hunterian MS. of the *Mirror*', *Neuphilologische Mitteilungen*, lxix (1968), 204–8.

Ek, K-G., *The development of OE æ̆ (i-mutated ă) before Nasals and OE æ in South-Eastern Middle English* (Acta Universitatis Lundensis; Sectio I, Theologica Juridica Humaniora, xxii, Lund, 1975).

Elene, ed. P. O. E. Gradon (Methuen's Old English Library, London, 1958).

Ellis, G., *Specimens of Early English Metrical Romances* (London, 1805; 3rd ed., revised J. O. Halliwell, 1848).

EPNS (Essex), see Reaney, P. H.

Feilitzen, O. von, *The Pre-Conquest Personal Names of Domesday Book* (Nomina Germanica, iii, Uppsala, 1937).

Fletcher, R. H., *The Arthurian Material in the Chronicles, Especially those of Great Britain and France* (Studies and Notes in Philology and Literature, x, Boston, 1906, 2nd ed., New York, 1966).

Floris and Blauncheflour, in *King Horn, Floriz and Blancheflur, The Assumption of our Lady*, re-ed. G. H. McKnight, EETS, os 14 (1901), 71–110.

—— ed. A. B. Taylor (Oxford, 1927).

Freymond, E., 'Artus Kampf mit dem Katzenungetüm', in A. Becker *et al.*, *Beiträge zur romanische Philologie, Festgabe für Gustav Gröber* (Halle, 1899), 315–17.

Fritzner, J., *Ordbog over det gamle norske Sprog* (Kristiania, 1883–96).

Generydes, ed. W. A. Wright. EETS, os 55, 70 (1878).

Geoffrey of Monmouth, *Historia Regum Britanniae*, ed. A. Griscom (London, 1929).

Godefroy, F., *Dictionnaire de l'ancienne langue française* (Paris, 1881–95), and *Complément* (1895–1902).

Gower, John, *The Complete Works*, ed. G. C. Macaulay (Oxford, 1899–1902).

Guddat-Figge, G., *Catalogue of Manuscripts containing Middle English Romances* (Munich, 1976).

Guy of Warwick (Auchinleck): *The Romance of Guy of Warwick, the first or 14th-century Version*, ed. J. Zupitza. EETS, es 42, 49, 59 (1883, 1887, 1891).

Hastings, J., *Encyclopedia of Religion and Ethics* (Edinburgh, 1908–26).

Havelok: The Lay of Havelok the Dane, ed. W. W. Skeat and K. Sisam (Oxford, 1915).

Heldris de Cornuälle, *Le Roman de Silence*, ed. L. Thorpe (Cambridge, 1972).

Heuser, W., *Altlondon, mit besonderer Berücksichtigung des Dialekts* (Osnabrück, 1914).

Higden, Ranulphus, *Polychronicon Ranulphi Higden*, ed. C. Babington and J. R. Lumby (Rolls Series, 41, London, 1865–86).

Hødnebø, F., *Rettelser og Tilleg* to Fritzner's *Ordbog* . . ., q.v. (I, Oslo, 1972).

Holland, W. E., 'Formulaic Diction and the Descent of a Middle English Romance', *Speculum*, xlviii (1973), 89–109.

Holmqvist, E., *On the History of the English Present Inflections, particularly -th and -s* (Heidelberg, 1922).

Holthausen, F., 'Zu alt- und mittelenglischen Texten', *Anglia Beiblatt*, xxxi (1920), 190–207.

Image of Ipocrysy, in *Poetical Works of John Skelton*, ed. A. Dyce (London, 1843), II, 413–47.

Jesperson, O., *Progress in Language, with Special Reference to English* (London and New York, 1894, 2nd ed. 1909).

Jocelyn of Furness, *Vita Kentegerni*, in *Lives of S. Ninian and S. Kentigern*, ed. A. P. Forbes (The Historians of Scotland, v, Edinburgh, 1874), 159–242.

Jolliffe, J. E. A., *The Constitutional History of Medieval England from the English Settlement to 1485* (London, 1937, 4th ed. 1961).

Jordan, R., *Handbuch der mittelenglischen Grammatik*, 2nd ed., revised H. Ch. Matthes (Heidelberg, 1934, 3rd ed. 1968).

Kaluza, M., Review of Kölbing's AM, *Litteraturblatt für germanische und romanische Philologie*, xii (1891), cols. 265–71.

Ker, W. P. *English Literature, Medieval* (New York, 1912).

King Horn, in *King Horn, Floriz and Blancheflur, The Assumption of our Lady*, re-ed. G. H. McKnight. EETS, os 14 (1901), 1–69.

King of Tars, The, ed. F. Krause, 'Kleine Publicationen aus der Auchinleck-Hs.; IX, The King of Tars', *ESt*, xi (1888), 1–62.

Kölbing, E., 'Vier Romanz Handschriften', *ESt*, vii (1884), 177–201.

Koeppel, E., Review of Kölbing's AM, *Anglia Beiblatt*, ii (1892), 105–7.

Kyng Alisaunder, ed. G. V. Smithers. EETS 227, 237 (1952–7).

Laȝamon, *Brut*, ed. G. L. Brook and R. F. Leslie. EETS 250, 277 (1963–78).

Langland, William, *Piers Plowman*, B-Text, Prologue and Passus I–VII, ed. J. A. W. Bennett (Oxford, 1972).

—— Lincoln's Inn MS. of A-text: unedited; see comments in W. W. Skeat's ed. of the A-Text, EETS, os 28 (1867), xxii–iii.

Lehmann, W. P., 'Comparative Constructions in Germanic of the OV Type', in *Studies for Einar Haugen*, ed. E. S. Firchow *et al.* (The Hague, 1972), 323–30.

Lestoire del saint Graal: The Vulgate Version of the Arthurian Romances, ed. H. O. Sommer, I (Washington, 1909).

Lestoire de Merlin: ibid., II (Washington, 1908).

Lewis, C. S., *The Discarded Image* (Cambridge, 1964).

Liedholm, A., *A Phonological Study of the Middle English Romance 'Arthour and Merlin'* (Uppsala, 1941).

Littré, E., *Dictionnaire de la langue française* (Paris, 1956–8).

Livre d'Artus, Le: *The Vulgate Version* . . ., VII (Washington, 1913).

Livre de Lancelot del lac, Le: ibid., III–V (Washington, 1910–12).

Livre de Marco Polo, citoyen de Venise, Le, ed. M. G. Pauthier (Paris, 1865).

Loomis, L. H., 'The Auchinleck MS. and a Possible London Bookshop of 1330–1340', *PMLA*, lvi (1942), 595–627.

Loomis, R. S., ed., *Arthurian Literature in the Middle Ages, a Collaborative History* (Oxford, 1959).

Louelich, Henry, the skinner, *Merlin*, ed. E. A. Kock. EETS, ES 93, 112, OS 185 (1904–32).

Luick, K., *Historische Grammatik der englischen Sprache* (Leipzig, 1914–40).

Lybeaus Desconus, ed. M. Mills. EETS 261 (1969).

Macrae-Gibson, O. D., 'The Auchinleck MS.: Participles in -*and(e)*', *English Studies*, lii (1971), 13–20.

—— 'Sir Walter Scott, the Auchinleck MS., and MS. Douce 124', *Neophilologus*, l (1966), 449–54.

Mahling, C., *Über Tonvokal+ht im Frühmittelenglischen* (Weimar and Leipzig, 1928).

Malory, Sir Thomas, *The Works of . . .*, ed. E. Vinaver (Oxford, 1947, 2nd ed. 1697).

Mannyng, Robert, of Brunne, *The Story of England*, ed. F. J. Furnivall (Rolls Series, lxxxvii, London, 1887).

Merlin, English Prose, ed. H. B. Wheatley. EETS, OS 10, 21, 36, 112 (1869–98).

Merlin, French Prose (Huth MS.), ed. G. Paris and J. Ulrich. SATF (Paris, 1886).

—— (Vulgate) see *Lestoire de Merlin*.

Metham, John, *Amoryus and Cleopes*, in *The Works of John Metham*, ed. H. Craig. EETS, OS 132 (1916), 1–81.

Micha, A., 'La Guerre contre les Romains dans la vulgate du *Merlin*', *Romania*, lxxii (1951), 310–23.

—— 'Les Manuscrits du *Merlin* en prose de Robert de Boron', *Romania*, lxxix (1958), 78–94.

—— 'Les Sources de la *Vulgate* du *Merlin*', *Le Moyen Âge*, lviii (1952), 299–345.

Michel, Dan, *Ayenbite of Inwyt*, ed. R. Morris. EETS, OS 23 (1866, revised P. Gradon 1965).

Moore, S., S. B. Meech, and H. Whitehall, *Middle English Dialect Characteristics and Dialect Boundaries: Preliminary Report of an Investigation based Exclusively on Localized Texts and Documents* (Essays and Studies in English and Comparative Literature by Members of the English Department of the University of Michigan; University of Michigan Publications, Language and Literature, xiii, Ann Arbor, 1935).

Morte Arthur, Le, see *Stanzaic . . .*

Of Arthour and of Merlin: *Arthour and Merlin: a Metrical Romance. Now First Edited from the Auchinleck-Ms.*, ed. W. Turnbull (Abbotsford Club, Edinburgh, 1838).

——: *Arthour and Merlin nach der Auchinleck-Hs. nebst zwei Beilagen*, ed. E. Kölbing (Altenglische Bibliothek, iv, Leipzig, 1890).

———: O. D. Macrae-Gibson, 'An Edition of the Middle English Romance *Arthour and Merlin*' (D.Phil. thesis, Oxford, 1964).

——— (Percy) see Percy Romances, etc.

Orrm, *Ormulum*, ed. R. M. White and R. Holt (Oxford and London, 1878).

Owl and the Nightingale, The, ed. J. W. Atkins (Cambridge, 1922).

———: *Das mittelenglische Streitgedicht Eule und Nachtigall*, ed. W. Gadow (Palaestra, lxv, Berlin, 1909).

Paston Letters and Papers of the Fifteenth Century, ed. N. Davis (Oxford, 1971–).

Percy Romances, etc.: *Bishop Percy's Folio Manuscript, Ballads and Romances*, ed. J. W. Hales and F. J. Furnivall (London, 1867–8).

Pope, M. K., *From Latin to Modern French* (Manchester, 1934).

Promptorium Parvulorum, ed. A. L. Mayhew. EETS, ES 102 (1908).

Ranulf de Glanvill (supposed author), *Tractatus de legibus et consuetudinibus regni Angliae tempore regis Henrici secundi*, ed. G. D. G. Hall (London, 1965).

Reaney, P. H., *The Place Names of Essex*. EPNS xii (Cambridge, 1935).

Reinbrun, Gij sone of Warwike, in *Guy of Warwick* (Auchinleck), q.v., 631–74.

Richard Cœur de Lion: *Der mittelenglische Versroman über Richard Löwenherz*, ed. K. Brunner (Wiener Beiträge zur englischen Philologie, xlii, Vienna and Leipzig, 1913).

Roland and Vernagu, in *The Taill of Rauf Coilyear, etc.*, ed. S. J. Herrtage. EETS, ES 39 (1882), 35–61.

Samuels, M. L., 'Some Applications of Middle English Dialectology', *English Studies*, xliv (1963), 81–94.

Seege or Batayle of Troye, The, ed. M. E. Barnicle. EETS 172 (1927).

Seven Sages of Rome, The, ed. K. Brunner. EETS 191 (1933).

Seynt Mergrete, in *Altenglische Legenden*, N.F., ed. C. Horstmann (Heilbronn, 1881), 226–35.

Sir Gawain and the Green Knight, ed. J. R. R. Tolkien and E. V. Gordon, 2nd ed., revised N. Davis (Oxford, 1968).

Sir Orfeo, ed. A. J. Bliss (Oxford, 1954, 2nd ed. 1966).

Sir Otuel, in *The Taill of Rauf Coilyear, etc.*, ed. S. J. Herrtage. EETS, ES 39 (1882), 63–116.

Sir Perceval of Gales, ed. J. Campion and F. Holthausen (Alt- und mittelenglische Texte, v, Heidelberg and New York, 1913).

Skeat, W. W., 'The Etymology of "Boast"', *Athenæum* (1906, I), 18.

Sklar, E. S., 'The Dialect of *Arthour and Merlin*', *ELN* xv (1977), 88–94.

Slettengren, E., 'On the Origin of the ME variant *diol*, OF *due(i)l*, and the Pronunciation of OF *-uel͂* in the Anglo-French Dialect', *Studia Neophilologica*, xiv (1941–2), 369–85.

Smithers, G. V., 'Another Fragment of the Auchinleck MS.', in *Medieval Literature and Civilization; Studies in Memory of G. N. Garmonsway*, ed. D. A. Pearsall and R. A. Waldron (London, 1969), 192–210.

Smithers, G. V., 'The Meaning of *The Seafarer* and *The Wanderer*', *MÆ*, xxvi (1957), 137–53, and xxviii (1959), 1–22.

—— 'Notes on Middle English Texts', *London Medieval Studies*, i (1939), 208–20.

—— 'Some English Ideophones', *Archivum Linguisticum*, vi (1954), 73–111.

—— 'Two Newly-Discovered Fragments from the Auchinleck MS.', *MÆ*, xviii (1949), 1–11.

Sommer, H. O., *The Vulgate Version of the Arthurian Romances: Index of Names and Places* . . . (Washington, 1916).

Stanzaic Morte Arthur: Le Morte Arthur, ed. J. D. Bruce. EETS, ES 88 (1903).

Tilander, A. G., *Lexique du roman de Renart* (Göteborgs Högskolas Årskrift, xxx, Göteborg, 1924).

Tobler, A., and E. Lommatzsch, *Altfranzösisches Wörterbuch* (I–II Berlin, III– Wiesbaden, 1915–).

Towneley Plays, The, ed. G. England. EETS, ES 71 (1897).

Vespasian Psalter, The, ed. S. H. Kuhn (Ann Arbor, 1965).

Vinaver, E., *The Rise of Romance* (Oxford, 1971).

Wace, *Roman de Brut*, ed. I. Arnold. SATF (Paris, 1938–40).

Wallenberg, J. K., *The Vocabulary of Dan Michel's Ayenbite of Inwyt. A Phonological, Morphological, Etymological, Semasiological and Textual Study* (Uppsala, 1923).

Walter de Bibbesworth, *Traité sur la langue française*, ed. A. Owen (Paris, 1929).

Wartburg, W. von, *Französisches etymologisches Wörterbuch* (Bonn, etc., 1922–).

Webster's New International Dictionary of the English Language, ed. W. T. Harris and F. Sturges Allen (London and Springfield, Mass., 1911).

Wells, J. E., *A Manual of the Writings on Middle English* (New Haven and London, 1916), and *Supplements* (1919–52); *A Manual . . ., based on . . . Wells . . .*, ed. J. B. Severs and A. E. Hartung (New Haven, 1967–).

Weston, J. L., *The Chief Middle English Poets* (Boston, New York, London, 1915).

William of Shoreham, *De Decem Preceptis, De Septem Sacramentis*, in *Poems*, ed. M. Konrath, Part I. EETS, ES 86 (1902).

Wilson, R. M., 'English and French in England, 1100–1300', *History*, xxviii (1943), 37–60.

Wright, T., and R. P. Wülcker, *Anglo-Saxon and Old English Vocabularies* (London and Marburg, 1884).

Ywain and Gawain, ed. A. B. Friedman and N. T. Harrington. EETS 254 (1964).

Zupitza, J., *Alt- und mittelenglisches Übungsbuch*, 11th edition, ed. J. Schipper (Vienna and Leipzig, 1915).

—— Review of Kölbing's AM, *Archiv für das Studium der neueren Sprachen und Litteraturen*, lxxxvii (1891), 88–94.

—— 'Zu Sir Torrent of Portyngale', *ESt*, xv (1891), 4–5.

In addition, though nowhere cited, the following important works of reference have been used:

Ackerman, R. W., *An Index of the Arthurian Names in Middle English* (Stanford, Calif., 1952).

Bossuat, R., *Manuel Bibliographique de la Littérature française du Moyen âge* (Melun, 1951), and *Suppléments* (Paris, 1955–61).

Bosworth, J., and T. N. Toller, *An Anglo-Saxon Dictionary* (Oxford, 1898), and Toller's *Supplement* (1921).

Brown, C., and R. H. Robbins, *The Index of Middle English Verse* (New York, 1943), and *Supplement* (Lexington, 1965).

Söderwall, K. F., *Ordbog öfver Svenska Medeltids-Spraket* (Lund, 1884–1918), and *Supplement* (1926–).

Verwijs, E., and J. Verdam, *Middelnederlandsch Woordenboek* (Gravenhage, 1882–1952).

APPENDIX 1

MARGINALIA OF THE MANUSCRIPTS

Recorded here, as far as they can be read, are all marginal annotations of **A** and **L** which relate to the text of the romance (see above, Introduction, pp. 39 and 41). References are to the lines beside which they occur; if 'above' or 'below' they are at the top or bottom of a page, and do not necessarily refer to the immediately adjacent lines. Matter which can be confidently read (apart from occasional doubt about contractions) is in roman; italic indicates tentative reading or interpretation of uncertain material, and angle brackets matter illegible, unintelligible, or cut off, any readings within them being contextual inferences, varying from the obvious to the speculative.

A

43–8	⟨*Cost*⟩ance had ⟨*cost*⟩ance ⟨*and*⟩ ambros and ⟨*vter*⟩ pendragoun
49–51	⟨*The el*⟩dest brother ⟨*was a mo*⟩nk that after ⟨*became*⟩ a kyng
53	Moyne
above 77	vortiger senescall
below 120	Angys of denmark *contra* nos Engist
231–2	⟨*Costan*⟩ceus capite ⟨. . . . . .⟩antur *contra* dice
233–5	Moyne
246–7	⟨*juventut*⟩e etatem
above 253	*Vortiger fit* Rex ⟨. . . . . .⟩ Sen*eschall* per prodi*c*
360–2	xij co⟨*nspirati*⟩
383	Suspens*us* per co⟨*rdam*⟩
below 428, 472	Vortiger et Angys participes
550–2	castrum vortigeri ⟨*non*⟩ potuit erigi
590–2	⟨*observati*⟩o Astronomorum
593–5	⟨. . . *su*⟩orum consilium ⟨. . . . . . .⟩onero
below 648	Incubus
703	Blasius
721–3	Incub⟨*us*⟩ inuitat Leona⟨*m*⟩[1] ad virgines in⟨*trare*⟩
730–1	adulterium mor⟨*e*⟩ dierum
777–9	⟨. . . .⟩cac⟨.⟩o ⟨.⟩o⟨.⟩tens *non Su*⟨. . . .⟩*at*
795–6	3ª soror apud blasium
901–2	3ª soror in tor⟨*tionem*⟩ citata

[1] Presumably error for *lenam*.

above 957	3ª soror *virgin⟨al⟩is* incarcerat⟨a⟩ quousque ⟨. . . . .⟩
978	partus
988–90	Merlynus baptizatus
1081–3	Mer accusat m⟨atrem⟩ iudicis
below 1044, 1088	Merlyny responsus pro matrem coram judicem et *num* b⟨. . .⟩os er*a*t
1195–7	Speculatores Vortigeri
below 1220, 1264	Merlyne
1443–4	⟨M⟩erlyn Vortigero
1454	*d*rachones
1594	Castrum erectum
1635–45	drachones quid ⟨s⟩ignificarint
below 1748, 1792	Vortiger adminiculum h*abet* ab Angis
1761–2	Vterpendragon a⟨d⟩ Wyntoniam
1767	Vexillum
1770–1	Leo Vterpend⟨rag⟩onis
1799–1800	vexillum
1816–17	⟨pro⟩elium inter ⟨Vt⟩erp. et Vortiger
above 1881, 1925	Vter vortigerum prosequitur ac igne cons*um*itur
below 1924, 1968	Vterp. misit quaesitum Merlynum
1931–2	Merlynus al⟨loquitur ad⟩ Speculatores V⟨ortigeri⟩
2000–2	⟨Me⟩rlynus alloquitur ⟨ad⟩ Vterp.

L

234–5	Vortiger made kinge
244	The comen
255–8	vter and his brother convoyed biyond sea
283–5	a battell be⟨tween the⟩ kinge[1] of ⟨denmark and⟩ men of ⟨england⟩
302–4	kinge Aungist neuer to ret*orne* into engl⟨and⟩
1081–4	The storye of Vter and pendrago⟨n⟩ and ther retorne agayne
1830	Winchester
1865–6	revolt of the people
1875–7	gret pr*i*veledg graunted to winchester
1908–9	Vortiger had xx*ti* to ane
1960–4	Vortiger driven to the castell vppon the playne of Salisburye

---

[1] Followed by a mark not wholly clear, but such that one would certainly read *kinges* if the word were in isolation. But this is not the only case in which one wishes to discount such a mark; see above, p. 43 n. 1.

APPENDIX 2

ERRONEOUS READINGS IN KÖLBING'S EDITION

Listed here are all cases, in passages also occurring in my edition, in which Kölbing's corrected reading[1] clearly misreports the manuscript, except as between long and short *i*, which are not distinguished in my text. Where there could be any doubt, I record the facts in my Apparatus. All discrepancies between the editions should thus be on record, and any which are not are likely to be undetected errors of mine, except in the following categories, in which I have taken notice only of significant differences:

(i) Differences of detail in the use of **P** to supply matter missing or illegible in **L**.

(ii) Different interpretations of minim sequences (applies almost exclusively in proper names).

(iii) Different treatments of MS. *ff-* (which Kölbing transcribes as *f-* everywhere).

(iv) Different treatments of what may represent *-e* in **D**.

(v) Differences of punctuation and word-division.

A919 it: *K* is   A961 þe: *K* the   A977 so: *K* to   A1362–3 And wraþfulliche . . . | ȝif: *K* wraþfulliche . . . | & ȝif   A1527 o: *K* a   A2297 Vlfin: *K* Ulfin   A2597 And: *K* An   A3689 And (*i.e.* MS. ȝ): *K* And *as though spelt out*   A4232 þat: *K* þas   A5437 þe: *K* The   A6551 Ih[es]us: *K* Iesus (*as though MS. correctly* ihūs; *in fact* ihus)   A6768 [¶]: *K reports* ¶ *present*   A7554 saun: *K* faun   A8969 heuedles: *K reports MS.* heuẹdeles (*third* e *in fact subpuncted*)   A9867 trespas: *K reports MS.* tresppas (*second* p *in fact subpuncted*)   A9916 xii: *K* vii

L98 seide: *K* saide   L141 elde: *K* olde   L603 out: *K* ut   L649 bytauȝht: *K* bitauȝht   L768 barst: *K* brast   L784 Ant: *K* And   L993 beo: *K* be   L1453 chaumbur[l]eyn: *K* chaumburleyn, *reporting* y *corrected from* l   L1599 somme (*i.e.* MS. sōme): *K* some   L1620 rested: *K corr.* restid, *though K text*

[1] See my vol. I, p. xiii. In addition, Kölbing corrects one misprint on p. 426, in his note to L868 (866 on his numeration).

rested   *Following* L1635: *K inserts* And þe white went away
L1804 зow: *K* yow   L1928 o: *K* a   L1932 seide: *K* saide

P1949 here: *K reports MS.* lere   P2061 kinge (*i.e. MS.* k:): *K*
king *as though spelt out so*   P2077 vs: *K* us   P2118 litle:
K little   P2359 moore: *K* more

D757 (= L634) The: *K* þe   D 912 (= L1073) The: *K* þe

APPENDIX 3

SPECIMENS OF
WYNKYN DE WORDE'S *MARLYN*

Printed here are the opening (lines 1–105), a section containing the most substantial passage in which this text uniquely preserves probable original AM2 matter (1457–1502), a section illustrating what is said in the Introduction on page 46 above (lines 1635–84), a section equivalent to the end of **L** and the beginning of the continuation otherwise only preserved in **P** (2235–66), and the final section (2761–86). I have made no corrections, even of obvious misprints. References to equivalent lines of the other texts are added in brackets.

f. A. i^v

CRyste on crosse his blode y̆ ble⟨dde⟩
    And lyfe for lyfe he layd to w⟨edde⟩
As it was his wyll
Graūt thē grace of myrthes r⟨yfe⟩
Ioye and blysse in all theyr ly⟨fe⟩   5
That me herkeneth tyll
I shall you tell solace and game
Frendes felawes sythe all in same
And herken of grete nobly
Sounde and sauffe than mote ye be   10
And all that herkeneth vnto me
What I shall you say
I shall you tell here afore   (L 5)
How Merlyn was goten and bore
And of his dedes also   15
And of other meruaylles many mo
Some tyme in Englonde was a kynge   (L 9, 11)
A noble man in all thynge
I warre he was ware and wys
Constanstyne the kynge hyght ywys   20
Sones he had full fayre thre   (L 25)
The fayrest that in londe myght be
The eldest sone that was his heyr ryght
Moyn he hyght
The medlest sone hyght Pendragon   25
He was a man of grete renon
The yongest sone hyght Vter ryght

A styffe man and stronge in fyght
Constantyne the kynge ywys
In euery place he bare the prys   30
In his tyme was reynynge in englonde
A grete syknesse I vnderstonde
In that syknes the kynge fell tho

f. A. ii^r

That out of this worlde he must nedes go   (L 35)
After erles and barons he lete call   35
Whan they were come before hym all
Than sayd the kynge to them all
Lordynge lefe and hende
Out of this worlde I must wende   (L 40)
I praye you syrs for the loue of me   40
And for goddes loue and saynt charyte
Whan I am dede and layde in clay
Helpe my chyldren all that ye may
And Moyn myn eldest sone   (L 45)
Make hym kynge and gyue hym crowne   45
The kynge called as ye may here
His stuarde that hyght Vortygere   (A 80)
Stronge he was wyse and daungerous
And false and fekle and full couetous
The kynge he had serued longe   50
For he was styffe and stronge
Whan Moyn was chosen kynge
In to denmarke the worde gan sprynge (L 70)
And whan angys worde had
Therof he was ryght glad   55
He sente after messagers in that tyde
Ouer all his londe on eche syde
For many a stoute man and stronge   (L 75)
Of genus and of danes londe
An hondred thousande and many mo   60
On hors and on fote also
Came to hym there letted none
For to warre on the yonge kynge Moyn (L 80)
Kynge angys wolde not abyde
Vnto shyp he wente in that tyde   65
And brought in to Englonde syn

f. A. ii^v

Meuy a doughty sarasyn
As Englonde was called that day   (L 85)
The more brytayne withouten nay
Worde anone aboute gan sprynge   70

How the denysshe kynge angys
Gan wyrche moche amys
Mony the kynge herde that it was so   (L 90)
He wente to syr Vortyger tho
With full grete mournynge chere   75
He prayed hym with good vygure
That he wolde be his gouernoure
Ayenst his fomen for to fyght   (L 95)
And he sayd that he ne myght
He made hym seke as traytour stronge   80
And neyther for ryght ne for wronge
Wolde he come in batayll
For his strength hym gan fayll   (L 100)
For his pourpose that he had on honde
Was to be kynge of this londe   85
The kynge wolde no more hym pray
But toke his leue and wente his way
His messengers he sente that tyde   (L 105)
Ouer all his londe on euery syde
To duke/Erle/Baron/and knyght   90
To come to hym in that fyght
And whan they were all ycome
And euerche had his armes nome   (L 110)
They prycked forth without fayle
And gaue the denysshe kynge batayll   95
There was broken many a crowne
And slayne was many a bolde barowne
Many a doughty man that tyde
Was slayne with woundes wyde
f. A. iii^r   And the denysshe kynge was so stronge   100 (D 110)
With speres and with knyues longe
All that they myght in that stounde   (L 115)
Were slayne and layed to grounde
So the englysshe folke that day
Were dyscomfyted and fledde away   105

                    .   .   .   .   .
f. D. iiii^r   Marlyn anone to them ran
And gret them as he well can
And sayd welcome messengers
That come fro syr Vortygers   1460 (L 1300)
Lo I am here that ye haue sought
Me to sle is your thought
For to bere the kynge my blode

That neuer sholde do hym good
For he that tolde hym that tydynge   1465 (L 1305)
On me lyeth a foule lesynge
He sayd my blode with grete wronge
Sholde make his werke styffe and stronge
Though his werke therewith were wet
It sholde stand eneuer the bet   1470 (L 1310)
The messagers hadde echone
And spake to marlyn anone
How canst thou knowe such preuyte
Tell vs sothe we praye the
Yes sayd marlyn I wote well   1475
The kynges councell euerydele   (A 1250)
And what is your pourpose for to do
And other aduentures many mo
Therfore sholde ye me not slo   (A 1255)
But to courte I wyll with you go   1480
I wyll saue you fro the dede
Hardely vpon my hede
And before the kynge yplyght
f. D. iiii^v   I shall tell the sothe a ryght
Why that his castell wyll not stonde   1485
And afterwarde I shall fonde   (A 1260)
To make the clerkes false echone
That hath demed me to be slone
Tho sayd the messagers rathe
To sle the it were grete scathe   1490
For thy wordes be good and hende
To courte with vs thou shalte wende
Tell vs what is thy name   (A 1268)
And what woman is thy dame
That we may haue veray tokenynge   1495 (L 1315)
To answere at home byfore our kynge
Marlyn led them forth a grete pace
Tyll he came there his moder was
And he them tolde his moder byfore
All how he was bygote and bore   1500 (L 1320)
And thorowe his wysdome and his rede
He saued her fro the dede

. . . . .

f. E. ii^v   Than was the kynge wonder wrothe   1635 (L 1445)
And eygrely he swore his othe
That she wolde be drawe and honge

But certes it were all with wronge
To sle a woman for a man
Thoughe she had mannes chothes on   1640
Therefore I pray you for the loue of me
For goddes loue and saynt charyte
Go to the kynge blyue

f. E. iii^r

Also fast as ye may dryue   (L 1450)
And saye vnto the kynge   1645
The quene hath made a stronge lesynge
Vpon his chamberlayne with wrake
Therfore bed hym that he do her take
And loke al aboute than   (L 1455)
He shall her fynde for a woman   1650
A knyght there was stoute and fre
He lepte vpon a good destre   (L 1460)
That he made no lettynge
Tyll he came byfore the kynge
And whan he came in to the hall   1655
Downe on knees he gan fall
And sayd to kynge Vortyger   (L 1465)
God the saue and thy power
Many a countre we haue wente
On thy message as thou vs sente   1660
To seke a chylde selcouth monde
Thanked be god we haue hym founde   (L 1470)
That chylde is fyue wynter olde
But ye sawe neuer sone so bolde
Wyse he is by crystes pyne   1665
And he hyght chylde merlyne
He can tell all thynge
That euer was without lesynge
And all thynhe that nowe is   (L 1475)
He can tell nowe Iwys   1670
Also he can tell ryght well
What destroyeth your castell
That it may not stande on the playne
And also of thy chamberlayne   (L 1480)
That thou hast thought to drawe & honge   1675

f. E. iii^v

For certes it were all with wronge
To sle a woman for a man
Thoughe she haue mannes clothes on
Therfore he sende the sayne   (L 1485)
Take anone thy chamberlayne   1680

And of her bondes her vnbynde
And a woman thou shalte her fynde
But yf it be so with all lawe
Do her to hange and to drawe   (L 1490)

. . . . .

f. F. iiii^r   Pendragon and syr Vther   2235
Prycked after Vortyger   (L 1965)
Whan they to the castell come
Wylde fyre anone they nome
And caste it ouer the wall anone
And also sone as it was within   2240
It gan to brenne as a fyre bronde   (L 1970)
That no man myght it withstonde
Tyll Vortyger was brente chylde & wyfe
And all that were within on lyfe
Beest and man with lyme and lede   2245
Brenned downe withouten rede   (L 1975)
That no thynge of them was founde
But dust that lay on the grounde
Whan Vortyger was so brente
Vther and pendragon togyder wente   2250
For to seche kynge Angys   (P 1870)

f. F. iiii^v   There he lay on his castell of prys
Thyder he was flowen for doute
And Pendragon with all his route
Bysette hym nyght and day   2255
That no man may scape a way   (P 1875)
But kynge angys in his castell
Was stored veray well
So well the castell was wrought
That no man it wynne mought   2260
Fyue barons with Vther were
That had ben with Vortygere
And tolde Vther & Pendragon before   (P 1885)
How Marlyn was bygote and bore
And how he coude tell all thynge   2265
That euer was without lesynge

. . . . .

f. G. viii^r   Of Englysshe men there were slayne   (P 2360)
But thre hondred ẙ ony man coude sayne
f. G. viii^v   Bytwene bath and brystowe tho
Thre myle myght no man go
Neyther in dale neyther in den   2765

But he trade on dede men   (P 2365)
Whan it was agaynst the nyght
Vther dyde dyscomfyte the fyght
With many an Erle and baroune   (A 2155)
And with knyghtes of grete renoune   2770
They wente home to theyr In
On $\overset{e}{y}$ morowe by the counceyll of Marlyn
Pendragon was out sought   (P 2370)
And in the erthe fayre Ibrought
Beryed he was full mery   2775
In the towne of Glastenbery
Thus ended the doughty kynge
God gyue his soule good endynge   (P 2375)
And after that Pendragon was dede
Vther was crowned by comyn rede   2780
And helde Englonde to ryght   (A 2162)
I praye to god full of myght
Graunte them heuen blysse aboue
Amen for his moders loue   (P 2379)
And gyue them all good endynge   2785
That haue herde this talkynge

⁋Here endeth a lytell treatyse of Marlyn whiche prophefyed of many fortunes or hap pes here in Englonde. Enprynted in Lōdon in flete strete at the sygne of $\overset{e}{y}$ sonne by Wyn kyn de Worde.the yere of oure lorde a.M. CCCCC.and.x.